'The topic is unquestionably of major importance, on a par with some of the most serious environmental dangers we face.' – **Adrian Guelke, Queen's University, Belfast, author of** *The Age of Terrorism*

'Calm, measured in tone, fair and balanced in its assessment of NBC terrorism, and reassuringly well-informed about the weaponry and about the major variations of currently active terrorist groups' – **Professor Paul Wilkinson**

Nadine Gurr, previously at the Centre for Defence Studies, King's College, London, is now an independent defence consultant. She is co-author with Sir Hugh Beach of *Flattering the Passions: Or, the Bomb and Britain's Bid for a World Role* (I.B.Tauris).

Benjamin Cole, formerly a Research Fellow at Southampton University, is also an independent defence consultant.

THE NEW FACE OF TERRORISM

Threats from Weapons of Mass Destruction

NADINE GURR

AND

BENJAMIN COLE

I.B. Tauris *Publishers*

LONDON • NEW YORK

Published in 2002 by I B.Tauris & Co Ltd
6 Salem Road, London W2 4BU
175 Fifth Avenue, New York NY 10010
www.ibtauris.com

In the United States of America and in Canada distributed by
St Martins Press, 175 Fifth Avenue, New York NY 10010

First published in 2000 by I B Tauris

ISBN 1 86064 825 8

A full CIP record for this book is available from the British Library
A full CIP record for this book is available from the Library of Congress

Library of Congress catalog card: available

Contents

Abbreviations

AAA	Animal Aid Association (Canada)
ALF	Animal Liberation Front (UK)
ANO	Abu Nidal Organization
ATCC	American Type Culture Collection
ATF	Alcohol, Tobacco, and Firearms Bureau (USA)
ANC	African National Congress
ARM	Animal Rights Militia (Canada)
BBC	British Broadcasting Corporation
BNP	British National Party
BTWC	Biological and Toxin Weapons Convention
BW	Biological weapons
BWAT	Biological Weapons Anti-Terrorism Statute
CBIRF	Chemical Biological Incident Response Force (USA)
CBRRT	Chemical Biological Rapid Response Teams (USA)
CBW	Chemical and Biological Weapons
CDC	Centers for Disease Control and Prevention (USA)
CIA	Central Intelligence Agency (USA)
CIO	Central Intelligence Agency (Zimbabwe)
CIS	Commonwealth of Independent States (FSU)

CSA	Covenant, Sword and Arm of the Lord (USA)
CW	Chemical Weapons
CWC	Chemical Weapons Convention
DEST	Domestic Emergency Support Team (USA)
DFP	diisopropyl flurophosphate
DIN	Dahm Y'Israel Nokam
DINA	secret service (Chile)
DMSO	dimethyl sulphoxide
DNA	deoxyribonucleic acid
DoD	Department of Defense (USA)
DoE	Department of Energy (USA)
EC	European Community
EEC	European Economic Community
ETA	Basque separatist group
EU	European Union
EURATOM	European Atomic Energy Authority
Europol	European Police Office
FBI	Federal Bureau of Investigation (USA)
FEMA	Federal Emergence Management Agency (USA)
FEST	Federal Emergency Support Team (USA)
FIS	Front Islamique de Salut
FSB	Federal Security Bureau (Russia)
FSU	the former Soviet Union
FYR	the former Republic of Yugoslavia
G7	Group of Seven industrialized nations (UK, Japan, Germany, USA, France, Italy, Canada)
G8	Group of Eight (the G7 states plus Russia)
GAO	General Accounting Office (US Congress)
GIA	Armed Islamic Group (Algeria)
HAZMAT	hazardous materials team (USA)
HEU	highly enriched uranium
HSE	Health and Safety Executive (UK)
HUA	Harakat ul-Ansar (Pakistan)
IAEA	International Atomic Energy Authority
INTERPOL	International Police (Organization)
IPE	individual protective equipment
IRA	Irish Republican Army
IRS	Internal Revenue Service (USA)
ISI	Inter Services Intelligence agency (Pakistan)
KGB	Soviet secret service
LEHI	Lotiamei Herut Yisrael (the Stern Gang)
LSD	lysergic Acid Diethylamide
MAF	Ministry of Agriculture and Forestry (New Zealand)
MB	Muslim Brotherhood
MIT	Massachusetts Institute of Technology

MoD	Ministry of Defence (UK)
MP	Member of Parliament (UK)
NAACP	National Association for the Advancement of Coloured People (USA)
NBC	Nuclear, Biological and Chemical (weapons)
NEST	Nuclear Emergency Search Team (USA)
NIF	National Islamic Front (Sudan)
NPT	Non-Proliferation Treaty (1974)
NRC	Nuclear Regulatory Committee (USA)
NSG	Nuclear Suppliers' Group
OTA	Office of Technology Assessment (USA)
PETN	pentaerythritol tetranitrate
PFLP	Popular Front For the Liberation of Palestine
PKK	Kurdish Workers Party
PLO	Palestine Liberation Organization
R&D	research and development
RAF	Red Army Faction
RAIDS	Rapid Assessment and Initial Detection Team (USA)
RCD	Rabbit calcivirus disease
RHD	Rabbit haemorrhagic disease
SEP	Slovak power utility
SIS	Italian Intelligence Service
SLA	Symbionese Liberation Army (USA)
SNLA	Scottish National Liberation Army
SWAPO	South West Africa People's Organization
TEU	Technical Escort Unit (USA)
TREVI	Terrorism Radicalism and Violence International
UN	United Nations
UNSCOM	United Nations Special Commission on Iraq
USAMRIID	United States Army Medical Research Institute of Infectious Diseases
WMD	Weapons of mass destruction
ZANU	Zimbabwe African National Union
ZAPU	Zimbabwe African People's Union
ZOG	Zionist Occupation Government

Introduction

On 11 September the world experienced the horrors of mass destruction terrorism when fanatical terrorists struck at the heart of the USA. Suicide bombers hijacked four Boeing passenger airlines and used them as bombs by flying them into the twin towers of the World Trade Centre in New York and the Pentagon in Washington. The fourth Boeing which seemed destined for the President's retreat at Camp David crashed in a field outside Pittsburg when its passengers attempted to regain control. Just over an hour after the Boeings struck the World Trade Centre, each tower collapsed reducing this symbolic landmark of US power and prosperity to a pile of smoking rubble. Approximately 3,000 people from many different nations are thought to have died in the World Trade Centre. A mere fraction of the 50,000 who could have died if the towers had collapsed immediately. This act went beyond any previously known boundaries into new realms of destruction. This new face of terrorism has not only changed the US, but has had a profound effect upon the whole world.

Since the beginning of the 1980s, terrorist violence has

escalated but this was the most destructive act of international terrorism to date. There is no doubt that regardless of their prime motivation, all international terrorist groups are becoming more destructive. What started with individuals and small groups setting bombs, has developed into highly skilled, well organised, well financed groups which are capable of sophisticated operations.

The perpetrators of the attack were believed to be fanatical Islamists, masterminded by the Saudi-born terrorist leader Osama bin Laden, and his al-Qaeda organisation. Their motives lay in the morass of Middle East politics especially in resentment of US support – political, financial and military – of Israel, and in the wider opposition to US hegemony in world politics and trade, and US action against Iran and Iraq, and opposition to pro-Western governments in the Middle East like Saudi Arabia. In the wake of the attacks President Bush declared that 'terrorist attacks may shake the foundations of the tallest buildings, but they cannot touch the foundations of America.' He took the decision to 'declare war' on terrorism and those states believed to be harbouring and supporting terrorists. The US and its allies launched a military attack on Afghanistan to destroy al-Qaeda and the Taliban government.

Even as the US pursued the war in Afghanistan, it was faced with a more insidious threat at home. A series of five letters containing bacillus anthracis, better known as anthrax, were sent to the offices of American Media, NBC, ABC, Senator Tom Daschle and Senator Patrick Leahy. In turn, these letters contaminated others in postal sorting offices, leading to contaminated mail turning up in many other places including the Supreme Court and the State Department. During September and October 2001 the FBI received over 2,300 reports of letters containing anthrax. Most of these cases turned out to be hoaxes, as were a number of cases in countries as far apart as Sweden, Norway, New Zealand, Israel, Egypt, Canada, Australia and the UK, but there was a significant number of genuine cases in the USA. This was the deadly threat that the USA had been anticipating for the previous decade, yet it proved not to be as terrible as many people had feared.

The attacks on 11 September, despite the horrendous effect, were basically 'low-tech' in concept involving primitive methods of murder in taking over the aircraft and using the planes themselves as weapons of mass destruction. But the attacks contributed massively to the fear of terrorist attack and the possibility of attack by nuclear devices and – a long-feared nightmare – of attack by chemical and biological weapons particularly smallpox.

Anthrax comes in three forms: cutaneous, respiratory and intestinal. The respiratory form is the most deadly, killing approximately 80–90% of those infected, whilst approximately 80% of those infected with the cutaneous form survive. Of those infected in the USA, the majority had the cutaneous form. The indiscriminate nature of the bacteria was evident from the diversity of the casualties. They ranged from postal workers in sorting offices, to office staff, to a seven month old baby who had been in the ABC news headquarters, as well as police officers and public health workers who had responded to the incidents. All three forms of infection can be treated with antibiotics which must be administered before patients develop symptoms of the disease. As a result none of the 40–50 staff who had been exposed in Senator Tom Daschle's office on Capitol Hill died. In contrast, the authorities were slow to appreciate the risks at postal sorting offices and delays in distributing antibiotics to certain categories of workers contributed to the deaths of a number of postal workers. In total there were only five deaths and the overall numbers of public infected was easily managed. Despite this, the degree of public anxiety and disruption caused by the letters far outweighed the number of casualties. Panic buying of gas masks and personal supplies of the antibiotic Cipro was reported as fear of further attacks spread. More disturbingly, public confidence in the ability of the administration to manage the crisis was severely undermined.

As officials and emergency response teams struggled to cope with the steady stream of letters and hoaxes, very little was known about the origins of the anthrax and the perpetrators. Al-Qaeda were the prime suspects but the targeting of the institutions of the federal government and a large number of hoaxes at abortion clinics coupled with the fact that the letters stopped suddenly without any clear link with Al-Qaeda being established, led the FBI to believe that a domestic right wing group or a lone sociopath might have been responsible. A number of reports suggested that the anthrax came from the USA, although it could equally have come from a number of other countries including the states of the former Soviet Union, the UK and Iraq. Although Ken Alibek, the former head of the Soviet bio-weapons programme suggests that 'If I were a terrorist, I would certainly not use a strain known to be from my country'. What was known was that the perpetrators had considerable technical know-how. The anthrax that was sent to Senator Tom Daschle caused considerable concern because senior law enforcement officials reported that it had been designed and milled specifically to stay in the air, increasing the chances of infecting people, with the deadly respiratory form. This only added to the confusion and anxiety.

The letter campaign suggests that anthrax has become the biological weapon of choice for terrorists. It is relatively easy to obtain, it can survive almost indefinitely, and it has now been proven to be extremely effective. So, the events of 11 September and the anthrax letters were dramatically linked. They seemingly confirmed many of the predictions and assumptions that had figured so prominently in national security debates over the previous decade. What until then had seemed a remote and hypothetical threat has now assumed an immediacy which could become the principle national security issue in many states for the foreseeable future.

1. The Emergence of the NBC Terrorism Debate

The United States and the 'third wave of vulnerability'

Throughout history, chemical and biological (CBW) weapons have been used by politically motivated individuals and groups, for purposes such as assassinations and generating terror. Since the successful development of the first nuclear weapons in 1945, debates about terrorism involving Nuclear, Biological and Chemical (NBC) weapons have been cyclical in nature, recurring in every decade, with varying levels of intensity. However, the debate in the 1990s was fundamentally different from those that preceded it, because of its persistence and its impact upon the mainstream national security debates in many states. Yet it has primarily been an American- led debate, with much of the most alarmist rhetoric and worst-case analysis originating from the USA.

Since the end of the Second World War, the USA has experienced three waves of vulnerability. The first followed the test of an atomic bomb (A bomb) by the Soviet Union in 1949; the second was a consequence of the spiralling superpower nuclear arms race that ensued; and, from 1995, the third has been NBC terrorism. At the end of the Second World War, the USA rested assured in the security offered by the awesome destructive power of the A-bomb that it had just created, and its monopoly of the knowledge of how to manufacture it. Under its protective umbrella, the USA de-mobilized a lot of its conventional military forces. This sense of security was suddenly shattered by the Soviet A-bomb test in 1949, years before it had been anticipated. This was followed by the outbreak of the Korean war in 1950, which was one of the seminal events in establishing the image of an aggressive, expansionist Communism, originating in the Soviet Union. Within ten years the Soviet Union had developed strategic bombers and intercontinental ballistic missiles (ICBMs) capable of launching nuclear weapons at the USA.

But whilst the Soviet Union had broken through this techno-logical barrier, the USA could at least feel safe in the knowledge that it had got there first, and had numerical superiority over the Soviet Union. But as the Cold War developed, the nuclear arms race between the two states meant that the Soviet Union matched, and eventually surpassed the number of US nuclear weapons. From that period onwards, the USA could no longer be assured of strategic superiority. However the end of the Cold War in 1989 alleviated this acute sense of vulnerability to the Soviet nuclear threat.

In the post-Cold War world, the USA remained as the only superpower and the pre-eminent conventional military power. For a brief period this generated a new sense of security within the USA, but the re-emergence of the NBC terrorism issue in the mid-1990s meant that it did not last long. The USA had previously experienced low levels of domestic terrorism, but it was international terrorism, the enemy 'out there,' which posed the greatest threat to its interests. What changed in the 1990s was the perception of a significantly increased threat from domestic terrorism, 'the enemy within.'

It is this new, and uniquely different, sense of vulnerability which drives the US debate on NBC terrorism. US President Bill Clinton has been noticeable in making strong public statements on this issue. In January 1999, he went on record as stating that the USA would be subject to a terrorist attack involving chemical weapons (CWs) or biological weapons (BWs) within the next few years, (1) whilst William Cohen, the US Defence Secretary, has stated that 'the question is no longer if this will happen, but when.' (2) This contrasts with the much more dis-creet approach of European leaders, who rarely make such sweeping comments.

The emergence of the 'third wave of vulnerability'
The issue of terrorism has been a particular problem since the 1970s, when ethno-nationalist groups such as the Palestine

Liberation Organization (PLO), the Popular Front For the Liberation of Palestine (PFLP) and the Abu Nidal Organization (ANO) and political groups such as the Red Army Faction (RAF) and Red Brigades (RB) were at their peak. But until the early 1990s, security debates in the West were dominated by the Cold War military and political stand-off with the Soviet Union. During this time, the balance of nuclear terror and the spread of Communism dominated debates. Concerns about terrorism and ethno-nationalist guerrilla movements assumed significance primarily because of concerns that the Soviet Union was using them as proxies to de-stabilize democratic regimes and spread Communism.

In the wake of the collapse of the Soviet Union and the end of the Cold War, the US defence community radically re-assessed the risks and challenges facing the USA, and the West in general. The outcome was that the primary threats to international security were perceived to come from a greater number of smaller, more amorphous sources, such as regional states seeking weapons of mass destruction (WMD) in pursuit of regional political ambitions, and transnational threats from non-state actors involving terrorism, crime, and narcotics. These threats had always existed but had previously been dominated by Cold War issues. All that happened was that there was a radical re-ordering of threats, and they rapidly rose to assume the primacy that the superpower confrontation had once held. To an extent some of these problems were interlinked, with many radical regimes in the developing world being profoundly anti-American, and actively seeking to limit US influence in their regions, which led to allegations of their sponsoring terrorism as a means of pursuing their foreign policy goals.

Inherent in this re-assessment of new security challenges was a search for new enemies. The 1979 Iranian revolution, with its direct challenge to Western and US influence in the Middle East, had already brought Islamic fundamentalism into the mainstream of the US national security debate. The exponential rise in Islamic terrorism during the 1980s and 1990s, which was frequently directed against US targets, served to confirm assessments that Iran would attempt to export its revolution throughout the Gulf Region and the Middle East, thereby threatening US strategic interests, such as the stability of Israel and oil supplies.

As a consequence of these developments some commentators were attracted to Professor Samuel Huntingdon's thesis, that the world was entering a period that would be marked by what he called a 'clash of civilizations.' (3) He suggested that in the post-Cold War World conflicts derived from cultural and religious divisions which would replace the ideologically driven conflicts of the Cold War. For some, perceptions of an expansionist Islamic Fundamentalism, to an extent, replaced expansionist Communism in threatening US global interests and national security. These perceived trends were also closely linked to the use of terrorism. Jessica Stern argues that the 'clash of civilizations' between the West and the rest, predicted by Samuel Huntingdon is unlikely to take place exclusively – or even principally – on the battlefield. Secretary of Defense William Cohen warned in 1997 'that some adversaries believe that their only way to fight America, given US military superiority, is to use WMD against US troops or civilians. Violent extremists have already recognized that they can impose significant pain through acts of terrorism. Right wing extremists and other domestic groups are also likely to participate in this clash.' (4)

Despite these fears, Huntingdon's thesis has never become reality, primarily because of the divisions within Islam and between different Muslim states. Islamic terrorist groups often do not work together, Muslim states have fought each other, and the West has managed to forge strategic alliances with some Muslim states. Although some Muslim states, such as Iran, and the leaders of some Islamic fundamentalist terror groups, do believe in some of the central tenets of his thesis. The rise of Islamic fundamentalism is partly derived from a belief that Islam is at a critical historical point. Globalization and the erosion of traditional values, along with widespread economic and political upheaval and inequality, has led to heightened levels of uncertainty about the future within many states. Faced by perceived threats from Western political, economic and cultural influence, Muslims believe that they must preserve their religious identity, and seize the moment to fundamentally alter their future. (5)

In conjunction with these changes in the international political system, the debate was also fuelled by a number of developments pertaining to terrorism and the proliferation of WMD. The 1991 Gulf War and the subsequent exposure of Iraq's WMD programme, provided conclusive evidence that the production of WMD is possible, despite international treaties and rigorous surveillance by the UN Special Commission on Iraq (UNSCOM). Concerns about Libya's intentions were also raised following the identification of an alleged CW facility at Tarhuna. These developments linked into broader concerns about the activities of so called rogue scientists who had previously been employed in the WMD programmes of the former Soviet Union (FSU), but who might have moved on to work for proliferator states for higher pay; and the opportunities that were afforded by rapid advances in biotechnology and genetic engineering, and the greater access to dual-use technology and expertise.

Concerns about the consequences of proliferation were heightened by the emergence of numerous ethnic-separatist wars in which civilians were deliberately targeted, and by the apparent links between proliferators and state-sponsored terrorism. Consequently, John Deutch, a former Director of the US Central Intelligence Agency (CIA), stated that the 'proliferation of nuclear, biological and chemical weapons and their potential use by states or terrorists is the most urgent challenge facing national security, and therefore the intelligence community in the post-Cold War world.' (6)

These developments established the context within which the debate flourished, but it was a number of specific terrorist incidents and trends in terrorist activity which highlighted perceptions of societal vulnerability to terrorism, and NBC terrorism in particular. First, US self-confidence was shaken in February 1993 by the bombing of the World Trade Centre in the US capital New York, by Islamic fundamentalists. This was followed in April 1995 by the bombing of the Alfred P. Murrah federal building in Oklahoma City USA by American far-right extremists. These two incidents made terrorism a national security priority, and challenged accepted beliefs and assumptions about terrorist activity in the USA. They prompted US Senator Richard Lugar to argue that 'From the tragedies of Oklahoma City and the World Trade Centre to the first act of nuclear terrorism requires but one small step.' (7) In rhetoric reminiscent of former US president Ronald Reagan's 'evil empire' speech during the Cold War (referring to the Soviet Union), President Clinton declared following the Oklahoma bombing, that 'one thing we owe those who have sacrificed is a duty to purge ourselves of the dark forces which give rise to this evil. They are forces that threaten our common peace, our freedom, our way of life.' (8)

The defining incident which brought the issues of terrorism and proliferation together however occurred (one month earlier than Oklahoma) in March 1995, when the Aum Shinrikyo or Aum Supreme Truth, a Japanese religious cult, staged an attack on the Tokyo subway system, using a CW called sarin. This shifted the significance of the debate from being purely academic in nature, to being policy-relevant, transforming the potential threat into something that was real and possibly increasing. In the immediate aftermath of the attack President Clinton issued Presidential Decision Directive 39, 'US Policy on Counter-Terrorism,' which stated that

> the development of effective capabilities for preventing and managing the consequences of terrorist use of

nuclear, biological or chemical (NBC) materials or weapons is the highest priority. Terrorist acquisition of weapons of mass destruction is not acceptable and there is no higher priority than preventing the acquisition of such materials/weapons or removing this capability from terrorist groups.' (9)

The apparent significance of these incidents was increased when they were viewed within the context of a number of trends in terrorist activity. Some analysts suggested that these incidents were symptomatic of deeper trends concerning the increasing lethality in terrorist attacks; the increasing numbers of indiscriminate terrorist attacks on population targets; and the rapid growth of religious-inspired terrorism. Individually and collectively, these trends were argued to point towards the increasing use of NBC weapons by terrorists.

For American citizens, these incidents underscored US vulnerability to terrorism, even from its own citizens. From that time, fear of 'the enemy within' was combined with the fear of the 'enemy out there.' This was an almost unique situation for the USA in particular, which fostered a new sense of vulnerability within the nation which, in the words of Richard Falkenrath, Robert Newman and Bradley Thayer, is 'America's Achilles Heel.' It also prompted knee-jerk reactions from the US establishment which blew the threat out of proportion. Congress declared in the Anti-Terrorism and Effective Death Penalty Act (1996) that 'international terrorism is among the most serious transnational threats faced by the United States and its allies, far eclipsing the dangers posed by population growth and pollution.' (10) Yet a reasoned analysis of the extent and impact of international terrorism simply does not bear this statement out. Therefore the debate on WMD terrorism dovetailed into broader and stronger concerns about the growth of terrorism in general.

The debate on NBC terrorism
In many aspects the arguments that were developed in the debate during the 1990s are not dissimilar to those in some of the literature from the late 1970s. During that period, secular terrorist violence was at its peak, with Palestinian groups, in particular, carrying out numerous high-profile attacks, and many Western European states experiencing political and ethno-separatist terrorism. Writing in 1977, David Rosenbaum argued that individuals with the necessary skills to develop nuclear weapons are easily found, and that 'Most revolutionaries now however seem to consider indiscriminate slaughter a primary tactic and one of which they are proud.' (11) Yet in the

1970s the debate was balanced out with analysts such as Brian Jenkins questioning terrorists' ability and motivations to procure NBC weapons: 'Nuclear terrorism is neither imminent nor inevitable ... simply killing a lot of people is not an objective of terrorism.' (12) It was argued that serious obstacles to NBC terrorism existed, and that the political and strategic disincentives for engaging in such attacks would be high. This seemed to be borne out by the fact that there were no public signs that any terrorist group had the will, or the capability, to engage in NBC violence. Studies assumed that terrorists needed political and material support for their organizations, and aimed to raise awareness of their cause in order to gain public sympathy and support. The view of many analysts was that the use of NBC weapons would stiffen governments' resolve not to accede to the terrorists' demands, and alienate potential supporters.

These types of arguments still permeated the debate in the 1980s, with Grant Wardlaw arguing that, 'The capability of killing on a grand scale must be balanced against the fear of widespread revulsion and alienating perceived constituents [supporters], of provoking a massive, publicly approved government crackdown.' (13) In the background papers for the 1985 International Task Force On the Prevention of Nuclear Terrorism, a multidisciplinary task-force of experts that was convened to undertake the first comprehensive analysis of the potential threat, Konrad Kellen argued that, 'terrorists believe their cause are positive aims designed to better the human condition. Thus, although violence is their weapon, mass killing is not likely to be attractive to most of them.' (14) Although Harvey J.McGeorge cautioned that 'The odious and insidious nature of chemical and biological agents suggests that they are potentially the most powerful and effective instruments of terror available. Circumstances suggest an evolution beyond explosives based violence is both necessary for terrorists and perhaps currently underway.' (15)

In direct contrast, the early years of the debate in the 1990s was marked by alarmist and worst-case analysis of the potential threat, and the sense of balance seemed to have been lost. The US discussions of the issue, in particular, generated apocalyptic visions of terrorist attacks involving WMD, spawning a whole new terminology of 'super terrorism,' 'catastrophic terrorism', 'ultimate terrorism' and 'ultraterrorism.'(16) US Senator Sam Nunn argued that , 'the threat of terrorist attack on American cities involving chemical, biological, radiological, or nuclear weapons has reached a point where a bold and vigorous effort is required. This is a clear and present danger to the American people that requires a timely response.' (17) Similarly, Kyle

Olsen argued that 'People must recognize that the threat from bioterrorism is not a curiosity but a grim reality as we enter the next century.' (18) In Spring 1997, the Director of the US Federal Bureau of Investigations (FBI), Louis Freeh, stated that 'The acquisition, proliferation, threatened or actual use of weapons of mass destruction by a terrorist group or individuals constitutes one of the gravest threats to the United States.' (19) This change in the nature of the debate was due to the political context within which the debate was taking place, which also served to heighten the significance that the debate itself assumed amongst the policy community and within the broader national security debate.

In the 1970s, articles about nuclear terrorism were merely an adjunct to broader debates about nuclear non-proliferation, following the Indian test of a nuclear weapon and the signature of the Non-Proliferation Treaty (NPT) in 1974. Moreover as such, the issue was lost alongside the more immediate concerns of policy makers to contain proliferation. Consequently, the issue failed to galvanize any significant response amongst them.

What is startling about the debate in the 1990s was that the sheer number of articles and other publications that were produced was significantly higher than in other decades. But more importantly, the issue became a debate in its own right, rather than remaining an adjunct to the broader debates on proliferation and terrorism. Consequently, activist legislators in the USA seized upon the issue and demanded action. The cumulative pressure from the debate in the policy community and the US Congress led to significant policy responses from the US administration, which were copied in other countries.

This change in political context was paralleled by developments in technology which served to broaden out the debate. In the 1970s the main focus was on nuclear terrorism, which culminated in the convening of the International Task Force On the Prevention of Nuclear Terrorism in 1985. Chemical and biological terrorism was a much lower concern at that time, despite the fact that CW are easier to develop than nuclear weapons. The threat of biological terrorism was also downplayed because BW had been used so rarely that precedent suggested they would not be used; that their use was so morally repugnant that no-one would consider using them; that the technology was too difficult for all but the most well equipped laboratories to master; and that the potential destructiveness of these weapons was simply too great for them to be considered. (20)

This concern about nuclear terrorism revived in the early 1990s when it became evident that there was a haemorrhage of nuclear materials from insecure nuclear facilities in the FSU.

But significantly, terrorism involving CBW had also begun to be considered as a threat equal to that of nuclear terrorism. By the mid-1990s developments in education and technology had made the development of all forms of NBC weapons relatively easier for non-state actors, but it was the explosive growth of the biotechnology industry, coupled with the potential casualty levels that BW can cause, which combined to put BW terrorism at the forefront of concern for the USA. In 1998, Richard Betts argued that 'Biological Weapons should now be the most serious concern, with nuclear weapons second and chemicals a distant third.' (21)

By the late 1990s, however, the debate was becoming more balanced and less alarmist in nature, with an increasing number of analysts downplaying the likelihood of a catastrophic attack involving a WMD, whilst accepting that it was a theoretical possibility. By the late 1990s Richard Falkenrath was arguing that WMD terrorism was 'a low-probability, high-consequence threat.' (22) Whereas at the beginning of the debate, analysts focused on the factors which made NBC terrorism more likely, by the late 1990s a larger number of analysts were looking at the factors which would inhibit NBC terrorism. Yet despite this, the US Commission on National Security still claimed in 1999 that 'the most serious threat to our security may consist of unannounced attacks on American cities by sub-national groups (such as drug cartels, cults, or criminal gangs) using genetically engineered pathogens.' (23)

The US response
During the Cold War the West, and the USA in particular, knew exactly who its enemies were, and there was a peculiar comfort and safety in this knowledge. Nuclear deterrence proved to be an effective means to counter the Soviet nuclear threat, whilst arms control and political rapprochement through detente (followed by glasnost) were pursued as a means of maintaining the stability of the deterrent relationship. In the 1990s however, the less monolithic, sometimes transnational and invariably shadowy nature of the threats to national security made them much more difficult to deal with. Analysis tended to over-emphasize the increasing vulnerability of technologically dependent states to terrorist violence, overlooking the fact that states have always been vulnerable, which is an accepted fact of life in many states.

This new sense of vulnerability was heightened by the fact that the traditional means of dealing with WMD threats through deterrence, arms control and political engagement were ineffective for dealing with these new threats. This prompted a radical re-assessment of how the USA should deal with national secu-

rity threats. Richard Betts argued that this new wave of vulnerability should be met with a strong civil defence programme, (24)
which had been all but rejected during the Cold War. Betts
argued that it should be easier to see the value of civil defence
in the context of more limited attacks, because during the Cold
War the lives that would have been saved seemed less salient
than the lives that would have been lost. (25) Yet civil defence is
an insular and reactive strategy, which can deal only with the
consequences of terrorist attacks.

This approach also involves an acceptance of America's state
of vulnerability, which does not sit well with the American psyche. As the sole remaining superpower, the US likes to be in
control of events, and perceives itself to be the foremost nation
in safeguarding and promoting democracy. The humiliation and
public embarrassment at being held hostage by small groups of
extremists who reject US values, is something which US society
and politics still needs to come to terms with, otherwise the US
government runs the risk of over reacting to terrorist incidents.

By the turn of the century the debate had become self-sus-
taining. Government studies and exercises to test and develop
response capabilities merely served to reinforce existing perceptions and misconceptions. US governmental planning proceeded on the basis of worst- case scenarios which invariably proved
that existing counter-measures were inadequate. In March
1998, for example, officials conducted an exercise to test
responses to the terrorist use of a BW along the Mexico-
American border. As the scenario unfolded thousands of people
fell ill, state and local officials were quickly overwhelmed, and
huge gaps were discovered in logistics, legal authority and medical care. (26) Yet the outcome of the exercise was dependent
upon its underlying assumptions, particularly that the terrorists
would develop a genetically modified BW which was resistant to
known vaccines, and that they were able to achieve effective dispersal of the agent. No-one seriously questioned the efficacy of
these assumptions.

Resultant publicity of these exercises and a massive increase
in sensational reporting in the late 1990s, served to heighten
public concern, and give activist legislators a means of pressur-
ing the administration. This provided the mass media with a
steady stream of alarmist stories which played upon public concerns. Yet the media has consistently failed to question the
validity of the worst-case scenarios which are underpinning
many of the current assessments of the threat and US vulnerability towards it.

The high profile accorded to the potential threat and the
emphasis on worst-case scenarios is also a consequence of the

dynamics that operate within the US bureaucracy. With the budgets of many of the agencies concerned with national security issues being cut in the post-Cold War world, they have sought new ways to maintain their funding base. The allocation of hundreds of millions of dollars to NBC terrorism-related programmes has made it the latest 'pork barrel' issue in US politics. Establishing a role for themselves in programmes to combat the threat of WMD terrorism became the latest issue over which various departments, agencies and other bodies could compete for funding. (27)

As a result of the large number of agencies attempting to enhance their role in this field, there has been a great deal of duplication as bureaucratic battles were fought to determine areas of responsibility. One consequence was that hazardous-materials response teams were established by the National Guard, the FBI, the army, the US Marine Corps and scores of police and fire departments. (28) The FBI wanted to build a multi-million-dollar biolab, despite the fact that the US army and the Centers For Disease Control already have more than a dozen such facilities. (29) Therefore it can be argued that as the different agencies compete for resources by highlighting inadequacies in their capabilities for dealing with the threat, they are also exacerbating concerns about the threat, which in turn maintains the high provision of funding.

The same is also true of commercial companies which have identified a lucrative market for their products in this area. In one instance, two members of a scientific panel which endorsed a plan to stockpile BW vaccines stood to financially gain from its implementation; and William Crowe, the former Chair of the Joint Chiefs of Staff who has been a strong advocate for establishing effective counter-terrorism programmes, is linked to Michigan Biologic Products, which is the sole manufacturer of an anthrax vaccine. (30) Anti-terrorism consultants have also acknowledged that this issue has become the latest gravy train.

Therefore there are actors both inside and outside of government who have a vested interest in emphasizing the worst-case analysis. As one cynical observer put it, 'The rising din about bioterrorism in the US is dominated by one faction – people who say the problem exists, and they should be trusted to deal with it.' (31) The influence of these actors invariably increases the difficulty of reaching a reasoned analysis of the potential threat, and how to respond to it.

The societal impact of the high profile that this issue has assumed can be gauged from its impact on peoples' everyday lives. This is most marked by its assimilation into the mainstream cultural media. There have always been books and films about NBC terrorism, but in the 1990s these types of books were making the bestseller lists, with one in particular, 'The Cobra Event,' by Richard Preston, even arousing President Clinton's interest. Whilst the film industry invested huge amounts of money in a number of high-profile films, such as the James Bond movie, 'The World is Not Enough,' and 'Mission Impossible 2.'

A side effect of all of this has been the emergence of a large number of hoaxers. At the end of 1998 Southern California USA, was hit by a spate of anthrax scares, with police being called out to at least seven alleged incidents in December alone. In one incident more than 750 people were detained in a US Los Angeles nightclub after an anonymous caller informed the police that a significant amount of the bacteria was in the club. Police accompanied by the FBI domestic terrorism team tested the air filters in the club and searched all the patrons, but the case proved to be a hoax. In all, a total of 3000 people have been affected by the hoaxes in California, and anthrax threats have also been reported in the US states Colorado, Kentucky and Tennessee. (32)

In 1999, US Senator Richard Lugar invested a considerable amount of money in a series of four TV commercials warning of the threat from nuclear terrorism, as part of his campaign to secure the Republican presidential nomination. (33) His belief that he could generate popular support on such a seemingly minor issue indicates the level to which he considered that it had permeated the US public consciousness. Certainly, a public opinion poll carried out by the Mellman Group for the Henry L. Stimson Center in 1997 discovered that 33 per cent of respondents considered that terrorists posed the greatest nuclear threat to the USA (compared to 9 per cent thinking it was Iran, and 12 per cent thinking it was Iraq). (34) As Jessica Stern observes, terrorism evokes an emotional response, because terrorists aim to make the target feel vulnerable, which in turn fuels public uncertainty. Consequently, those that choose to exploit the issue can easily tap into a groundswell of public unease. (35)

This sense of unease is also driven by the strong psychological reaction that NBC weapons evoke. Fear of disease and poison are deep rooted within the human psyche – both psychologically and culturally. This partly derives from a historical fear of disease which goes back to the Middle Ages, when Europe experienced a number of great plagues. One commentator observed that, 'It plays on primal human fears of past and future – of Dark Ages, plagues that science was supposed to have conquered, and of modern microscopic Frankensteins unleashed by out-of-control genetic engineers.' (36) Fear of unusual diseases is much stronger than fear of common diseases, tending to occupy the public imagination to a much greater extent, even if they only kill a few people. Equally, catastrophic risks are disproportionately feared, and receive more coverage in the press despite their rarity, and events that are uncontrollable and inequitable invoke the greatest dread. Jessica Stern argues that 'We feel a gut-level fear of nuclear, biological and chemical terrorism, and we want to eradicate the risk entirely, with little regard to cost.' (37)

When the issue became policy-relevant, US congressmen put considerable pressure on the US administration to take action, which has led to a strong policy response within the USA. The Republican party, in particular, had been pressing for action for several years, with the result that it became one of the few policy areas where President Clinton received congressional support. This political pressure was sustained by activist legislators, some of whom arranged publicity stunts, such as that sponsored by Republican Curt Weldon, in which the US Marine Corps' chemical, biological incident response force conducted a full-blown exercise on Capitol Hill, with the avowed aim of influencing congressmen to approve funding for more equipment for firefighters and the Marines. (38)

Legislators have readily agreed to the budgetary demands of implementing a programme of counter-measures, partly it would seem because they do not want to be held responsible for inadequate response capabilities should an attack actually occur. However this has led to a situation in which critics argue, that funding is based upon fear and perceived vulnerability, rather than a rational assessment of the real threat. The resultant sudden investment of resources before an adequate foundation plan had been established merely led to duplication and confusion. (39)

The debate in other countries
In Russia, the issue has nowhere near the profile that it does in the West, despite the fact that Russia also began to experience a uniquely new sense of vulnerability in the late 1990s. This is probably due to the low profile which terrorism previously held in Russian security debates. There had been few signs of terrorism in Russia until the 1990s, when the dissolution of the Soviet Union unleashed a wave of religious and nationalist sentiment. This included a large growth in right-wing terrorism, which has primarily been directed against Russia's Jewish population. (40) But the main source of concern has been the violent ethnonationalist separatist movements within Russia. Initially, terror-

ist acts by these groups tended to remain confined to the region of the insurgency, but in 1999, Islamic fundamentalists fighting for the independence of Dagestan, bombed a number of apartment blocks in Moscow, killing hundreds of civilians. This led to a fundamental change in Russian security doctrine, which by 1999 clearly identified terrorism, particularly international terrorism, as a serious threat to Russia's security. (41)

The security forces in Russia and the other states of the FSU were unable to contain these outbreaks of violence, because effective law enforcement had been undermined by endemic problems derived from fragmented political and legal authority and pervasive corruption throughout the government, bureaucracy and the security forces themselves. This left the security forces unable to cope with the widespread disregard for the law, or contain the Russian mafia which has infiltrated many part of government, politics and the economy.

This general malaise within Russian government and society also created the conditions which make NBC terrorism a real danger. The main problem that Russia faces is its decaying military infrastructure, which has spread to affect its WMD infrastructure. In particular, there are suspect security and accounting procedures at nuclear facilities, shortages of trained personnel and modern equipment, inadequate provision for the transport of nuclear materials, ineffective material control procedures, and inadequate storage facilities for nuclear materials. These deficiencies, coupled with plummeting morale and poor pay amongst Russian military personnel and workers in the nuclear industry, has created the conditions in which bribery, corruption and the theft of nuclear materials and other types of materials and equipment associated with NBC weapons has become much more likely.

Partly as a result of the low threat perception of terrorism, but also because of a lack of resources, the Russian government response to the threat has been limited. For members of the Russian parliament the Duma, security debates have been dominated by the Strategic Arms Reduction Treaty (START), NATO expansion and the general weakness of the Russian armed forces, although some official sources have expressed concern about the potential threat. As early as 1992, the Ministry of Security warned that the threat of nuclear sabotage was real and that there had been threats against three nuclear power plants. This was also supported by the Defence Ministry which stated that 'We cannot exclude possibilities of unauthorized access (by individual terrorists and terrorist groups) to Russian nuclear warheads in storage or in transportation in the future.' Yuri Luzhkov, the populist mayor of Moscow, has also expressed concern about sabotage at nuclear power plants, (42) but the issue still does not have the same political ramifications as it does in the USA.

Russian academic literature is also dominated by issues related to START and other arms control issues, particularly non-proliferation. However the academics who have worked on the subject generally reflect views prevalent in the USA. Vladimir Orlov considers that,

> The growth of national radicalism and the appearance of religious sects similar to Aum in Japan, as well as ethnic wars and low intensity conflicts in the geopolitical space of the Former Soviet Union, together with the absence or inefficiency of border controls within the CIS and the large number of poorly guarded strategic facilities, has made Russia and her CIS neighbours more vulnerable to the threat of terrorism involving WMD than other regions of the world, even those with a higher incidence of terrorist activity. (43)

Writing in 1997, Oleg Bukharin considers terrorist threats to nuclear facilities to be real and increasing, but maintained that the possibility of the detonation of a nuclear explosive device appeared to be hypothetical. (44) Masha Katsva argues that,

> Chemical Weapons in Russia are becoming an even more dangerous tool for terrorism because of instability, inadequate storage of CW, the ongoing economic crisis, and the lack of appropriate legislation in the Russian Federation ...The availability of toxic materials and the devastating effect of the use of small amounts of the extremely toxic agents could attract terrorists to the use of agents and toxins. Terrorists may also choose CBW because organization of population and individuals protection is difficult and finding out the source of the attack is hard. One of the aspects which makes CBW such an attractive weapon for terrorists is their ability to induce panic. In general terrorists thrive off the shock factor of their activities and chemical warfare exhibits a high level of shock value. (45)

In the wake of the 1999 Moscow bomb blasts, the Russian press also expressed concerns about the security of nuclear installations. (46) Yet despite the fact that Russia is significantly more vulnerable to NBC terrorism than the USA, there has not been the same sense of urgency and hysteria experienced in the USA. Moreover whilst the threat is generally acknowledged to be a real one within Russia, it is kept firmly in proportion. In contrast to the USA, which focuses on the most dangerous potential threat, the Russian debate focuses on what is perceived to be the most immediate and realistic one. Hence, the principal focus in the Russian debate is terrorist attacks on nuclear power plants, which now receives only limited attention in the US debate.

For some other states, this sense of vulnerability is not a new phenomenon. The UK has been under threat from domestic and international terrorism for decades, and the British public has directly experienced atrocities carried out by the Irish Republican Army (IRA) and other terrorist groups. Therefore the experience in the USA also contrasts sharply with that in the UK, where the issue is being dealt with in a much more low-key fashion. For example NBC terrorism exercises are regularly conducted in the UK, but until very recently the assumptions on which they were planned, and their results, were not publicized. For example in 1995 the emergency services conducted operation 'Fire Storm' in the city of Manchester. Very little is known about the exercise, but indications suggest that it involved a scenario of terrorists unleashing a canister of anthrax. One police officer commented, 'The press are not invited ... it's private.' On whether it was a BW exercise, another officer commented. 'There is no publicly available information on that type of exercise.' The emergency planning authorities also conduct a number of much smaller exercises a year about which very little is known. (47) On the 1st July 2000 however, these restrictions were relaxed a little, when the media was briefed on a major CW terrorism exercise conducted in London. This served the purpose of heightening public awareness, even though officials were careful to downplay the potential threat.

This high level of secrecy is also reflected in official government statements in Parliament. In response to one question concerning what studies the UK Ministry of Defence (MOD) had carried out in response to the threat from nuclear terrorism, a defence minister replied, 'My Department keeps the possibility of such a threat under constant review. It would not be appropriate, for reasons of national security and defence, to provide more specific details of any studies in this area and the information is therefore withheld.' (48)

In addition, differences in the legislative process in the UK mean that policy responses have been internally generated by the government rather than being the result of pressure from legislators. In fact, UK members of parliament (MPs) have been markedly less active on this issue than have some congressmen and senators in the USA. No MPs have brought this issue to the forefront of the UK security debate as Senators Sam Nunn and Richard Lugar have in the USA. Those MPs that are interested in issues related to terrorism focus instead on issues that are of immediate and direct interest, such as Northern Ireland and the provisions of anti-terrorism legislation. Partly because of the different nature of the two legislatures and party political processes, British MPs have fewer official opportunities than their American counterparts to pursue specific issues. But, even so, there have been very few incidences where issues associated with NBC terrorism have been raised in parliament, (49) therefore there has been less external pressure on the British government to act, and programmes of counter-measures have been instituted in a much more relaxed political environment. This is reflected in a different approach to combat the threat within the UK, which places the imperative on intelligence warning rather than civil defence.

The UK academic community is also generally more downbeat about the threat than their American counterparts. (50). Although some individuals reflect the views being expressed in the US. Professor Frank Barnaby has been highlighting the dangers of nuclear terrorism since the early 1990s, and Professor Paul Rogers wrote an article entitled 'The Next Terror Weapon Will Be Biological. And It Could be Used Soon' for the *Guardian* newspaper (51). In general though, whilst there is a widespread acknowledgement that it is a real threat, most academics in the UK consider that it has been over hyped in the American literature. (52) Therefore, despite occasional articles in the press, there is no major public concern about the potential threat within the UK.

Israel is potentially one of the states most under threat from NBC terrorism. From the time of its founding it has experienced a grave threat from Palestinian and Muslim terrorism, originally from the Secular PLO and its offshoots, which by the 1990s were largely replaced by Muslim fundamentalist groups such as Islamic Jihad and Hamas. This was coupled with increased concerns about Jewish terrorism and extremist religious cults.

Yet despite potentially facing the gravest threat, there is very little published material on this issue coming from Israeli Universities and non-governmental think-tanks. As is the case in Russia, the Israeli national security debate is dominated by immediate and most likely threats, such as Israel's relations with its neighbours, the conventional force balance in the Middle East, the proliferation of WMD in the Middle East, and conventional forms of terrorism. A public opinion poll on National Security, conducted by Bar Ilan University, indicated that of all the threats they faced, Israelis were most concerned about suicide bombings by Islamic militants, and NBC terrorism was not mentioned. (53)

As a consequence, there is no undue sense of alarm within Israel. The threat is acknowledged, but is merely an adjunct to the broader debate on terrorism, rather than being a debate in its own right. Boaz Ganor argues that 'Many scholars who have studied terrorism agree today that it is only a matter of time, now that the Supreme Truth Cult in Japan has paved the way for others of its ilk, until other such groups use non-conventional weaponry in their attacks. (54) In contrast, Ehud Sprinzak of the Hebrew University of Jerusalem, who wrote one of the most influential articles in the late 1990s, argues that a WMD attack is neither inevitable nor likely. This is primarily because the world has not entered a new era of terrorist chaos, and there are only a very small number of groups likely to resort to using WMD. He blames the hype in the US debate on sloppy thinking, vested interests and morbid fascination. (55) Since Israel already has strong counter-terrorism policies, and civil defence programmes to counter NBC threats, there is no need for a debate to generate political pressure for counter-measures, in the same way as has occurred in the US.

Conclusion

There is little doubt that in the 1990s there were inflated claims of the threat posed by WMD terrorism, but in the aftermath of the attacks on 11 September the USA was the target for the first ever sustained bio-terrorism campaign. As a result, the differences between the various national debates began to disappear and the perceptions that characterised the debate in the USA became more universally accepted. However, there were some attempts at keeping a sense of proportion. Robin Cook, the leader of the House of Commons in the UK, stated that the 'possibility of a BW attack is assessed as low. It is important to keep it in perspective. We are not aware of a specific threat, we are not anticipating it, but it is important that we are ready.'

The events of September and October 2001 proved that the threat from WMD terrorism is a very real one, apparently confirming a number of assumptions and preconceptions that have driven policy in many states. These include:

- Trends in terrorist activity make further incidents involving NBC weapons and WMD possible.
- The disincentives for terrorists to use NBC weapons are weakening, whilst the motivations to use them are increasing, for a greater number of groups.

•Technologically, it is becoming increasingly possible for non-state actors to develop NBC weapons.

•Secular groups are not interested in using NBC weapons, especially because of concerns that it will lose them political support.

•Religious terrorists are most likely to use NBC weapons, and will use them if they can acquire them, because they operate under fewer constraints.

Despite these assumptions and preconceptions that permeate the debate, until the anthrax attacks in the USA many academics argued there were boundaries to terrorist activities involving WMD. Events have now taken the debate to a new level. With disease having been used as a weapon, a psychological threshold has been crossed and the significance of psychological factors in using NBC weapons has to be reassessed. There is little doubt that the face of terrorism has changed and there is no turning back. The world has to face the fact that one terrorist or group is capable of staging a bio terror campaign in the heart of the USA. Any sense of security that the public previously enjoyed has collapsed, creating strong political pressure for tougher counter terrorism measures and more proactive use of military force to attack terrorists in other countries. Whilst the frequency and destructiveness of future attacks remains unknown, there is little doubt that some terrorists will continue to try and use NBC weapons. As a result, this vulnerability will continue to be a central feature of national security debates for the foreseeable future. The following chapters in this book will explore the strengths and weaknesses of these assumptions, to reach conclusions about the nature of the threat and the means of countering it.

Notes and references
1. Michael Evans, 'Russians Help to Make Chemical Arms', *The Times* (25 January 1999)
2. William Cohen, US Defence Secretary, quoted in Ehud Sprinzak, 'The Great Superterrorism Scare', *Foreign Policy* (Fall 1998) p 111
3. Samuel P. Huntingdon, *The Clash of Civilisations and the Remaking of the New World Order* (New York: Simon & Schuster 1996)
4. Jessica Stern, *The Ultimate Terrorists* (Harvard University, 1999) p 5
5. Gavin Cameron, *Nuclear Terrorism: A Threat assessment for the Twentieth Century* (Basingstoke: MacMillan, 1999) p 78
6. John M. Deutch, Speech to Harvard-Los Alamos Conference on Nuclear Biological and Chemical Weapons Proliferation and Terrorism, Washington, DC (23 May 1996)
<speeches/archives/1996/dci_speech_052396.html>
7. International Physicians For the Prevention of Nuclear War, 'Crude

Nuclear Weapons: Proliferation and the Terrorist Threat', *IPPNW Global Health Watch Report* 1, p 42

8. Thomas J. Badey, 'US Anti-Terrorism Policy: The Clinton Administration, *Contemporary Security Policy* 19/2 (August 1998) p 52

9. Ron Purver, 'Chemical and Biological Terrorism: New Threat to Public Safety?', *Conflict Studies* 295 (December 1996–January 1997) p 20

10. Badey: 'US Anti-Terrorism Policy, p 52

11. David M. Rosenbaum, 'Nuclear Terror', *International Security* 1/3 (Winter 1997) p 147

12. John F. Murphy, 'Co-operative International Arrangements: Prevention of Nuclear Terrorism and the Extradition and Prosecution of Terrorists', in Paul Leventhal and Yonah Alexander (eds), *Preventing Nuclear Terrorism* (Lexington, MA: Lexington Books, 1986) p 374

13. Quote by Grant Wardlaw *Political Terrorism* (1983) found in Alison Jamieson, *Terrorism* (Hove: Wayland 1991) p 44

14. Konrad Kellen, 'The Potential For Nuclear Terrorism: A Discussion', in Leventhal and Alexander (eds): *Preventing Nuclear Terrorism*, p 113

15. Harvey J. McGeorge, 'Reversing The Trend On Terror,' *Defence and Foreign Affairs* (April 1988) p 22

16. Ehud Sprinzak, 'The Great Superterrorism Scare,' *Foreign Policy* (Fall 1998); Ashton Carter, John Deutch and Philip Zelikow, 'Catastrophic Terrorism,' Foreign Affairs (November–December 1998); W.D. Brackett, *Holy Terror, Armageddon in Tokyo* (New York: Weatherhill, 1996) p 45

17. Sam Nunn, Terrorism Meets Proliferation: A Post-Cold War The Convergence of Threats', *The Monitor* 3/2 (Spring 1997) p 4

18. Quoted in Robert Taylor, 'All Fall Down', Special Report, *New Scientist* (11 May 1996) p 32

19. Statement by Louis Freeh, Director, Federal Bureau of Investigation, before the United States Senate Appropriations Committee Hearing on Counterterrorism, (May 13, 1997) <http://www.fbi.gov>

20. D.A. Henderson, 'Bioterrorism As A Public Health Threat', *Journal of Emerging Diseases* 4/3 (June–September 1998) p 1

21. Richard Betts, 'The New Threat of Mass Destruction', *Foreign Affairs* (January–February 1996) p 27

22. Richard Falkenrath, 'Confronting Nuclear, Biological and Chemical Terrorism', *Survival* 40/3 (Autumn 1998) p 44

23. 'New World Coming: American Security in the 21st Century', Report of the US Commission on National Security (15 September 1999) <www.nssg.gov>

24. Betts: 'The New Threat of Mass Destruction', p 27

25. Betts: 'The New Threat of Mass Destruction', p 37

26. *Guardian* (28 April 1998)

27. In one example, federal money for health and human services is tight but the Department of Health and Human Services still received an additional $144 million, compared to its existing $14 million, to cope with the bioterrorism preparedness. 'Bioterrorism Panic Rises, But Is It Truly Justified?, *The World's Nuclear News Agency* (26 March 1999)

28. 'Agencies May Be Getting Fat Off Bioterrorism Fear', *The Salt Lake Tribune* (31 October 1999)

29. 'Bioterrorism Panic Rises, But Is It Truly Justified?'

30. Sprinzak: 'The Great Superterrorism Scare', p 117

31. 'Bioterrorism Panic Rises, But Is It Truly Justified?'

32. Christopher Reed, 'Hoax Callers Spread Anthrax Scare', *Guardian* (29 December 1998)
33. 'Lugar Unveils Ads on Nuclear Terrorism', *USA Today* (4 November 1999)
34. 'Voters' Attitudes To Nuclear Weapons', The Mellman Group (6 November 1997) <http://www.stimson.org/policy/pollmemo.htm>
35. Stern: *The Ultimate Terrorists*, p 12
36. Sydney J. Freedberg and Marilyn Werber Serefini, 'Be Afraid, Be Moderately Afraid', *The national Journal* 31/13, p 807
37. Stern: *The Ultimate Terrorists*, pp 34, 35, 41
38. 'Fake Nerve Gas Attack Wednesday in Rayburn', Roll Call (28 April 1997)
39. 'Agencies May Be Getting Fat Off Bioterrorism Fear'
40. Mathew Engel, 'A History of Hate', *Guardian* (16 August 1999)
41. 'National Security Doctrine Stresses Multipolar World', *The Moscow Times* (13 January 1999)
42. Vladimir Orlov, 'Preventing The Threat of Nuclear Terrorism: The Case of Russia', *Disarmament Diplomacy* (November 1997) p 15
43. Orlov: 'Preventing The Threat of Nuclear Terrorism', p 13
44. Oleg Bukharin, 'Problems of Nuclear Terrorism', *The Monitor* 3/2 (Spring 1997), Center For International Trade and Security at the University of Georgia, p 8
45. Masha Katsva, 'Threat Of Chemical and Biological Terrorism in Russia', *The Monitor* 3/2 (Spring 1997) p 14
46. 'Could Terrorists Hit Sosnovy Bor?', *The St Petersburg Times* (2 November 1999)
47. Wendy Barnaby, *The Plague Makers: The Secret World of Biological Warfare* (London: Vision Paperbacks, 1997) pp 36–37
48. Reply to question from Llew Smith MP, by Mr Arbuthnot, *Parliamentary Debates* 288, 1996–7, Col. 310 (16 January 1997)
49. See parliamentary questions by Llew Smith, *Parliamentary Debates* 288, 1996–97, Col. 310 (16 January 1997); David Chaytor, *Parliamentary Debates* 302, 1997–98, Col. 548, (10 December 1997); David Chaytor, *Parliamentary Debates* 304, 1997–98, Col. 213 (14 January 1998); Julia Drown, *Parliamentary Debates* 335, 1998–99, Col. 534 (27 July 1999); Robert Key, *Parliamentary Debates* 1998–99, Col. 277 (7 July 1999)
50. Bruce Hoffman, 'Terrorism and WMD: Some Preliminary Hypotheses', *Nonproliferation Review* (Spring–Summer 1997)
51. Paul Rogers, 'The Next Terror Weapon Will Be Biological, And It Could Be Used Soon', *Guardian* (18 August 1998)
52. Interviews: Dr Alistair Hay (28 April 1999); Dr Trevor Findlay (8 December 1999): Interview, name withheld by request (2 November 1998)
Similarly, Alan Meale MP and Ian Haworth both stressed that the dominant threat to society from religious cults was the threat to the individual, rather than NBC terrorism: Interviews (14 April 1999)
53. 'New Public Opinion Poll On Terrorism and Israeli National Security', *BESA Bulletin*, Bar Ilan University No.10 (November 1999)
54. Boaz Ganor, 'Non-Conventional Terrorism: Chemical, Nuclear, Biological' <http://www.ict.org.il/articles/article1.htm>
55. Sprinzak: 'The Great Superterrorism Scare', pp 111–114

2. Trends in Terrorist Activity

One of the core assumptions underpinning much of the published analysis of NBC terrorism threats is that specific trends in terrorist activity indicate, or even prove, that increased use of NBC weapons by terrorists is highly likely, or even inevitable. The general conclusion is that current trends are leading to an increase in the number of terrorist groups that are both capable and interested in causing mass casualties. The two principal trends that have been identified are the steadily increasing lethality of terrorist attacks and the growth of religious terrorism. Causal links are frequently drawn between the two, because religious terrorists are considered to be more prone to engage in acts of indiscriminate violence. This chapter will also explore the past record of NBC terrorism, to look for possible trends, as well as other themes and issues which might provide insights for assessing the future threat.

Trends in terrorist attacks: fewer incidents, greater casualties
Figures collated by the US Office of Technology Assessment (OTA) show that during the 1970s there were a total of 8,114 terrorists incidents worldwide, which resulted in 4,978 deaths

and 6,902 injured. During the 1980s there were 31,426 incidents, resulting in 70,859 deaths and 47,849 injured. (1) The RAND-St Andrews, joint-university, database of international terrorist incidents, which has been in operation since 1968, records 2,536 incidents in the 1970s, resulting in 1975 deaths, and records 3,658 incidents in the 1980s, resulting in 4,077 deaths. These figures indicate that casualty levels are increasing at a faster rate than the number of incidents, and therefore that individual incidents are becoming more lethal. During the 1980s the number of international terrorist incidents was about 50 per cent more than in the 1970s, and twice as many people were killed. (2) During the 1990s the number of international terrorist incidents actually began to fall. A record 484 incidents occurred in 1991, which fell to 343 in 1992, then to 360 in 1993, to 353 in 1994 and finally to 278 in 1995. Yet as these figures fell, a greater percentage of incidents were resulting in fatalities.

These figures relate only to international terrorism, but the evidence in respect of domestic terrorism is more problematic. Whilst there are some indications that domestic terrorism is also following this trend, particularly in Algeria and Sri Lanka, this is not borne out by groups such as the IRA and the Basque Separatist group, Euskadi Ta Askatasuna (ETA). Richard Falkenrath, Robert Newman and Bradley Thayer, however, believe that the levels of violence which terrorists believe is necessary to achieve their goals is rising. (3)

Whilst all of these figures highlight the fact that terrorist attacks are becoming more lethal, hidden within them is a more dramatic assessment which lies at the heart of the contention, that the trend towards increasing levels of lethality will result in the increasing use of NBC weapons. Writing in 1990, Professor Paul Wilkinson identified a trend, that originated from 1982, of increasingly indiscriminate and lethal attacks in which ordinary civilians were targeted. He pondered:

> How does one explain this increase in indiscriminateness? In part it results from the terrorists' ever more desperate desire for publicity. With the media and the public satiated with reports of violence around the world, terrorist leaders have concluded that they must commit greater atrocities to capture the headlines. Another key factor is the growing attraction of soft targets to terrorists, increasingly aware of the greater risks that face them if they seek to attack high prestige targets ... Some experienced observers have suggested that another major element may be a shift inside terrorist organizations away from the more

pragmatic 'politically minded' terrorist leaders to
fanatical hard men, obsessed with vengeance and
violence. (4)

His assessment was confirmed in 1996, by John Deutch a former Director of the CIA, who argued that 'Where once terrorists
undertook relatively small operations aimed at attaining specific political objectives, today they are more likely to inflict mass
casualties as a form of revenge.' (5)

Yet Richard Falkenrath drew the conclusion from looking at
previous terrorist incidents according to the number of casualties that were incurred, that terrorist attacks which seek to kill
large numbers of people are actually quite rare. (6) He found
that there have been only 16 terrorist incidents since 1925 that
have incurred more than 100 casualties. (7) In fact, nine of these
attacks occurred in the 1980s, and only four in the 1990s. So
statistically, attacks at the higher end of the casualty spectrum
reached a high point in the 1980s and have since declined in
number. However, these figures do not include failed attacks,
and attacks where there was an intention to kill large numbers
but which failed to achieve that goal. The other main observation from these attacks is that the targets in many of them were
discriminate in nature, such as the 1984 bombing of the US
Marine Corps barracks in Beirut, the Lebanon. Of the four
attacks which occurred in the 1990s, only two of them – the
series of ten bombs detonated in India's capital Bombay in
1993, and the destruction of a Russian apartment block in the
capital Moscow 1999, were indiscriminate in nature. So even
when terrorists are willing to kill large numbers of people, they
will not necessarily choose an indiscriminate target, which will
in turn impact upon the type of weapon that they will consider
using for the attack.

Falkenrath concludes from the data that there has been a
general aversion amongst most terrorist groups to causing mass
casualties. He suggests that this is due less to technical inca-
pacity, than a conscious decision on the part of many terrorist
groups to kill fewer people than they could, because of fears that
such attacks would undermine political support, raise the risk
of unfettered government reprisal, and because such violent
attacks do not make it easier for terrorists to achieve their aims.
(8) Therefore the general increase in the lethality of terrorist
attacks has not included an increase in the number of the most
lethal attacks. It is also worth noting that there is also no correlation between these most lethal attacks and the general trend
towards increasing numbers of indiscriminate attacks. This
must prompt questions about the extent to which terrorists,

ingeneral, are interested in causing mass casualties. It has always been the case that terrorists have killed fewer people than they were capable of, even with the conventional weapons at their disposal. For many groups, there is every reason to believe that this will continue to be the case.

Therefore, the data itself does not prove that terrorists will attempt to procure NBC weapons in order to perpetrate indiscriminate attacks involving mass casualties. Yet contained within these figures are four key incidents in the 1990s which underpin the debate on NBC terrorism: the bombing of the World Trade Centre in New York; the sarin attack on the Tokyo subway; the bombing of the Alfred P. Murrah building in Oklahoma City; and the more recent 1998 bombing of the US embassies in two African capital cities, Nairobi, Kenya and Dar-es-Salaam, Tanzania. They are important not only because of the number of casualties involved, but also because of what they represent – the underlying intent of the attack, their political impact and their symbolic value.

The bombing of the World Trade Centre in New York, was carried out on 26 February 1993, using a 1-ton truck bomb. The terrorists' aim was to make the twin towers collapse by destroying their main support columns, with the intention of killing as many of those in the towers as possible. Significantly, the terrorists also tried to release cyanide gas in the explosion; however the sodium cyanide burned in the explosion, instead of vaporizing, with no effect. (9) The police eventually discovered that the attack was carried out by an Egyptian Islamic fundamentalist group, led by Ramseh Youssef, (10) that was linked to the Muslim cleric Sheik Omar Abdel Rahman, who was suspected of complicity in terrorist attacks in Egypt. The group also planned to kill thousands more US citizens with attacks on New York's major landmarks and bridges, as well as blowing up 12 US airliners. (11) Intelligence sources believe that the group were financed and backed by the world's most wanted terrorist, Osama bin Laden, who it is believed has organized and financed an international Muslim terror network. (12)

The attack killed six people, and injured more than 1,000. But had the bomb managed to undermine the structural foundations of the building, then many more of the 50,000 people in the building could have been killed, a fact which Youssef would have been well aware of. Therefore, despite the fact that this incident does not figure among the list of incidents which resulted in more than 100 deaths, there was an intent to kill numbers of people far in excess of any previous terrorist incident.

The attack on the Tokyo subway was carried out in March 1995 by a Japanese pseudo-Buddhist-Hindu religious cult called Aum Shinrikyo, or Aum Supreme Truth, using sarin nerve agent. (13) It represents the first major attack by a terrorist group using a CW. It was actually the last in a series of attacks and attempted attacks by the cult using CBW, but it was the most effective and spectacular. During the morning rush hour on 20 March, five cult members carried several packages of sarin on to three subway trains converging on Kasumigaseki station in central Tokyo. The bags of sarin were placed on the floor, and then punctured with sharpened umbrella tips, releasing the gas. (14) The attack killed 12 people and injured approximately 5,500. However the death toll would have been much higher if the Aum Shinrikyo chemists had produced a purer form of sarin, or if it had been dispersed by means of an aerosol generator. (15) It is interesting to note that the Aum Shinrikyo did not present the Japanese authorities with any demands prior to the attack.

As is the case with the World Trade Centre bombing, this does not figure on the list of incidents which resulted in more than 100 deaths, but the intent was also to cause fatalities far in excess of what any of those incidents could have achieved. This incident generated a belief that extremist cults place very little value on human life, because they believe that they are on a divine mission to carry out acts of extreme violence that have been ordained and sanctioned by a higher deity. This has placed them firmly at the forefront of concern about NBC terrorism. The most significant outcome of this attack was symbolic in nature. It is perceived to have weakened the unspoken taboo against non-state actors using NBC weapons against mass population targets. The significance of the attack is perhaps best summed up by the American journalist D.W Brackett:

> With few exceptions only two groups of people understood that a horrible bell had tolled in the Tokyo subways, one that the world will surely hear again. The first group to realize the enormous implications of the Sarin-gas attack was the small handful of counter terrorist experts who daily monitor the activities of the world's known terrorist organizations. They understood immediately that the Tokyo gassing crossed an unprecedented threshold of terrorist violence. Weapons of mass destruction, specifically chemical and biological agents had been produced by a small group of religious terrorists with the will to use them. The counterterrorists also knew that the odds were good that other terrorist groups would try to copy the new form of terrorism pioneered by Aum Shinrikyo. The second group to instantly recognize

the underlying importance of the Tokyo attack was the international terrorist groups themselves, those who pursue political and religious goals at the expense of human life and suffering. They too realized that a new chapter in terrorist violence was opened on that March morning in Tokyo. Terrorist do not follow rules of engagement in their operations but they do absorb the lessons to be learned from successful acts of violence. A successful terrorist operation is one that receives broad publicity for the death, injury and destruction it causes. By that standard, the Tokyo gassing was a huge success. With that precedent setting example before them, many terrorist groups will now feel free to use chemical and biological weapons, if they can acquire them. With those weapons, they can conduct terrorism on a scale so horrific that all the bombings, assassinations, and skyjackings that have gone before will pale into insignificance. (16)

Despite its severity, the impact of the attack should not be overstated. It was not an act of WMD terrorism; and whilst there were a few threats that followed this, that appear to have been inspired by it, it did not spawn a sudden rush of copy cat attacks, and the taboo against the use of NBC weapons still exists. The implications of the Aum Shinrikyo attacks therefore remain ambiguous.

The bombing of the Alfred P. Murrah building, in the US city of Oklahoma on the 19th April 1995, resulted i the deaths of 169 adults and children. Despite initial speculation that it was the work of Islamic fundamentalists from the Middle East, the perpetrator was discovered to be a US citizen, Timothy McVeigh. He was linked to white supremacist, far-right extremist groups, and a Christian Identity church in Oklahoma. He was primarily motivated by hostility towards the federal government, which is perceived by the right to be in league with an international conspiracy to enslave American citizens, (for fuller details of these beliefs see Chapter 6). McVeigh was eventually convicted of the bombing and sentenced to death. This was America's worst ever case of domestic terrorism, (17) and led to the emergence of a new term: the 'McVeigh factor', in debates on terrorism. The principal significance of the incident was its impact on US perceptions of terrorism, directly fuelling the debate on NBC terrorism, by prompting the question 'What if McVeigh had used anthrax?' (18)

The last incident was the simultaneous bombings of the American embassies in Nairobi, Kenya and Dar-es-Salaam, Tanzania. On 7 August 1998, a huge car bomb was detonated in the car park of the American embassy in the heart of Nairobi's commercial capital. Adjacent offices and banks were full of workers and the streets were full of commuters, cars, buses and shoppers. Hundreds of office workers had been drawn to their windows by the sound of an exploding grenade, and were then injured by a second bomb. Almost simultaneously, another bomb exploded in Dar-es-Salaam, capital of neighbouring Tanzania. According to newspaper reports the bombing in Kenya killed 201 and 5,500 people were injured, whilst the bomb in Tanzania killed 11. The security at the embassies was lax compared to the fortress mentality exhibited in more troubled parts of the world, because neither embassy was considered to be a major terrorist target.

Following the bombings western intelligence services managed to piece together a picture which showed that the culprits behind the terrorist bombings were part of a group called 'The Base'. Like the perpetrators of the World Trade Centre bombing, this group was also linked to Osama bin Laden, and their intention was to strike at the West by targeting Americans and Britons wherever they might be. The significance of this incident lay not only in the level of casualties that it caused, but in the willingness of the terrorists to inflict large numbers of indiscriminate casualties, which also included African Muslims working in the embassies.

Yet this apparent increasing interest in causing mass casualties does not necessarily equate with an interest in NBC weapons. It is possible to kill substantial numbers of people with conventional weapons, but terrorists have not yet reached the full potential for mass killing using conventional weapons. Therefore if terrorists are systematically moving towards attacks intended to cause mass casualties, it should initially be manifest in more mass-casualty attacks involving conventional weapons. Yet this has not been the case, and such attacks remain rare.

The growth of religious terrorism

A common link between the majority of the incidents which have involved fatalities exceeding 100, and these four specified attacks, is religion. As will be discussed in greater depth in Chapter 6, religious extremism has now become the most serious issue regarding international terrorism. Whilst many terrorist groups such as the IRA and the PLO, have had a religious component, it was their political goals which were dominant. For a new generation of terrorists that emerged strongly in the 1990s, the religious imperative is paramount. This involves all of the world's major religions, from Christian right-wing white supremacists, radical Jews, militant Sikhs, and Islamic fundamentalists, and has been manifested all around the world: from Europe, North America, the South Asian Subcontinent, Northeast Asia, to the Middle East. (19) Of these groups, those that have been most responsible for this trend are Islamic fundamentalists; millenarian religious cults and Christian orientated right-wing groups, notably in the USA.

According to Bruce Hoffman, in 1968 none of the 11 identifiable international terrorist groups could be classified as 'religious.' In 1980 the first modern religious terrorist groups emerged following the Iranian revolution, but comprised only two of the 64 active terrorist groups. By 1992 that number had risen to 11, comprising a quarter of all the terrorist groups that carried out attacks in that year. By 1994, the trend had accelerated, and 16 (or one-third) of the 49 identifiable groups could be classified as religious in character or motivation. In 1995 that number had risen again to 25 out of 58 known active terrorist groups, or 42 per cent. The linkage between this trend and the trend towards increasing lethality in terrorist attacks is evident from the fact that although religious terrorists committed only 25 per cent of the recorded international terrorist incidents in 1995, they were responsible for 58 per cent of the fatalities and carried out all of the attacks in 1995 where there were more than eight fatalities. (20) These figures indicate that religion is fast becoming the prime motivation for terrorist acts.

One thing that has become clear is that the rise in lethality of religiously derived violence is primarily linked to the growth of Islamic fundamentalist groups. Since 1980, Shi'a terrorist groups have been responsible for over a quarter of the deaths from terrorism, (21) and between 1982 and 1989 were responsible for 30 per cent of the total fatalities despite committing only 8 per cent of all attacks. (22) Despite the rapid growth of the religious far right in the USA, its adherents have not been responsible for many terror attacks involving fatalities. The level of destruction caused by the Oklahoma City bombing was exceptional, and could be categorized as an isolated incident which, whilst precedent-setting, did not fit into a wider strategy of attacks intended to indiscriminately kill large numbers of people. (Although they are under heavy surveillance, and may have been prevented from executing other lethal attacks.) Similarly, despite the high level of concern about religious cults in the lead-up to the millennium, this same observation can also be made in respect of millennial cults. Their record of outward directed violent acts is even less than that of the US far right. Whilst there has been a steady trickle of plots and threats, the Aum Shinrikyo attacks can also be better categorized as isolated incidents. But, whilst Islamic fundamentalist groups have committed more of these attacks than any other type of religious group, a wide spectrum of religious groups have engaged in such attacks, albeit sporadically.

One of the underlying reasons for the differences in the debates on NBC terrorism during the 1970s and 1990s is this change in the nature of terrorist motivations. During the 1970s, conclusions about NBC terrorism were derived from an analysis of the strategies and objectives of secular terrorists. In the 1990s the focus shifted to religious terrorists. The perceived differences between the two have contributed to the different tenor of the debate. Bruce Hoffman argues that the different characteristics, justifications and mindsets of religious and quasi-religious groups suggest that they might be the most likely types of group to use NBC weapons, because they have radically different value systems, mechanisms of legitimization and justification, concepts of morality and world view. (23)

Many of them have less comprehensible nationalist or ideological motivations than their secular counterparts, embracing far more amorphous religious and millenarian aims which in their eyes are divinely sanctioned. In some instances their aims go far beyond the establishment of some theocracy amenable to their particular deity, to embrace mystical, almost transcendental and divinely inspired imperatives, or a vehemently anti-government form of populism, reflecting far-fetched conspiracy notions, based on a volatile mixture of seditious, racial and religious dictums. (24) These groups are less cohesive organizational entities, that decentralize and compartmentalize their activities, and have a more diffuse structure and membership, than secular groups.

According to Hoffman, religious terrorists have engaged in more lethal attacks primarily because they perceive violence to be a sacramental act, or divine duty, executed in direct response to some theological demand or imperative. He therefore argues that its perpetrators are unconstrained by the same kind of political, moral and practical constraints that influence secular terrorists, who often perceive indiscriminate violence to be counter-productive or morally wrong. For them, religion is a legitimizing force, and clerical sanction is an important component of their campaigns of terror. Second, religious terrorists differ in their constituency because they are at once activists and constituents, who execute their acts for no one but themselves. Therefore the restraints which secular terrorists apply to themselves in order to appeal to their constituency are not relevant, 'Moreover, this absence of a constituency in the secular terrorist sense leads to a sanctioning of almost limitless violence against a virtually open ended category of targets – that is, any one who is not a member of the terrorist's religion or religious sect.' In fact they frequently seek the elimination of broadly defined categories of enemies, and therefore regard large-scale violence not only as morally justified but as a necessary expedient for the attainment of their goals. Religious terrorists aim to guarantee the attainment of the greatest possible benefits for themselves and their co-religionists only, an aim which further engenders a tremendous disparity between ends and means, with the religious terrorist viewing violence as an end in itself. They see themselves as outsiders, and seek fundamental changes to society and politics, rather than attempting to correct flaws in existing systems. This sense of alienation enables the religious terrorist to contemplate far more destructive and deadly types of terrorist operations than secular terrorists and allows them to embrace a far more open-ended category of enemies to attack. (25)

The significance of the increase in religious terrorism can be seen in the fact that all of the attacks during the 1990s which have incurred more than 100 casualties were perpetrated by religious groups, whilst several of those in the 1980s, such as the December 1988 bombing of Pan American Airways (Flight 103) over the Scottish village of Lockerbie in which 270 people were killed, were secular in nature. (26) Yet the convergence of the trends in increasing casualties resulting from terrorist attacks, and the growth of religious terrorism, is not matched by a similar upward trend in the number of attacks resulting in more than 100 casualties, nor has it led to an increase in the number of indiscriminate targets amongst these attacks.

This can be partly explained by the fact that what is defined as religious terrorism is rarely wholly apolitical. Many religious groups seek tangible political objectives, especially in the short and medium term. Many Islamic groups want changes in US foreign policy in the Gulf region, and the Christian far right in the US has a clear political and social agenda. The majority of them also have to take some account of political factors related to gaining popular support, in determining their tactics and strategies. Therefore, groups that are defined as religious in nature, do not necessarily renounce all of the commonly accepted strategies, tactics and constraints of secular terrorists – who themselves have been prone to occasional acts of indiscriminate violence. The strategy of the Lebanese Islamic group, Hezbollah, is to strike primarily at Israeli military targets, and it claims to attack civilian targets only in retaliation for Israeli airstrikes. It must also be borne in mind that the target in Kenya was the US embassy, which is not an indiscriminate target. Therefore, whilst religious terrorists might be more prone to strike at indiscriminate targets than secular terrorists, they still display a tendency to strike at targets which are integral to the power and security of their opponents. This indicates that religious terrorists are willing to limit casualties when it suits them, although the Kenya embassy bombing suggests that they might also be willing to accept high levels of collateral casualties.

As a consequence, it is only really possible to talk about groups that are predominantly religious in character according to the characteristics identified by Hoffman, and groups that are predominantly secular in character. Only some religious cults can be considered to be wholly apolitical, but even some cults have demonstrated an interest in political objectives.

Whilst the correlation between the increasing lethality of terrorist incidents and the growth of religious groups is a cause for concern, the most worrying feature of religiously inspired violence, is that on occasion such groups have renounced all limits on the casualty levels that they are prepared to inflict. The four principal incidents cited earlier have challenged common assumptions about the nature of terrorism. In one sense they symbolize the fact that conventional forms of terrorism have grown more lethal, but beyond that what has emerged from these extraordinary acts, is that a new style of terror has been born. Perhaps the two key incidents have been the Aum Shinrikyo attack and the World Trade Centre bombing. Whilst neither resulted in large number of deaths, both had the potential and the intention to cause fatalities far in excess of any other previous terrorist incident. Both occurred in the 1990s but it is not certain that they constitute a trend, because they were not followed by a spate of similar attempts. Instead, all that can be observed is that religious terrorists have a greater propensity to attempt indiscriminate mass casualty attacks, possibly running into thousands, but such attacks are not necessarily their primary tactic.

NBC terrorism – the past record
Despite the large number of cases linking terrorists to NBC weapons, only a small proportion of them actually led to the use of an NBC weapon. The US Monterrey Institute database of NBC terrorist incidents identifies 282 cases, but only 26 per cent of them involved the actual use of a weapon. (27) Of the rest, there are difficulties in differentiating between what are genuine cases of terrorists attempting to acquire NBC weapons with a serious intent to use them; cases where groups made threats with no intent to develop or use such weapons; and reports which are little more than hearsay. Some cases on the public record are supported by an incontrovertible corpus of facts, particularly

when those involved are brought to trial. Yet uncorroborated reports in the press cannot be dismissed out of hand as mere hearsay, because for many years CBW experts and governments have been keeping a low profile on the issue for fear of encouraging the very threats that they were discussing. This copy cat phenomenon was apparent in 1995, when following the Aum Shinrikyo attack on the Tokyo subway, there were threats by Chilean right-wing groups to release sarin in the Santiago underground if General Manuel Contreras, the former head of the Secret Police, was imprisoned, and claims by Canadian Micmac Indians involved in a fishing dispute in New Brunswick that they possessed stockpiles of chemicals including sarin. (28) In both instances the threats never materialized, even when General Contreras was jailed.

Incidents involving CW constitute approximately 52 per cent of the previous cases of NBC terrorism, (29) but there have been many more threats and conspiracies than cases where terrorists actually managed to execute an attack using a CW. In analysing those attacks that did not happen, it is probably fair to assume that some of the reports could have been fabrications based on hearsay and speculation, other efforts to acquire CW could primarily have been conceived of as threats by groups with an underlying lack of intent to actually use them, but some of the plots could have been serious threats that were prevented from occurring only by the security forces of the state.

There has been an increase in both the number of plots and threats, and also the number of times that terrorists have actually acquired or used CW, in the 1990s. The increase in the number of cases of acquisition and use was due almost entirely to the large number of attempted attacks by Aum Shinrikyo. The list of incidents contained in the Appendix also indicates that a whole spectrum of groups, including nationalist separatist movements, Islamic fundamentalists, religious cults and the racist far right, have at some time shown an interest in CW, and interest is by no means dominated by religious groups. Equally as significant, is that many of the attacks were, or were intended to be, discriminate in nature, against individuals or the occupants of specific buildings or sites. Several, however, were indiscriminate in nature, with the intention to kill larger numbers of people than could typically be achieved with conventional weapons, although significantly, none of them succeeded.

In technical terms, the types of agent that have been used are very small in number: primarily cyanide, sarin, arsenic and mustard gas, with some instances of other agents. At no time has a group developed what could be defined as a WMD. Only Aum Shinrikyo has ever got close to engineering its CW into a

WMD, but their inability to achieve this appears to have been due a to technical inability to disperse or use it effectively. Most of the attacks have had to rely on using chemicals as contaminants, particularly in food and drink, which has greatly restricted the potential casualties that they could cause.

Incidents involving BW constitute approximately 25.9 per cent of the previous cases of NBC terrorism. (30) As is the case with CW, a relatively small number of pathogens and toxins keeps reoccurring: primarily anthrax, botulinum and ricin, with a few of incidences of typhoid, plague and salmonella. There have only ever been five confirmed cases of terrorists actually using BW, although the increasing trend of successful acquisition of BW in the 1990s is even more pronounced than is the case with CW. There also appears to have been a gradual shift in the type of groups attempting to procure these weapons, from predominantly secular and ethno-nationalist groups in the 1970s and 1980s, to predominantly religious groups in the 1990s. Perhaps the most worrying aspect of these developments is the fact that, unlike with CW, it is not entirely owing to the activities of Aum shinrikyo, because of the success of individuals on the Christian far right in the USA in developing ricin, and the use of salmonella typhimurium in salad bars, by the Rajneeshpuram religious cult in the USA. (See Appendix for details)

A greater proportion of the incidents where groups acquired BW appear to have been directed against indiscriminate targets than is the case with CW, although in the cases where the agent was not used it is sometimes impossible to determine what the target actually was, or if the group had a serious intent to carry out the attack. But whilst this seems to indicate a greater interest in indiscriminate targeting, no group has managed to engineer its BW into a WMD. From the known details of the cases involving the Christian far right in the USA, it appears that they possessed the pathogen or toxin, but had to rely on using it as a contaminant. Aum Shinrikyo attempted to engineer BW into a WMD but failed, although the known details of their programme do not indicate how close they actually were to effectively weaponizing their pathogens. All of these previous attacks were singularly unsuccessful, with no confirmed fatalities, (although the Polish resistance claimed to have killed 200 Germans during the Second World War using BW – see Appendix for details).

There has been a much lower incidence of nuclear terrorism than is the case with CBW, (approximately 3.7 per cent of previous cases of NBC terrorism). From known conspiracies it appears that no terrorist group has even attempted to develop a nuclear explosive device, and there have been only a few cases of groups attempting to purchase a nuclear device. Instead, the use of radioactive materials for contamination, either through a contamination bomb or otherwise, has been the preferred option for nuclear terrorism. But what few incidents have occurred, have mainly been in the 1990s, although it is too early to determine whether this constitutes a possible trend towards a greater number of incidents.

Conclusion

The past record demonstrates a small but significant history of NBC terrorism. Unsubstantiated reports comprise over half of the recorded incidents, but even accounting for the reports that have remained uncorroborated, there have been a small but regular number of cases where groups or individuals have actually acquired NBC weapons. Of the corroborated incidents nuclear weapons hardly featured, and there were a lot more CW than BW incidents.

The history of terrorist incidents involving NBC weapons suggests (but does not prove) that further incidents are inevitable. But it does not establish a case that an incident involving a WMD is inevitable or even likely, since no group has ever posed a credible WMD threat. The most significant observation in respect of NBC terrorism is the increasing acquisition of these types of weapons. The actual use of NBC weapons has not been very great, although there has been a demonstrable increase in the 1990s. Yet this does not clearly constitute a trend in increasing use of NBC weapons by terrorist groups. Actual attacks have been rare enough to suggest that further cases might fit into a pattern of occasional isolated incidents, rather than constituting a trend. Although the setting of key precedents, such as the use of CW against indiscriminate population targets, has been a highly significant development. There are no indications, however, of different groups' intent to use these weapons in the cases where they threatened to use them but never actually conducted an attack. It is possible to argue that a large number of them were mere threats, intended to intimidate governments and their populations, and to generate propaganda; but with at least some of them there was probably an underlying intent to follow through on the threat.

This record also raises questions about the technical problems which non-state actors face in developing NBC weapons: the Aum Shinrikyo attempted to carry out a very large number of CBW attacks but with only a very low success rate. Equally, as far as is publicly known, no group has managed to develop or otherwise acquire a WMD, and only the Aum Shinrikyo managed to weaponize a CBW weapon with an effective delivery mechanism. Most of these plots involved the use of agents and pathogens as contaminants. The main significance of the Tokyo subway attack was as an indicator that non-state actors are getting closer to developing a WMD. Yet it would be wrong to claim that the Aum Shinrikyo programme itself represents a trend towards eventual development and use of WMD by terrorists, because it remains an isolated incident.

The discriminate nature of many of these plots and attacks – targeting individuals, installations and buildings, means that the majority of them were not intended to kill many more people than conventional weapons. There is however, a significant number of cases, principally through contaminating the water supplies of large residential areas, where there was an intent was to cause high enough levels of casualties sufficient to be labelled 'mass destruction.' Whatever the feasibility of achieving this through contaminating water supplies, the intent of the perpetrators is what is important.

Members from across the whole spectrum of terrorist groups have attempted to acquire these weapons. This includes: secular political groups and individuals on the far right and left, and religious cults, national liberation movements and Islamic militants. But of these groups, it is religious cults who have been responsible for the largest number of incidents where actual possession of an NBC weapon has been involved, followed by Christian far-right groups and individuals in the USA. Islamic fundamentalists along with national liberation movements such as the Kurdish Workers Party (PKK) and the Palestinians have been responsible for a few each. Whilst this indicates that some groups might represent more of a threat than others, it also indicates that the whole spectrum of terrorist groups represents a threat. It must also be noted, however, that very few of these groups appear to have undertaken long-term systematic programmes to develop and use NBC weapons. This suggests that in many cases, interest in acquiring and using NBC weapons has partly been driven by opportunity and circumstances.

Whilst these trends are useful as a partial and general explanation of why there will probably be further terrorist incidents involving NBC weapons, there are no causal links between them. There appears to be a correlation between the increase in religious terrorism and the increased acquisition of BW because of a number of cases involving cults and the Christian far right in the USA, but this does not tie in very strongly to the trend of increasing lethality in terrorist attacks, since these groups do not have histories of systematic campaigns of violence against indiscriminate population targets. Islamic fundamentalist groups are primarily responsible for the increasing lethality of religious terrorism, but they do not figure very prominently in the history of NBC terrorism. Similarly, the increasing acquisition and use of NBC weapons has not significantly contributed to the trend towards increasing lethality of terrorist incidents. This in turn suggests that the trend towards increasing lethality is not necessarily driving terrorists towards increasing use of NBC weapons. Equally, whilst there has been a general trend towards increasingly indiscriminate targeting of populations, in all of the cases in the past record where targeting intentions are known, the majority have been intended for discriminate targets, although a significant number have also been intended for indiscriminate targets. It is only in the case of BW that there appears to be a strong correlation with causing indiscriminate casualties.

Therefore, whilst these trends suggest broad directions in terrorist activity, they are of little use for determining the nature and extent of the future threat. The frequency and lethality of future attacks cannot be gauged with any certainty from these trends. They suggest that some types of groups are more likely to procure specific NBC weapons for specific purposes but, equally, they also suggest that any of the other possible contingencies could also occur. Hence, trends and statistics in themselves prove nothing, the nature of the likely future threat can be determined in greater detail only by exploring key themes in greater depth, such as technical opportunities and constraints acting on terrorists attempting to develop NBC weapons, terrorist motivations to use these weapons, the likely disincentives to using these weapons, the strategies and tactics which different terrorist groups employ and psychological issues associated with using such weapons.

Notes and references
1. Frank Barnaby, *Instruments of Terror: Mass Destruction Has Never Been So Easy* (London: Vision Paperbacks, 1996) pp 52–5
2. Barnaby: *Instruments of Terror*, p 52
3. Bruce Hoffman, *Inside Terrorism* (Indigo, London) 1998) p 47
4. Richard Falkenrath, Robert D.Newman and Bradley Thayer, *America's Achilles Heel*, (Cambridge, MA: MIT Press, 1998), pp 3–4.
5. Paul Wilkinson, 'Terrorist Targets: New Risks to World Order', *Conflict Studies* 236 (December 1990) p 7
6. John Deutch, 'Worldwide Threat Assessment Brief to the Senate Select Committee on Intelligence,' Statement for the Record (22 February 1996) p 1
7. Richard Falkenrath, 'Confronting Nuclear, Biological and Chemical Terrorism', *Survival* 40/3 (Autumn 1998) p 52
8. The terrorist incidents in the twentieth century which have incurred more than 100 casualties are:
1999: The bombing of a Moscow apartment block – 119 dead
1998: The bombing of the US embassies in Kenya and Tanzania – 212

dead

1995: The bombing of the Alfred P. Murrah building, Oklahoma City – 168 dead

1993: A co-ordinated series of ten bomb explosions in Bombay – 235 dead.

1989: The bombing of an Avianca aircraft in Bogota – 107 dead

1989: The bombing of a French UTA airliner in Niger – 171 dead.

1988: The bombing of Pan Am flight 103 over Scotland – 278 dead

1987: The Tamil Tigers' shooting of Sinhalese civilians on a number of buses – over 100 dead

1987: A car bomb in a bus station in Sri Lanka, – 113 dead

1987: The bombing of a South Korean Airliner on the Thai-Burma border – 117 dead

1985: The bombing of an Air India airliner over the Irish Sea – 328 dead

1983: The derailing of a train in India – over 200 dead

1983: The bombing of the US Marines barracks in Beirut – 241 dead

1979: An arson attack on a cinema in Abadan, Iran – 477 dead

1946: The poisoning of German POWs by the Jewish reprisal organization Nakam – 100s dead

1925: The bombing of a cathedral in Sofia, Bulgaria – 160 dead

Falkenrath: 'Confronting Nuclear, Biological and Chemical Terrorism,' p 52

9. The judge at the trial stated that if the sodium cyanide had vaporized it would have been sucked into the North Tower, killing everyone inside. Quoted in the prepared statement of John F. Sopko and Alan Edelman, Permanent Sub-Committee on Investigations in Senate Hearings 104–422, Global Proliferation of Weapons of Mass Destruction , Part III, Hearings Before the Permanent Sub-Committee on Investigations of the Committee on Governmental Affairs, US Senate, 104 th Congress, 2nd session (Washington, DC : US Government Printing Office, 1996). However, Falkenrath, Newman and Thayer question to the technical basis of this assessment by suggesting that the bomb could not have disseminated the sodium cyanide effectively and the amount present was too small to be lethal except in a confined space. Falkenrath, Newman and Thayer: *America's Achilles Heel*, p 32

10. The FBI believe his real name to be Abdul Basit Karim, and that he goes under many assumed names

11. Youssef is also alleged to have been responsible for a bomb attack in Iran which killed 25 people, an explosion on a plane in the Philippines,and plots to assassinate Pope John Paul II and Benazir Bhutto. Barnaby: *Instruments of Terror*, p 86

12. Osama bin Laden is a former Saudi construction tycoon turned terrorist Islamic warrior. Born into a wealthy Saudi Arabian family (his estimated personal fortune is in the region of 200 million pounds), he was exiled from both Saudi Arabia and his own family for opposing the Saudi regime and its support for the USA. He moved to Afghanistan to join the war against the Soviet invaders. Once there, he set up a series of training camps in remote mountains and valleys. The defeat of the Soviet Union was seen by all Muslims as a victory for Islam, and inspired bin Laden to believe he could also defeat the USA. In 1991 he returned to Saudi Arabia. He was already profoundly anti-American because of its

support for Israel, and it was at this time that his mission to target Americans began. In 1994 his Saudi citizenship was revoked and he moved to Sudan, developing close ties with the radical Sudanese government, the National Islamic Front. He brought considerable wealth to the Sudan and spent millions of dollars building roads and an airport. Behind this public facade he developed an international terrorist network.He set up training camps, and formed his organization from a coalition of groups from Uganda, the Philippines, Ethiopia and Egypt. When US troops entered Somalia in December 1992 on a UN peacekeeping mission, bin Laden inspired and backed attacks on them, claiming that the US presence was unjustified aggression. The USA finally withdrew, defeated, after two of its helicopters were shot down and 18 US servicemen killed. Sudan supported bin Laden, but US pressure eventually forced the Sudanese to expel him, and he was exiled to Afghanistan. From this Afghan refuge, he runs an army of Arab veterans of the Afghan war, the Mojahedin, and is suspected of bankrolling Islamic militants throughout the Middle East and beyond. He is wanted by American investigators in connection with the truck bombing of the Khobar Towers US barracks in Saudi Arabia June 1996, and an attack onUS military buildings in Riyadh in 1995, and also for various terrorist attacks carried out in Egypt and the Philippines. There have also been allegations of a plot to assassinate President Clinton. In a television interview June 1998 bin Laden vowed to carry out more attacks against Americans. Intelligence sources indicate that 20 countries now harbour terrorist groups supported by bin Laden's terror network.

13. Sarin (GB) or isopropyl methylphosphonofluoridate is a stable nerve agent which is easy to disperse, emits little smell and is highly toxic. Nerve gas such as sarin attack the central and peripheral nervous system. Symptoms are progressive and include breathing difficulties, sweating, vomiting, cramps, involuntary bowel movements, fainting and confusion usually leading to coma and death. Robert Guest, 'Cult's Commune of Torture', *Daily Telegraph* (24 March 1995, p 16). Sarin is 20 times more deadly than potassium cyanide, killing in minutes by attacking and crippling an individual's nervous system. Only a tiny amount is needed, a fatal dose is 0.01 milligram per kilogram of human body weight. Barnaby: *Instruments of Terror*, pp 126–27

14. Gwen Robinson (from Tokyo) 'Nerve Gas Solvent found as Police Swoop on Sect', *The Times*, London (23 March 1995) p 10

15. Edward M. Spiers, *Chemical Weaponry* (New York: St Martin's Press, 1989); Edward M. Spiers, *Chemical and Biological Weapons* (New York: St Martin's Press, 1994)

16. D.W. Brackett, *Holy Terror, Armageddon in Tokyo* (New York: Weatherhill, 1996) pp 5–7

17. Gururaj Mutalik, MD, 'Crude Nuclear Weapons, Proliferation and the Terrorist Threat', International Physicians for the Prevention of Nuclear War Global Health Watch, Report 1 (1996) p 41

18. Richard K. Betts, 'The New Threat of Mass Destruction', *Foreign Affairs* (January–February 1998) p 26

19. Brackett: *Holy Terror*, p 46

20. Hoffman: *Inside Terrorism*, p 48

21. Andrew Hubback, 'Apocalypse When? The Global Threat of Religious

Cults', *Conflict Studies* 300, Research Institute For the Study of Conflict and Terrorism (June 1997) p 2

22. Hoffman: *Inside Terrorism*, p 94

23. Hoffman: *Inside Terrorism*, p 94

24. Hoffman: *Inside Terrorism*, p 47

25. Hoffman: *Inside Terrorism*, pp 48–49

26. The two culprits charged with the bombing were alleged to have been agents of the Libyan secret service

27. Jonathan B.Tucker & Amy Sands, 'An Unlikely Threat', *The Bulletin of the Atomic Scientists* (July/August 1999) p 48

28. Ron Purver, 'Chemical and Biological Terrorism: New Threat to Public Safety?', *Conflict Studies* 295, Research Institute For The Study of Conflict and Terrorism (December 1996–January 1997) p 14

29. Presentation by Dr Amy Sands, 'CBRN Terrorism: Assessing the Threat', The Seventh Carnegie International Non-Proliferation Conference, Washington DC (11-12 January 1999) <http://cerp.org/programs/hpp/Powerpoint/Carnegie—Amy/index.htm>

30. Sands, 'CBRN Terrorism: Assessing the Threat'

31. Sands, 'CBRN Terrorism: Assessing the Threat'

3. Technical Opportunities and Constraints

Whilst current trends in terrorist activity suggest that future incidents involving NBC weapons are probably inevitable, they provide no indication of the nature of the future threat. One of the fundamental issues in assessing the frequency and nature of the threat is the ability of terrorist groups to develop or otherwise acquire different types of NBC weapons – and, equally as significant, the lethality of the weapons that they prove to be capable of developing. Analysts are now almost unanimous in concluding that it is becoming increasingly easy for terrorist groups to develop NBC weapons, yet there is a dichotomy within the literature over exactly how easy it is. Some analysts consider that terrorists could develop NBC weapons very quickly once they set their minds to it, yet others consider that developing WMD is a long and involved process because certain aspects of the technology are still not widely known, and various elements of it are difficult to gain access to. In addition, some analysts suggest that the level of technological difficulty does not vary much between the three types, (1) whilst others consider that some are more difficult to develop than others, with CW being the easiest to develop and nuclear weapons the most difficult.

Despite the low incidence of actual terrorist use of NBC weapons, individuals with links to extremist organizations have frequently been apprehended in possession of CBW, and several clandestine programmes to develop such weapons have also been discovered by the security forces in some states. Possession of a weapon does not indicate an intent to use it, but the fact that a greater number of terrorists and other individuals are managing to develop NBC weapons does increase the likelihood that they will be used. But equally, the fact that some individuals have also been apprehended whilst still in the process of developing CBW suggests that it may not be as easy as some analysts are suggesting. This chapter will examine the technical factors involved in developing NBC weapons, in order to reach an objective assessment of how easy it could be for terrorist groups to develop the three different types. By assessing the difficulty of developing different types of weapon, it will be possible to identify which types terrorists are most likely to develop, and hence the likely nature of future threats.

The increasing availability of information
The starting point for any state or terrorist group attempting to develop NBC weapons is to gather together and master the relevant theoretical knowledge. It is now considered that the core theoretical knowledge required for developing all three types of weapon is available from open sources. Academic journals contain much of the information they require, and an exhaustive literature search through sources such as *Acta Scandinavia* and the Merck Index can provide the information that they need. Aum Shinrikyo began its CBW programme with an exhaustive literature search, which included downloading the entire protein data bank from the Brookhaven National Laboratory in the USA, which included details of the chemical breakdowns of various toxins. (2)

The internet has also become a dangerous source of information for terrorists. Using this resource it is not difficult to find detailed technical information on developing NBC weapons, such as formulas for CW agents like sarin, and chemical equations for precursor chemicals. An American citizen using the pseudonym 'Uncle Fester' has become notorious for posting the production process for ricin, which can be used as a BW, on the internet. (3) Similarly, one of the easiest means of manufacturing the VX nerve agent, using the chemical empta is now posted on the internet. It was originally developed by US scientists in the 1950s, and the patent was declassified in 1975, on the premise that any good chemist would only need to know the chemical name of VX in order to guess a way of preparing it. (4) However the internet is not a wholly reliable source of information. Whilst some of the available information is very accurate, much of it is erroneous and even hazardous to the health of the individual attempting to use it.

Whilst the relevant theoretical knowledge is available, it still needs to be converted into a functional weapon. This is an engineering process which will be dependent upon the skills of the engineers engaged on the project. Nowadays, more and more people are being equipped with the necessary skills to undertake such projects because of the greater educational opportunities that are available, and the greater ease with which knowledge now diffuses. Some sources indicate that the techniques for making nerve agents are similar to those used for insecticides; (5) whilst the explosive growth of basic biological research and biotechnology has made the development of BW significantly easier for both states and non-state actors. (6) What was once considered to be esoteric knowledge about how to culture and disperse infectious agents has now spread amongst tens of thousands of people. In the USA the award of life science PhDs increased by 30 per cent between 1975 and 1991, to more than 5700 a year, the number of PhDs rising by 144 per cent between 1994 and 1996. (7) In 1994 the UK had 5,700 biology graduate students. There are over 1,300 biotechnology companies in the USA, and about 580 in Europe, whereas 25 years ago there were none. (8)

This trend is matched by the increasing numbers of highly educated individuals who are being drawn into sub-state and terrorist groups. Aum Shinrikyo, for example, recruited hundreds of trained scientists and engineers. In addition, following the dissolution of the Soviet Union, large numbers of engineers who had previously worked on developing WMD were made unemployed or simply not paid by the governments of the successor states. Some of these engineers have allegedly become available for hire. The allegations primarily link these engineers to proliferator states such as Iran and Libya, but it is not inconceivable that some unscrupulous individuals might be willing to sell their skills to terrorist groups for purely financial reasons, owing to religious beliefs, or because of political and nationalist convictions.

The task is made easier by the fact that as technology progresses, new ways of developing some types of NBC weapons are emerging, some of which are easier than the old ways. (9) However, the openly available information is not enough to guarantee the successful development of a weapon. There are certain 'tricks of the trade' in engineering these weapons, which have not been codified explicitly. Terrorist groups will have to learn these processes through the experimentation and development process, unless they can find an experienced practitioner to show them. The tricks of the trade can be learned, especially by skilled engineers, but it takes time. But once they have been learned, the process can then be operated by engineers of a lower calibre, (10) and can be passed on to other engineers by word of mouth. Consequently, there is still a technological barrier which terrorists are going to have to cross by themselves. Whether this will prevent them developing NBC weapons or merely increase the amount of time it takes them, is dependent upon a number of factors which will be explored below.

Nuclear weapons

Nuclear weapons are extremely difficult to manufacture, even for a modern state with all of the necessary resources. However a distinction must be drawn between the kind of military weapons which states strive to develop and the rougher types of device which terrorists would be satisfied with. The US, OTA argues that,

> A small group of people, none of whom has access to the classified literature, could possibly design and build a crude nuclear explosive device. They would not necessarily require a great deal of technological equipment or have to undertake any experiments. Only modest machine shop facilities, that could be contracted for without arousing suspicion, would be required. The financial resources for the acquisition of necessary equipment on the open market need not exceed a fraction of a million dollars. The group would have to include as a minimum, a person capable of researching and understanding the literature in several fields and a jack of all trades technician ... There is a clear possibility that a clever, competent group could design and construct a device which would produce a significant nuclear yield (i.e. a yield much greater than the yield of an equal mass of high explosive). (11)

There are two types of nuclear weapon that terrorists could attempt to develop. The easiest to develop are radiological bombs, in which radioactive materials are packed around a conventional bomb and an incendiary material. With this type of weapon the explosion leads to a fireball, shooting the radioactive material up into the air, which then falls back to earth, scattering over a wide area. The primary purpose of such weapons is to spread radioactive contamination rather than cause casualties through blast effects.

Much more difficult to develop are nuclear weapons, in which the explosive core of the bomb comprises an amount of 'fissile material.' The optimum fissile materials for nuclear weapon design are plutonium-239 (Pu-239), or uranium enriched to approximately 94 per cent, uranium-235 (U-235), otherwise known as highly enriched uranium (HEU), although plutonium-240 (Pu-240) and uranium of lower enrichment levels can also be used. These weapons are designed to cause casualties through blast effects, although the dispersion of radioactive contamination is also a major secondary consequence. The minimum amount of material required for the explosive core is known as the 'critical mass.' These weapons are based upon two basic design principles: implosion or the gun device. With implosion devices, conventional explosives are used to compress a sphere comprising a sub-critical mass of fissile material into a smaller, critical mass which initiates the explosive chain reaction. With the gun design, two sub-critical masses of fissile material are fired together, becoming a critical mass, initiating the explosive chain reaction. The gun design is the easiest of the two to develop, with the implosion design requiring a greater range of equipment and skills and a lot of testing.

Some analysts consider that a Physics PhD student could design a crude nuclear device. But while schematic drawings of basic nuclear weapons similar to those dropped on the Japanese cities of Hiroshima and Nagasaki in 1945 are readily available, the detailed design drawings and specifications that are essential for fabricating actual parts are not. Nuclear weapon design is a serious problem, but not if the group has access to individuals with the right skills. Preparing such drawings requires the direct participation of individuals thoroughly versed in several quite distinct areas such as the physical, chemical and metallurgical properties of the various materials, as well as the characteristics affecting their fabrication; neutronic properties; radiation effects; technology concerning high explosives and/or chemical propellants; some aerodynamics, electrical circuitry and others. (12) This suggests that a team of at least three members needs to be involved. Terrorist groups might have some difficulty building a team with such diverse skills, but people with the necessary skills can be found in the general technical community, and therefore it can be done. A crude device might weigh a tonne or more, while a sophisticated device might weigh a few hundred pounds. (13)

The critical mass of fissile material that would be required varies according to the efficiency of the design of the weapon, whether it uses Pu-239 or HEU, the shape of the material (a sphere is the optimum shape), the density of the material, the purity of the material and the physical surrounding of the material. The amounts required for a 20 Kt bomb would be in the order of 5–6 kg of Pu-239, and at least 25 kg of HEU, as an absolute minimum. (But if used in their metal form, even more would be required because some of it would be lost in the machining process.) (14) A more recent estimate puts the amount required by a state possessing a low technical capability at 6 kg of plutonium or 16 kg of HEU. With the most sophisticated designs it is estimated that only 3 kg of Pu-239, or 5 kg of HEU is enough. (15)

Because of the high levels of security surrounding virtually all states' stockpiles of Pu-239 and HEU, terrorists will probably find it easier to acquire Pu-240 (otherwise known as reactor-grade plutonium because it is one of the main by-products of nuclear power generation, in nuclear fuel rods) and uranium of less than 94 per cent U-235. Whilst both are capable of being used in nuclear weapons, significantly more material would be required – perhaps in the order of 7–15 kg of Pu-240, and the finished device would be capable of producing only a low-yield explosion. (16) Victor Gilinsky, an American Nuclear Regulatory Commissioner, argued that:

> so far as reactor grade Plutonium is concerned, one fact is that it is possible to use this material for nuclear warheads at all levels of technical sophistication. In other words, countries less advanced than the major industrial powers but, nevertheless, possessing nuclear power programs can make very respectable weapons ... Of course, when reactor grade plutonium is used there may be a penalty in performance that is considerable or insignificant, depending on the weapon design. But whatever we might once have thought, we now know that even simple designs, albeit with some uncertainties in yield, can serve as effective, highly powerful weapons – reliably in the kiloton range. (17)

The ease with which a nuclear weapon could be constructed by a terrorist group was discussed in detail by Carson Mark, Theodore Taylor, Eugene Eyster, William Marman and Jacob Wechsler for the 1985 International Task Force on Prevention of Nuclear Terrorism. They argued that crude nuclear devices (that are guaranteed to work without the need for extensive theoretical or experimental demonstration) could be constructed by a group not previously engaged in designing or building nuclear weapons, provided a number of requirements are met. The amounts of fissile material necessary would tend to be large – certainly several times the minimum quantity required by expert and experienced weapon designers. The weight of the complete device would also be large – not as large as the first atomic devices (about 4.5 tonnes), which required aerodynamic cases to enable them to be handled as bombs, but probably more than a tonne.

The devices considered by Mark and his colleagues are similar to those dropped on Hiroshima and Nagasaki which had yields of approximately 20 Kt, but much cruder designs that are more unpredictable and inefficient, but which can still provide a powerful explosion are also achievable. The likely yields of these crude weapons are impossible to determine, but Frank Barnaby estimates that some may achieve only a few tens of thousands of tonnes of TNT, others might achieve hundreds of tonnes, or a few thousand tonnes, and 1 Kt is not impossible. (18) Whilst this is considerably smaller than the military weapons deployed by the nuclear weapon states, it is still a lot larger than conventional explosives, and will also guarantee a significant level of radioactive contamination. It is even theoretically possible to produce a nuclear explosion by dropping two pieces of plutonium on to each other from a suitable height. (19) However the likely yield from such a crude approach is likely to be very small, but it would cause a certain amount of radioactive contamination.

The option of using oxide powder, (whether of uranium or plutonium) directly, with no post-acquisition processing or fabrication, would seem to be the simplest and quickest way to make a bomb. However the amount of material required would be considerably greater than if metal was used, perhaps 35 kg. (20) The plutonium oxide would be contained in a spherical vessel in the centre of a large mass of conventional high explosive armed with a few detonators, arranged to go off simultaneously. When detonated, the shock wave would compress the plutonium enough to produce some fission, with a potential explosive yield in the order of tens or hundreds of tonnes of TNT, along with substantial radioactive contamination. (21) In a primitive device no effort would be made to focus the shock wave and so the high explosive would be simply stacked around the plutonium. (22) Reducing the oxide to metal form would take a number of days, and require specialized equipment and techniques, but could be within reach of a technologically sophisticated group. (23)

There are a number of potential hazards in developing nuclear weapons, including those arising from the handling of a high explosive; the possibility of inadvertently causing an explosion, especially when putting the feed material into a solution and conducting a number of other chemical processes; and the chemical toxicity or radiological hazards inherent in the materials used. (24) Failure to foresee all possible needs on these points could lead to failure, yet these problems are not insurmountable. The potential radiation doses from plutonium, including reactor-grade plutonium oxide, would not deter a person from handling it. Whilst plutonium is radioactive, it emits alpha particles, which cannot penetrate the skin, and HEU is not radioactive at all. The high toxicity of the metal and its extreme chemical radioactivity would necessitate the use of glove boxes, suits and masks, (25) but little shielding is necessary, and sensible precautions against achieving criticality accidentally could also be taken. (26)

Sophisticated designs would require less fissile material; however it is extremely unlikely that terrorists would be able to develop such weapons, because it took weapons laboratories in the nuclear weapon states many years of experimentation and testing with a whole cadre of highly experienced personnel. Since such weapons would require much higher levels of skill and considerably more experimentation to complete, (27) there is also more likelihood that they would fail, therefore terrorists are more likely to opt for a crude design.

Radiological weapons, or contamination bombs, (28) can utilize any radioactive material, although the more radioactive the material, the better. Some suitable isotopes such as strontium-90, caesium-137 and cobalt-60, have already been smuggled out of the FSU. (29) Strontium is particularly hazardous because it becomes congested in the bones, and can cause cancer. Caesium-137 causes many problems for decontamination because it sticks to surfaces, and Cobalt-60 emits gamma rays of high energy which produce hazardous radiation levels for a long period of time. Plutonium is also capable of being scattered from these devices, in the form of small particles that are capable of being inhaled, irradiating surrounding lung tissue and possibly causing lung cancer. The half-life of plutonium is 24,000 years, therefore once it is in the environment it stays there. This threat of dispersion is perhaps the most likely danger that would follow the illegal acquisition of plutonium, therefore the mere possession of nuclear material by a terrorist group is a significant threat. (30) Other means of dispersing radioactive isotopes include introducing them as powders into the ventilation systems of a building, or through blowers in the atmosphere, or merely by dumping them into the discrete water supplies of buildings. (31)

Chemical weapons

CW are lethal man-made poisons that can be disseminated as gasses, liquids or aerosols. There are four basic types: (32) the first comprises choking agents such as chlorine and phosgene which damage lung tissue causing the lungs to fill with fluid. The second category comprises blood gases such as hydrogen cyanide and cynanogen chloride. These attack an enzyme preventing the synthesis of molecules used by the body as an energy source, or interfere with the transport of oxygen in the blood, causing vital organs to shut down. The third category comprises vessicants, or 'blister' agents, such as mustard gas and Lewisite which cause burns and tissue damage to the skin, the inside of the lungs and other tissues throughout the body. The fourth category comprises nerve agents which are the most lethal of the CW, and kill by disabling crucial enzymes in the nervous system. These are divided into two groups – G-agents which mainly cause death after inhalation such as tabun, sarin and soman; and a V-agent, VX. Soman is the most lethal and rapid of the G-agents, sarin is three times more lethal than tabun, (33) whilst VX is more lethal than all of them. There are three methods of producing chemical casualties: through inhalation, skin effects and the digestive tract. Sarin is an example of an inhalation agent. One of the most dangerous agents relying on the skin route is VX and cyanide in potassium or sodium form is a common ingestion agent. The other significant feature of CW is that some, such as soman, mustard gas and VX, are persistent, whilst others, such as sarin and tabun, are not. In addition, many commercially available chemicals or insecticides such as organochlorine insecticides, herbicides and carbamates, can be used as CW. Hydrogen cyanide, cyanogen chloride and arsine are all industrial chemicals, which have been used as CW in the past. (34)

The effectiveness of a CW depends considerably on the nature of the agent and the conditions under which it is used. Hydrogen cyanide evaporates so quickly that its use outdoors is limited, whilst mustard gas and VX are not so volatile and are more suitable for use outdoors. (35) Even those agents that are suitable for use outdoors must be delivered in huge doses in order to inflict mass casualties. The required amounts of sarin reaches hundreds of thousands of kg per square km, depending on the weather conditions; it would require 4 tonnes of VX to cause several hundred thousand deaths if released in aerosol form in a crowded urban area; whilst 10 tonnes of potassium cyanide would need to be introduced into a 5 million-litre reservoir to kill a person drinking 100 ml of untreated water. (36) Therefore, even assuming perfect dispersal, the use of different

CW would involve various levels of lethality: 48 ounces of chlorine can produce 5,000 lethal casualties; 25 ounces of hydrogen cyanide and a third of an ounce of sarin would be enough to produce the same effect. (37) A poor delivery mechanism will lessen the effectiveness of these agents even further.

CW are amongst the easiest NBC weapons to produce, with some agents being easier to develop than others: hydrogen cyanide is very easy to produce, whilst tabun is the easiest of the G-agents to produce. Large-scale production facilities are unnecessary, and it requires only an individual who has a sound knowledge of organic chemistry and access to a laboratory with some sophisticated equipment. Certain CW can even be manufactured in a kitchen or basement, in quantities sufficient to cause large numbers of casualties. The production processes for some agents are simple, accurately described in publicly available sources, and require only commonly available laboratory glassware, good ventilation and commercially available chemicals. Sarin dates from the 1930s, and can now be made in more than a hundred different ways, most of which are fairly simple processes which would not tax the abilities of an average graduate-level chemist. The most difficult step is probably finding the formula, but it is now so old that it is not a problem. (38) Greater expertise and some specialized equipment is required for producing the most toxic CW agents, but they are within reach of some technically capable terrorist groups. (39)

Laboratory-scale production however, will yield only small quantities of an agent, and it would take some time before a laboratory-scale production programme could produce enough agent for an effective mass casualty attack against an outdoor target. (40) Therefore, should terrorists succeed in developing CW in the laboratory, they face two additional technical problems: improving the yield of the production process, and scaling up the process to produce larger amounts. (41) Some processes may produce only low yields of an agent in proportion to the quantities of precursors being used, and having to procure large quantities of precursors will increase the cost and potentially attract attention. Aum Shinrikyo, however, discovered that the production of agents in laboratory conditions is significantly easier than large-scale production. Taken together, these two factors indicate that terrorists will face significant practical difficulties in producing the large quantities of an agent required for indiscriminate 'mass-destruction' attacks. This limits the attractiveness of CW for some terrorist roles.

Equipment and safety requirements also vary with the agent being produced, the synthesis path chosen and its purity. A high-agent purity would be difficult to achieve by some production processes without specialized equipment. But equipment needs can be minimized by choosing specific agents and production paths that avoid high-energy, high-pressure and high-temperature reactions.(42)

The Aum Shinrikyo provides a useful case study of terrorist development of CW. It was vastly wealthy, had 300 engineers among its membership and had access to much of the dual-use equipment and materials required for CW production. Therefore the limitations evident in this programme should apply with greater effect to groups with fewer resources. Whilst Aum Shinrikyo engineers successfully produced sarin, tabun, VX, mustard gas and hydrogen cyanide, it took them approximately one–two years to produce the first batches of sarin. (43) The group then attempted to switch to large-scale production in a specialized building that was equipped with automated and computerized high-tech manufacturing equipment, designed to be capable of producing 2 tonnes of sarin in a day. (44) But when it attempted to use this facility there were repeated leaks of toxic substances, some of which were massive, overcoming workers and escaping the confines of the building. As a result, Aum Shinrikyo produced perhaps only 30 litres of sarin in total. (45) The batch of sarin which it used in the attack on the Japanese town of Matsumoto was very pure, but when it switched to industrial-size manufacture the quality of the sarin dropped to approximately 39 per cent because of problems in the manufacturing process (see Appendix for details).

Other terrorist groups with fewer resources will probably have to rely on lower technology, and smaller-scale facilities, to achieve similar results. Therefore it seems unlikely that most groups will be able to manufacture a good-quality agent in bulk. Consequently, groups intent on using CW to inflict large numbers of casualties will probably be forced to produce agents in small batches, and stockpile it until they have enough for their purposes.

Biological weapons
There are three main categories of biological agents which can be used in weapons. The first comprises weapons which disseminate viruses, which are microorganisms that invade the target, multiply inside it and destroy it. In people this includes the range of viruses that cause yellow fever, smallpox, typhoid, plague, diphtheria, ebola, cholera, dysentery, dengue fever and encephalitis, which are spread through coughing, sneezing and contact with body fluids. In animals viruses can cause rabies, swine fever, canine distemper, foot and mouth disease and vesticular stomatitis. In plants they cause mosaic diseases in toba-

cco, tomatoes, soya beans and sugar beat curly top. The second category comprises bacteria which cause illness by invading tissues and reproducing themselves, or by producing toxins. Bacterial toxins include botulinum, ricin, tetanus, diphtheria, shiga (which causes dysentery) and staphylococcus (which causes food poisoning). The diseases they cause include anthrax, brucellosis, cholera, pneumonic plague, tulameria (similar to plague), and typhoid. These diseases are considered to be primarily useful against people (although anthrax was used during the Second World War to attack cattle), whilst in plants, bacteria can cause rice and corn blight. The third category comprises rickettsia, which lie between viruses and bacteria. They are bacteria but they can live only inside host cells, like viruses. They are carried by insects such as lice ticks, fleas, and are also carried on mice. In people rickettsia can cause typhus, Q-fever, psittacosis and Rocky Mountain spotted fever. In animals such as goats and sheep they cause heart water. In animals, fungi can produce a mycotoxin (aflatoxin) which causes the respiratory disease aspergillosis in poultry, whilst in plants, fungi cause potato blight, black stem rust in cereals and rice blast. (46)

Along with plutonium, the FBI list two biological agents – botulinum and ricin – as the three most toxic substances in the world. (47) BW are colourless and odourless which means that unless the terrorists are caught in the act of releasing a pathogen, an attack will go unnoticed until people start falling ill. Some BW such as anthrax, for example, are not contagious, but others such as plague are. The result of a BW attack would be a largely simultaneous outbreak of disease after an incubation period of a few days (depending on the agent used and the dose inhaled), which would spread rapidly if a highly infectious agent were used. Because of their ability to multiply inside the host, BW can be fatal in minute quantities. But without an effective system of dispersal, BW cannot easily cause massive numbers of casualties.

Toxin weapons differ from microbial BW agents in that they are non-living, which means that potential casualties will be restricted to those directly infected by the weapon. Gram for gram they are less deadly than certain living pathogens because they do not reproduce themselves within the victim, and since they are not contagious they cannot spread beyond the victims that are immediately exposed.

It is theoretically possible to introduce enough pathogens into the air to infect a large area of territory. The particles of bioweapons are very small (approximately 1–5 microns in diameter), and because they are light and fluffy they do not fall to earth very quickly; given the right weather conditions a bioweapon will drift for up to a hundred miles. Their tiny size means that they are sucked deep into the lungs, where they stick to the membranes and then enter the bloodstream where they begin to replicate. One particle of some pathogens is enough to kill, although the lethality of others is dependent upon inhalation of a sufficient quantity. Like CW, they can also be differentiated by their degree of persistence. Sunlight kills bioweapons, and like radioactivity they have a variable half-life, which is known as the 'decay time'. Some pathogens such as anthrax have a long decay time, but others such as ricin and botulinum have a relatively short decay time.

As is the case with CW, the development of BW requires no particularly specialized technology. The laboratories of universities and the biotechnology industry are adequate for the purpose, and information on the necessary science and technology is now openly available. Culturing microorganisms or growing and purifying toxins is inexpensive and can be accomplished by anyone with university-level training and good laboratory skills. A few hundred kg of a properly weaponized bacterial agent, when dried and milled to a precise particle size, has the potential to wipe out the inhabitants of an entire city. There are now many more people who are technically trained to complete such a task, and the methods of culturing large quantities of bacteria are well worked out and commonly employed: 'A person who is smart, determined, trained in basic microbiological techniques, and willing to take a few short cuts on safety, and go at a few technical problems in mildly unconventional ways, could conceivably do some horrible things.' (48)

There are safety hazards for individuals working these pathogens, and specialized state-run facilities have rigorous safety mechanisms and procedures to protect staff. At the UK's Biological and Chemical Weapon Defence Establishment at Porton (in Wiltshire), staff are individually protected from the effects of BW through individual protective equipment such as protective biological containment suits, and they work in highly secure conditions that are specifically designed to handle dangerous pathogens. Before entering the laboratories workers have to decontaminate under showers, and they work in pairs. The air pressure in the laboratories is kept extremely low, which will prevent any pathogen escaping the laboratory, because the lower air pressure will ensure that it is sucked back inside. (49)

There is no reason to suggest that an individual with the necessary skills to successfully culture and work with these pathogens would not be aware of basic safety mechanisms and procedures that would enable them to work with a reasonable degree of safety. Yet this was not always the case with Aum Shinrikyo: its scientists working with botulinum allowed particles of the toxin to flake into the air as they were grinding it into a powder. They were protected by contamination suits, but afterwards they simply took their suits off without decontamination: one worker commented that, 'If the powder had worked, we would be dead.' (50) Others have also previously worked on BW with little or no protection, and survived. During the Second World War British production of anthrax weapons was undertaken behind sheets of glass, and the workers had no respiratory equipment, and UNSCOM inspectors discovered that Iraqi engineers had been working on microorganisms in straightforward laboratory cabinets. (51)

Therefore, in some respects, BW might look a lot easier to develop than some forms of CW, in terms of access to the necessary materials and the level of expertise required, but there are some key technical problems which have to be solved in order to produce an effective BW. The nature of these problems can be discerned from the case of developing an anthrax weapon, where the key is to create and disperse spores containing particles of exactly the right size for inhalation and dispersal – between 1 and 5 micrometres. An OTA report indicates that transforming *bacillus anthracis* into a weapon is a low-technology procedure, in which the technical problems are not insurmountable. The tricky part is not culturing the agent but processing the crude slurry into a form suitable for dispersal (i.e. to dry it, adjust the particle size and load it into a dispersal mechanism). At some stage it would also be wise for the group to test its weapon to make sure that it worked effectively. A project of this complexity would require months of systematic effort, practical engineering skills and also luck. Basic microbiology skills that an undergraduate would learn should be sufficient to isolate *bacillus anthracis*, and using a 100-litre culture vessel several kilos of crude slurry containing billions of spores could be brewed up in a few days. Drying the slurry is a difficult procedure, but basic freeze-drying procedures can be used as potential options. Grinding the powder to particles of the desired diameter is the most demanding part of the whole process, mostly because of the danger of contamination. (52)

A few essential details of these procedures are not commonly known. The degree of difficulty is evident from the fact that despite years of development time, the Iraqis never mastered the art of weaponizing their bacterial agents. Following the Gulf War, UNSCOM inspectors found crude BW preparations mounted on conventional bombs and missiles. Aum Shinrikyo was equally unsuccessful in weaponizing any pathogen. It operated a BW laboratory from 1990, in which it attempted to aerosolize botulinum toxin and anthrax and Q-fever, but failed. (53) One suggestion is that the spores may not have been properly incubated, (54) others believe that they grew weak strains of *clostridium botulinum*, and *bacillus anthracis*, and had difficulty aerosolizing them into a respirable particle size. (55) But even in their crude form, these pathogens are still deadly. In one possible scenario, if anthrax slurry were left in an underground railway tunnel, the wind from passing trains would dry it out and disperse the spores, possibly leading to thousands of casualties. (56)

The effectiveness of a BW will be affected by factors such as the particular bacterial strain, its growth conditions, the age of the culture and the methods of preparing and preserving it, all of which will affect its ability to survive spraying. (57) Most BW are vulnerable to humidity, dessication, oxidation, air pollution, heat and shock and ultraviolet light (whilst CW are not), (58) although some are less susceptible than others – anthrax, for instance, being quite robust.

There has been considerable speculation about the prospect of terrorists developing genetically modified pathogens which combine DNA from different pathogens to produce a new pathogen with different characteristics such as increased lethality, greater ease of weaponization, greater resistance to antibiotics, or greater resistance to environmental factors. The FSU led the way in developing such weapons, and deployed modified forms of plague and anthrax in its strategic arsenal. Smallpox is another pathogen which is very amenable to genetic engineering. It also means that new variants of pathogens can be engineered which are resistant to the vaccines and antibiotics.

A certain amount of caution must be expressed about terrorists' ability and interest in exploitation of this technology. Genetic engineering is at the cutting edge of biotechnology research, requiring modern laboratory facilities, and terrorists already face huge technological problems in developing existing forms of pathogens. Whilst the Soviet Union was successful, it took a considerable amount of time to 'find the right place for the insertion of foreign genes into the smallpox virus,' and it required a whole industrial complex, employing numerous scientists, who conducted large numbers of tests on live animals. (59) The Aum Shinrikyo procured sophisticated molecular design software, the purpose of which is to 're-engineer the molecular structure of chemicals or micro-organisms'. Seiichi Endo, an Aum Shinrikyo microbiologist, was deeply interested in biotechnology and genetic engineering. (60) Yet Aum Shinrikyo never even got beyond cultivating and weaponizing natural pathogens, and doubts have to be expressed about what it could have achieved with this equipment even in the medium term. Genetically modified pathogens are frequently weaker than the original, because modifications which might strengthen some characteristics, such as penetration, could weaken other features. (61) It is generally agreed that reliable genetic engineering of pathogens cannot be guaranteed because not enough is known about the interactions between the different characteristics of pathogens, but this could change. (62)

Whilst it remains a theoretical threat, questions need to be asked about what terrorist groups with very small facilities and resources can achieve. Dr Alistair Hay questions whether terrorists would even make the basic choice to attempt to develop a genetically modified pathogen, considering the number of easily obtainable natural pathogens with the requisite lethal potential that are available. (63) Over time, however, these considerations might change as the biotechnology industry becomes more sophisticated and spreads around the globe.

Acquiring the materials to develop WMD
The relative ease, or difficulty, with which a terrorist organization can acquire the raw materials to produce NBC weapons varies considerably according to the type of device that is being sought. CW precursor chemicals are the easiest to acquire (if development is taking place in a developed state), BW are slightly more difficult and nuclear materials are by far and away the most difficult to acquire.

Acquiring fissile material is the most difficult element of nuclear weapon development. Natural uranium needs to be enriched in order to make an effective bomb, because natural uranium comprises only 0.7 per cent uranium-235. Equally, plutonium is not a naturally occurring substance but is created in the fuel rods of nuclear power reactors during the energy production process, and has to be separated from the other elements of the fuel rod.

The uranium enrichment process requires highly specialized equipment such as gas centrifuges. Establishing a clandestine facility to enrich uranium will take considerable time and expense, even assuming that manufacturers will supply such equipment to individuals who are not affiliated with major nuclear facilities or institutions. Plutonium can be separated from nuclear fuel rods through a series of chemical processes, which are relatively easier to master than the enrichment of uranium. This does not necessarily require industrial-scale facilities: laboratory-size facilities called 'hot cells' can be used to separate small quantities. With these two processes, the smaller the facility, the longer will be the time required to separate the necessary amount. The longer the time, the greater the risk of detection. Equally, the bigger the facility, the greater the risk of detection. However these are extremely complex processes even for states to master, and the thought of small terrorist cells building and running such facilities clandestinely is almost inconceivable, as is the use of existing facilities. (64)

Instead, the most likely means for terrorists to acquire fissile material is to either steal it, or buy it on the black market. Since 1991, the principal source of nuclear material for the black market has been the states of the FSU. (65) Russia possesses stockpiles of 125–165 tonnes of plutonium, up to 1200 tonnes of HEU and 640 million cubic metres of radioactive waste which contains uranium and plutonium. It also continues to produce large quantities of fissile material annually, for its civil and military programmes, as well as low-enriched uranium for commercial sale. Following the break-up of the Soviet Union, the accounting, control and physical protection measures required for the effective management and security of nuclear materials at the nearly 1000 sites that hold enriched uranium or plutonium, and at the facilities which hold other nuclear materials, began to break down. (66) Many Russian facilities are very old and in a state of considerable disrepair, which in certain cases enables relatively easy access to intruders and insiders interested in smuggling nuclear materials out. Since the end of the Soviet era, workers in the Russian nuclear industry have lost their privileged status and are now very poorly paid, in some cases going unpaid for months. In conjunction with a chronic lack of funding this has led to a general decline in management efficiency at many facilities. Lack of investment has meant that these problems were unable to be rectified, and the problems became so deep-seated that massive amounts of investment would be required to ensure high enough levels of security.

In conjunction with these problems in the Russian civil and military nuclear infrastructure, endemic corruption, the breakdown of the Russian administration and the criminalization of Russian society has created conditions which increase the incentives and opportunity to smuggle nuclear material. The persistence of Russia's economic crisis means that the conditions which generate the motives and opportunity to steal nuclear materials are likely to endure. Export controls are no longer fully effective, officials can be bribed and the law enforcement agencies are overstretched and underfunded. Faced with intense economic hardship, individuals have had to look after their own interests, which was reflected in the early cases of theft and smuggling, which were perpetrated by amateurs seeking to improve their economic situation. Most worryingly this has included disaffected employees at storage and production facilities. Between January 1993 and August 1994, 300 employees were arrested in Russia for illegally possessing, stealing, or transporting radioactive waste. (67) Bruce Hoffman and David Claridge point to 'the dangerous confluence of insiders and fences, serving and former intelligence officers with equally nefarious characters earning their livings as international arms dealers, black marketeers and criminals potentially points to developing "professionalism" among traffickers which is both alarming and will prove increasingly difficult to counter.' (68)

The problem is made more difficult by the fact that the lack of national or even site- specific inventory systems means that it is not even known how much nuclear material Russia and the other FSU states possess. Sources indicate that 10 per cent of all nuclear material was hidden during the Soviet era, and facility managers used to withhold some surplus material from accountancy in case there were production shortfalls in subsequent years. The present governments do not know where this material is located, (69) which means that there are caches inside FSU states which are unaccounted for, and can enter the black market with no risk of detection. (70)

One British intelligence source has stated that, 'The smuggling is unpreventable, unstoppable and one of the greatest threats to the future security of the West.' (71) It is made easier by the relatively small amounts that are required to make nuclear weapons, with a critical mass being somewhere between the size of an apple and a grapefruit. (72) In each year since 1991, there have been numerous reports of a wide range of nuclear materials being offered for sale on the black market. However it is difficult to separate fact from fiction in assessing the reports of this trade. In late 1996 the *Washington Times* alleged that 50–60 kg of a larger shipment of HEU being transported from Kazakhstan to the USA went missing, and the *Sunday Times* reported that a large cache of radioactive material including plutonium-239 and uranium-235 had disappeared from a site in Chechnya, along with a large amount of highly radioactive nuclear material (possibly waste). (73) The veracity of these reports is difficult to determine since official confirmation was not forthcoming. All that can be done is analyse the confirmed cases that have occurred.

According to the database of the International Atomic Energy Authority (IAEA) the number of confirmed and intercepted attempts to smuggle nuclear material went up from 43 in 1993 to a high point of 44 in 1994. This included four detected attempts to smuggle weapons- usable fissile material – three in Germany and one in Prague. But in all cases the amounts involved were extremely small – at least an order of magnitude smaller than the amount necessary to build a bomb. The largest amount was the 2.73 kg of HEU (enriched to 87 per cent) seized by Czech police in December 1994, whilst the largest amount seized in Germany was 363 g of plutonium in August 1994. (74) In 1995 the reported number of smuggling incidents declined to 27 in 1995, and then fell to 17 in 1996. Of 114 incidents of nuclear smuggling between 1993 and 1995, 72 involved natural, depleted or low-enriched uranium (although the precise levels of enrichment are frequently not made public). The amounts were mostly in gramme quantities, although the largest was a consignment of 149.8 kg of 3.3 per cent enriched uranium.

In all, since the collapse of the FSU there have been six confirmed cases involving gram or milligram quantities of plutonium, and several other reports of seizures which lack corroborating evidence. (75) There has not been a single confirmed case involving an amount of fissile material that could be considered significant for the purposes of constructing a nuclear weapon. But despite the fact that most of the material has not been fissile or weapons grade, a lot of it is still adequate for the construction of a radiological weapon or the poisoning of water supplies. In addition, very little is known about the potential purchasers, although at least one of the cases in Germany appears to have been a sting operation being run by the Russian foreign intelligence services. (76) There is no confirmed case of a terrorist being arrested in the act of purchasing fissile material, and no terrorist has been caught in possession.

Professor Phil Williams, however, argues that in all illicit markets only the tip of the iceberg is visible, with most remaining hidden. For instance, only 40 per cent of the illicit narcotics entering the USA is intercepted. Therefore the full extent of this trade is unknown, which leaves a considerable degree of uncertainty about the nature and quantities of the materials that have leaked into the black market but were not intercepted. The General Accounting Office (GAO) of the US Congress states that the samples that have been intercepted have more to do with luck than skilled detection. (77) Like other commodities, smuggling routes for nuclear materials are inherently flexible and alternative routes out of the FSU are continuously emerging.

Since 1992 the IAEA and the USA have been attempting to help Russia re-establish strong accountancy and control procedures, which has been matched by a decline in the number of seizures of nuclear material, including a dramatic decline in seizures of fissile material, with no cases being reported in 1997. (78) Whilst seizures of fissile material declined, a significant number of cases involving nuclear materials suitable for use in a radiological weapon continue to surface each year. This decline in seizures suggests that security at the facilities holding such material has become considerably more effective, but it does not necessarily indicate a decline in the volume of material being smuggled. There are also concerns that more professional smugglers have taken over, and fewer are now being apprehended. At a conference held at Dijon in France, to discuss the prevention of trafficking in radioactive material in late 1998, representatives from several participating organizations reported a shift in smuggling radioactive materials from individuals to organized crime. (79) There are still concerns about the material being held in the Russian civil nuclear sector, and potentially unaccounted for stocks. It is highly likely that there have been further leakages of fissile material other than those reported, and considerably more resources and work are required in order for Russia to secure its facilities. This indicates that the supply side of the black market continues to be filled. Yet just because nuclear materials are more available than they were in the 1970s and 1980s, this does not mean that terrorists will be able to acquire them. They need to make contact with the smugglers, be able to outbid any rival buyers and be sure that what they are being sold is what it is claimed to be.

The states of the FSU, however, are not the only possible source of nuclear materials. All states which operate nuclear industries have stockpiles of nuclear materials and there is a burgeoning materials trade with some state's spent reactor fuel being reprocessed in other states and nuclear fuel being transported globally. This all offers potential for terrorists to attempt to steal nuclear material. In particular, some of the isotopes that are suitable for use in radiological bombs also have civilian applications, particularly in hospitals. Therefore terrorists intent on building a radiological bomb could potentially steal the necessary material from such sources in any number of states. Since only small quantities of isotopes are used for medical purposes, it would be extremely difficult to acquire large quantities from these sources, but if a group were content with a small-scale radiological weapon, this could be an alternative source.

In certain states biological pathogens can be acquired from biological supply services such as the American Type Culture Collection (ATCC) in Maryland, USA. Regulations concerning the release of pathogens from these sources have been tightened considerably, but most pathogens and toxins can also be collected or synthesized from natural sources. In 1992 members of the Aum Shinrikyo visited the African state of Zaire on a medical mission to treat ebola victims, but government officials believe that their real purpose was to obtain a sample of the virus. Brucellosis and tulameria can both be acquired from natural sources. The plague virus can be obtained from fleas on rats; anthrax spores can be recovered from contaminated soil; ricin is developed from protein from castor beans; tricothene mycotoxins are derived from corn; aflatoxin from peanuts; and saxitoxin is an organic chemical synthesized by blue-green algae. (80) Consequently, toxins such as ricin are fairly easy to produce, which partly accounts for the number of white supremacists that have been arrested in the USA for being in possession of ricin (see Appendix for details), although recovering pathogens and toxins from natural sources does take time.

In industrialized states, chemical precursors for CW are easily available because most of them are standard industrial products, and because of their dual-use nature there are few, if any checks on sales. Exports of certain chemicals need export licenses under the rules of the Australia Group, which attempts to regulate the sale of chemicals which might be diverted to use for CW. (81) There are some key chemicals, however, which would indicate possible production of CW. One of the main pieces of evidence that the USA used as justification to destroy the Shaifa chemical factory in Sudan in 1999 was the presence of the chemical empta in soil samples taken at the site, the sole use of which is the production of VX. (82) In addition, some potential CW agents can be procured directly from industrial sources. Phosgene oxime which was one of the original CW agents, is now a commonly used toxic industrial chemical.

Just as the states of the FSU pose a risk of nuclear leakage, Russia also faces similar problems in controlling its CW and BW facilities. Frank Barnaby argues that there is undoubtedly a black market in the materials required to produce CW and BW. (83) Ken Alibek, the former First Deputy Chief of Research and Production for the FSU's BW programme, suggests that rogue scientists may already have taken samples of a modified anthrax to proliferator states. Russia has approximately 40,000 tonnes of CW which are scheduled for destruction under the provisions of the Chemical Weapons Convention (CWC), (84) but there are concerns about its safety. Storage facilities for CW are as inadequate as those housing nuclear materials. Photographs show old, rusty and leaking munitions. Some blister munitions are stored together with their fuses, and protection and control systems do not exist at the stockpiles. Old CW are also being dumped at a large number of sites which could be easily raided. (85) A lot of CW agents, however, are stored in bulk form, in 1-tonne containers, which greatly reduces the risk of leakage. Much of it is also very old, and has deteriorated, making it unsafe to handle or use. There is also little knowledge of the location of chemical munitions and agents that had been stored for use at testing sites in the FSU. In Kazakhstan there were several production facilities and research institutes for CBW, as well as a number of other major facilities. In Russia, one BW facility in the city of Tobolsk has been run down, but its by-products and burial grounds (where amongst other weapons, anthrax has been dumped) could be a target for terrorists. (86)

Russian biological research centres are not as vulnerable as nuclear facilities, because essential biosafety measures restrict access to the critical areas, greatly reducing the opportunities for theft and easing the task of physical protection, although the threat from insiders is still a concern. However there have been no reports so far of terrorists exploiting these weaknesses.

Much of the material and facilities for CBW production are dual-use, with the same technologies being used for peaceful purposes. Organisms and precursors which are used for pesticides, solvents, vaccines, medicines, beer and even some household products can be used to produce CBW. Ricin, botulinum and diphtheria toxins are now being considered for use as therapies. (87) The Aum Shinrikyo procured much of the specialized dual-use equipment such as air filtration equipment, molecular modelling equipment and sophisticated lasers openly in the USA. (88) This means that the procurement of many of the necessary materials and technologies will not necessarily raise any concerns within the supplier companies.

Delivery mechanisms for WMD

If a terrorist group manages to develop a CBW it then faces the problem of weaponizing it so that it can be delivered effectively. This technology is complex and involved. Previous incidents show that a significant number of groups have succeeded in developing CBW agents and pathogens, but hardly any managed to weaponize them effectively. Nuclear weapons are the easiest of the NBC weapons to deliver, because they can simply be loaded into trucks and driven to their target. This is one of the most common methods by which terrorist groups deliver bombs. It poses no technological problems, and consequently increases the attractiveness of nuclear weapons to terrorists, especially since the method of delivery for CBW can have a radical affect on the effectiveness of an attack. In fact, many analysts consider that developing effective dispersal mechanisms is actually more difficult than developing some forms of CBW agents themselves. Aum Shinrikyo came closest to effectively weaponizing a CW, but its engineers discovered that producing sarin was easier than disseminating it. The first two attempts to kill Daisaku Ikeda of the Japanese Soka Gakkai sect, with sarin, failed owing to a faulty delivery mechanism. (89) These problems greatly reduced the number of casualties in the attacks. The most effective dispersal method is spraying the agent into the air as a gas, which requires raising its temperature, which is time-consuming and dangerous. Aum Shinrikyo engineers originally converted a truck which contained a mechanism by which the sarin was dripped onto a heater, it would vaporize and then be blown out of the truck by a fan. (90) The system was used in the Matsumoto attack in 1994, but the system malfunctioned and caught fire, leaking gas fumes into the truck. (91) It has been speculated that the problem lay in the mechanism that turns the liquid sarin into sprayable gas. It took months to resolve this problem, through developing a computer-controlled spraying system that contained three tanks to hold the sarin, a heater to generate the right temperature and a fan to disperse the atomized agent. (92) The Tokyo subway attack however, was planned and executed in haste, which forced the Aum Shinrikyo engineers to improvise a dispersal mechanism of putting sarin into plastic bags which were pierced with sharpened umbrella tips, leaving the sarin to gradually leak out and vaporize.

In another attack an improvised delivery mechanism involved a bag containing a condom full of sodium cyanide, and a condom full of hydrochloric acid. The acid would eat through the rubber, and produce cyanide gas when it mixed with the sodium cyanide. The effectiveness of such a crude system is unknown, but a simulation concluded that the gas would have been sucked into the ventilation system, and out onto a nearby platform, killing up to 20,000 people. (93)

To maximize casualties the terrorist ideally needs to ensure that the target receives a continuous exposure to the agent. A single release of an agent will be rapidly dispersed as the agent is blown downwind, and basic civil defence measures would be effective in minimizing its effects. Instead, what is needed is a high enough concentration of the agent in an area for a period of time; the best way of achieving this is by a continuous release of the agent, (94) ideally through an aerosol apparatus. In addition, it has to be released at a high enough altitude to spread over the target, but not so high that it passes over it. Merely releasing it from the top of the nearest tall building is not good enough to maximize casualties.

Developing a delivery mechanism adds an additional layer of difficulty to CW production. It is unlikely that a chemist will also have the necessary skills to develop an aerosol dispersal mechanism, preferably with a remote-control firing mechanism. He, or she, would need a partner with engineering and electrical engineering skills. Whilst many individuals with the necessary skills can be found within industry – for example, within the refrigeration industry, or those developing hair and fly spray, (95) the terrorist group will have to identify and recruit such an individual, which entails risks for the success of their enterprise. Without such an individual, the group would have to fall back on a cruder dispersal mechanism, with a concomitant loss of lethality.

The most efficient aerosolization systems for BW require considerable technological sophistication, and remain beyond the reach of most states and terrorist groups. However less efficient aerosolization techniques are commercially available, and could be mastered by some highly capable groups, but would lead to a reduction in effectiveness, since mechanical stresses can kill many microorganisms. (96) But as time goes by, aerosolization systems that are more suitable for the dispersal of CBW will become increasingly available as their commercial applications increase: in the coming decades, delivery will not be the problem that it currently is. (97) Whilst several groups have previously succeeded in developing BW, it is not known whether they ever succeeded in engineering those pathogens into a form that was capable of use in an efficient aerosol mechanism. Inability to mill the particles to the correct size could also force terrorists to use their pathogens as contaminants. Whilst being relatively easy to develop, ricin is a particularly difficult agent to weaponize, which might account for why white supremacists in the USA have been apprehended in possession of the agent without any form of delivery mechanism. Aum Shinrikyo produced an aerosol dispersal system for botulinum which fitted into a briefcase. It held vinyl tubes of a solution containing the toxin. Using the power from dry batteries, the toxin was converted into steam, which was then blown out of the case by a small electric fan. (98) It remains unknown whether the device would have worked because of Aum Shinrikyo's problems with the toxin itself.

The operational use of CBW in open spaces is also subject to the vagaries of the weather. These weapons do not have an 'all-weather capability', and conditions must be exactly right in order to carry out an attack in the open air. For instance, during the first Aum Shinrikyo attack at Matsumoto, the wind went in the wrong direction, which reduced the number of casualties. (99) Therefore terrorists would also need a good knowledge of how these conditions might affect the lethality of their weapon, in order to maximize casualties.

There are also a number of more unconventional delivery methods which are open to terrorists. Ken Alibek describes one such scenario, of a terrorist who has been inoculated against a specific form of infectious BW carrying a sample of the agent onto an aeroplane bound for New York. During the course of the flight all of the crew and passengers would be infected, and once at the airport they would disperse throughout the city or even travel on to other cities before the first symptoms became apparent. (100)

It is also considered possible to use BW to inflict mass casualties by contaminating foodstuffs or liquids. Yet introducing biological agents into food-processing plants assumes that the agent will not be killed in the production process or identified by existing quality control procedures which are in place to detect the presence of bacteria such as salmonella. It would be possible to contaminate some foodstuffs or liquids after production, but contaminating large numbers of individual packages would be a time-consuming task, and would be less appealing and effective as a means of causing mass casualties. Similarly, agents could be introduced into food in restaurants; however, nearly all microorganisms are killed by heat, therefore they would have to be added to food after cooking, which is why the Rajneeshpuram cult disseminated *salmonella typhimurium* through salad bars. This would restrict casualties to the patrons of those specific restaurants, but this approach is theoretically capable of causing large numbers of casualties – if, for instance, several busy, fast-food restaurants were targeted simultaneously. Alternatively, targeting a range of different individual venues over an extended period of time could also serve terrorists' purposes by disrupting commerce and everyday life.

The popular scenario of terrorists poisoning water supplies is also a poor method of disseminating an agent. It would require large amounts of NBC materials or agents to produce a level of contamination sufficient to inflict mass casualties because the volume of dilution, in even small reservoirs, would drastically affect the amount of the agent needed. It could perhaps require tonnes of a material to be effective as a contaminant, although one estimate suggests that it would require 0.5 kg of *salmonella typhi* or 5 kg of botulinum toxin in a 5 million-litre reservoir to kill an individual drinking 100 ml of untreated water. (101) However most BW die in water owing to sunlight and chlorine, and the harm done by those that remained would depend upon the dose, rate of consumption and the resistance of the individual. (102)

There are also a number of other factors related to the reservoir itself which would impact upon the effect of a contaminant. These include variable in-flow and down-flow rates; thermal stratification of reservoir waters and seasonal turnover; other biological activity that might remove the contaminant or reduce its concentration; and potential reactions of the contaminant with chemicals naturally present in the water. In addition, a number of filtration and purification systems operate at water treatment plants which would further reduce their effectiveness. (103) In 1999, the threat by the Leader of the Scottish National Liberation Army (SNLA) to contaminate water supplies in the UK attempted to bypass these systems by pumping paraquat directly into water mains via fire hydrants. But even so, toxicologists argued that there would be little danger, with kidney dialysis patients who require a great deal of water in their treatment being at greatest risk. (104)

Contaminating the discrete supply of a specific installation or building is a more feasible option, as is contaminating air conditioning systems. (105) This might be relatively easier than outdoor attacks but it still requires knowledge of ventilation systems. The precise number of casualties from such an attack would depend upon a number of factors, including the rate at which air is exchanged, the number of cubic feet serviced by the system and the precise dosage required to kill an individual. These are complex calculations, and without a detailed understanding of them, the success of an attack depends upon a fair amount of luck. (106)

Lack of an effective dispersal mechanism will force terrorists to use any CBW agents that they manage to develop as contaminants. Yet even used in this fashion they are capable of inflicting significant numbers of casualties. Equally, lack of knowledge of some of the other complex practical aspects of each form of delivery could also severely limit casualty levels. Therefore the scenario of mass casualty attacks in the open air remains the most technologically difficult to master. In the short term this has two potential effects: to conceivably put WMD beyond the reach of some groups, and to reduce the effectiveness of attacks by NBC weapons. Technologically sophisticated groups, however, over time, could prove capable of developing, or acquiring, efficient dispersal mechanisms.

Finance

Assessments of the likely costs of developing NBC weapons vary depending upon the nature and scale of the exercise. Nuclear weapons are the most expensive for a terrorist group to develop, primarily because of the cost of acquiring the fissile material and the specialized machinery. Of the cases of nuclear smuggling that have been uncovered in Germany, HEU was being offered at prices between US$1 million and $60 million, whilst plutonium was being offered at prices between $700,000 and $1 million, (107) even though none of the quantities involved consti tuted a critical mass.

CBW are the cheapest weapon types to develop, especially in small-scale production operations. In particular, the raw materials are much cheaper. The American white supremacist, Larry Wayne Harris, paid only $240 for three vials of bubonic plague from the ATCC. (108) One source puts the start-up costs of a BW programme as less than $1 million, and botulinum toxin could be produced for $400 per kg; another source estimates that the production of 1000 kg of sarin in a small laboratory could cost about $200,000. Many of these estimates, however, do not specify whether they include additional costs such as the need to procure equipment and materials. (109) These weapons require only the hiring of laboratory-scale production facilities. The greater the quantity of CBW that a group intends to develop, the higher the cost. Producing enough CW for a mass-destruction attack on a state will require industrial-scale production capacity, involving considerably higher costs, although the degree of technical difficulty in developing specific types of CBW will affect the cost of the exercise. Similarly, developing effective delivery mechanisms will add to the cost.

From an analysis of the technology it is apparent that terrorist groups do not necessarily have to be well funded to develop NBC weapons. There are low-cost options available which can provide a reasonable assurance of success: in fact, the more basic technology of some of the lower-cost options probably provides a higher assurance of success. Therefore, assuming that a group's engineers make reasonable technological choices, finance should not be an inhibiting factor, except perhaps if the group intends to produce the weapon on an industrial scale. Although it is probably also true to say that the more money a group has at its disposal the better the weapons it can potentially produce, adequate financial resources is not enough in itself to guarantee success.

The nature of the threat

From this analysis of the technology and the various other factors involved in developing NBC weapons, it is clear that there are varying levels of difficulty associated with developing and employing the different types. The past record of terrorists managing to develop CBW indicates the same agents cropping up a number of times: ricin, anthrax, botulinum, cyanide, sarin and VX. The list of agents that groups have attempted to develop is only a little longer. This indicates that previously groups have succeeded in developing specific agents, and made specific technical choices, for a number of reasons: the group's strategic objectives, the ease of acquiring raw materials and the relative ease of development. It suggests that a small group of CBW are relatively easier to develop than the others, and the failure to develop other types hints at the difficulties involved in developing them. With the technological problems involved, terrorists are going to have to undertake systematic, long-term programmes to develop even the simplest forms of NBC weapons. The fact that Aum Shinrikyo took approximately two years to develop its first batches of sarin provides a useful indicator.

There are three general levels of threat.
Most common threats:
This is the threat which governments are most concerned with in the short term, and represents the weapon types which the largest number of terrorist groups would be able to develop. This is the category into which the vast majority of the previous cases of NBC terrorism fit. It comprises the most technologically easy of the NBC weapons to develop, because of ease of access to the necessary production facilities, raw materials and expertise. It includes all of the basic types of CW and some crude BW which have been poorly produced. Most are likely to be usable only as contaminants, although some might be crudely weaponized. The persistent leakage of nuclear materials from the FSU also puts radiological weapons into this category, although acquiring this material could still prove to be more difficult than developing CW and crude BW.

Intermediate threats:
These involve a greater degree of technical expertise and access to more specialized production facilities. These threats are going to be much less frequent than the common threats and will probably occur intermittently over a longer timeframe. This group of weapons includes the most complex CW, coupled with reasonably effective efficient delivery technology. This is the category into which the Aum Shinrikyo attacks on Matsumoto and the Tokyo subway fit.

Least common threats:
These are the WMD, which at worst are likely to occur only very rarely. It will be restricted to the groups which have the highest technological skill levels and financial resources. This group of weapons includes nuclear weapons, as well as efficiently weaponized CBW. No group in the past record of NBC terrorism appears to fit into this category, although Aum Shinrikyo might have achieved it given more time.

In categorizing these threats there are a number of independent variables in play. The biggest assumption is that a rogue state will not deliberately supply a WMD to a terrorist organization. This is a theoretical risk which is impossible to quantify, and is examined in greater depth in Chapter 8.

The second variable is that terrorists might steal or otherwise acquire a complete NBC weapon from a possessor state. Following the break-up of the FSU, reports circulated that a number of its nuclear weapons had gone missing, but these reports remain unconfirmed. (110) However there have been some concrete reports of the smuggling of CW from the FSU. In August 1996 a sting operation run by the Turkish authorities resulted in the seizure of 19 containers of mustard gas and one container of sarin from a smuggler in Istanbul who claimed he had acquired them from a KGB officer in Russia. (111) But if freelancing individuals or criminal gangs did manage to steal a WMD they would presumably sell it to the highest bidder, and a proliferator state should always manage to outbid a terrorist group. All possessor states will hold their WMD under very tight control, but it would still be unwise to consider that this scenario will never happen, especially if the group can gain assistance from insiders.

The third variable is that terrorists can gain the assistance of scientists and engineers who had previously worked on the WMD programmes of any of the possessor states. This variable means that some terrorist groups could acquire NBC weapons much quicker than if they had to rely on engineers who had never previously produced an NBC weapon – and, more significantly, even low-technology groups could leapfrog into the equation if they gained access to such individuals. There are already considerable concerns that engineers in the FSU are selling their skills to proliferators. Fortunately, they appear to be commercially driven rather than ideologically driven, and few groups will have the financial resources to pay them more than a state would. Serious questions must also be asked about whether these people would be so unscrupulous as to assist a terrorist organization, even for money. There is a significant difference between assisting a proliferator state and assisting an unpredictable terrorist group which is highly likely to use a WMD. A more likely scenario is that a religious cult will actively recruit these people – the continued activities of Aum Shinrikyo in Russia (see Chapter 6) suggest that this could be a real possibility. Of the independent variables, this is the most likely to influence events, and is a real concern.

The potential list of CBW that terrorists could develop is enormous, but the most likely BW to be developed include anthrax, botulinum toxin, bubonic plague, tulameria and ricin; and the CW most likely to be used include commercially available chem icals such as hydrogen cyanide or phosgene, as well as mustard gas, sarin, tabun, and perhaps VX. It will remain uncertain whether terrorists are most likely to prefer CW or BW, because whilst CW might be relatively easier to produce, BW are theoretically capable of producing a higher number of casualties. Since CW are typically less deadly, and can be more controllable than most BW, they are better suited to operations with restricted objectives. The Aum Shinrikyo possibly focused on CW because of the problems they encountered in weaponizing BW, but then it went for a CW which, whilst relatively low-technology in nature, was not the absolutely easiest to develop.

Ron Purver argues that the selection of an agent would depend upon its toxicity, the ease of manufacture or other means of acquisition, cultivation and dissemination, hardiness, immunity to detection and counter-measures, rapidity of effect and contagiousness. (112) The weight which a group would attach to any of these criteria will vary depending upon a number of factors. It is also worth considering whether terrorists are likely to opt for the weapon types which are best suited to their requirements, or those that they are most capable of developing. Groups with a limited technical capability might be tempted to go for the easiest technological options such as tabun and hydrogen cyanide: it is not clear that the additional technological difficulty of developing a more effective agent such as sarin would be enough to deter them from attempting to do so. In respect of BW, experts believe that terrorists would be more likely to choose a bacteriological rather than a viral or rickettsial agent which are easier to treat, more difficult to cultivate and do not live long outside of a host. In addition, some toxins are attractive because they are more stable, as is anthrax. (113) Right-wing US groups may have chosen ricin because there is a ready supply of castor beans from which to extract it, the processes for extracting and purifying the toxin are all well known and relatively easy and also perhaps because it is extremely toxic, works quickly and chemical toxicologists will not necessarily recognize it because it is difficult for them to pick up on. (114) Therefore it is both an easy technological option and also a desirable one.

Terrorists have a wide range of technological choices available to them which they will have to weigh against their intended objectives,. But this does not necessarily mean that a group will choose to develop the specific type of weapon which is best suited to the intended role. Aum Shinrikyo was intent on committing genocide, but nuclear weapons or BW would have been superior to sarin for this objective. The Aum Shinrikyo case indicates that where groups fail to develop the type of weapon which best meets their requirements, they will develop and use a less effective alternative. This analysis also suggests that if terrorists opt for the easiest NBC weapons to develop, the level of casualties that terrorists might be able to inflict with their early weapons will be limited. But when a wider range of weapon types comes within their reach, as they gain greater skills and access to better facilities and materials, the potential level of casualties that they will be capable of inflicting will increase.

Technical indicators of clandestine programmes
It is evident that terrorist groups can clandestinely develop some forms of NBC weapons with very little chance of detection. Some of the activities involved in developing some types of NBC weapons, however, will leave tell-tale technical indicators that a group might be developing them. One of the most telling aspects of the Aum Shinrikyo case was that its CW programme produced strong indicators of what the cult was up to, but the security forces were not looking for any such indicators and therefore overlooked their significance when they were reported. In general, it will be impossible to locate and identify small-scale clandestine NBC weapon programmes by technical means, and by looking for technical indicators: only routine monitoring of suspects, sites and group activities, in conjunction with technical indicators, could give the security forces enough time to work out what a group might be up to.

The greatest problem facing non-state actors developing WMD is the length of time which it will take them. The greater the length of time it takes, the higher the chances of detection because of the higher likelihood of a security breach, which gives the security forces greater time to identify key individuals and look for relevant patterns in their activities to indicate their involvement in NBC weapon development.

Some weapon types, together with technical routes for developing them, contain a higher number of indicators than other weapon type of development routes. By far the greatest number of unequivocal indicators arise in respect of clandestine nuclear weapon development. Acquiring fissile material by theft or purchase will provide an unequivocal indicator of intent. The acquisition of related production facilities and other key materials, while essentially dual-use in nature, are more equivocal indicators. Yet they are indicators of potential intent which security forces can act upon. If a group managed to steal fissile material there are a number of factors which could lead to detection – these include a defection from the group and a massive search which would be instituted for the stolen material, although it would be difficult to locate its storage place. The material needed for neutron shielding – boron polycarbonate brick or sheet – is uncommon and its acquisition would attract attention. Inexperience in the team, will also lead to time penalties, which increase the risk of detection. (115)

The dual-use nature of most CW and BW materials and facilities means that security forces are likely to identify only equivocal technical indicators. There are a few key materials for some nerve gases such as phosphoryl chloride and dimethlamine, but these are required only in small quantities. By making careful choices a group could develop an agent which does not leave such indicators. Similarly, procuring BW pathogens from biological supply houses can be monitored, but procuring them from the environment will leave no indicators. The acquisition of personnel, particularly if they are not already in the group, could be the most significant indicator that a group provides, but only the monitoring of the activities of key individuals enables technical indicators to be put into context.

Chemical suppliers, particularly in the West, know who they are dealing with, and are careful in who they sell to. The CWC requires international declarations of production, and use, of precursor chemicals, controls, and reporting on all facilities that use more than 1 metric tonne of a defined set of high-risk precursors, and 30 metric tonnes of a defined set of dual-use precursors on an annual basis. This means that some precursors are easier to acquire than others, and many can be obtained in small quantities without arousing suspicion, there is little control and reporting and terrorists can cover their tracks with cover stories. (116) Overall, potential indicators can be masked, especially by purchasing small quantities of precursors and choosing specific agents and production processes, although this can lead to greater costs or complexity. CW production, however, is likely to produce noxious odours, as might some BW processes, (117) although there are fewer indicators of BW production.

The most unequivocal indicators are likely to occur only by chance, such as terrorist defections, attempts to recruit engineers that fail, and are reported, along with fires explosions or other accidental leaks from their clandestine facilities.

The greater the sophistication of the programme, and the larger its scale, the greater the number of indicators that will be given away. Aum provided a number of significant indicators from the industrial-scale manufacture of sarin by procuring a significant amount of specialized dual-use equipment, which any CW specialist would have identified as being usable to produce CW. Small-scale operations will leave fewer indicators, because the procurement of small quantities of precursor chemicals is easier for security services to miss and report on. The former director of the CIA, James Woolsey, told the US Senate Foreign Relations Committee that, 'The chemical weapons problem is so difficult from an intelligence perspective that I cannot state that we have high confidence in our ability to detect non-compliance, especially on a small scale.' (118) Consequently, the least number of indicators will arise from small-scale, basic CBW production. Ironically these lie in the first order of threats. Some of the most dangerous threats, particularly industrial-scale production of CW and nuclear weapon development, will potentially leave the highest number of indicators.

Consequently, a technologically sophisticated terrorist group, which exercises a great degree of caution, could choose to pursue technological options which will minimize the number of technical indicators that are likely to be noticed. Taking the options which leave fewest indicators will greatly complicate the task of developing specific types of NBC weapons, which may not necessarily be consistent with the goals of the group. For instance, the Aum Shinrikyo had to undertake industrial-scale manufacture of sarin because of its genocidal objectives. Therefore depending upon the roles which the NBC weapons are required for, some groups could be forced into following routes that leave a higher number of indicators.

Conclusion
Analysts are correct to conclude that the technology to develop NBC weapons is now theoretically within reach of a large number of terrorist groups. Therefore technological factors are not an insurmountable obstacle, particularly to technologically sophisticated groups such as the Aum Shinrikyo, and well-funded groups such as Osama bin Laden's terrorist network. Yet technological factors will continue to pose serious barriers to terrorist groups attempting to develop NBC weapons. The fact that Ramseh Youssef, the leader of the team responsible for the bombing of the World Trade Centre in 1993, apparently attempted to turn the bomb into a CW by packing hydrogen cyanide around the explosive, indicates that his group lacked the technical expertise to weaponize CW agents. The raw materials for developing CBW have always been available in the West, yet several groups have failed to produce CBW for a number of reasons, one of which is technical, and this situation will continue to pertain into the future.

Therefore it cannot be assumed that any terrorist group will be able to develop NBC weapons as soon as it sets its mind to it. One of the biggest assumptions is that terrorists will automatically attract individuals with the necessary skills merely because increasing numbers of skilled people exist in the community. The precise nature of the future threats will partly depend upon the skills of the engineers that terrorists manage to recruit. WMD threats will emerge only if a group can successfully build a team which is capable of effectively weaponizing an NBC weapon. Yet even if a group does manage to assemble such a team, it is not a simple task, it is difficult to do things safely and effectively and will take time. This will increase the risk of detection, but the less time that a group spends, the poorer the weapon that it is likely to produce.

Technological constraints indicate that lower-level NBC threats will be considerably more likely than WMD threats. This first order of threats consists primarily of most CW, and crude forms of BW or toxins, which have not been weaponized effectively. The second order of threats derives from more sophisticated CW, and BW which have been more effectively weaponized. Nuclear technology poses serious technological problems, perhaps even insurmountable ones, for terrorists. The principle threat of nuclear terrorism appears to derive primarily from radiological weapons, which are amongst the first order of threats. Equally, because it is easier to undertake smaller-scale production operations, the initial threats are likely to be small-scale in nature, from limited quantities of CBW. Therefore the most likely threats are CBW with poor delivery mechanisms, which are primarily usable only as contaminants. The development of WMD capable of causing extremely large levels of casualties is the least likely threat to emerge.

For governments attempting to counter the threat, it is evident that they will not necessarily receive any clear-cut technical indicators of clandestine NBC programmes. A sophisticated group which maintains its security and makes careful technological choices concerning the type of NBC weapon that it is attempting to develop can virtually eliminate any significant technical indicators of its activities. The more ambitious the programme, however, the more indicators that are likely to emerge, although accidental indicators are the most likely to lead to detection of a clandestine programme. In general, technical indicators cannot be relied on in isolation. They need to be linked to identified terrorist suspects. It is not through technical indicators that clandestine programmes will be identified, it is by monitoring the groups, and then interpreting their observed actions.

Notes and references
1. Interview with Professor Frank Barnaby (25 January 1999)
2. David Kaplan and Andrew Marshall, *The Cult at the End of the World* (New York: Crown Publishers, 1996) p 102

3. Real name Steve Kreisler, 'Uncle Fester' is an amateur scientist and former convict who worked out how to make ricin in his own kitchen, and subsequently published a book on it. Both his book and his internet website are popular. In the UK, the Defence Evaluation and Research Agency and the Chemical and Biological Defence. Establishment at Porton Down have examined Kreisler's work and claim it is highly dangerous. Kreisler argues that knowledge of how to make ricin should be made known because of the right of freedom of information. He admits that there is no moral line in his book and advocates experimenting on family pets. Kreisler also claims he would not be unhappy if his work inspired a BW attack, provided innocent victims were not hurt. *The Plague Wars* 1 (1989)

4. 'Patent Blunder', *Scientific American* (November 1998) p 25

5. Ron Purver, 'Chemical and Biological Terrorism: New Threat To Public Safety', *Conflict Studies* 295 (December 1996–January 1997) p 4

6. The essence of biotechnology is growing large numbers of cells under controlled conditions. At its simplest it involves the use of living organisms in agriculture, food and other industrial processes. The biotechnology industry is now thriving in many industrialized states.

7. Richard Falkenrath, Robert D. Newman and Bradley Thayer, *America's Achilles Heel* (Cambridge, MA: MIT Press, 1998) p 172

8. Robert Taylor, 'All Fall Down', Special Report, *New Scientist* (11 May 1996) pp 32–33

9. 'New Routes to Old Poisons', *Guardian* (4 November 1998)

10. Interview, name withheld by request (23 March 1999)

11. Nuclear Proliferation and Safeguards, US Congress Office of Technology Assessment (Washington DC: Office of Technology, 1977)

12. J. Carson Mark, Theodore Taylor, Eugene Eyster, William Marman and Jacob Wechsler, 'Can Terrorists Build Nuclear Weapons?', in Paul Leventhal and Yonah Alexander (eds), *Preventing Nuclear Terrorism* (Lexington, MA: Lexington Books, 1987) p 58

13. Mark et al: 'Can Terrorists Build Nuclear Weapons?', p 55

14. Mark et al: 'Can Terrorists Build Nuclear Weapons?', p 58

15. Leonard S. Spector, Mark G. McDonough and Evan Medeiros, Tracking Nuclear Proliferation (Washington DC : Carnegie Endowment for International Peace, 1995) p 10

16. Mark et al: 'Can Terrorists Build Nuclear Weapons?', p 57

17. Frank Barnaby, 'Nuclear Terrorism', *Safe Energy* 95 (June–July 1993) p 11

18. Frank Barnaby, *Instruments of Terror: Mass Destruction Has Never Been So Easy* (London: Vision Paperbacks, 1996) p 170

19. Interview with Professor Frank Barnaby (25 January 25 1999)

20. Barnaby: *Instruments of Terror*, p 169

21. International Physicians For the Prevention of Nuclear War, 'Crude Nuclear Weapons: Proliferation and the Terrorist Threat', Global Health Watch, Report 1 (1996) p 5

22. Frank Barnaby, 'Issues Surrounding Crude Nuclear Explosives,' p 9

23. Robert Mullen, 'Nuclear Violence', in Leventhal and Alexander (eds): *Preventing Nuclear Terrorism*, p 56

24. Mullen: 'Nuclear Violence', pp 60–63

25. Falkenrath, Newman and Thayer: *America's Achilles Heel*, p 136

26. Frank Barnaby: 'Issues Surrounding Crude Nuclear Explosives', p 10

27. Mark et al: 'Can Terrorists Build Nuclear Weapons?', p 64

28. These types of devices have also been referred to as 'dirty bombs' and 'dustbin bombs'

29. Barnaby: *Instruments of Terror*, p 173; other suitable isotopes include polonium-210, lithium-6 and americium-241

30. Barnaby: 'Nuclear Terrorism', p 12

31. Jessica Stern, The Ultimate Terrorists, (Cambridge Ma: Harvard University, 1999) p 56

32. A potential fifth category comprises 'incapacitating agents', such as hallucinogens, CS, BZ or other psychochemical agents. However these agents are not designed to kill or injure but to cause disorientation to the individual, and their effects are relatively short-term. Therefore their interest value to terrorists is limited, with their primary value perhaps lying in how their use might generate media attention.

33. Barnaby: *Instruments of Terror*, p 134

34. Stern: *The Ultimate Terrorists*, p 24

35. D.W.Brackett, *Holy Terror: Armageddon In Tokyo* (New York: Weatherhill, 1996) p 114

36. Purver: 'Chemical and Biological Terrorism', p 2

37. Purver: 'Chemical and Biological Terrorism', p 113

38. Brackett: *Holy Terror*, p 109

39. Richard Falkenrath, 'Confronting Nuclear, Biological and Chemical Terrorism', *Survival* 40/3 (Autumn 1998) p 48

40. Interview with Dr Alistair Hay (28 April 1999)

41. Interview, name withheld by request (23 March 1999)

42. Falkenrath, Newman and Thayer: *America's Achilles Heel*, p 107

43. Aum started its CW programme in 1992, and the first attack using sarin occurred in the Spring of 1994

44. Kaplan and Marshall: *The Cult at the End of the World*, p 121

45. Brackett: *Holy Terror*, pp 116, 117

46. Wendy Barnaby, *The Plague Makers: The Secret World of Biological Warfare* (London: Vision   Paperbacks, 1997) p 23

47. Barnaby: *Instruments of Terror*, p 136

48. Taylor: 'All Fall Down', p 33

49. DERA, Chemical and Biological Defence, *Protecting Through Scientific Understanding*, DERA Brochure (1997)

50. Kaplan and Marshall: *The Cult at the End of the World*, p 53

51. Wendy Barnaby: *The Plague Makers*, p 45

52. Taylor: 'All Fall Down', p 34

53. Brackett: *Holy Terror*, p 114

54. Kaplan and Marshall: *The Cult at the End of the World*, p 96

55. Stern: *The Ultimate Terrorists*, p 68

56. Taylor: 'All Fall Down', p 35

57. Falkenrath, Newman and Thayer: *America's Achilles Heel*, p 123

58. Stern: *The Ultimate Terrorists*, p 51

59. Al J.Venter, 'Spectre of Biowar Remains,' *Jane's Defence Weekly* (28 April 1999) p 23

60. Kaplan and Marshall: *The Cult at the End of the World*, p 233

61. Interview with Dr Alistair Hay (28 April 1999)

62. Wendy Barnaby: *The Plague Makers*, p 129

63. Interview with Dr Alistair Hay (28 April 1999)

64. In the background papers of the 1985 Task Force, Robert Mullen provides an indication of what establishing a plutonium separation facility would involve: 'To build that facility, they need a site and the planning and design of the facility by architects, engineers and plutonium chemists. They would need to survey, grade, and excavate for the four major elements of the facility: the spent fuel feed handling area, the hot processing line, the plutonium clean up and storage area, and the waste handling operation. Once the site was prepared skilled workers would be required to pour a lot of concrete; other skilled workers would have to install specialized mechanical, plumbing, and electrical systems, including the radiation shielding and remote handling equipment. The terrorists would then have to acquire, store, and install the processing equipment.' The complexity of this task increases the likelihood of failure: secrecy would be hard to maintain, the theft of spent fuel would trigger a massive search, the number of people involved raises security risks, there is a danger of defections from the groups considering the hazardous nature of the undertaking and its consequences, and then there are the dangers associated with the process itself. Consequently, Mullen concluded that separating plutonium was not a credible option for a terrorist group. Mullen: 'Nuclear Violence', p 232

65. For a fuller account of nuclear smuggling from the Former Soviet Union, see Graham T.Allison, Owen R. Cote Jr, Richard A.Falkenrath and Steven E.Miller, *Avoiding Nuclear Anarchy* (Cambridge Ma: MIT Press 1996)

66. Barnaby: *Instruments of Terror*, p 162; Bruce Hoffman and David Claridge, 'Illicit Trafficking in Nuclear Materials', *Conflict Studies* 314/315, Research Institute For the Study of Conflict and Terrorism (January–February 1999) p 10

67. Hoffman and Claridge: 'Illicit Trafficking', p 12. This includes cases in 1992, when 3.7 lb of HEU were stolen from the Luch Scientific Production Association and in 1993 when 10 lb was stolen from Murmansk naval base, although the Russian authorities apprehended both perpetrators.

68. Hoffman and Claridge: 'Illicit Trafficking', p 16

69. Barnaby: *Instruments of Terror*, p 165

70. John Sopko, 'The Changing Proliferation Threat', *Foreign Policy* 103 (Winter 1996–97) p 10

71. Barnaby: *Instruments of Terror*, p 159

72. Allison et al: *Avoiding Nuclear Anarchy*, p 45

73. *PPNN Newsbrief* (Fourth Quarter 1996) p 14

74. Summary Listing of Incidents Involving Illicit Trafficking in Nuclear Materials and Other Radioactive Sources (4th Quarter 1996), attached to IAEA's Letter of 29 January 1997, Reference N4.11.42

75. For fuller accounts of these incidents see the Nuclear Material Trafficking sections of PPNN Newsbrief, particularly 25–32, 1994–95; and for unsubstantiated reports see 36, 44 , 46, 47

76. *PPNN Newsbrief* (First Quarter 1997) p 11

77. Barnaby: *Instruments of Terror*, p 163

78. *PPNN Newsbrief* (First Quarter 1998) p 18

79. *PPNN Newsbrief* (Third Quarter 1998) p 25
80. 'New Routes to Old Poisons', *Guardian* (4 November 1998); Purver: 'Chemical and Biological Terrorism', p 7
81. The Australia Group is a cartel of chemical producers which operate an informal export control regime, based upon lists of chemical precursors. Under the rules of the group, the export of any listed chemicals from a member group will be denied if there concern that it might be used in a CW programme.
82. *Guardian* (23 September 1998)
83. Barnaby: *Instruments of Terror*, p 139
84. For a fuller description of the convention, see Chapter 9
85. Masha Katsva, 'Threat of Chemical and Biological Terrorism in Russia', *The Monitor* (Spring 1997) p 15
86. Katsva: 'Threat of Chemical and Biological Terrorism'
87. Sopko: 'The Changing Proliferation Threat', p 9
88. Sopko: 'The Changing Proliferation Threat', p 11
89. Kaplan and Marshall: *The Cult at the End of the World*, p 132
90. Kaplan and Marshall: *The Cult at the End of the World*, p 139
91. Brackett: *Holy Terror*, p 29
92. Brackett: *Holy Terror*, p 29
93. Kaplan and Marshall: *The Cult at the End of the World*, pp 279–80
94. Interview with Dr Alistair Hay (28 April 1999)
95. Interview with Dr Alistair Hay (28 April 1999)
96. Falkenrath, Newman and Thayer: *America's Achilles Heel*, p 123; Falkenrath: 'Confronting Nuclear, Biological and Chemical Terrorism', p 47
97. Interview with Julian Perry Robinson (23 February 1999)
98. Kaplan and Marshall: *The Cult at the End of the World*, p 235
99. Brackett: *Holy Terror*, pp 32–33
100. *Sunday Telegraph* (8 March 1998)
101. Purver: 'Chemical and Biological Terrorism', p 2
102. Karl Lowe, 'Analyzing Technical Constraints on Bioweapons: Are They Important?', in Brad Roberts (ed), *Terrorism With Chemical and Biological Weapons: Calibrating Risks and Responses* (Alexandria Va: Chemical and Biological Control Institute, 1997) p 54
103. Purver: 'Chemical and Biological Terrorism', p 6
104. 'Water Terror Plot Foiled', *Observer* (11 July 1999)
105. Purver: 'Chemical and Biological Terrorism', p 6
106. Lowe: 'Analyzing Technical Constraints', p 55
107. Hoffman and Claridge: 'Illicit Trafficking', p 17
108. Sopko: 'The Changing Proliferation Threat, p 6.
109. Purver: 'Chemical and Biological Terrorism', p 4
110. In 1991 a secret operation by the environmental organization Greenpeace called Loose Cannon apparently came within weeks of taking delivery of a Russian nuclear weapon. Greenpeace offered a Soviet soldier $250,000. Just before the exchange was to take place the British, US, German or Russian intelligence services picked up on Greenpeace's communications and the Russian army officer was apprehended. In September 1996, a number of Russian soldiers were killed when the warhead of a missile they were probably trying to steal exploded at a military base in Komsomolsk-on-Amur in Russia's far east.

According to Frank Barnaby who quotes intelligence sources, a number of FSU nuclear weapons are missing. In the mid-1980s, before the FSU began to break up, there were about 30,000 nuclear weapons on Soviet territory. The majority of these weapons may still be secure, while they are in the hands of the military, but given the fact that many Russian troops are extremely badly paid, if paid at all, there is a risk that a device could fall into the wrong hands. Steve Boggan, 'For Sale: A Russian Nuclear Bomb, A Snip at $250,000, One Careless Owner, *Independent* (25 July 1998)

111. Purver, 'Chemical and Biological Terrorism', p 16. The KGB was the secret police of the former Soviet Union
112. Purver: The Threat of Chemical and Biological Terrorism', p 7
113. Purver: The Threat of Chemical and Biological Terrorism', p 6
114. Interview with Dr Alistair Hay (28 April 1999)
115. Mark et al: 'Can Terrorists Build Nuclear Weapons?', p 236
116. Falkenrath, Newman and Thayer: *America's Achilles Heel*, pp 103–04
117. Falkenrath, Newman and Thayer: *America's Achilles Heel*, pp 110, 123
118. Barnaby, *Instruments of Terror*, p 139

4. Strategic And Tactical Motivations and Disincentives to Using NBC Weapons

If a terrorist group is technically capable of exploiting NBC weapon technology, it is commonly assumed that tactical and strategic imperatives will at some stage drive it to attempt to develop NBC weapons. The analysis of NBC weapon technology indicates that the types of weapons which terrorists are likely to be able to develop will be constrained by technological factors, which will undoubtedly have an impact upon how a group might be able to employ any NBC weapon that it managed to develop. But, equally, a group's strategy and tactics will also play a key role in determining the technological options that they might attempt to exploit, because different weapon types will be more suited to specific tactics. But whilst the procurement of NBC weapons will undoubtedly provide terrorist groups with new tactical options, question marks remain over whether some groups would necessarily want those options.

The consequences of the use of NBC weapons
The question of whether the use of NBC weapons would further terrorist objectives is primarily dependent upon the consequences of their use. The first impact would be the immediate

physical damage and casualties, but an attack could also have potentially profound repercussions for the economy of the state, its internal politics and perhaps even longer-term effects on the nature of society itself. The intensity of the consequences, however, will vary according to the type of weapon that is used. Richard Falkenrath identifies seven consequences of a WMD attack. (1)

The primary consequence of the use of any of the categories of NBC weapon identified in Chapter 3 is casualties. The exact numbers will depend upon the kind of weapon that is employed, the quality of the weapon (including its delivery mechanism), how it is employed and the environmental conditions under which it is used.

There is a considerable amount of uncertainty about likely casualty levels from a CW attack, and overestimates are common. CW attacks involving third-order WMD in optimal weather conditions have the potential capacity to kill hundreds or thousands and injure many more. An illustration of likely casualty levels from second-order weapon types in the open air is provided by some of the Aum Shinrikyo attacks. The attack on the town of Matsumoto resulted in the death of seven people, and injured more than 200 others, (2) whilst the attack on the Tokyo subway killed 12 and injured over 5500. Pumping agents through the air conditioning of a building has the potential to maximize the lethality of an agent. In one exercise in 1998 the US government estimated that a release of sarin into the corridors of the Pentagon would result in 26 deaths and 100 others being exposed to the agent. (3) The OTA estimate that 1 kg of VX released inside a large building could kill 500 people of the 1000 exposed; tens of kg of phosgene would have the same effect; whilst hundreds of grams of VX in a subway car could kill 50–100. (4) The OTA estimate fatalities between 60 and 200 from a release of 300 kg of sarin in a normal urban area in moderate wind conditions. (5) Therefore the number of deaths from CW attacks is likely to be equivalent to some of the most destructive attacks using conventional weapons, and even this would require amounts of agent that were larger than could be produced in a basement lab.

The effects of BW can be more variable, but also significantly more lethal. Only a few pathogens are known to have the potential to cause deaths exceeding those that could be caused by CW and nuclear weapons. Some agents such as anthrax kill nearly 100 per cent of untreated victims, but brucellosis kills only 5 per cent of untreated victims. (6) At the higher end of the spectrum, fatalities in the low tens of thousands are feasible with unsophisticated weapons, whilst a more advanced BW could kill or injure hundreds of thousands. Neil Livingstone states that half of an ounce of type-A botulinum toxin, properly dispersed, could kill everyone in North America. (7) In another example, 130 grammes of ricin effectively dispersed, is enough to kill thousands of people. (8) The Advanced Concepts Research corporation of Santa Barbara in the USA calculated that an aerosol attack with anthrax spores on New York city could kill over 600,000. (9) Representative figures for multiple points of attack using 100 kg of dry anthrax powder are 1–3 million deaths, and from a single source using 30 kg of dry powder 30,000–100,000 deaths. Use indoors can achieve very high casualty rates. US military tests in the 1960s indicated that crude dispersal of anthrax on the New York subway would kill hundreds to thousands of people, (10) whilst the US Law Enforcement Assistance Administration warned in the 1970s that an ounce of anthrax introduced into the air conditioning system of a domed stadium could kill 70,000–80,000 spectators within an hour. More recent figures from the OTA estimate that an indoor attack with 1–100 litres of anthrax would cause 8,000–40,000 deaths, and brucellosis would cause 160–800 deaths. As is the case with CW, precise casualty levels will depend upon how well the BW has been prepared, and a number of operational factors including the effectiveness of the delivery mechanism, whether a single or multiple point of attack was used, the type of pathogen and the weather conditions prevailing at the time of the incident. In addition, potential casualty levels from CBW will be affected by the speed and effectiveness of the medical response, since treatment is possible for all of the easily used bacteriological agents, as well as many toxins.

The potential number of casualties caused by nuclear weapons is less sensitive to the method of delivery and conditions of its use, and is primarily dependent upon the explosive yield of the device and the nature of the area in which it is used. There are considerable uncertainties concerned in estimating potential casualty levels from a nuclear explosion because of a lack of empirical evidence. The 20 Kt weapon dropped on Hiroshima in Japan, killed somewhere between 90,000 and 120,000 people, with 91,000 injured, whilst Theodore Taylor estimates that the detonation of a crude nuclear weapon with a yield of 0.5 Kt in New York, could kill up to 50,000 people. (11)

By their very nature, NBC weapons have the potential to cause large numbers of indiscriminate casualties, but significantly, they are also capable of being used in a number of different operational roles. If used in a controlled fashion, they are equally capable of causing small numbers of casualties, or large numbers of discriminate casualties. Consequently, the nature of the casualties – low or high, discriminate or indiscriminate will also depend upon how the terrorists use the weapon at their disposal.

The second effect of the use of NBC weapons is contamination. With third-order WMD, very large geographical areas could be contaminated, rendering them uninhabitable for varying periods of time. Under optimal conditions it has been estimated that biological pathogens could drift for hundreds of miles on the wind, whilst the area of contamination caused by a nuclear weapon would primarily depend upon its yield, and the weather conditions prevailing at the time.

The levels of contamination likely to be caused by first- and second-order NBC weapons are likely to be much smaller than those caused by third-order WMD. Most of these threats involve crude dispersal mechanisms which mean that whilst the contamination would probably be quite severe, it would be confined to relatively small geographical areas. The likely effects of contamination from introducing an agent into the air conditioning of a building is illustrated by an incident in February 1981, in which there was an accidental leak of dioxins in an 18-storey office block in New York. By late 1982 the building was still empty and millions of dollars had been spent on decontamination. (12) Another indication of the effects of radioactive contamination emerges from an incident at Goina, Brazil, in 1987, when a caesium source which was found in an abandoned medical clinic was broken open and 17 g of powder were released. Four people were killed and thousands of cubic metres of soil had to be removed and decontaminated. (13) A possible exception in this order of threats are radiological weapons, which have the potential to spread contamination over a wide area. It has been estimated that if a radiological weapon had been used in conjunction with the World Trade Centre bomb, a large area of lower Manhattan would still have been uninhabitable in 1998, and another analysis by Peter Taylor and David Sumner, who modelled a release of 35 kg of plutonium in a major population centre, using a crude dispersal mechanism, estimated that an area of 900–5000 km2 would need to be evacuated. (14)

Decontamination would be a costly and lengthy process, which will vary according to the toxicity and persistence of the contaminating pathogen or agent. The level of contamination caused by the dispersal of radioactive materials will vary according to factors such as the physical and biological half-lives of the agent, modes of radioactive decay, specific radioactivities of starting and end-use materials; physical and chemical forms of starting and end materials, the medium into which the material is dispersed and environmental factors. (15)

The third effect is panic. Hospitals are likely to be overwhelmed with people claiming infection and ill effects. It is likely to lead to the migration of people away from infected areas, disrupting personal, social and economic life. However the effects of panic following an attack should not be overstated. Mass panic is likely to be a consequence only of a third-order WMD attack. This is illustrated by the immediate aftermath of the accidental leakage of chemicals from the Union Carbide Pesticide plant at Bhopal in India, in 1984, when somewhere between 70,000 and 200,000 people out of a population of 900,000 fled the city. (16) In contrast, the Tokyo subway was up and running again shortly after the Aum attack, and it was still used by large numbers of commuters, although some time after the incident hundreds of commuters on the subway suffered copy-cat symptoms of the sarin attack, including breathlessness, which psychiatrists argue was caused by mass hysteria as a result of the memory of the attack. Consequently, the level of panic will vary according to the lethality and precise circumstances of a future attack.

The fourth effect is degraded response capabilities, because government personnel trained to deal with the emergency may themselves become casualties or be prevented from responding in other ways. Unless trained and equipped, first-responders such as police and medical personnel will become casualties, whilst congested roads caused by mass panic will cause havoc. This will increase the number of casualties resulting from any attack, and increase the amount of time that it takes to deal with an incident. However, the Tokyo attacks also proved that response units in most developed states should be able to cope with first- and second-order NBC threats. Second-order threats will probably stretch their capabilities, but it is only third-order WMD threats which are likely to threaten a breakdown of response capabilities.

The fifth effect is economic damage. Besides the death of workers, business premises could be rendered unusable or destroyed, and commerce will be disrupted. Again this will vary according to the location of the attack, the type of NBC weapon that is used and how it was used. The explosion of the Chernobyl nuclear reactor in Ukraine was the most expensive accident in human history, with both immediate and long-term consequences, because of the loss of considerable tracts of agricultural land. The FSU put the cost up to May 1988 at 10 billion rubles but western experts estimate it to be much higher. (17) The cost of the destruction of the financial sector of a major city such as London or New York would be even higher. Again, though, levels of economic damage are going to vary according to whether a first-, second- or third-order weapon is used, but it seems likely that only third-order WMD threats are likely to cause massive economic damage.

A potential sixth effect could be loss of strategic position. The victim state might be reluctant to engage in regional crises, or might otherwise reduce its international commitments and interests, for fear of provoking a further terrorist attack. This will be especially true of states that already have isolationist tendencies. This potential effect should not be overstated because states very rarely act in isolation in dealing with international crises, and these risks will generally be shared. Therefore it remains to be seen whether powerful states would be intimidated into adopting a lower international profile. It would also only seem likely to apply to attacks involving third-order WMD, although it is conceivable that the use of first and second-order weapons might intimidate states into changing their foreign policies, if they feared the terrorists would escalate to using a WMD.

The seventh effect would be social-psychological damage and political change. The continuing risk of attack after a successful incident could have a profound effect on the target population, and on the nation's politics and law. Richard Falkenrath argues that public expressions of paranoia, xenophobia, isolationism and vengeful fury could become powerful influences on foreign policy. There could be a loss of confidence in the government because of its inability to prevent the attack, and society would demand action from its government. This phenomenon already occurs in the USA, where the administration was forced into punitive military action in the aftermath of the Kenya and Tanzania embassy bombings in 1998. President Clinton authorized cruise missile strikes against targets linked to Osama bin Laden which ultimately achieved little, but assuaged US public opinion. Other responses could involve curtailing the civil liberties that form the basis of democratic society. But, again, likely reactions to first- and second-order threats are likely to be less hysterical. Japan and Tokyo survived without such extreme consequences following the Aum attacks, therefore, potential reactions would also depend upon the robustness of the population of the state that was attacked.

Consequently the precise intensity and implications of any of these consequences will be variable. But for the majority of future NBC weapon threats, which will consist primarily of first-order weapons, and a smaller incidence of second-order weapons, the consequences should be manageable by many states. It is only in the very rare cases when terrorists might acquire a third-order WMD that the consequences will be so severe that states might not be able to cope with them. All NBC weapons have both short- and long-term effects which are considerably more damaging than are achievable with conventional weapons. These characteristics will make NBC weapons the weapons of choice for some tactics and strategies, but not for others. It cannot be assumed, however, that terrorists would always use NBC weapons in ways that reflect their technical characteristics.

Terrorist strategies and targets

Terrorist groups generally seek specific political, religious or social objectives, and will employ violence to achieve those objectives in a number of complementary and often interlinked strategies and tactics, that are designed to intimidate and coerce governments, increase the cost for the state of continuing the conflict, and to win a political victory over the state.

Propaganda

Terrorists use violence as a means to generate propaganda, to demonstrate to their constituency, their enemies and the world at large, that their cause is still alive, and that the group is still active. Terrorists need propaganda to maintain and build their support base, and to keep political pressure on the state(s) that they are in conflict with. All terrorist attacks serve this objective, although terrorists also have to consider the potential propaganda losses from their actions. It has been argued that should the influence of a group begin to decline, it could be tempted into more extreme attacks in order to demonstrate its continued effectiveness.

The dynamic interrelationship between violence, propaganda, and the political environment in which terrorists operate is illustrated by the case of the PLO. Along with other Palestinian groups, it was hugely successful in generating propaganda during the late 1960s and early 1970s with audacious attacks, such as the killing of eleven Israeli Athletes in Germany, at the Munich Olympics in 1972, and hijackings such as the seizure of three airliners that were diverted to Dawsons Field in Jordan, in 1970, and subsequently blown up. But by 1973 Yasser Arafat and other PLO leaders were worried by the adverse effects that the large number of attacks were having on world opinion, and attacks on moderate Arab states such as Saudi Arabia threatened its financial backing. As a result, the notorious Black September group, which was part of the PLO, ceased its operations, and when Arafat saw the potential for a diplomatic victory following the 1973 Arab-Israeli war, he sought to implement an even stricter prohibition on terrorist activity. This left only the hardliners such as the Popular Front For the Liberation of

Palestine (PFLP), and the ANO to continue the campaign of indiscriminate terrorism. (18)

In deciding how to generate propaganda, terrorists have to choose what levels of violence and categories of targets would most suit their objectives. Higher levels of violence would not necessarily alienate popular and international support, particularly if their constituency believed that high levels of violence were justified, although increased indiscriminate attacks against population targets could. Therefore escalation is probably safest against institutional targets. Adverse publicity, however, might be better than none at all, especially if the group is in decline. This might serve to remove constraints on both the levels and the targets that it is directed against. Yet some groups do not seek publicity, especially when the media reports unsavoury incidents. The 1987 Enniskillen bomb in Northern Ireland, in which 11 civilians were killed, did not affect the IRA's core support, but the uncommitted were devastated by it. Polls in the UK also showed a steep reduction in support for a withdrawal from Northern Ireland, from 61 per cent to 40 per cent. In addition, media attention is rarely vital to the continued existence of many groups, therefore the media is more important to some groups than others. (19) Some groups might also choose to act against public opinion if they believed that their ideology or politico-strategic circumstances demanded it. Hence, the Real IRA chose to continue the war in Northern Ireland, despite the consensus for the peace process. Decisions will vary between different groups.

Extortion
As a means to commit extortion, by threatening or committing specific acts in order to coerce governments into making concessions. To achieve this objective, different terrorist groups have committed acts across the full spectrum of violence. A core objective of the RAF in West Germany during the 1970s was to secure the release of their comrades held in prison. They attempted to achieve this by taking hostages such as businessmen and diplomats, yet after an initial success, the West German government refused to release the most dangerous prisoners that it held. (20) This strategy gradually lost effectiveness during the 1970s, as more and more states refused to accede to hijackers' and kidnappers' demands, and specialized anti-terrorist units were used to secure the release of hostages, although the Islamic Jihad allegedly received concessions from the USA, France and West Germany, in return for the release of hostages that it held in Beirut during the 1990s.

Defeating the security forces
To defeat the security forces of the state. Terrorists are engaged in an ongoing war against the security forces of a state, and consequently these personnel are high on the list of terrorist targets. It is impossible for the terrorist to defeat the security forces of a state because of the disproportionate balance of power between the two. Consequently, attacking the security forces is a tactic within a wider strategy of breaking the will of the government and people, and generating propaganda, which will lead to a political victory. A good example of this was the truck bombing of the US Marine Corps barracks in Beirut, in 1983, which killed 241 marines and which, in conjunction with the bombings of the French barracks and the US embassy in Beirut, led to the withdrawal of the multilateral force that was overseeing the ceasefire in the Lebanese civil war. The essence of this strategy is that constantly killing soldiers heightens the cost of the conflict, thereby generating public and political pressure on states to accede to their demands. The targeting of soldiers also enables the terrorists to legitimize their activities to a higher degree, helping them to maintain political support for their cause.

Attacking economic targets
A major strategy of many terrorist campaigns has been to attempt to defeat the state economically, by attacking targets, such as property and economic infrastructure, in order to increase the cost of war and force concessions from the government. A key element of IRA strategy has been to increase the economic cost of continued British engagement in Northern Ireland. This led to a number of bombing campaigns in the City of London, and other commercial centres which caused billions of pounds worth of damage. (21) Similarly, the most effective tactic of the Islamic Group in Egypt has been to target the tourist industry by attacking foreign tourists. In 1992 this led to a 53 per cent decline in tourism, damaging Egypt much more than any of their other tactics. (22) This strategy reached its height in 1997, when 58 foreign tourists and four Egyptians were massacred at Luxor. Whilst killing large numbers of people is not necessarily a pre-requisite of such a strategy, this single incident brought the Egyptian tourist industry to almost a complete halt for a short period of time.

Deterrence
As a means to deter the state from pursuing various courses of action, such as further repressive policies. Yitzhak Shamir argues that in Palestine during the 1940s, the Jewish terrorist

group Lotiamei Herut Yisrael (LEHI), otherwise known as the Stern Gang, used violence for the purpose of deterring the British authorities from taking or damaging Jewish lives. (23) Although, groups could also attempt to deter through mere threats to escalate the level of violence that they are currently employing.

Polarizing Communities
Many ethno-nationalist groups, have engaged in indiscriminate acts of terror in order to polarize the communities in which they live. The theory behind this strategy of 'polarization' is that these attacks will force the government to respond with harsh counter-measures, which broaden the campaign of violence to encompass the whole of society, dividing society and driving one part of the divided community into more active support for the group. (24) Whilst many groups eventually move away from this strategy, as the IRA did, some do not. Among the most extreme examples of the generation of terror as an end in itself is occurring in Algeria, where guerrillas of the Armed Islamic Group (GIA) have massacred whole communities following the installation of a military government after the annulment of elections which gave Islamic fundamentalist parties a majority. Whilst attacks need not necessarily necessitate the killing of large numbers of people in order to generate terror, it can generally be considered that the more people that are killed, the higher the levels of terror that can be generated.

Breaking the government's will
All of the previous strategies can also be part of an integral part of a broader strategy to use terror as an end in itself to break the will of government and people to continue the struggle. Terrorist groups can pursue this objective in several ways: the perpetration of attacks which result in large numbers of discriminate casualties, acts which lead to large numbers of indiscriminate casualties, individual assassinations and acts involving the discriminate or indiscriminate killing of small numbers of people. For these purposes, indiscriminate terrorism is most effective because people have problems explaining such events, which generates heightened levels of uncertainty and fear because everyone becomes a potential target. Most terrorist groups have resorted to such a strategy at some stage in their campaigns. The IRA attempted to achieve this in the mid-1970s when bomb explosions were an almost daily occurrence in Northern Ireland and many, such as the Birmingham pub bombings on the UK mainland, were indiscriminate in nature. (25) This campaign

involved a large number of incidents which though indiscriminate, typically resulted in relatively small numbers of fatalities. Generating fear and uncertainty amongst the target audience does not necessarily require large numbers of casualties.

Analysing terrorists' strategies and tactics
In analysing terrorists' strategies and tactics, it is important to differentiate between attacks in which the target is discriminate, and attacks in which the target is indiscriminate, in nature. Many previous terrorist attacks involving high levels of casualties were discriminate in nature, targeting government and military facilities. The attacks on the Oklahoma City federal building and the US Marine Corps barracks, and the US embassy in Beirut, are examples of attacks intended to kill and injure discriminately, because the terrorists were targeting people in specific sites, which by their nature classified those people as 'legitimate' targets. The 1998 attacks on the US embassies in Kenya and Tanzania have also been cited as examples of indiscriminate mass killing, but these attacks actually fit into the same category as the Oklahoma and Beirut bombings. Whilst the bombers were clearly prepared to accept a number of indiscriminate casualties, the intention of the attacks was to kill the occupants of the embassies. Therefore the actual outcome of the attack should not be confused with the terrorists' intentions. In contrast, the attacks by the GIA in Algeria, the bombing of the World Trade Centre and the Tokyo subway attack, are all examples of indiscriminate attacks, aimed at the general population of a state

In pursuing these strategies and tactics, terrorist violence is typically directed at targets with symbolic value; (26) they have a wide range of lucrative targets to choose from including:

- High-profile individuals in government and society, such as judges, politicians, and senior military figures;
- Military and other security force personnel;
- Weapon storage sites;
- The population of the state;
- Commercial sites such as shopping centres and the financial districts of major cities, and other economic related targets such as transportation systems;
- Government buildings and headquarters;
- Nuclear and chemical installations.

There are innumerable targets within any state that are of interest to terrorists. Attacking any of these targets will fit a number of terrorist strategies and tactics, and typical terrorist campaigns will generally involve most of these target types. Many terrorist campaigns evolve over time, moving through different phases in which different tactics and strategies are pursued and then rejected, depending upon the capabilities of the group, the perceived effectiveness of each tactic, the attitudes of its leadership and its politico-strategic situation at any given time. Therefore terrorist groups will differ on which target types are more important than others, and at which time. Merely generating hysteria and media attention is perhaps enough for some groups at certain times; whilst for others attacking the organs of the state will be most important. Others, that might not think that they are achieving their goals, might come to believe that escalation to new levels of violence, or targets, might be necessary. It is also generally true that the better defended a target is, the less likely a terrorist is to attack it. This is not necessarily to say that they are deterred, but because they have so many potential targets open to them they can simply choose a less defended one.

Ends and means
The past record of terrorist use, or intent to use NBC weapons, shows that some groups have used or intended to use them for indiscriminate mass-casualty attacks, whilst others used or intended to use them in a controlled fashion against specific targets. One of the major tactical disincentives to using NBC weapons could be their inherent uncontrollability, because terrorists generally seek certainty and control in many of their operations. Yet this is not borne out by the evidence, since the majority of the past incidents of NBC terrorism were attempts to use weapons in a controlled fashion. Whilst NBC weapons, and WMD in particular, are the optimum choice of weapon for achieving some goals and attacking some target types, their utility for attacking the whole range of potential target types is questionable, although the ways in which terrorists might employ NBC weapons will also be determined by the technical characteristics of the weapon that they prove to be capable of producing. In particular, failure to effectively weaponize CBW will restrict terrorists to using their agents as contaminants. In general, though, answers to questions about whether terrorists would use NBC weapons will partly be determined by the operational advantages that their use might be perceived to confer, weighed against the operational disadvantages that their use might incur.

Assassinations

The assassination of political, judicial, military and other individuals is a traditional terrorist tactic. For maximum impact these attacks need to kill only the target and minimize incidental casualties which could undermine domestic and international support for the cause. This serves the important function of enabling the terrorist group to justify its actions to its constituency and the international community at large. Numerous incidents throughout history have demonstrated that CBW are a highly effective method of committing criminal murders or political assassinations. In operational terms this might require injecting the victim with the agent using a syringe, contaminating food, or even introducing the CBW into the target's home. Yet terrorists have always enjoyed considerable success in conducting assassinations using firearms and conventional bombs, and therefore it is difficult to understand why they would choose to use NBC weapons to assassinate an individual when other means with which they have had much more experience, are easier to use, are significantly more controllable, and are much more readily available to them. Although it is conceivable that in some scenarios, where it is difficult to get close enough to the target with a firearm or bomb, to have a high enough assurance of success, using a CBW could offer tactical advantages, particularly for getting past metal and explosives detectors.

White supremacist groups in the USA have intended to use them for just this purpose. One plot to kill government officials by members of the Patriots' Council in 1992, involved spreading ricin on their doorknobs; and an interesting observation about the Aum Shinrikyo attacks between 1994 and 1995 was that many of them were targeted against specific individuals, and failed. The group would have been better off using firearms or bombs which would have provided a higher assurance of success.

Therefore, the use of NBC weapons for conducting assassinations confers few, if any, operational advantages to the terrorist, and incurs several disadvantages. What probably drives terrorists decisions to use NBC weapons for this purpose is a number of other factors. Aum Shinrikyo's decision to use CW was primarily derived from the fixation of Shoko Asahara, the leader of the cult, with technology and poison gas, as well as a practical need to test their weapon before undertaking larger-scale indiscriminate attacks. The use of an NBC weapon also increases the intimidation element of an attack, because of the latent threat that next time the group might develop a WMD capability and inflict higher numbers of casualties. There is also a propaganda element in such attacks, because their novel nature will attract more media attention. Last, there is perhaps also a psychological dimension. There is the possibility that individuals or groups might become fixated with NBC weapons, and consider using them even to the extent of ignoring operational considerations.

Attacking military facilities
Attacking military facilities is a typical means for terrorists to kill members of the security forces. When terrorists specifically target military facilities it is assumed that they are intending to be discriminate in who they kill, in order to be able to legitimize their actions. NBC weapons could be used discriminately, to attack military facilities in several ways: the most obvious example is a truck bomb parked outside of a facility. However, there are limits to the extent to which it would be possible to cause discriminate casualties by using third-order WMD. The massive blast and radiation effects of nuclear weapons means that they cannot be used in this role, and the use of CBW in the environment will lead to additional indiscriminate casualties if the target is in a built-up area. Therefore third-order CBW can be used discriminately only in the open air, if the targets are isolated enough that environmental factors do not spread the agent over populated areas. So unless the group was willing to accept large numbers of indiscriminate casualties (in which case they would really be perpetrating an act of indiscriminate violence), it would have to use weapons against facilities in isolated areas. Alternatively, if access can be gained to a facility, water supplies can be poisoned, or CW and pathogens released into air conditioning systems. This enables casualties to be restricted to the occupants of the facility and, depending upon the quality of the weapon, it could also be the optimum means to maximize the potential casualties from an attack because it makes fewer demands on a delivery mechanism and is not subject to the vagaries of the weather.

NBC weapons do not seem to offer terrorists the capability to achieve complete victory over the security forces, but they do offer more spectacular victories because of their potential capacity to kill more people. This would help to achieve the objective of heightening the cost of the conflict, and generating public and political pressure on states to accede to their demands. The 1983 attacks on the US Marine Corps barracks and embassy in Beirut seem to indicate that the greater the number of casualties, the greater the political impact, and likelihood that the group will achieve its overall goal, although it must also be borne in mind that the withdrawal of the multilateral force was primarily a function of the political context within which the attacks took place. US domestic opinion was already questioning the Beirut mission, and politically the USA was in a position where it could easily concede the goals of the group. There are limits to what can be achieved by inflicting mass casualties on discriminate targets, particularly in states that have been subjected to prolonged campaigns of terrorist violence, and where public opinion has become hardened. An equally telling example in respect of the USA is the Oklahoma City bombing, which did not result in the Federal government making any concessions to the Christian Far Right. US public opinion is likely to harden in the face of such acts as it gains greater direct exposure to terrorism, and the government and public opinion know that they cannot accede to the demands of these groups.

Terrorists, however, have had plenty of success with these tactics, using conventional explosives. Therefore NBC weapons would not necessarily be the weapon of choice for even this type of target. In fact, similar results can be achieved with conventional weapons which are easier to obtain, harder for the authorities to detect, probably safer to use, and more familiar to the terrorists, (27) whilst the potentially indiscriminate effects of NBC weapons makes them more difficult to use in a controlled fashion. The controlled use of conventional weapons, such as truck bombs, makes it relatively easier to limit indiscriminate casualties (although the attack on the US embassy in Kenya in 1998 demonstrated how difficult it is to control even the effects of conventional weapons). In some scenarios, NBC weapons might offer a means of defeating counter-measures. Against targets which are protected against truck bombs, NBC weapons might confer an operational advantage to the terrorists, particularly if a group is capable of penetrating a facility. As is the case with the use of NBC weapons for assassinations, there is also an intimidatory and propaganda value in their use for these objectives, particularly in generating fears that the terrorists might switch to using these weapons against indiscriminate population targets. This might be the most telling factor in future decisions by terrorists to use NBC weapons against this target type.

Indiscriminate attacks on population targets
Indiscriminate attacks on population targets can take two general forms: those where the intent is to limit casualties and those where the intent is to kill as many people as possible. NBC weapons are suitable only for the former if they can be controlled effectively. This would be impossible in an open-air attack, although they could be used in a controlled fashion by being introduced into the air conditioning systems and water supplies of buildings. WMD, in particular, are the weapons of choice for attacks aimed at causing indiscriminate mass casu-

alties, because they have the potential to inflict casualties far in excess of what is achievable with conventional weapons. The capabilities of nuclear weapons and BW make them particularly suited to use for genocidal or apocalyptic objectives. The consequences of such an attack on the willingness of societies and governments to continue the struggle against the terrorists has never been tested, but it is generally assumed that the greater the level of terror and casualties inflicted, the more likely that states will concede to terrorist demands (assuming that the groups' demands can be met).

However, for many groups, a number of operational factors will constrain their use of NBC weapons in this role. Since the use of NBC weapons against population targets in the open air is indiscriminate in nature it will kill any of the terrorists' own people who happen to be in the immediate vicinity of the weapon. For instance, the use of a third-order BW in Jerusalem would probably infect a large number of Muslims, even if the attack took place in a Jewish quarter. As has been stated earlier, terrorists have always been willing to accept a certain level of incidental casualties in order to achieve their goals, but the potential incidental casualties resulting from the use of a third-order WMD will be significantly higher. This could prove to be a significant inhibitor on terrorists' willingness to use WMD against population targets, although careful target selection would probably limit the significance of this factor. In addition, public opinion can also harden in response to indiscriminate killings.

Therefore NBC weapons offer significant operational benefits in this role, which outweigh the operational problems that will be encountered. For most objectives such as propaganda and intimidation, the greater the number of casualties caused by indiscriminate attacks on population targets, the greater the effect, although third-order WMD are not necessarily the weapon of choice for indiscriminate attacks in which terrorists want to limit the number of casualties.

Economic damage
Attempting to extract concessions from governments by causing levels of economic damage which the government is unwilling to bear has been a feature of many terrorist campaigns, but has typically been unsuccessful . The IRA was never able to inflict an economic cost that was sufficient to compel the UK government to unconditionally withdraw from Northern Ireland. That this strategy failed could be argued to have been a consequence of the limited destructive capacity of conventional explosives, even though truck bombs still caused billions of pounds' worth of

damage. Instead, the key factor in the failure of the strategy was probably the British government's ability to prevent regular attacks, its steadfast political commitment to the principle of refusing to give in to terrorism, and its willingness to bear the cost by underwriting insurance claims on terrorist bomb damage.

The greater destructive and contamination effects of NBC weapons suggests that they would be significantly more useful than conventional weapons for causing economic damage. The blast effects of nuclear weapons are greater than that of even the largest conventional bombs that have previously been used, and makes them ideally suited to causing long-term damage to whole industrial and commercial centres, whereas current truck bombs can damage only specific sections of those centres. CBW are less effective for this purpose because they rely on contamination. The effectiveness of contamination from all NBC weapons for causing economic damage depends upon the amount, toxicity and persistence of the material or agent used, and how effectively it is dispersed. But even a few days' disruption to a major financial centre like London's 'square mile', which is the city's financial nerve centre, would result in the loss of millions of pounds. Yet blast damage from large conventional bombs would have a higher economic impact than some forms of CBW contamination if rebuilding takes longer than decontamination. Attacks on nuclear and chemical facilities are a double-edged sword, because they are economic targets in themselves, which when attacked could also spread contamination over surrounding areas. Damage to a state's economy could also be caused by the indiscriminate killing of skilled workers, who could not be replaced quickly or easily. Terrorists' willingness to use NBC weapons for causing economic damage could, however, be constrained if the territory on which the target is situated has some value to the terrorists, and if the people in the surrounding areas contained their supporters, although the IRA sought to avoid casualties in its economic attacks by providing warnings to the police, which enabled the area to be evacuated.

Perhaps the most likely method of causing economic damage using NBC agents, is to contaminate export products. Criminal and terrorist contamination of goods, such as Chilean grapes or Israeli oranges, has been fairly common, and has caused significant economic damage to particular companies or industries Yet the level of economic damage that was inflicted, was never seriously damaging to the state itself, since these industries would recover over time. Perhaps as a result, no terrorist group has engaged in a long term, systematic strategy of product tampering, and such attacks have only ever resulted in limited economic damage and short term media exposure.

In addition, some pathogens kill only livestock and destroy crops. The significance of anti-crop pathogens was identified as early as the 1960s, and Iraq attempted to develop anti-crop BW such as wheat smuts. These pathogens can potentially lead to massive decreases in crop yields, costing states vast amounts of money. The past record of BW terrorism indicates very few threats to use anti-crop BW, and only the Kenyan nationalist movement, the Mau Mau, have used a BW against livestock. (See Appendix for details). However, for groups which might object to causing indiscriminate casualties, anti-crop and live-stock BW could be perceived as a means of executing a potentially devastating BW attack, without the moral dilemmas associated with killing people – although if the goal of the group is to seize control of the state, they would not wish to contaminate its environment with pathogens which could persist for some period of time. Therefore the use of such weapons might only really be acceptable against another state, perhaps as an incentive to withdraw support for the regime the group is fighting against.

Blackmail and intimidation
The potential levels of destruction and panic caused by the threat of using any form of NBC weapon theoretically makes them ideally suited to use for blackmail purposes. The traditional means by which terrorists blackmailed governments are now of limited utility, especially because governments have become a lot tougher (at least publicly) in refusing to give in to terrorist demands since the 1970s. Airplane hijackings now occur only infrequently, and hostage situations frequently result in the deaths of the kidnappers when special forces attempt to free the hostages. This occurred in the 1981, Iranian embassy siege in London, and the 1996 seizure of the Japanese embassy in Peru. Whilst it is not entirely certain that successful blackmail relies on making increasingly violent threats, when states refuse to accede to terrorists using traditional threats, escalating the level of violence inherent in blackmail threats might be considered as the only means by which states can be successfully blackmailed.

Blackmail involving NBC weapons is not a new phenomenon, and has been a concern for decades. For decades, criminal extortionists have contaminated consumer products as a means of extorting money from shops and manufacturers, which occasionally resulted in a number of deaths. Similarly, many of the past threats to use NBC weapons appear to be primarily for intimidation or blackmail. What has changed since the 1980s is that it could be perceived by terrorists as a means to replace the traditional methods of blackmail and intimidation. The potential consequences of a terrorist attack involving an NBC weapon, especially third-order WMD, will make governments extremely sensitive to the potential costs of calling the terrorists' bluff and getting it wrong, and therefore theoretically more inclined to give in to their demands. Even first-order NBC weapons could have a powerful intimidatory effect, because of the latent threat that the group might move on to develop a WMD.

The RAF apparently discussed the use of nuclear weapons in this role. Michael Baumann, a member of the Second of June Movement, (the RAF's sister organization), stated that 'During their attack on the Stockholm Embassy the RAF people noticed that the government no longer gives in.' He went on to claim that they were capable of acquiring a nuclear weapon and that 'If you had a thing like that under your control you can make the Federal Chancellor dance the can-can on colour TV.' (28)

A number of potential problems have been identified with using WMD for coercion. The terrorists would have to establish the credibility of the threat, in order to demonstrate that they had the capacity to follow it through. Equally, they would have to convince the government that they had an interest in negotiating, therefore their demands would need to be commensurate with the threat. Consequently, they might opt for more limited demands which governments could accede to, although, if the government could not be assured that the threat would be dismantled after the demands had been met it would have little incentive to negotiate. However, the terrorists would need to maintain the threat indefinitely in order to ensure a permanent change. (29) It could also be argued that groups would be less interested in some forms of NBC threats because they might not want to threaten something they would not want to carry out, particularly if it involved large numbers of indiscriminate casualties.

The question of whether NBC weapons would enhance blackmail tactics remains unanswered. Many criminal extortionists fail to get what they want, although some undoubtedly have succeeded. But whether they actually enhance these tactics or not, some terrorists might still be inclined to attempt to use them in blackmail threats anyway.

Propaganda

In the 1970s, Brian Jenkins argued that 'terrorists want a lot of people watching and a lot of people listening, and not a lot of people dead', (30) suggesting that the use of an NBC weapon will not necessarily be compatible with the objective of generating propaganda. Writing in the 1980s however, Harvey J.McGeorge argued that populations were becoming desensitized to conventional forms of terrorism, which was reducing its ability to generate propaganda. He suggested that the use of CBW could reverse this trend. (31). This line of thinking was pursued by Frank Barnaby, who argues that terrorists constantly have to escalate the level of violence in order to achieve the same levels of propaganda, which means that they will eventually be forced to escalate to use third-order WMD, in order to achieve the levels of propaganda that they require. (32)

One of the easiest ways to catch people's attention is to commit an atrocity. This was what occurred in the immediate aftermath of the sarin attack on the Tokyo subway: the eyes of the world were upon Japan, and Aum Shinrikyo received massive media coverage. What this also demonstrates is that the use of NBC weapons need not necessarily kill a lot of people in order to generate propaganda. The threat, or use, of any order of NBC weapon, in any of the aforementioned ways, would be a massive propaganda coup, that might help to rally supporters, and guarantee that the group's cause would gain heightened prominence in the public eye and on the agenda of politicians and the international community. Since the use of such weapons is still rare, the use of even first-order NBC weapons will generate publicity: even a demonstration of the capability that does not result in any deaths will have a profound propaganda effect. The psychological effects of NBC contamination amongst the population suggest that even after it has been cleared, the consequences derived from fear amongst the public will remain for some time. Therefore Jenkins' argument might be relevant only to the use of third-order WMD.

Yet propaganda can be generated in a number of ways which do not rely on NBC weapons or WMD. It is not necessarily true to say that propaganda levels always have a direct relationship to casualties. It might be enough to simply kill victims of direct interest to the foreign media. Alternatively, during the conflict in Northern Ireland, the IRA was always able to ensure regular and powerful propaganda coups through the judicious and timely choice of targets, rather than the level of casualties caused by their attacks. 'Spectaculars' such as the assassination of Lord Louis Mountbatten (a member of the British Royal Family), truck bombings in the City of London, the bombing of the British cabinet in Brighton in 1984 and the mortar bombing of Downing Street, the prime minister's official residence in 1991, were fairly infrequent occurrences, but they always generated significant levels of propaganda because of their rarity, and the choice of high- profile targets.

A number of other factors are also relevant in terrorists calculations of whether to resort to using NBC weapons for propaganda purposes. If the terrorists' objective is to maintain and enhance public and international support for their cause, the threat, or use, of an NBC weapon will not necessarily guarantee this. Widespread public antipathy and revulsion towards NBC weapons in the western world suggests that the public and the majority of international opinion would probably turn against a group that resorted to the use of such weapons. Although in the second Chechen War in 1999–2000, both the Chechen insurgents and the Russians attempted to manipulate international political opinion by claiming that the other side had used CW. This might also help to explain why no terrorist groups which have been in decline have ever attacked nuclear and chemical facilities as a response. Rather than discouraging terrorists from using NBC weapons, these factors might instead influence the type of weapons that they use, and the targets that they select. If terrorists consider using them for this purpose, first-order weapons used against institutional targets and causing discriminate casualties would be the preferred option because they would not attract the negative publicity that would arise from killing large number of civilians.

In broad terms, NBC weapons do provide terrorists with an enhanced capability to generate propaganda, and in many cases groups have merely had to threaten to use any order of NBC weapon, or provide some other indication of their capability, in order to be successful. The primary consequence of US white supremacists being apprehended in possession of ricin has been to give them a much higher profile in debates about NBC terrorism. Therefore, mere threats may be enough, and a group may never escalate to actual use. Whether a group would actually use them for propaganda purposes will depend upon what the group wants to achieve with its propaganda. If it merely wants press coverage, the use of a WMD would certainly guarantee it. But assuming there is some purpose to generating press coverage, such as winning public and political support, the levels of violence that groups employ might need to be restricted unless the support that they seeking to generate will actually respond favourably to an act of mass destruction.

Attacking key buildings and sites
NBC weapons do not appear to enhance terrorists' capabilities to destroy buildings. Only nuclear weapons have the capacity to physically destroy a building, although buildings can also be rendered unusable by contamination from any form of NBC weapon. Unless access can be gained to the building or site when it is empty, it seems unlikely that they would be used in

this role unless the group also wanted to kill everyone inside, in which case the attack would fit into one of the previous categories. Use of CBW in the ventilation systems or water supplies of a building could be a means of defeating truck bomb defences.

Deterrence

Richard Falkenrath. Robert D. Newman and Bradley Thayer consider that deterrence is not a rational use for NBC weapons. But whilst legitimate questions might be raised about how a group could deter a state, what is important is that the group might think in terms of deterrence. The Chechens certainly seem to have considered their use in this role. During the first Chechen War, the insurgents buried radioactive materials in a Moscow park as a deterrent to the Russian government on escalating the war in Chechnya. Despite the severity of the war in Chechnya and the privations suffered by Chechen civilians, the insurgents did not follow through on their potential capability to use a radiological weapon in Russia. Instead, the Chechen leader Jokhar Dudayev issued a clear deterrent threat; when asked whether they had any WMD, he replied, 'We won't use them, unless Russia uses nuclear weapons.' (33)

Terrorist attacks on nuclear and chemical facilities

Terrorist groups, particularly those with little technical capacity, have the option of producing similar results to those caused by the use of NBC weapons by attacking commercial nuclear and chemical facilities. Terrorists can conduct such attacks using their traditional techniques of sabotage and truck bombings. States can physically protect such facilities, but whilst most possess a manageable number of nuclear facilities, there are generally a large number of potential chemical targets in most states, many of which use highly toxic compounds, such as phosgene and cyanide.

In the background papers for the 1985 International Task Force On the Prevention of Nuclear Terrorism, Daniel Hirsch identifies two threats: the truck bomb and the insider threat. (34) Truck bombs have proved enormously successful and destructive in past terrorist attacks such as Oklahoma, Beirut and Kenya (discussed at length in Chapter 2). The use of a truck bomb could result in considerable damage to a nuclear facility and lead to a release of radiation, contaminating the surrounding area. But even if adequate security measures could be instituted to protect against truck bombs, it is difficult to contain the threat from insiders because facilities employ large numbers of people who must have access to sensitive areas. (35) In the USA the original Nuclear Regulatory Committee (NRC) regulations provided only for attacks by three external attack-ers, on foot, armed with hand-held automatic weapons and with the help of perhaps one insider. A considerable number of facilities, including research reactors and those in urban areas were exempted from these requirements. In the mid-1980s Sandia National Laboratory in the USA was contracted by the NRC to evaluate the threat and suggest easily implemented and cost effective safeguards mechanisms. (36) Its report indicated that nuclear facilities were extraordinarily vulnerable, and unacceptable damage to vital reactor systems could occur from relatively small charges at close distances, and from larger but still reasonable-size charges at large setback distances which were greater than the protected area for most plants. However the cost was a lot more than was originally anticipated and the response was limited. (37)

Oleg Bukharin agrees that in most cases of attack against a research reactor or nuclear fuel cycle installation there would not be a release of radioactive material off-site, but concedes that Chernobyl-scale incidents could be caused. He argues that 'A global catastrophe is possible as a result of sabotage of a nuclear power reactor with its large inventory of radioactivity and high rates of energy generation.' A technologically knowledgeable attacker will probably seek to damage the reactor's main core, (38) and there are numerous systems within nuclear plants which can be switched off, or sabotaged, particularly coolant systems, in order to cause a release of radiation. The sabotage of any nuclear plant is generally seen in terms of terrorists ability to overcome the reactor security forces. It is assumed that terrorists can achieve this, and overcome other relevant factors such as security contingency plans and procedures that would come into play only during an incident, and the integration of reactor plant operations with security operations during a security contingency event. (39) US reactors, however, have extremely strong physical security measures, and are generally designed to enable the reactor to be shut down from at least two locations, and consequently it is extremely difficult to envisage how terrorists could effect a radioactive release in an attempt to sabotage a plant through a frontal assault. (40) It is virtually inconceivable that terrorists could overcome the integrated security and operational measures at US power stations, and even if they did whether it would lead to a major public health consequence, (41) although, this might well not be the case in other states, particularly with older stations.

To cause only economic damage there are the easier methods, such as toppling key pylons on the primary distribution line outside of nuclear power plants, or using rockets at some key buildings which might lead to a shutdown. These attacks would also generate publicity. But in the absence of assistance from an insider, an off-site release of radiation would be minuscule. Most of the critical areas are in well-sealed areas, which would require substantial amounts of explosives to breach. Therefore any scenario of possible terrorist explosive attack seems unlikely. (42)

Terrorists could also attempt to attack radioactive material in transit. Such materials are transported in casks that are constructed to shield the population, and be immune to accidents. Numerous experiments have also been conducted to test their vulnerability to explosives, and the results showed that casks were neither ruptured nor penetrated. Casks that did not have water jackets could be breached by a number of different explosive charges, if enough was known about the design, and the explosive was used in the optimum way. Although it was also estimated that the potential radioactive release from such attacks would constitute a zero-to-small health hazard. (43)

The number of deaths caused by attacking nuclear and chemical facilities will vary, according to the precise results of the attack and the location of the facility. But several previous incidents provide useful indications. Two people died in the 1986 explosion at the Chernobyl nuclear reactor, although several more received lethal doses of radiation in the immediate aftermath and an unquantifiable number of others received radiation poisoning, which could lead to lethal cancers in the longer term. In contrast, the accident at the Union Carbide plant in Bhopal, in 1985, killed over 2,800 people, and up to 180,000 received medical assistance for related ailments. (44) The level of contamination caused by attacking nuclear and chemical facilities will also be variable. Following the Chernobyl disaster, the Soviet authorities established a 30 km exclusion zone around the plant which was evacuated, and later a further 113 villages outside of the zone were evacuated. But it appears as if the Soviet authorities accepted levels of radiation higher than would have been accepted in the West. In addition, unofficial analysis of satellite photographs indicated that an area much larger that the 30 km zone had been abandoned by farmers, with some land as far away as 100 km from the plant being abandoned. (45) In the mid-1960s the Brookhaven National Laboratory in the USA assessed the potential casualties from a large reactor accident, and concluded that casualties could be as high as 45,000 with significant radioactivity levels over 10,000–100,000 km2. (46)

Conclusion

This analysis demonstrates that whilst NBC weapons can be adapted for use in a wide range of tactics and strategies, they are not necessarily the optimum weapons available to terrorists for their purposes. The technical capabilities of NBC weapons – and especially third-order WMD – make them the weapon of choice for two strategies – causing indiscriminate mass casualties against population targets, and generating propaganda. But very few groups have previously shown an interest in conducting mass-casualty attacks against population targets. For most types of attack, the technical and operational factors favour the use of conventional weapons. Yet terrorists already have a history of using NBC weapons in roles for which conventional weapons and tactics are more suited, and in certain cases would provide a clearer guarantee of success. Therefore it cannot be guaranteed that terrorists would refrain from using NBC weapons just because conventional weapons are more suited to the task, familiar to the terrorist and more readily available. It is perhaps the propaganda value of these weapons which might prove to be the driving factor behind their use in these roles. Their use by non-state actors is still so novel, and they generate such levels of anxiety, that even using them in highly discriminate ways, such as assassinating individuals, will guarantee press coverage, and have an impact beyond that from the use of conventional weapons. Consequently, tactical motivations and disincentives will play a key role in determining what kinds of NBC weapons terrorists might acquire, and strong pressures will exist for the use of low-level NBC weapons rather than WMD.

Notes and references
1. Richard A.Falkenrath, 'Confronting Nuclear, Biological and Chemical Terrorism', *Survival* 40/3 (Autumn 1998) pp 48–50
2. Jonathan Annells and James Adams, 'Did Terrorists Kill with Deadly Nerve Gas Test?', *Sunday Times* (19 March 1994) p 15
3. 'US Takes Steps To Defend Vital Interests From Terrorist Attack' (31 February 1998), International Policy Institute for Counter Terrorism, internet site <http://www.ict.org.il/articles/isl-terr.htm>
4. Richard Falkenrath, Robert D. Newman and Bradley Thayer, *America's Achilles Heel* (Cambridge, MA: MIT Press, 1998) p 149
5. Washington, DC, US Government Printing Office (August 1993) p 53
6. Falkenrath, Newman and Thayer: *America's Achilles Heel*, pp 151–52
7. Neil Livingstone, *The War Against Terrorism* (Lexington, MA: Lexington Books, 1982) p 110
8. John F. Sopko, 'The Changing Proliferation Threat', *Foreign Policy* 103 (Winter 1996–97) p 8

9. Ron Purver, 'Chemical and Biological Terrorism: New Threat To Public Safety?', *Conflict Studies* 295, Research Institute For the Study of Conflict and Terrorism (December 1996–January 1997) p 2

10. Purver: 'Chemical and Biological Terrorism', p 2

11. Gururaj Mutalik, 'Nuclear Terrorism - Prevention is the only Cure', International Physicians for the Prevention of Nuclear War, 'Crude Nuclear Weapons and the Terrorist Threat', IPPNW Global Health Watch, *Report 1*, (1996) pp 43, 52

12. Robert Mullen, 'Nuclear Violence', in Paul Leventhal and Yonah Alexander (eds), *Preventing Nuclear Terrorism* (Lexington, MA: Lexington Books, 1987) p 244

13. Sopko: 'The Changing Proliferation Threat', p 7

14. Peter Taylor and David Sumner 'The Effects of a Crude Plutonium Dispersal Weapon,' International Physicians for the Prevention of Nuclear War: 'Crude Nuclear Weapons', p 38

15. Mullen: 'Nuclear Violence', p 243

16. *Keesing's Record of World Events* XXXI (March 1985) pp 33467–68

17. Maxine Angela Roberts, 'The Chernobyl Incident of 1986: Its Impact on Soviet Agriculture', MSc dissertation, Wye College, University of London (July 1993) p 27

18. Christopher Dobson and Ronald Payne, 'Terror International: Hostages, Hijackings and Bombings in the Early 1970s', *War In Peace*, pp 1509–15

19. C.J.M. Drake, *Terrorists' Target Selection*, (London: St Martin's Press, 1998) pp 157–58

20. Adrian Guelke, *The Age of Terrorism and the International Political System* (London: I.]B Tauris, 1998) pp 88–91

21. Drake: *Terrorists' Target Selection*, p 161 – 1992 City of London bomb – £350 million; February 1996 Docklands bomb – £75–150 million

22. James Adams, *The New Spies: Exploring the Frontiers of Espionage* (London: Hutchinson, 1994) p 185

23. Yitzhak Shamir, *Summing Up: An Autobiography* (London: Wiedenfeld & Nicolson,1994) pp 22–23

24. Conor Gearty, *Terror* (London: Faber & Faber, 1991) p 39

25. Tim Pat Coogan, *The IRA* (London: Harper Collins, 1995) pp 383–4

26. Gavin Cameron, 'Nuclear Terrorism: A Real Threat?', *Jane's Intelligence Review* (September 1996) p 138

27. Cameron, 'Nuclear Terrorism', p. 245

28. Michael Baumann, 'The Mind of A German Terrorist', *Encounter* 51/3 (September 1978) p 87

29. Brian Jenkins, 'Will Terrorists Go Nuclear?,' *Orbis* 29/3 (Fall 1985) pp 514–15

30. Brian Michael Jenkins, 'International Terrorism: A New Mode of Conflict', in David Carlton and Carlo Schaerf (eds), *International Terrorism and World Security* (London: Croom Helm, 1975) p 15

31. Harvey J.McGeorge, 'Reversing the Trend On Terror,' *Defense and Foreign Affairs* (April 1988) p 16

32. Interview with Dr Frank Barnaby (25 January 1999)

33. 'Terms of War and Peace', *Time* (4 March 1996) p 37

34. Daniel Hirsch, 'The Truck Bomb and Insider Threats to Nuclear Facilities', in Leventhal and Alexander (eds): *Preventing Nuclear Terrorism*, p 207

35. Hirsch: 'The Truck Bomb', p 207

36. Hirsch: 'The Truck Bomb', p 209

37. Hirsch: 'The Truck Bomb', p 210

38. Oleg Bhukarin, 'Problems of Nuclear Terrorism', *The Monitor* (Spring 1997) p 9

39. Mullen: 'Nuclear Violence', p 237

40. Mullen: 'Nuclear Violence', p 239

41. Mullen: 'Nuclear Violence', p 239

42. Mullen: 'Nuclear Violence', p 241

43. Mullen: 'Nuclear Violence', p 242

44. *Keesing's Record of World Events* XXXI (March 1985) pp 33467–68; XXXIV (April 1988) p 35839

45. Roberts: 'The Chernobyl Incident', p 42

46. Hirsch: 'The Truck Bomb', p 215

5. Strategic and Political Disincentives to Using NBC Weapons

One of the key anomalies in the past record of NBC terrorism is the small number of actual cases in which these weapons have been used, even accounting for the occasions where security forces have prevented attacks from taking place. Chapter 3 indicated that NBC weapons have technologically been within the grasp of an increasing number of terrorist groups for some time, and that in technological terms it will become increasingly easy to develop them. This suggests that some groups, which are technologically capable of developing NBC weapons, have deliberately chosen no to do so. Potential reasons for some groups' apparent lack of interest can be sought in the disincentives to using NBC weapons that might play a role in terrorists' decision making. Those disincentives lie in the political goals that the group wants to achieve, and the strategies that it employs to achieve those goals, coupled with the perceived consequences of using NBC weapons. What is more uncertain is the extent to which these potential disincentives will hold up during the course of terrorist campaigns, and precisely how strong they are in the first instance.

Limited goals – limited violence

Bruce Hoffman argues that, 'Contrary to popular belief and media depiction, most terrorism is neither crazed nor capricious ... it is also conceived and executed in a manner that simultaneously reflects the terrorists group's particular aims and motivations, fits its resources and capabilities and takes into account the "target audience" at which the act is directed.' (1) Despite many differences, terrorist groups have one common trait: none commits actions randomly or senselessly. Each wants maximum publicity from its actions, as a means of intimidating the government and population of the state.

Groups that are predominantly secular, or political, in character, are generally considered to be the least likely type of terrorist group to use NBC weapons. This belief is derived from the political objectives of the majority of such groups. The goals of most secular left- and right-wing groups, as well as many ethno-nationalist and other separatist groups, is to re-structure the existing political system of states according to the tenets of their own political ideology. They primarily deny the legitimacy of the institutions of the state – or even of the state itself, in the case of ethno-nationalist separatist groups, which means that the principal target of these types of groups is the regime of the particular state in which they operate.

As a consequence, many secular terrorist groups focus on a narrowly defined target set, which typically includes political and military targets, as well as individuals and institutions associated with the regime or the existing order. This enables them to legitimize casualties according to their ideology and goals. These types of groups can also engage in indiscriminate acts of violence against population targets, but their purpose is symbolic, to communicate a message, rather than being an end in itself. Consequently, many of the anti-American attacks planned by the RAF in West Germany, were intended to cause mass casualties. (2)

Whilst left-wing groups had their heyday in the 1970s and early 1980s, one of the features of the post-Cold War World has been the growth of the extreme right wing. In Europe, this has consisted mainly of a disparate collection of small secular groups, with no long-term systematic programme of violence to achieve their political goals. They mainly engage in indiscriminate, unstructured violence against immigrants and opposing political groups, although some of these groups and individuals are used by more sophisticated neo-Nazi organizations which give their violence some form of structure, (3) and some have engaged in short-term bombing campaigns. Because of this, right-wing violence has often been characterized as the least dis-

criminate and most senseless form of contemporary political violence. To an extent this is borne out by statistics, which show
that in the 1980s right-wing attacks were considerably more
lethal than those of their left-wing counterparts. (4)

The primary goal of secular right-wing terrorists is to replace
the liberal democratic state with some form of national socialist
or fascist regime. They see violence as the catalyst to achieve
this, often by generating chaos which might lead to civil war.
One fascist group in Italy pursued a 'strategy of tension', which
stated that,

> Our belief is that the first phase of political activity
> ought to be to create the conditions favouring the
> installation of chaos in all the regimes structures.
> This should necessarily begin with the undermining
> of the regimes economy as a whole so as to arrive at
> confusion throughout the whole legal apparatus. This
> leads on to the situation of strong political tension,
> fear in the world of industry and hostility towards the
> government and political parties. (5)

The other defining feature of the majority of right-wing groups
is their racism. They do not necessarily espouse any specific
programme of reform, but instead tend to concentrate on crude
nationalist and racist slogans, calls for the expulsion of immigrants, and the need for strong government. They criticize liberal states for their social welfare policies, tolerance of diverse
opinion and immigration policies.

Yet right-wing violence is not completely random or indiscriminate. Whilst in the 1980s it was more lethal than left-wing
violence, there were relatively few indiscriminate attacks, and
most of them were directed at left-wing targets or immigrants.
(6) The targets of right wing groups are also determined by their
ideology and the need to maintain and develop the support of
their constituency. The pattern of right-wing violence has
remained roughly the same since the 1970s, with sporadic
attacks against particular types of target. With the exception of
a few major indiscriminate bombings, they have also attempted
to keep their violence within limits. The more sophisticated of
them act like the left-wing groups, carefully selecting targets,
recognizing the value of symbolic acts of violence and accepting
that violence itself will reap rewards only if it is carefully mod-
erated.

Many groups that are predominantly religious in character,
also pursue political objectives. One of the principal developments which has brought the issues of Islamic fundamentalism
and NBC terrorism together is the emergence of the network of

terrorist groups that is financed and run by the exiled Saudi Arabian millionaire, Osama bin Laden. This network, called the 'International Islamic Front for Jihad against the Jews and the Crusaders', (the Front), has both an anti-Christian and an Anti-western orientation. The Front has assumed a major significance in the debate on NBC terrorism because of persistent allegations about its efforts to procure nuclear weapons, fissile material, and CBW, as well as the apparent attempt by one of its affiliated groups to convert the World Trade Centre bomb into a CW, using sodium cyanide.

Bin Laden's initial objective is primarily political in nature: the expulsion of the USA from Saudi Arabia and the Persian Gulf region. According to his 'Declaration of War Against The Americans Occupying the Land of the Two Holy Places' that was published in 1996,

> the latest and the greatest of [the] aggressions, incurred by the Muslims since the death of the Prophet ... is the occupation of the two Holy Places – the foundation of the House of Islam, the place of the revelation, the source of the message and the place of the noble Ka'ba, the Qiblah of the Muslims – by the armies of the American crusaders and their Allies.

The Declaration is presented as the first step in 'correcting what had happened to the Islamic world in general and the Land of the Two Holy Places in particular ... Today ... the sons of the two Holy Places, have started their Jihad in the cause of Allah, to expel the occupying enemy out of the country of the two Holy Places.' (7)

Similarly, the fatwa that was publicly presented in the name of the leaders of the Front, in May 1998 states the primary reason for the declaration of jihad against Americans to be the fact that 'for seven years the US has been occupying the lands of Islam in the holiest places, the Arabian peninsula, plundering its riches, dictating to its rulers, humiliating its people, terrorizing its neighbours, and turning its bases in the Peninsula into a spearhead through which to fight the neighbouring Muslim peoples'. The second reason is the devastation of the Iraqi people, and the third is the American role in serving the 'Jews' petty state' and its occupation of Jerusalem. (8)

The Front relies heavily on conventional terrorist strategies and tactics. In his public statements, bin Laden frequently cites the forced withdrawal of the USA from Lebanon and Somalia as precedents that he wants to emulate. These defeats were inflicted on the US following attacks on US servicemen, and as a result, groups that are allegedly affiliated to the Front have attacked a number of high profile discriminate targets, such as US servicemen in Saudi Arabia and the US embassies in Kenya and Tanzania. The precedents set in Lebanon and Somalia, suggest that the objective of expelling US military forces from the Gulf region using these tactics, and then moving on to overthrow of the Saudi regime and replacing it with an Islamic government, is a realistic goal, and there is no need to engage in widespread indiscriminate violence. (9)

Groups with ethnic enemies
Ethno-nationalist groups and racist groups on the far right differ from other secular groups in that although they also generally have limited goals, their target set also includes specific ethnic communities. The genocidal nature of the ethnic conflicts in the former Yugoslavia (FYR), Rwanda and Sri Lanka, during the 1980s and 1990s prove that racial motivations can drive groups to extreme levels of violence.

However, such groups may not necessarily target their ethnic enemies indiscriminately – or if they do, it may not necessarily be the core component of their strategy. Conor Gearty argues that for some ethno-nationalist groups such as ETA in Spain and the PLO, the purpose of their violence is primarily symbolic in nature, to communicate a message. In contrast, other groups, such as the various republican and loyalist groups in Northern Ireland, the Ellalan Force of the Liberation Tigers of Tamil Ealam (otherwise known as the 'Tamil Tigers') in Sri Lanka and Sikh nationalists in the Punjab, have all at some stage used violence for intimidation. The objective of this strategy is to enforce the separation of their communities and provoke a government backlash leading to further polarization (although this has never been the prevalent tactic amongst the groups in Northern Ireland). (10)

Therefore, despite having similar goals, these types of groups can have radically different perceptions of the purpose of violence, which in turn will affect the nature of their campaigns. Whilst most of these types of groups have engaged in indiscriminate acts of violence, for those that are attempting to communicate a message such attacks are not a major element of their campaign, and casualties are frequently limited. In contrast, for those that aim to polarize communities, indiscriminate attacks are a more dominant feature of their campaigns, and they are generally willing to inflict significantly higher numbers of casualties. The Tamil Tigers have perpetrated two indiscriminate attacks which resulted in over 100 deaths, and the Sikh nation alists have perpetrated one, with one other failure when a bomb placed on an airliner exploded only after the plane had landed. (11)

Consequently, for many ethno-nationalist groups there has been a conscious recognition that only if their violence is properly calculated and in some way regulated, will they achieve their objectives. Many do not attempt to use indiscriminate violence in any systematic way to heighten tension and polarize their societies, and as a result, many groups operate well below their potential capacity for violence. For instance, in 1999, official UK sources estimated that the IRA in Northern Ireland had enough weapons and equipment to equip 500 men to carry out the equivalent of a full-scale war for six months. (12) But even before all of the paramilitary groups operating in Northern Ireland implemented a ceasefire as part of the Irish peace process, levels of IRA violence were nowhere near the capacity offered by this arsenal.

An exception to this analysis would appear to be religiously orientated ethno-nationalist groups, yet even some of these groups have demonstrated a willingness to limit their violence. The two prime examples are the Chechen insurgency in Russia and the Sikh nationalists in the Punjab in India. The Chechen insurgents are a diverse mix of individuals, driven by a range of political and religious motivations, from pure nationalism to Islamic fundamentalism. Despite the generalized characterization of them as being Islamic 'extremists', they largely restricted their campaign to military targets within the borders of Chechnya. Occasionally, they have conducted raids into Russia which resulted in taking civilian hostages, but these were generally isolated incidents, and they did not attempt to undertake a systematic campaign of terrorism inside Russia itself. Chechen interest in constraining their violence was illustrated by their burying caesium-137 in Moscow and threatening to detonate radiological weapons, but never following through on the threat. This could be interpreted as an attempt to generate propaganda; Bruce Hoffman and David Claridge argue that it 'was undoubtedly sufficient to cause considerable alarm and attract world-wide attention to the Chechens, their cause and their demands – precisely terrorism's primary objectives'. (13) But it can also be interpreted as a coercive threat to Russia to limit its own violence. It therefore appears that the Chechen leadership deliberately attempted to constrain their violence, whilst keeping open the option to escalate as a deterrent threat.

The Sikh nationalists in India who were fighting to achieve independence for the Punjab also placed some constraints on their violence. In common with other religious terrorist groups, their leader, Sant Jarnail Singh Bhindranwale, was willing to sanction violence against an open-ended range of targets. He once commented that, 'I only finish [kill] those who are enemies of the Sikh faith like policemen, government officials and Hindus.' (14) Therefore, besides attacking the police, government officials and other opponents, the Sikh militants also attacked Hindu civilians to coerce them into leaving the Punjab. Much of this indiscriminate violence comprised shootings and bombings which caused relatively low numbers of casualties. (15) But like the Chechens, the Sikhs generally restricted their violence to within the borders of the Punjab. Following the battle for the Golden Temple in Amritsar in 1984, in which Bhindranwale was killed and the backbone of his movement destroyed, Sikh tactics appeared to change. They were blamed for the 1985 bombing of an Air India passenger airliner over the Irish sea in which 328 people were killed, and another failed attempt to down an airliner a few hours later. But whilst the casualty levels from their campaign have risen steadily since the attack on the Golden Temple, most have been incurred in small-scale indiscriminate bombings and shootings. (16)

Some secular groups, however, do seem to be less willing than others to place limits on their violence. In particular, the various Palestinian factions which split from the PLO following its tacit acceptance of the existence of Israel, and its policy of political compromise, have consistently resorted to acts of indiscriminate violence. One of the most prominent of these has been the ANO, which has adopted a much broader set of revolutionary objectives than the PLO. In an interview Abu Nidal stated that,

> I want to tell you what I dream about: about a single Arab people, living in freedom, justice and equality. My enemies are the Zionist occupation of my homeland. My enemies are imperialism in all its forms, the division and divisiveness of my Arab people, and the chaos in our Arab society. (17)

The more revolutionary nature of these objectives does not necessarily establish a basis for conducting indiscriminate attacks; instead, what it signifies is that the group does not believe that such attacks will be detrimental to achieving these objectives.

The other main type of group which is less inclined to limit its violence is secular racist groups on the far right. Concern about the potential genocidal goals of these groups is heightened by their involvement in previous incidents of NBC terrorism, which have been targeted at ethnic minorities. The growth of the right-wing has been most noticeable in the USA, and has been popularized in works of fiction such as William Pearce's Turner Diaries, which tells the story of a race war, which ends when white revolutionaries take over the USA by force. As a result, the racist far right is the most dangerous domestic terrorist threat that the USA faces. Besides perpetrating indiscriminate attacks against individuals, their violence has been directed against Jewish banks, TV stations, gay nightclubs, black churches and abortion clinics.

In 1999, US intelligence sources identified more than 2,000 right-wing extremist groups across the USA, with more than a million full-time supporters and thousands more supporting them through hundreds of internet websites. They comprise a wide range of different racist secular groups, including white supremacists, national socialists, white nationalists and separatists. (18) The Simon Wiesenthal Centre in the US which monitors right wing activity, also estimated that there were 400 race hate groups in the USA, with a membership of between 20,000 and 40,000, (19) although many of these groups are predominantly religious in nature, and are described in more depth in Chapter 6. This makes white separatism one of America's fastest growing political affiliations.

The target group that these groups hope to attract are extreme right-wingers who oppose gun control, who believe that abortion is a sin, that homosexuality is an abomination, that race mixing contaminates the Aryan blood line and who want to keep the USA white. (20) Amongst the most violent of these groups are The National Alliance and the Aryan Brotherhood. Yet individual groups have different viewpoints, and do not necessarily engage in systematic campaigns of indiscriminate racist violence to achieve their goals.

Using violence as a means to generate popular and political support
The principal goal of the majority of secular and ethno-nationalist groups is the objective of winning popular and political support. Bruce Hoffman argues that 'Terrorism, therefore, may be seen as a violent act that is conceived to attract attention and then, through the publicity it generates, to communicate a message.' (21) That message is directed towards a diverse audience: the government of the state; public opinion within the state; the international community; and the domestic constituency of the group itself. But whereas the message aimed at the government of the state and public opinion is intended to intimidate and coerce, that same message is also directed towards the international community in order to gain political support, and as a

means to maintain and enhance the support that the group receives from its constituency.

At one level, some groups seek to generate international political support for their cause, either as a means of applying pressure on the regime to make concessions, or for gaining direct support, such as arms supplies (for a fuller analysis of state sponsorship of terrorism, see Chapter 8). Depending upon which state(s) the group is attempting to win support from, this can serve as a powerful inhibitor on the level of violence that a group employs, and the targets that it is directed against, because its acts of violence would need to be legitimized to the governments and public opinion of those states. This is particularly the case with groups that are attempting to win support from western states, where public opinion can be sympathetic to many causes, but can be opposed to the use of violence. The IRA has been notably successful in calibrating its violence to a level which does not alienate its public and political support in the USA. Islamic groups and others which might deny the legitimacy of western liberal democracies look instead to gain support from radical regimes in the developing world.

At the other level, Bruce Hoffman argues that the overriding tactical and ethical imperative for left-wing terrorists has been to tailor the level of violence that they employ to their perceived constituencies. Killing innocent civilians was seen by some left-wing groups as tarnishing their image as a revolutionary vanguard in the pursuit of social justice. In their perception, violence should be used to gain publicity for their cause and educate the public. (22) Therefore left-wing violence has tended to be highly discriminate and limited and indiscriminate acts of violence have not been one of their core strategies.

Yet some campaigns of indiscriminate violence have been specifically intended to mobilize popular opinion. For example, Italy which has been the western European country most affected by neo-fascist violence, experienced several 'stagi', or massacres, between 1969 and 1986. This included the bomb attack on Bologna railway station in 1980, which killed 85 people and injured 200. Resorting to indiscriminate violence represented a qualitative escalation of political violence in Italy, but the aim of the campaign was to persuade the public through the very climate of insecurity that it helped to create (alongside the activities of left-wing groups such as the Red Brigades) to accept the need for an authoritarian government. (23) Similarly, Chris Hani, the former leader of South Africa's African National Congress (ANC) armed wing, Spear of the Nation, stated in the 1980s that he allowed bomb attacks on white civilian targets because, 'If we don't increase our level of violence, we'll risk losing the support of young Blacks in the townships.' (24)

It is commonly assumed that the terrorist groups that are predominantly religious in character, which have emerged since 1980, differ from the predominantly secular groups because they do not attempt to appeal to a constituency, and consequently are more willing to engage in indiscriminate attacks, against a broader range of targets. Currently, only religious cults really fit this description. Others, such as Islamic fundamentalists, Sikh nationalists, Jewish extremists and the Christian right wing in the USA do have constituencies which they purport to represent, and to some degree their activities reflect a need to mobilize that constituency.

Osama bin Laden argues that his bombing campaigns in Saudi Arabia had important propaganda effects for mobilizing his constituency. He suggests that,

> Most important amongst these is the awareness of the people to the significance of the American occupation of the country of the two sacred Mosques, and that the original decrees of the regime are a reflection of the wishes of the American occupiers. So the people became aware that their main problems were caused by the American occupiers and their puppets in the Saudi regime. They also had a larger strategic purpose, these missions also paved the way for the rising of the voices of opposition against the American occupation from within the ruling family and the armed forces; in fact we can say that the remaining Gulf countries have been affected to the same degree, and that the voices of opposition to the American occupation have begun to be heard at the level of the ruling families of the ... Gulf countries. (25)

Provoking a response from their enemies by such acts also serves to generate propaganda and support. In response to the attacks on the US embassies in Kenya and Tanzania in 1998, the USA launched cruise missile attacks on several of bin Laden's bases in Afghanistan and the Shaifa pharmaceutical plant in the Sudan which was linked to bin Laden, and alleged to have been a CW production facility. Doubts about whether the Shaifa plant was a CW production facility, coupled with widespread international criticism of the attack, turned it into a propaganda victory for the Sudan and bin Laden, sparking worldwide demonstrations by Muslims. The anger that it generated heightened concerns of further terrorist attacks, and turned bin Laden into a hero and a symbol for Islam.

The need for these groups to win popular support has been most evident in Egypt, where indiscriminate attacks on tourists

by the Islamist Al Gamaa Islamiya and Al Jihad groups, pro-
voked widespread public hostility which left the militant groups
in a state of disarray. This prompted the leadership of Al Gamaa
Islamiya to abandon the strategy, because it had lost them too
much public support. (Although not all members of the leadership accepted this view, and some continued to believe that
high-publicity attacks such as that at Luxor in 1997, would
highlight the group's cause and weaken the Egyptian government.) (26) Equally, Islamic Jihad distinguishes between civilians, and soldiers or settlers, in its attacks, by trying to avoid
civilian casualties. This may be because it wants to win support
amongst Palestinians who oppose the killing of civilians,
although this is not the prime objective of the group. (27)

Similarly, the Christian white supremacists in the USA also
have a constituency amongst the white population, which they
have to nurture and appeal to for support. Whilst they accept
that some white people have 'sold out' to the Zionist occupation
government and the new world order, they are generally
attempting to mobilize the white race in the USA. They cannot
afford to conduct indiscriminate mass casualty attacks, without
risking killing so-called 'innocent' white people, which is likely to
alienate potential support for their movement. Therefore if they
attempt to use NBC weapons to precipitate a race war, they will
either have to use them in a discriminate fashion, or if they did
choose to use NBC weapons for indiscriminate attacks, they
would have to choose their targets carefully in order to minimize
collateral casualties.

There is, however, an apparent difference between the way
that groups which are predominantly religious in character
appeal to their constituencies, and the way that predominantly
secular and ethno-nationalist groups appeal to theirs. Secular
terrorists believe that whilst the general population might not
actually support their cause, they are a potential source of support, which can be mobilized by increasing their awareness of
the cause the group espouses, through carefully calibrated violence that does not alienate them. In contrast, groups that are
predominantly religious in character appear to believe that
mobilizing their constituency is best achieved not by limiting
violence, but in pursuing heightened levels of violence directed
against clearly defined enemies, which their constituency also
identifies as their enemy. For Islamic fundamentalists, this is
achieved by any acts of violence against Israel and the USA,
which the vast majority of Arabs in the Middle East already perceive to be their enemies.

In addition, it can also be argued that many of these groups
that are predominantly religious in character are less interested

in generating international political support than secular and ethno-nationalist separatist movements. For many ethno-nationalist separatist groups, gaining the support of powerful western states such as the USA is the main objective – or, failing that, powerful regional actors. Bhindranwale, the former leader of the Sikh militants in the Punjab in India, recognized the importance of propaganda for both rallying his supporters and winning international support. He was always anxious to give interviews to foreign correspondents and have the activities of his followers filmed. The British journalist Mark Tully recounts one meeting with Bhindranwale:

> I explained to the Sant that we would like to film his congregation the next day and interview him. He liked the idea until I told him that the interview would only last about ten minutes. 'Ten minutes,' he replied. 'It should be at least two hours. There are lots of Sikhs in England, you know, who would like to see me for two hours. (28)

In contrast, Islamic fundamentalists have little interest in winning political support from western states because they perceive all non-Islamist regimes to be illegitimate. Instead, the main focus of their violence is their constituency, which they hope will gain awareness through their actions, and eventually inspire them to overthrow the 'illegitimate' regimes under which they live. Although they do have an interest in forging links with the small number of radical regimes which might supply them with material support. Consequently, their violence is not generally limited by concerns about gathering international political support. Similarly, religious cults and Christian white supremacists commit their acts for none but themselves and their constituency.

Using NBC weapons and generating popular support
NBC weapons are the optimum means of committing indiscriminate mass casualty attacks, but because this is not a common tactic of most of the terrorist groups that are predominantly secular in character, they should theoretically have limited interest in procuring and using such weapons. Therefore, one of the primary disincentives to the use of NBC weapons is the sheer numbers of indiscriminate casualties that WMD can potentially cause. As has been stated earlier, Brian Jenkins argues that killing lots of people is not necessarily a major objective of most terrorist groups, because it would be counter-productive for pursuing their political objectives. This would particularly be the

case for groups that are predominantly secular in character, whose primary concern is that they are more likely to lose support than gain it, by causing huge numbers of casualties. For this reason, many analysts consider that secular terrorist groups on the left and right would be reluctant to use NBC weapons, for fear of alienating the political support on which they depend. The only type of groups that might fall outside of this explanation are groups which identify a racial enemy.

In many states there exists a societal revulsion towards the use of NBC weapons, which is significantly stronger than with conventional weapons. There is also a sense in which NBC weapons are uniquely terrible because of the nature of the injuries they cause, and the lingering effects of the contamination that they leave. Therefore it is generally considered that using NBC weapons against any target would evoke a negative public reaction in the majority of states, even amongst potential supporters.

The relationship between committing acts of indiscriminate violence and generating propaganda, however, is not clear-cut. This is evident from the 1972 Munich massacre in which members of the Palestinian Black September group killed two Israeli athletes and then kidnapped a further nine at the Munich Olympics, who were all then killed during a shoot-out with the police. The operation was a failure because it did not achieve its objective of securing the release of Palestinian prisoners, and the righteousness of their cause was tarnished because international opinion was almost unanimous in condemning the attack. What the episode did demonstrate, however, was that even when an operation fails in all its objectives, it can still be counted as a success if it is dramatic enough to capture the attention of the media. In these terms, Munich was an unequivocal success. (29) What this episode suggests is that even negative publicity can prove useful. Whilst an NBC attack might evoke universal revulsion, leading to a loss of political sympathy and support, it would still be highly effective in gaining media attention, focusing worldwide attention on the cause of the group that perpetrated the attack. This was what occurred with the Aum Shinrikyo after its attack on the Tokyo subway, even though generating propaganda was not an objective of the attack.

Yet despite these powerful arguments that groups which are predominantly secular in character would not be interested in using NBC weapons, some of this type of group have previously been involved in plots involving NBC weapons, or are alleged to have been involved in such plots. For instance, the left-wing German group the RAF (Baader Meinhof Gang) were implicated in five allegations of CBW plots during the 1970s and 1980s, including one where Botulism was allegedly produced. Similarly, secular right-wing groups have also sporadically been linked to CBW plots. Yet as far as is publicly known, none of these types of groups has ever undertaken a long-term, systematic effort to procure NBC weapons. This seems to suggest that whilst considering the options, their interest in NBC weapons was determined more by opportunity and circumstance than by longer-term strategic or tactical requirements.

Whilst concerns about alienating political support would seem to rule out most groups that are predominantly secular in character, from using NBC weapons in indiscriminate mass casualty attacks against population targets, Chapter 4 indicated that NBC weapons are capable of being used in a number of discriminate roles, such as assassinating individuals or attacking specific buildings through their air conditioning systems. Hence, by selecting what they could justify as 'legitimate' targets, terrorist groups could still consider using NBC weapons and gain a massive propaganda effect. Whether this would alienate members of their constituency is a matter of pure speculation. Some people would probably be repulsed by the use of an NBC weapon, even in this role, but others might accept it. This might help to account for the occasional interest of secular left- and right-wing groups in procuring these weapons, and why some individuals and groups such as the Christian white supremacists in the USA have procured ricin in order to assassinate individuals, even though it would have been more effective to use conventional weapons for that purpose.

It is difficult to draw substantive conclusions to support these contentions from analysing the past record of secular terrorism and NBC weapons. In several cases in which groups were allegedly attempting to acquire CBW, there were no details of potential targets, and it is difficult to differentiate the threats where there was an underlying intent to acquire and use NBC weapons, and those which were just a bluff. But in the cases where targets were identified, there have been slightly more cases where the targets were discriminate in nature than those involving indiscriminate targets. Several of the latter cases can potentially be discounted because the threat appears to be little more than a bluff, and cases of contaminating foodstuffs such as Israeli oranges and Chilean grapes can be discounted, because the intent was not to kill large numbers of people, but to spread alarm and undermine exports of those products. This leaves a small hard core of cases where the threat to cause indiscriminate casualties was real. After weeding out these cases the disparity between terrorists targeting discriminate and indiscriminate targets is much greater.In contrast, because religiously motivated terrorists perceive their constituency differently, and attempt to mobilize it through different means, they might be more willing to consider perpetrating indiscriminate mass-casualty attacks involving NBC weapons. Although they would still have to tailor their attacks to avoid alienating their constituency, they would have an interest in restricting mass-casualty attacks to what can be identified as 'legitimate' targets, just as the Oklahoma City bombing was legitimized as an attack on the federal government. If right-wing groups attempted to use NBC weapons to precipitate a race war, they would either have to use them in a discriminate fashion, or if they did decide to use NBC weapons for indiscriminate attacks, they would have to select their targets carefully in order to minimize collateral casualties. Therefore concerns that members of their constituency would be accidentally killed, could be addressed by careful target selection, which for Islamic fundamentalists could perhaps be as simple as choosing a target on the mainland USA.

Operational disincentives to using NBC weapons
At the operational level, terrorists are unfamiliar with using NBC weapons, and their effects can be unpredictable. This raises concerns about the safety of both the terrorists and their supporters. Terrorists tend to be risk averse in conducting their operations, with the survival of the group being an overriding imperative. Therefore, if the use of NBC weapons exposes the group to greater risks it will militate against their use. There is some evidence to support these contentions. When challenged over whether the Chechens would attack Russian nuclear power plants during the Russian-Chechen war of 1999–2000, Salman Raduyev, a prominent Chechen warlord, claimed that they would not, 'because the consequences of this cannot be predicted'. (30) Whether this was actually the main reason or not, the Chechens never did attack a nuclear power station, despite the severity of the war.

In the Middle East, it could not be guaranteed that the use of NBC weapons in Israel would not impact upon Arab communities because of the close proximity of the two peoples. The Koran prohibits the killing of Muslims by fellow Muslims, and threatens harsh punishments for those that do so. The Lebanese guerrilla movement ,Hezbollah, however, has got around this ruling by seeking religious sanction for any attacks which might involve Muslim deaths, in order to assess whether each attack was consistent with Islamic Laws. (31) Since different Islamic scholars could interpret Islamic law differently, the sanctioning of any specific attack would be dependent upon the individual scholar that the terrorists consulted. There may not, however, be that much scope for interpretation of this ruling. In one specific instance, Hezbollah received clerical sanction to attack an Israeli prison, despite the presence of Muslim prisoners, on the principle that the end justifies the means, but it was permitted only if the enemies' toll of casualties exceeded the Muslim casualties. (32) A religious edict to this effect was passed, and the attack was carried out. It would be a big step for an Islamic scholar to go from this precedent to sanctioning an indiscriminate attack against a population target using an NBC weapon, in which many Muslims could potentially be killed.

In operational terms, this means that discrete targets would have to be identified for indiscriminate attacks if a group was concerned about killing its own people. Similarly, for any group attempting to achieve independence for their territorial homeland, the contamination effects of using NBC weapons would be incompatible with their ultimate objective. Therefore, for the Islamic Group Hamas, the Chechens and the Sikh militants in the Punjab, who all operate primarily on their own territory, any consideration of the use of NBC weapons would necessitate changes in their strategy. These factors will all be powerful inhibitors in making decisions on whether to use NBC weapons. In certain circumstances groups might still consider that the advantages that would accrue from using these weapons, could outweigh the disadvantages of using them on their own soil, but it might constrain them to use these weapons in specific, highly controlled ways, such as spreading CBW through the air conditioning of government or military buildings.

Another possible disincentive for some groups to use NBC weapons is the fear of provoking an unprecedented government backlash. Some terrorist groups operate within a fairly permissive environment, which would be threatened if they carried out an attack of such magnitude. For instance, during the course of the conflict in Northern Ireland many terrorist activists from both sides were known to the security forces, but were left at liberty for lack of evidence to convict them of any specific crime. If it had felt compelled to act, there were several legal and even extra-legal measures which the British government could have employed to clamp down on terrorist activity, such as internment or even a shoot to kill policy (as has regularly been alleged by the republican movement). Similarly, the Indian government was extremely unwilling to act against the former Sikh leader, Bhindranwale, and was goaded into attacking his base in the Golden Temple of Amritsar only by a series of high-profile terrorist attacks and threats.

Yet it is precisely such backlashes which some terrorist groups are attempting to provoke. When governments clamp down on terrorist activities they invariably encroach on civil liberties, and in some states even human rights. This undermines the legitimacy of the government in the eyes of the population, drawing support to the terrorist cause. Religious terrorists might also want to provoke a harsh response because it fits into their belief system of an apocalyptic life and death struggle between themselves and the establishment. Therefore different groups, at different times, are less likely to be deterred by potential backlashes.

Yet this strategy need not necessarily involve large numbers of indiscriminate casualties in order to be successful. The IRA conducted a highly personal campaign to provoke the British prime minister, Mrs Thatcher, into over reacting and invoking widespread repression which would drive moderate nationalists to support the IRA. This was achieved through killing British servicemen and close colleagues such as the Conservative Party politicians Airey Neave and Ian Gow. The most dramatic example of this was the attack on the Grand Hotel in Brighton, where delegates from the Conservative party conference were staying in 1984, and which nearly killed Mrs Thatcher herself. (33)

In other circumstances, indiscriminate atrocities have been perpetrated in order to provoke an adverse reaction from their target audience. Hamas attempted to undermine the Middle East peace process with indiscriminate attacks on Israeli civilians in order to turn Israeli public opinion against it; similarly the Jewish extremist Baruch Goldstein attempted to turn Arab opinion against the process with an attack at the Cave of the Patriarch which killed 30 Muslim worshippers. (34) Therefore groups could conceivably use NBC weapons in either discriminate or indiscriminate attacks, precisely in anticipation of evoking just such a response.

Yet an act of terrorism that successfully provokes a backlash from the government might also result in a potential loss of international support for the group. For some groups this might not be a concern, but it will be a factor for others. Governments themselves can also lose international support by invoking harsh measures to suppress terrorism, whatever the provocation. When Russia invaded Chechnya in 1999, in retaliation for the Moscow apartment block bombings, it incurred considerable criticism from the West and the Muslim world. The invasion, and the atrocities carried out by the Russian army, was a propaganda defeat for Russia. It was never able to regain the moral high ground, despite constantly trying to justify its actions as a legitimate campaign to wipe out domestic terrorists.

Conclusion

The past record of plots where individuals or groups acquired NBC weapons, but never followed through by using them, can be partly explained by reference to considerations of losing the support of the international community and alienating their domestic constituency. These factors will inhibit some secular groups, in particular, from using NBC weapons for indiscriminate mass-casualty attacks. These considerations will not necessarily inhibit them from using them in more discriminate roles; in fact, the strong propaganda value to be gained from using such weapons could make them distinctly attractive for use in these roles. These factors might just shape the nature of tactics, prompting their controlled use against discriminate targets. Nevertheless the racist goals of some secular groups; some groups led by hardliners, such as the ANO; or groups with amorphous constituencies, such as ad hoc groups bent on revenge rather than achieving political goals means that not all secular groups have a predisposition to limit their violence. Therefore the disincentives for secular groups to using NBC weapons are not universal, and neither are they particularly strong. They are strongest in respect of non-racist secular groups and indiscriminate mass- casualty attacks. In all other circumstances, other considerations may override them.

Notes and references
1. Bruce Hoffman, *Inside Terrorism* (London: Indigo, 1998) p 157
2. C.J.M. Drake, *Terrorists' Target Selection* (London: St Martin's Press, 1998) p 34
3. Gavin Cameron, *Nuclear Terrorism* (Basingstoke: MacMillan, 1999) p 103
4. Cameron: *Nuclear Terrorism*, p 115
5. Drake: *Terrorists' Target Selection*, p 48
6. Cameron: *Nuclear Terrorism*, p 115
7. Ely Karmon, 'Bin Laden Is Out To Get America!', The International Policy Institute For Counter-Terrorism, internet site: <http://www.ict.org.il/articles/isl-terr.htm> (29 October 1998)
8. Karmon: 'Bin Laden'
9. Karmon: 'Bin Laden'
10. Conor Gearty, *Terror* (London: Faber & Faber, 1991) pp 102, 106, 120–21
11. Gearty: *Terror*, p 105
12. 'IRA Arms May Go To Rogue Factions', *Sunday Telegraph* (4 July 1999)
13. Bruce Hoffman and David Claridge, 'Illicit Trafficking in Nuclear Materials', *Conflict Studies* 314/315, Research Institute For The Study of Conflict and Terrorism (January–February 1999) p 28
14. Mark Tully and Satish Jacob, *Amritsar: Mrs Ghandi's Last Battle* (London: Jonathan Cape, 1985) p 102

15. Official government figures put the number of Hindus killed at 165 in the first 22 months of Bhindranwale's campaign. Tully and Jacob: *Amritsar*

16. Gearty: *Terror*, p 105

17. Yosi Melman, The Master Terrorist: The True Story of Abu Nidal (London: Sidgwick & Jackson, 1986) p 68

18. 'Frequently Asked Questions: White Power', Aryan Nations webpage www.christian-aryannations.com

19. 'Attack is Tip of Hate Crime Iceberg', *Guardian* (11 August 1999)

20. Daniel Jeffreys, quoted in *Daily Mail* (21 November 1998) pp 12–13

21. Hoffman: *Inside Terrorism*, p 131

22. Hoffman: *Inside Terrorism*, p 158

23. Adrian Guelke: *The Age of Terrorism and the International Political System* (London: I.B. Tauris, 1998) p 65

24. Drake: *Terrorists' Target Selection*, p 171

25. Karmon: 'Bin Laden'

26. Richard Engel, 'Egypt Digs for the Truth', *Jane's Defence Weekly* (24 February 1999) p 2

27. Cameron: *Nuclear Terrorism*, p 891

28. Tully and Jacob: *Amritsar*, p 126. On another occasion, the international press were invited to the wedding of six young Sikh fighters in the Sikh's holiest site, the Golden Temple of Amritsar. Tully and Jacob: Amritsar, p 135

29. Hoffman: *Inside Terrorism*, pp 72–73

30. 'Sergeyev: Troops Won't Stop at Terek', *Moscow Times* (13 October 1999)<http://www.moscowtimes.ru/13-Oct-1999/stories/story1.html>

31. Hala Jaber, *Hezbollah: Born With A Vengeance* (London: Fourth Estate, 1997) p 89

32. Jaber: *Hezbollah*, p 89

33. Gearty: *Terror*, p 121

34. Between April 1994 and March 1996 Hamas killed 130 in 13 attacks on buses and queues at bus stops. Drake: *Terrorists' Target Selection*, p 159; Cameron: *Nuclear Terrorism*

6. Political and Theological Motivations to Using NBC Weapons

NBC weapons can be used in a number of tactical roles, although Chapter 4 indicated that the strength of the tactical incentives to use them varies according to the type of target, or outcome, that the terrorists desire. Yet whether a group will choose to exploit those tactical incentives will depend upon the strength of the political and strategic motivations which drive them. These are derived from the belief system of the group, and the goals that it seeks to achieve; they would also have to be stronger than the political, ideological and tactical disincentives to using NBC weapons that would also be an influence on the group. It would appear that groups which are predominantly secular in nature typically operate under strong political and strategic disincentives to using NBC weapons. Chapter 2 highlighted the link between groups that are predominantly religious in character, and the steady increase in the lethality of modern terrorism, which has fuelled the perception of an increased risk of the use of NBC weapons. Yet these groups are not wholly apolitical, and also operate under a number of perceived political, strategic and theological constraints. This chapter will explore the potential political, theological and strategic motivations for using NBC weapons, focusing particularly on the predominantly religious orientated groups.

Islamic fundamentalists
Islamic fundamentalist groups are closely linked to the steady rise in lethality of terrorist incidents. The dynamic hard core of modern-day religious terrorism are the militant Islamic groups, including radical offshoots of the Muslim Brotherhood (Ikhwan) such as Islamic Jihad and Tafkir wa'l Hijra; the Groupe Islamique Armée (GIA); Al Jihad; Al Gamaa Islamiya; the Islamic Resistance Movement (Hamas); and the Party of God (Hezbollah) that all emerged in the Middle East and North Africa. In the late 1990s the tide of Islamic militancy in the Middle East appeared to be receding, and instead was becoming more manifest on the fringes of the Muslim world, particularly in the Caucasus and Central Asia. Islamic fundamentalism, however, is not a homogeneous movement, with differences between groups sometimes being as evident as their similarities, although they typically share many common beliefs and objectives.

To understand the Muslim terrorist cause it is necessary to understand the background to Islamic fundamentalism. Islamism refers to the movements and ideologies that claim Islam, as they interpret it, as the basis for restructuring contemporary states and societies according to an idealised image of Islam's founding period 1400 years ago. Consequently, the short- to mid-term objective of many groups is to Islamize the nation states in which they operate, or were born in. As a long-term objective, though, many Islamists talk about the need to return to a 'golden age,' (1) through the revival of the Muslim empire and the unification of the Muslim world as one nation. This is considered to require the implementation of Islam in society as a whole, since individual adherence to the faith cannot in itself lead to the creation of an Islamic society. Islamists believe that Islam encompasses 'three Ds': din (religion); dunya (life); and dawla (state); which has to be implemented in its entirety. Deviation from this 'golden age' paradigm is tantamount to jahiliyya, or pre-Islamic ignorance

Since the 1970s, many Middle Eastern and North African regimes have failed to relieve the social tensions and dislocation that resulted from the highly uneven economic development, rapid urbanization, and accelerated liberalization of their states. This has resulted in a decline in the popular legitimacy of many regimes. Within this political vacuum, Islamist groups proposing that the creation of Islamic states was the only answer to the profound political, social and economic problems affecting Muslim peoples' lives, found a receptive social base. (2)

For Islamic fundamentalists, the un-Islamic aspects of the contemporary world are represented by 'a monster with four heads.' (3) The first head is that of 'the Jew, the eternal schemer against God.' The second head is symbolized by the Cross. Islamic fundamentalists believe that the Crusades never ended, so that there is a perpetual state of war between the Muslim world, and the Crusaders' political culture, in which the Christian powers are attempting to eliminate Islam from the world. Consequently, the socio-cultural element of Islamist teachings is peppered with hostility towards the West, Israel and the Jews. The third head of the monster is atheism, the chief contemporary manifestation of which is communism. Both atheism and Communism are considered to have been devised by the Jews. The fourth head represents secularism. To Islamic fundamentalists, all secular governments are inherently illegitimate, since legitimacy can be conferred only through the adoption of Islamic Shari'a law. (4) Secularism can also mean many things, including the advocacy of the separation of Church and state, and even the idea that Islam should be propagated and enforced by example, rather than terrorism. Therefore, Islamist groups are also engaged in an ongoing conflict with secular Arab regimes. Their members believe that they are soldiers in the service of Allah, fighting an enemy which is everywhere, including deep inside the Muslim world, in the form of corrupt governments and diseased cultures.

These negative perceptions of the West and the international system as a whole play an important role in defining the nature of the Islamist terrorist groups. The USA is identified as the primary enemy of Islam, and is held responsible for all of the problems in the Middle East through its support for Israel, and other reactionary regimes. But Islamists view the West as an enemy not only for political and religious reasons, but also for socio-economic and cultural ones. Therefore, the contemporary crusaders are considered to comprise a wide range of western writers, poets, businessmen, film makers, diplomats, politicians, musicians, and artists who all spread western culture and values. Most of the Arab regimes facing an Islamist challenge are also supported by the West, which in turn increases their illegitimacy in the eyes of the Islamists.

Since the war against the Crusaders is considered to be the consequence of a western-Jewish conspiracy against Islam, the Islamist belief system defines it as a war of self-defence. Islamists perceive themselves to be encircled by enemies, and on the defensive because of their lack of economic and military power. In 1996 Sheik Fadlallah, the spiritual leader of the Lebanese group Hezbollah, justified Islamic terrorism by arguing that: 'We are not preachers of violence ... Jihad in Islam is a defensive movement against those who impose violence.' (5) Many reactions in the Muslim press to the bombing of the US embassies in Kenya and Tanzania in 1999 considered that US behaviour towards fundamentalist Islam and Muslim states in general, had encouraged such attacks. The double standard that the USA is perceived to apply in the Middle East, and its leniency towards Israel, are particularly strong grievances. (6)

Whilst Islamists' ultimate aim is to establish God's rule on earth, through the creation of Islamic regimes, the Koran itself can be interpreted in a number of ways. As a result, Islamic terms and symbols are used by both secular Muslim regimes and Islamist groups, to convey diverse meanings, in order to serve their different political objectives. But whilst secular Muslim rulers and regimes attempt to base their political legitimacy on Islam, Islamist activists accuse them of deviating from true Islam, and of serving the interests of their enemies. The 'clerics of the regime' (Ulama'al-Salatin) who are appointed by secular regimes are perceived to be subordinate to their political masters, and their religious rulings (fatwa) are often denied by the Islamists.

Some of the Islamist groups that follow the teachings of Ayatollah Khomeini have their own clerics who issue religious rulings on Islamic principles. Known as Wali al-Faqih, these figures interpret the teachings of the Koran, and determine the religious dimension of virtually all aspects of everyday life. The power of the Faqih is such that:

> We must obey the Wali al-Faqih, disagreement with
> him is not permitted. The guardianship of the Faqih
> is like the guardianship of the Prophet Mohammed
> and of the Infallible Imam. Just as the guardianship
> of the Prophet and the Infallible Imam is obligatory,
> so too is the guardianship of the Faqih.

Each group can have a different Faqih, who can potentially interpret the teachings of the Koran slightly differently. (7) Although this concept is hotly disputed by other Shi'a leaders.

From one perspective, the very nature of fundamentalism suggests that Islamists are incapable of compromising on their underlying goals and principles. Amir Taheri argues that, 'Islamic Fundamentalism has always viewed itself as a force capable of conquering the contemporary world from without. It cannot conceive of either coexistence or political compromise. To the exponents of Holy Terror, Islam must either dominate or be dominated.' (8) Yet as is the case with predominantly secular groups, Islamist groups have at times shown a willingness to re-formulate their goals and adapt to changing circumstances. The leadership of Hezbollah, for instance, has departed from its manifesto by declaring that the liberation of South Lebanon and Jerusalem are two separate enterprises. It now talks of co-oper-ating with Palestinian rejectionists, although more militant members remain committed to a military struggle until Palestine is liberated. (9) It has also recognized the multi-confessional nature of Lebanese society, and has participated in elections resulting in its members serving in the Lebanese parliament. These factors can have a significant impact upon the strategies which Islamist groups adopt, and the political options that are available to states attempting to engage them.

The strategies of Islamic fundamentalists
The defining characteristic of the strategy pursued by Islamic Fundamentalists, is the goal of achieving political power. Islamists regard this step as crucial if they are to succeed in re-shaping the politics, society, economy and culture of the state. Whilst all Islamists share the goal of creating an Islamic state, they differ over how they should achieve this. One method is militant and radical, the other, political and legal. Political Islamists believe that violent struggle is futile and self-defeating, and reject the assumptions of urgency advocated by militants. Political Islamists include the Ikhwan al-Muslim, the Muslim Brotherhood (MB), founded by Hassan al-Bana in Egypt in 1928, the Front Islamique de Salut (FIS), Hezbollah and the Hizb al-Isah (Reform Party).

Militant leaders, who tend to be much younger than those of the MB, combine ideological purity and deep contempt for polit-ical compromise with a keen sense of urgency for direct action. Their main objective is to bring an end to what they consider to be the oppressive conditions under which true Muslims have become a tiny minority. They believe that their primary obliga-tion is to fight against those states which embody 'jahiliyya.' They therefore reject the current political and social order entirely, their aim being to wage a war of attrition against the state for as long as it takes to overthrow it.

The primary strategic aim of Militant Islamists, is to under-mine the principal foundation of the state: its hybah – the per-ceived invincibility that it cultivates amongst its people. To undermine this hybah, the militants attempt to demonstrate the failure of the state to protect its key leaders and strategic instal-lations. The second strategic aim of the militants is to weaken the foundations of the state, particularly by striking at its sources of revenue. This has resulted in militant groups attacking the gas and oil industries in Algeria, and tourism in Egypt. This will weaken the state's ability to provide the necessary services to its citizens, resulting in a decline in popular support for the regime. The third objective is to provoke the ruling elites to strike back indiscriminately with emergency laws and other extreme measures, which would alienate the population by disrupting normal life. By demonstrating its inability to deal efficiently with violent challenges, the legitimacy of the regime will decline even further. The resulting popular resentment is intended to fuel opposition and create a social atmosphere that is receptive to militant ideas. Militants thus challenge not only the regime, but also other Islamists who accept the idea of reforming existing systems from within.

In pursuing these objectives, militant leaders such as Osama bin Laden, Omar Abdel Rahman in Egypt and Abdel Rahman al-Zaytouni (the leader of the GIA in Algeria) start from the premise that existing regimes will not respond to humanitarian appeals, eloquent sermons, party political practises, legal petitions or peaceful marches. For them, jahiliyya must be confronted and eradicated through insurrection, directed by a new believing minority, who form the vanguard of a Quaranic generation. According to Islamist ideologue Sayyid Qutb, this vanguard should comprise the select few who know what nobody else knows. (10)

An additional major strategic goal for many Islamist groups is to strike at US and Western targets around the world, in order to force a withdrawal of their political, military and economic support from secular regimes in the Middle East, as well as to hold back on their cultural 'invasion' of Muslim states. Therefore Islamists are seeking nothing less than complete western disengagement from the Muslim world. They consider that just as the infidels fight using contemptible and foul methods, the Islamic answer should be to use all possible means of self-defence, including indiscriminate terrorism. (11) It has also been suggested that the violence perpetrated by some of these new Islamic groups is not political in nature, but driven by revenge, as a punishment and an end in itself. (12) Although the precise motives for any attack are difficult to establish, and revenge could be just one motive tied in with other political and strategic motivations.

Islamic fundamentalists and NBC terrorism
From an examination of the goals and strategies of Islamist groups, it is apparent that they do not operate under any overwhelmingly strong political or theological motivations to perpetrate acts of 'mass destruction', or NBC terrorism. From one per-

spective, the theological underpinning of the Islamist belief system can provide a strong motivation for conducting indiscriminate mass- casualty attacks. Amir Taheri states that Islamist teachings pronounce that 'those who adamantly refuse to convert to Islam are, to all intents and purposes, enemies of Allah Himself.' (13) This establishes a moral imperative, and strong justificatory mechanism for perpetrating indiscriminate attacks against non-Muslim targets. Yet the Koran also states that if Muslims enter the enemy's territory, they must not kill women and children, or destroy crops and trees. (14) It urges Muslims to 'Fight in the cause of God against those who fight you, but do not transgress limits. God does not love Transgressors.' (15) As a result of this dichotomy within Islamic teachings, different Islamist groups have adopted a range of tactics.

Many have undertaken acts of controlled violence in order to achieve limited goals. This is evident from their strategic goals to drive western political and military influence out of their states, and to undermine secular regimes. In the process, some of them deliberately try to avoid civilian casualties. Conventional weapons are more suited for attacking military, political and economic targets, because of the operational problems associated with using NBC weapons in a controlled yet effective manner. Indeed, their successes using conventional weapons in these roles means that there is no overwhelming tactical imperative for them to escalate to using NBC weapons.

Yet despite all of this, at least one Islamic cleric has argued for the use of BW against western governments. Omar Bakri Muhammad has declared that 'If any Muslims are under occupation by a western force, they can use any weapon to survive and that includes biological weapons.' He gave no indication of how they might be used discriminately against governments, but appeared to rule out their use for indiscriminate attacks against population targets by stating that 'We have no problem with the western people and we wish them peace. We have problems only with the action that is committed by western governments.' (16) Because of the operational problems associated with using BW discriminately, threats to use them in this role probably have more to do with attempting to heighten the level of intimidation involved in the threat, rather than because they are perceived to confer any tactical advantage.

In conjunction with perpetrating acts of controlled violence for limited goals, some groups have provided rhetorical indications of their willingness to perpetrate acts of indiscriminate violence, and even genocide. Hussein Mussawi, the former leader of Hezbollah, once commented that 'We are not fighting so that the enemy recognizes us and offers us something. We are fighting to wipe out the enemy.' (17) Similarly, Antar Zoubari, a leader of the GIA, argues that God does not negotiate or engage in discussion. He couches the GIA's campaign of violence in terms of an 'all-out war' with an absolute goal to establish an Islamic state. If innocents should perish in pursuing this divinely ordained goal that is an acceptable consequence, whilst the killing of 'apostate,' or those not part of the Islamic movement, was a duty. This is justified by reference to verses in the Koran which state that   'I am innocent of those killed because they were associated with those who had to be fought.' (18) Hamas uses similar rhetoric of all-out war until the enemy is totally and utterly vanquished. Its covenant states that 'Israel will continue to exist until Islam will obliterate it.' Moreover, Article 7 of its Covenant displays clear millenarian overtones: 'The time [of redemption] will not come until the Muslims fight the Jews and kill them, and until the Jews hide behind rocks and trees when the call is raised: "Oh Muslim, here is a Jew hiding come and kill him." (19) There is a lot of similar genocidal rhetoric amongst Islamic groups concerning the Jews. The use of WMD would clearly fit in with these goals.

The World Trade Centre bombing was a powerful indicator that at least some groups are willing to perpetrate acts of indiscriminate mass killing. But even the perpetrators of this attack were pursuing a mix of limited goals and unconstrained violence. A letter discovered by FBI investigators stated the goals of the group to be stopping the end of all US military, economic and political aid to Israel; the ending of US diplomatic relations with Israel; and for the USA not to interfere in the domestic affairs of any Middle Eastern state. Yet the letter went on to argue that 'The American People are responsible for the actions of their government and they must question all of the crimes that their government is committing against other people. Or they – Americans – will be targets of our operations that could diminish them.' (20) Therefore despite pursuing limited aims, the group believed that indiscriminate violence was justified in meeting those objectives.

This dichotomy in Islamist motivations is also evident in the strategy being pursued by Osama bin Laden's, International Islamic Front for Jihad against the Jews and the Crusaders, (The Front). Apart from the bombing of the World Trade Centre, all of the targets in the attacks attributed to the Front were discriminate in nature, ranging from assassinations of the Pope, the prime minister of Egypt and Crown Prince Abdullah of Jordan, to attacks on US servicemen in Yemen, Saudi Arabia and an attack on the Egyptian embassy in Pakistan. (21) Many of the warnings of impending attacks by the Front identify western embassies as the targets. (22) Yet despite this, the basic anti-Christian and anti-western nature of the Front establishes a potential motivation to undertake mass-casualty attacks against western population targets. Therefore there have also been allegations of interest in blowing up passenger airliners and acquiring nuclear weapons. (23) In December 1998, following air strikes on Iraq, in which the USA and UK attempted to destroy Iraq' s residual stocks of WMD, *Asharq al-Awsat*, the London-based daily, quoted bin Laden denouncing,

> the Jews and the crusaders, especially the Americans and British who did not care about the rights of any child, elderly man or woman in Iraq ... The British and the Americans people have widely voiced their support for their leaders decision to attack Iraq which makes all these people who occupy Palestine, into people warring [against God]. Every Muslim should confront and fight them. Anything that can be taken by them by force is a prize for the Muslims. (24)

Religious cults
Traditional thinking has viewed religious cults as a sociological, psychological or theological phenomenon. Concerns were primarily expressed about their impact on the individual, focusing on issues such as how they recruit and control individuals; strip them of their financial assets; separate them from their families; or even engage in sexual abuse. Mass suicides such as the 1978 'Jonestown Massacre' of the members of the People's Temple in Guyana heightened these concerns, but they were never really perceived to be threats to national security. A growing number of incidents, however, has led to a gradually broadening perception of the potential threat that cults can pose to society as a whole. It is now known that some of them also have political agendas, sometimes operating within the institutions of the state; (25) whilst others reject both state and society, which occasionally finds expression in violently anti-social acts.

For Ian Haworth, the founder of the Cult Information Centre in the UK, the most salient feature of post-war religious cults is their use of mind-control techniques, which give the leader, or leadership clique, complete control over the lives of the cult members. (26) The all-powerful role of the leader within the cult, coupled with the use of mind control, means that the membership will unquestioningly follow the leader's directives. Consequently, cult members are compelled to live out the imperatives of the religious doctrine which the leader espouses, which is invariably heavily influenced by his or her personal fantasies, delusions and intentions. Because of the bizarre nature of the beliefs of some cults, it is generally assumed that it is unintelligent, weak and mentally ill people who are drawn into cults. This might be an accurate description of some cult members, (27) but it is in general terms a misconception. Healthy minds that are intellectually alert and inquisitive, and perhaps idealistic, are in fact the easiest to recruit and control. In addition, individuals do not join cults, but are actively sought out and recruited. Hence, many intelligent people become members of cults, including professional people such as doctors, teachers and engineers. (28) Aum Shinrikyo sent recruiters to universities with instructions to target the young and the bright. (29) Once they join, mind control brings them under the control of the leader, and they could end up engaging in activities which they might otherwise have rejected. The highly intelligent membership of Aum Shinrikyo which developed and used sarin is testament to this fact.

Cults are inherently volatile entities which by their very nature are violent. This is primarily psychological violence, owing to the use of mind control and other forms of coercion, (30) but there have also been numerous documented cases of physical abuse within cults, and even of cult members being murdered. The most visible manifestation of cult violence has been the phenomenon of mass suicides. There has always been a small but steady number of cult-related mass suicides, which increased slightly during the 1990s in the run-up to the millennium. However, there has also been a steady number of incidents where a cult violently lashes out at society. Although these cases occur very infrequently, with no perceptible upward trend.

The central theme in the belief system of dangerous cults is the concept of the end of the world. The core of this belief is that an act of divine intervention will create a cataclysm which only the righteous will survive. It is very common for cults to have an apocalyptic focus, particularly pseudo-Christian groups, but the concept has now reached further than Judaeo-Christian theology, even appearing in Far Eastern cults, such as the Aum Shinrikyo and the Falun Gong in China. (31) Belief in an impending apocalypse does not necessarily mean that a group will engage in physical violence, and neither are there any objective criteria by which it is possible to determine whether a cult will implode in mass suicide, or explode into outward-directed violence. Although Jessica Stern suggests that the nature of a cult's core myth is an important indicator. Those that model themselves on an avenging angel or vindictive god – Christ with a sword, Kali (the Hindu goddess of terror and destruction) or Phineas (the avenger priest from the Old Testament) – are more likely to lash out than those where the core myth is a suffering messiah. However some cults switch myths when under pressure – for example, because of the millennium, or the state of mind of the leader. (32)

Another feature of cults is that they can appear very quickly, almost overnight, whilst established groups can take a radical turn, perhaps under the authority of a new leader. Hence, threats to society can appear and disappear very quickly. Andrew Hubback argues that because cults have no rational objective they can quickly come into conflict with a society which they perceive to be sinful and lost. (33) Equally, the local populations amongst which cults live generally tend to be wary of them, and negative reactions from local populations can create the conditions in which cult leaders can develop persecution complexes and crises can develop. It is not a coincidence that the Rajneeshpuram cult and the Branch Davidians in the USA, as well as the Aum Shinrikyo, all lashed out in violence when they faced threats from the legal system (see Annex).

Whilst the US Christian Identity cult, the Covenant, Sword and Arm of the Lord had plotted to poison the water supplies of major US cities in the USA (see Appendix for details), it was the Aum Shinrikyo's use of CW which marked a watershed, not only because it was the first systematic use of CW by a non-state actor, but also because it focused attention on religious cults as potential terrorist organizations. In the run-up to the millennium this concern about religious cults was ratcheted up many times over, but whilst this focus on religious cults is justified, there is an inherent danger of exaggerating the threat. Whilst the activities of the Aum Shinrikyo, the Rajneeshpuram cult and the Covenant, Sword, and Arm of the Lord, in acquiring and using CBW, indicate that there is a threat to society from religious cults, the main threat they present is still to the individual. Despite acknowledging that another incident similar to the Aum Shinrikyo's use of sarin is something that could quite possibly re-occur, cultwatchers in the UK still consider that it is the individual who is most at risk from these groups, and perceive them to represent a very small threat to national security. (34)

Aum Shinrikyo
Aum Shinrikyo has a pivotal importance in debates about NBC terrorism, because of its total indifference to human suffering, and because it moved terrorist activity in a new and more dangerous direction. Brian Jenkins argues that,

> Terrorism is imitative behaviour. A spectacular event
> invited repetition. The Tokyo attack has already had

an inspirational effect, as reflected in new threats and reports indicating that some terrorists may now at least be thinking about chemical weapons. The probability of a second event exceeds the probability of the first, but we have no gift of prophecy to state what that probability may be. Nor, despite increased attention of the possibility of chemical attack, can we be certain that authorities would be able to identify and thwart any new attack. It could come form any group resembling the Aum Shinrikyo, it could come from an entirely new direction. (35)

Yet Aum Shinrikyo began its existence like many other small, harmless religious cults and sects. After a troubled early life, its founder, Shoko Asahara, sought a spiritual meaning for the problems which were affecting his life. He turned to traditional Chinese medicine, fortune-telling, astrology and the writings of a new religion known as the God Light Association. But as he read more, he came across the writings of the scholars of 'Early Buddhism.' This was a more idealized form of Buddhism which differed from Zen Buddhism and traditional Buddhism, which is more popular in Japan and the West.

These writings were the foundations of the Aum Shinrikyo belief system. From studying these works, Asahara came to believe that everything in the world is sin. In 1985 he claimed to have been visited by the Hindu God Shiva, who appointed him 'the God of Light who leads the armies of the Gods,' and charged him with building an ideal society, called the Kingdom of Shambhala. This is an ancient concept appearing in Hinduism, Islam and Buddhism. Asahara adopted a Tantric Buddhist portrayal of the concept, which spoke of a hidden valley populated by spiritual adepts. According to this tradition, a messiah king will appear in Shambhala, defeat the infidels in war, and establish a universal reign of Buddhism.

This formed the basis of Asahara's belief that he was a messiah who would have a leadership role in the inevitable Armageddon. By 1989, he was arguing that the world was sliding towards an Armageddon, which might take the form of a nuclear war, towards the end of the century. By the 1990s Asahara's obsession with Armageddon was becoming the focal point of the Aum Shinrikyo belief system. But equally as significant was his stronger portrayal of an Armageddon in which atomic and CBWs would wipe out 90 per cent of Japan's population.

In some ways this fixation with a war of Armageddon specifically involving WMD makes the Aum Shinrikyo belief system different from many of the other cults which merely predict a general war of Armageddon. Whilst Aum Shinrikyo was not unique in espousing that belief, not all cults proffer such a clearly defined vision of Armageddon. What is significant is that the belief system of the cult provided clear indicators of what Asahara was planning, if only the Japanese security forces had matched Asahara's writings with the technical indicators of the Aum Shinrikyo CW programme which they had managed to gather. What this also indicates is that compared to traditional terrorist groups, religious cults can be more open about their intentions.

Less than four years after its leaders were arrested following the Tokyo subway attack, the Aum Shinrikyo began recruiting new members from Japan's disaffected youth, raising fears that economic recession has created an ideal breeding-ground for the cult. Moreover, according to security experts, it has raised billions of yen through commercial activities, and rebuilt much of its domestic and overseas network. This revival comes despite the fact that it was classified as a terrorist organization in the USA, and has been under police surveillance since 1995. In Japan there has long been a demand for a spiritual alternative to Japan's materialistic lifestyle. Now, however, in a period of record unemployment and rapid social change, social commentators fear that cults such as the Aum Shinrikyo may hold a powerful attraction for young people with uncertain prospects. (36)

Millenarianism and the resurgence of religious cults
The most dangerous religions are messianic ones which preach that man can hasten the coming of a prophesied messiah. They believe that the end of the world is coming because God has promised that it will, and that He will save the righteous or chosen ones. This is known as millenarianism or millennialism. Most religions are prepared to wait for these events to happen, but some fundamentalist religions attempt to hasten the event by stressing the significance of individual actions in shaping events. (37) The moment is important in millennialism, and for this reason violence may not be steady, but rather occasional, sudden and extreme. Former members of the Covenant, Sword, and Arm of the Lord, stated that

> We thought there were signs of Armageddon, and we
> believed that once those signs were there it was time
> for us to act, to make judgements against those who
> were doing wrong or who refused to repent. We felt
> you could kill those people, that God wanted us to kill
> those people. The original timetable was up to God,

> but God could use us in creating Armageddon. That
> if we stepped out things might be hurried along. You
> get tired of waiting for what you think God is plan-
> ning. (38)

However it must be remembered that not all millenarianism is violent. Cults have always existed within societies, but occasionally changes in economic, political and social conditions can create an environment in which cults become much more prevalent. Historically, they have tended to proliferate at times when the world is unstable and chaotic, perhaps undergoing rapid and painful change. Therefore there were upsurges of cult activity after the fall of Rome, during the English civil war, and during the French Revolution. Some of the cults which emerged at these times grew to become new religious movements such as the Mormons and Jehovah's Witnesses, whilst others faded into obscurity.

Living in an uncertain environment, people are forced to make fundamental adjustments to their way of life, and in the process can become disorientated, frightened, credulous and hysterical, as well as angry and bitter. When peoples' lives are in turmoil and subject to considerable uncertainty, charismatic cult leaders have been able to gather supporters by offering simple and attractive solutions to their problems. As a result, cults are constantly springing up, especially in states where poverty, ignorance and frustration within society are coupled with ineffective governments. These cults and extremist sects espouse a wide range of belief systems, which incorporate phenomena such as the resurrection of the dead; the second Coming of Jesus Christ, or their particular religious leader; a war of Armageddon; or the end of the world and the appearance of the Anti-Christ. (39)

These types of conditions have affected many states at different times, but since the fall of communism and the dissolution of the Soviet Union, Russia has exhibited all of the indicators required for an explosion of cult activity and millenarian beliefs. Since 1991 it has experienced a prolonged period of control by weak governments, which have implemented devastating political and economic changes without warning, and were themselves subject to sudden and dramatic change. This political uncertainty was exacerbated by widespread economic deprivation following the transformation to a market economy; the existence of widespread corruption; a breakdown in law enforcement; and endemic violence within society.

Russia is a deeply religious society where formal religion conceals hidden depths of superstition. It is a state with a long tradition of charismatic monks, mystic preachers, weird sects and utopian communities. After years of communist repression, mysticism and superstition underwent a renaissance after faith healers were allowed to appear on Russian television. But one of the most worrying cult trends in Russia has been the rise of anti-semitic propagandist groups, which reject the Jewish origins of christianity and espouse a violently racist and xenophobic ideology. (40)

Yet the Russian experience also demonstrates that the threat from cults should not be overstated. Russia has experienced very little cult-related terrorism. Aum had a large membership in Russia, which allegedly procured precursors and other equipment for the cult's CBW programme. Members of the Russian army's radiation, biological and chemical protection troops, together with influential political figures, were also alleged to have been members. (41) Yet there was no Aum Shinrikyo-related violence in Russia to coincide with its campaign in Japan.

Whilst cults can thrive in any state when the conditions are right, the single event which is most closely linked to the global growth of cult activity, is the millennium, which is deep rooted in the Judaeo-Christian tradition. Hints of it appear in the Old Testament, in the book of Daniel and Epoch, and in Psalm 90. It is spelled out in the Bible, in the Book of Revelations, Chapter 20. This predicts an apocalyptic war of Armageddon, in which the armies of God will come to earth and defeat the Anti-Christ and the armies of the kings who have turned against God. This will be followed by thousand-year period of blessedness associated with the Second Coming of Christ. After the thousand years are over Satan will return to earth, and the final battle between good and evil will take place, in which Satan will be defeated by the armies of God. After the battle, the Final Judgement will take place, in which everyone will be judged according to how they had lived their lives.

According to millennialists, the Bible states that 1000 years is a day, and since the world was in existence for 4000 years prior to Jesus' birth, the world is about to enter the seventh millennium. Before the start of the millennium, God will lift his chosen people up to heaven for a seven-year period during which he will wreak destruction on the rest of humanity. The chosen ones will then be returned to earth to be part of Jesus' 1000-year reign. (42) Consequently, millennial notions are a mixture of hope and fear. In the early church, where millenarian beliefs were strong, zealous Christians associated the millennium not only with joy and the coming of Christ, but also with apocalyptic warfare and terrifying events, a time of trial, judgement and reckoning.

As a result, the world experienced an explosion of cult activity towards the end of the twentieth century. In some states this was also a time of great uncertainty because of political and economic crisis, and the impending millennium merely reinforced the impact of other societal problems. This latest resurgence of cult activity, however, was fundamentally different from that which has occurred before, because of the sheer numbers of groups involved and their use of mind-control techniques, (43) which made it a much more threatening proposition. The millennium established a focus which enabled cults and other pseudo-religious figures to tap into the emotions of the disaffected, and attract 'lost' people, who were experiencing a spiritual vacuum. For some individuals, the millennium created a sense of impending crisis, which could potentially have exploded into mass hysteria or even violence. The problem was compounded by the fact, that the established churches did not know how to handle the millennium phenomenon. Many of the cults were waiting for the Second Coming, but if the Messiah did not turn up as expected, it was feared that the more volatile of these cults might take matters into their own hands, and initiate their own personal apocalyptic war of Armageddon through acts of terrorism.

Whilst most states were affected by the millennium phenomenon, the primary focus of cult activity was Israel, which was expecting the arrival of five million pilgrims for the millennium, including some of the most extreme religious cults. (44) Of particular concern was the security of the Temple Mount, known to Muslims as Haram-as-Sharif, or the Noble Sanctuary, within the Old City of Jerusalem. This is one of the most sensitive sites in the whole of the Middle East, because it is considered to be the site of the first and second Jewish temples, and is the location of the Dome of the Rock Mosque and the Al Aqsa mosque, which is Islam's third holiest site. Some Christian cults believe the destruction of the mosques will lead to the rebuilding of the Jewish temple, hastening the end of the world and the Second Coming. The Temple Mount is so sensitive a site that any assault upon it would be likely to trigger communal violence within Israel, undermining the Arab-Israeli peace process. Fears that Jewish or Christian extremists might attack the Mosques were realized in early 1999 when Israel deported two immigrants who were preparing just such an attack in order to precipitate Armageddon, (45) and the Israeli police were investigating a possible conspiracy by the Concerned Christians, from the US, to instigate a 'big provocation' on the Temple Mount aimed at sparking a war between Arabs and Jews that would culminate in the biblical Armageddon and final judgement (46) but in the event, the anticipated explosion of cult-related violence did not occur. To a great extent the threat was overstated anyway, because of the confusion over when the millennium actually falls. Whilst most people accept it to be the beginning of the year 2000, mathematically, the period of 1000 years actually falls at the beginning of the year 2001. And in any case, many groups work on their own timescales – one group called The Family is forecasting the end of the world in the year 2006 or 2007, (47) whilst Shoko Asahara variously predicted the years 1997, 1999, 2000 and 2003. (48) Therefore cult leaders are predisposed to pick any date they wish for Armageddon or the Second Coming. Consequently, threats from Millennial cults might reach a peak in the years 2000 and 2001, but the potential threat will not simply disappear as time passes.

Ian Haworth argues that it is not the date which is important anyway: 'If it [the cult] uses mind control techniques then it has control over the members and so the leader has control to start with. He doesn't need to persuade people to do this because it is the year 2000 or 2001 depending upon when you see the millennium start.' (49) Therefore it is the acceptance of the principle of Armageddon, coupled with the use of mind control, which creates the danger, not specific dates. In addition, a failed prophesy can also bind a group closer together. The leader works harder to erase his feelings of guilt for letting the group down, and slightly re-writes the prophecy. This can give the group new vigour as the modified message is put out. (50) Therefore violent cults will continue to emerge when their internal dynamics reach crisis point, as was proved by the murder and mass suicide of 780 members of The Movement for the Restoration of the Ten Commandments in Uganda, during March and April 2000. (51)

Religious cults and NBC weapons
It is a commonly held belief that an NBC attack will probably not come from a typical terrorist group, but it is more likely to emanate from a group who have placed themselves above conventional morality. The RAND Corporation in the US, have stated that

> Terrorist groups with more millennial aims, as opposed to those operating on behalf of concrete political programmes, may be less constrained in their actions and hence more willing to cause or risk mass casualties. These more fanatical and extreme terrorist groups tend to hold apocalyptic views, devoid of specific political content and seek the creation of new and continuing disasters as the precondition for the emergence of a new heavenly order on earth. (52)

The lack of violence over the millennium indicated that the potential threat of any form of overt violence from cults is very small. Yet since the 1970s there have been three cases of religious cults intending or attempting to use CBW in pursuit of their goals – the Rajneeshpuram Cult, the Covenant, Sword, and Arm of the Lord and the Aum Shinrikyo. The significance of these cases lies not in their small number, but the fact that two of them were intent upon perpetrating acts of indiscriminate mass destruction. Therefore they rank amongst the most serious of the previous incidents of NBC terrorism.

The overriding religious belief in Armageddon establishes a strong motive for some cults to use NBC weapons, but unlike other terrorist groups their belief systems can incorporate no incentives to be discriminate in choosing their targets. In believing that the righteous (specifically themselves) will be saved from destruction, or will receive redemption, they are defining the whole of society as a target. Therefore, once a group decides to lash out, it could impose no limits on its violence, and might use whatever weapons it has at its disposal. Cults are also unique because many of them do not operate under any of the other practical or moral constraints which can inhibit other types of terrorist groups. They have no constituency apart from themselves, and neither are they in a bargaining relationship with the authorities, because they want nothing more than the destruction of existing society. (53)

The other crucial factors in assessing the potential threat from religious cults are that many of them are capable of funding the research and development of NBC weapons, because of the great wealth that they acquire from their membership. In addition, because they actively go out and recruit members, a leader intent upon committing acts of NBC terrorism could specifically target the kinds of people who possess the skills required to develop NBC weapons. Once part of the cult, the use of mind control would force these engineers to put their skills to the task of developing NBC weapons. Therefore it is possible to argue that cults are more likely than other types of terrorist groups to recruit individuals who possess the skills required to develop NBC weapons.

This mixture of motivations and potential capabilities places religious cults at the forefront of concern about NBC terrorism. Previous incidents indicate that if a cult intends to lash out violently, it will use NBC weapons if it can acquire them, although the Rajneeshpuram cult's choice of salmonella, rather than the typhoid which it also had access to, demonstrates that some cults are willing to place constraints on their violence, depending upon their goals and sense of morality. However not all cults are interested in violence and of those that are, most will implode. Therefore, whilst they represent a very small danger, they are amongst the most extreme threats.

The Christian right wing

One of the features of the post-Cold War world has been the growth of the extreme right wing. In Europe, this has mainly consisted of a disparate collection of small secular groups with no coherent programme of violence to achieve their political goals. The most dangerous developments in the far right, however, have originated in the USA, with the growth of a wide diversity of Christian orientated groups, such as the Ku Klux Klan (KKK), Aryan Nations, Aryan Brotherhood, the US Nazi party, and citizens militias. The KKK were the original terrorist group to organize white racism in the USA. For over 100 years they have indulged in violent acts of terror in the name of white supremacy. The KKK believe in positive hate and positive racism, and argue that the white race should be separated from people of colour. Modern day followers of Klan-style groups frequently engage in acts of indiscriminate terror similar to those which the Klan have engaged in since 1860. The threat has also increased significantly, because the Klan are no longer isolated to one state in the South but have joined a larger white supremacy movement. By 1999, these organizations were operating in 44 out of the 50 states in the USA. Whilst they share many of the same traits as secular European groups, US groups differ from most of them, in that scripture and religious edicts underpin their belief system. They also tend to be more revolutionary than the 'old' forms of right-wing terrorism which were mainly authoritarian and counter-revolutionary, in their focus on anti-communism and immigration. This means that they are directly confrontational with the state, whereas the old right-wing terrorism tended to target only the state when it came to the aid of its victims. (54) This has resulted in escalating levels of violence in the USA, where the number of white supremacists has grown by 20 per cent since 1989, and has been matched by an increase in the number of hate crimes.

The Christian Identity movement

Whilst the different groups comprising the US far right advocate a broad mix of paranoid, seditious and racist beliefs, the common thread between many of them is a religious movement called Christian Identity. Because of this, there is a close interrelationship between some of these groups and religious cults. Originating in England in the eighteenth century, Christian Identity contends that Christ was an Aryan; as were the ten lost tribes of Israel, which had migrated to Europe and the UK. The settling of America by the British is interpreted as the fulfilment of a directive by God to create a promised land, where Jesus Christ will make his Second Coming. It is a strongly racist religion, preaching that the Jewish people are the seed of Satan; that people of colour have no souls; and that the white race is superior to all others, in being God's 'chosen people.' Consequently, they do not consider the non-white races to be really human.

Christian Identity teachings are the basis for the millenarian imperatives and apocalyptic visions, which influence many right-wing groups in the USA. They preach that there will a day of reckoning as predicted in the Book of Revelations, which will take the form of a race war, between the 'Godly' Aryans and the Satanic people of colour and Jews. Therefore, followers of Christian Identity perceive themselves to be the righteous, in a perpetual struggle with the forces of evil, who control government and society. (55) These beliefs are particularly strong amongst the advocates of Dominion theology, which is the latest re-interpretation of Christian Identity. As well as being anti-semitic and racist they argue that it is incumbent upon each individual to hasten redemption, by actively working to ensure the return of the messiah. By accelerating the inevitable apocalypse, the tribulations which currently afflict the white race will end, ushering in a period of 1000-year rule by Christians, at the end of which Christ will return to earth. (56) To this end, many of them welcome the prospect of a future nuclear war.

By the late 1970s, Christian Identity churches had sprung up across the USA. They provided support for the more orthodox groups such as the KKK and secular neo-Nazis, as part of a process of taking over the leadership of America's far right . They also attempted to establish a greater degree of cohesion between the disparate groups by inviting members of right-wing organizations to Identity events, and subsequently maintaining these contacts in preparation for the coming 'revolution.' (57)

The two key figures in the Christian Identity movement were William Gale, who went on to found the violent anti-state groups, Posse Comitatus (Power of the County) and Committee of the States, which were forerunners of the militia movement; and Richard Butler who transformed one of the original churches into the Aryan Nations and its military wing – the Order. This group is at the nexus between Christian Identity, Christian patriotism and the militia movement. It presents itself as the embodiment of the ongoing work of Jesus Christ to re-gather his people, preserve the white race and bring about the creation of His kingdom on earth. According to Aryan Nations, only the white race descends from Adam, and there are literal children of Satan in the world who are the result of Eve's original sin. (58) These developments paved the way for the continuing wave of right- wing violence, which originated in the 1980s. (59) There are two distinct but closely interlinked strands to this violence: opposition to the federal government and racism.

Christian Identity racism and anti-federalists.
The cornerstone of anti-federalism is the principle that the US government, the financial centre in New York, and the media are controlled by Jews. This is referred to as the Zionist occupation government (ZOG), which the right wing claim is usurping the rights of US citizens. The eventual goal of the ZOG is perceived to be the establishment of a new world order, using the UN and other international organizations, which will operate for the benefit of international banking interests, the Jews, Freemasons and other 'dark forces'. Consequently, these groups do not believe in any form of government above the local level; opposing federal income taxes and the federal judiciary.

Evidence of this alleged conspiracy was identified in two seminal events, which presaged the upsurge of the far right, and led directly to the Oklahoma City bombing. (60) At Ruby Ridge in October 1982, a Christian Identity activist, Randy Weaver, saw his wife and young son killed in a shoot-out with federal marshals. The movement swore that its members would not be left to the mercy of the authorities again, and the militia movement was created as an instrument for self-defence. At Waco from March to April 1993, the Alcohol, Tobacco, and Firearms Bureau (ATF) and the FBI laid siege to the compound of the Branch Davidian cult led by David Koresh, following a botched raid to seize a cache of guns. The siege ended with an assault, during which a fire broke out in the main building, killing 75 cult members, including Koresh and 25 children.

For a small minority of Americans the Branch Davidians were martyrs, and the federal government was perceived to be undermining the constitutional and religious rights of ordinary citizens. Christian Identity activists caught a mood amongst many Americans who were revolted by the actions of the ATF and FBI, as well as those who opposed gun controls, and many others who merely shared a general distaste for the federal government and the perceived new world order. (61) Therefore, the militia movement attracted many people, including non-whites, who did not necessarily share Christian Identity goals, but were attracted by the militia's eclectic combination of traditional right-wing fears of an elitist cabal, strong anti-communism, a Protestant work ethic, a strongly millenarian view of history and other core American values such as patriotism. (62) This made the movement attractive to a wide number of people, with the result that by 1995, it had grown so strong that it had moved to a position of influence on the fringe of the Republican party and the mainstream American right. Yet it also enabled the movement to become a link between Christian Identity and broader society and a mechanism to introduce people to more radical ideas. Christian Identity activists amongst the militia's leaders sought out individuals from amongst their ranks, who they recruited into terrorist cells.

The belief system of these groups is fuelled by rumours and paranoia concerning the alleged activities of the ZOG. As one example, the Aryan Nations identify the Federal Emergence Management Agency (FEMA) as the organ through which the federal government would usurp political power and deprive US citizens of their constitutional rights. FEMA is the body which is tasked to take control in any security emergency that might confront the federal government. The Aryan Nations argue that 'Under FEMA, the Executive Orders which are already written and is the current law of the land, calls for the COMPLETE suspension of the United States constitution, all rights and liberties, as they are currently known.' It claims that FEMA has already established internment camps which will be brought into use during a federal government-inspired national emergency in which over one million Americans who would oppose the new world order will be rounded up. (63)

The linkage between opposition to the federal government, racism, and Christian Identity theology, lies in their belief that the federal government and the New World Order have made the eradication of the white race and its culture one of their foremost objectives. (64) Consequently, another goal of Christian Identity is the creation of a national state where the white race can preserve its culture and live out its destiny. To this end, it considers that the use of terrorism against the ZOG will be the prelude to a racial war of Armageddon, which will result in the establishment of Christ's kingdom on earth. (65)

Using scriptures to justify the principle of white separatism, the Reverend Roy Masker of the Aryan Nations states that his members 'are in disobedience to our Father and God, Yahweh, for allowing the Nation he gave us to become the mongrelized cesspool in which we now find ourselves ... Indeed it is incumbent upon us to BUILD A NEW, ALL-WHITE NATION! We are under command to do so! All scripture demands it.' (66) Whilst some individuals and groups espouse the complete religious and racial purification of the USA, others such as Richard Butler, the founder of the Aryan Nations, favour the 10 per cent solution, in which the North West corner of the USA would be set aside for whites.

Rather than using constitutional means to achieve these goals, Aryan Nations' promotional literature proclaims its desire to 'make clear to ourselves and our enemies what we intend to do: We will have a national racial state at whatever price in blood is necessary.' (67) What this might actually mean in practice was spelled out by Robert Matthews, the deceased leader of the Order, who once declared that in order to prevent the white race being overrun by immigrants, all Jews, Blacks, Hispanics, and other 'mud people' along with white 'race traitors' must be exterminated in 'a racial war of Armageddon.' (68) indicating that at least some elements in the US right wing harbour genocidal fantasies.

Christian Identity has also been linked to a shadowy, hard core, ideological group called the Phineas Priesthood. These are the self-appointed terrorists of the movement, claiming to have been appointed by God. The Phineas priest is mentioned in the Bible, and praised for the killing of an intertribal (or mixed-race) couple. In the scriptures, God promises that the Phineas priesthood would live on. Their self-appointed mission to impose God's law on earth includes the enforcement of prohibitions on interracial marriage, homosexuality and abortion, and an end to the federal banking system. (69) In the late 1990s, the FBI began to identify signs of the Phineas priesthood on documents found at the scenes of terrorist acts.

The development of a terrorist organization
Despite many years of preparation to fight the final conflict, groups linked to Christian Identity did not turn to terrorism until 1983, when the Order, along with other groups, began to lay the foundations for a terror campaign by accumulating weapons and cash. This first campaign of violence failed because they chose to build popular support by creating permanent survivalist camps, which were located and monitored by the FBI. Attempts to create a national network of groups rather than allow clandestine cells to operate independently, left a trail of written and telephone communications that compromised the movement, enabling the FBI to infiltrate the groups. (70)

According to the authorities, right-wing groups have already laid plans for a massive assault on the federal government. A federal grand jury indictment, stated that plans were announced at the Hadyn Lake meeting in the 1980s, for the violent overthrow of the federal government, and the creation of a separate Aryan nation within the USA. The indictment charged that the white supremacists planned to 'carry out assassinations of federal officers, politicians, and Jews as well as bombings and polluting municipal water supplies.' (71)

Many of the strategies and tactics of the far right are derived from traditional guerrilla and terrorist doctrines. The militia of Montana's blueprint for battle planned to paralyse America's economy and transport system; assassinate leading personalities in sport and the arts for propaganda; eliminate spies and traitorous government officials; and generally ferment 'an air of nervousness, discredit, insecurity, uncertainty, and concern on the part of the government.' One of their main tactics has been to target federal buildings. In 1996 federal officers prevented a bombing campaign by the Arizona-based Viper militia, which had intended to attack federal buildings such as the offices of the FBI, the Internal Revenue Service, the Secret Service, National Guard, and police departments. That same year a group linked to the West Virginian Mountain militia was arrested on charges of plotting to attack a new FBI fingerprint centre.

The Oklahoma City bombing was an unequivocal sign of these strategies being put into practice. It was also a watershed in the campaign against the federal government, because for the first time it signalled a willingness to perpetrate acts of indiscriminate mass killing. Since the bombing, domestic terrorism in the USA has increased, although without reaching the level of violence witnessed in Oklahoma. It also represented a watershed in the fortunes of the Christian Identity movement, which has since come under greater scrutiny by federal law enforcement agencies. It prompted many members of right- wing groups to re-assess their beliefs and actions, with some leaving the movement.

Not all of these groups are the same, however. Only some of them are violent, and even these are not universally dangerous or effective. Others are largely inactive in their wait for the messiah, contenting themselves with training and disseminating hate mail and propaganda. In addition, they can also go through phases of activity and inactivity depending upon the moment, (72) and in their quiet phases tend to withdraw from society. Even the groups that are disposed towards terrorism have not undertaken a coherent plan of violence, despite the plans and the rhetoric. Oklahoma was not part of a systematic campaign, and in general these groups have not sought to cause mass casualties, but have mostly killed only small numbers. (73).

The global far-right movement
There are numerous links between far-right groups in different countries, and this has led to the transmission of some of these religious beliefs and ideas from the USA, to groups in other

countries. There are close links between right-wing groups in the USA and German neo-Nazis, who share a common hatred of their governments, and a belief that the rights of white men are being infringed by multi-cultural societies. Similarly, in the UK, a number of extreme right-wing splinter groups have begun to adopt the pseudo-millennial, anti-Zionist philosophies of the American far right.

In April 1999 the UK experienced an escalation in right-wing violence when three nail bombs exploded in areas of London at the heart of the Black, Asian and gay communities. The perpetrator was working alone, but was a member of the far right groups, the British National Party (BNP) and the National Socialist Movement. He was also an adherent of the anti-semitic Kingdom Identity Ministries in the USA. (74). His favourite book was the *Turner Diaries*, and he had hoped that the bombs would trigger a race war in the UK. His arrest brought an end to the attacks, but they were a portent of a possible change within the far right in the UK, which has previously confined itself to unstructured street thuggery and which is so infiltrated by the security services and other watchdog groups that its ability to function covertly is severely restricted.

The far right in the UK had been in decline since its heyday in the 1970s when the National Front (NF) threatened to achieve electoral success. The party split in a bitter division which saw the emergence of the BNP and the National Democrats. Since then it has been riven by fundamental disagreements over its core tactics: the bullet or the ballot box. Phil Andrews, a former NF Political Soldier, stated that, 'There were always elements from the grass roots who wanted us to move towards terrorism, but these demands were always resisted by the leadership ... It wasn't that they necessarily had any moral problems with it, more that they were worried the tactic would backfire.' They were also made extremely paranoid by the infiltration of the movement, and distrusted anyone proposing a campaign of terrorism as being a potential agent provocateur. (75).

The BNP, which by the 1990s was the dominant group on the far right, focuses on electoral politics, attempting to broaden its support base outside of the disadvantaged inner cities. But the dispute over tactics led to the emergence of a number of radical splinter groups, such as Combat-18 (C-18), and the White Wolves which comprised a hard core of fundamentalists who are disillusioned with the other far-right groups.

In 1996, the far right conducted a letter-bomb campaign against British celebrities in mixed-race marriages, as well as leaders of some far right groups including C-18. (76). But it was not until the 1999 nail bomb campaign that the rhetoric of the far right finally threatened to be matched by a cohesive campaign of structured terrorism. However, it did not trigger a wider wave of terrorism. C-18 in particular, was paralysed during the 1990s by an internal power struggle for control of profits from the neo-Nazi music industry. (77). It became a diffuse organization with no defined membership (in 1999 police sources put its hard core activists at about 30, with perhaps several hundred active supporters). (78). It has been so heavily infiltrated that most of its members' identities are known to the law enforcement agencies, and the Security Service MI-5 has been successful in breaking up its activities.

The burgeoning pseudo-millennial rhetoric of some of these groups was evident from a statement issued by the White Wolves, which falsely claimed responsibility for the 1999 nail bombs. It stated that, 'Notice is hereby given that all non-whites (defined by blood, not religion) must permanently leave the British Isles before the year is out. Jews and Non-whites who remain after 1999 has ended will be exterminated when the clock strikes midnight on 31/12/99.' (79). In common with US groups, an internal White Wolves document outlines the core of their strategy as being to start a race war:

> Our main line of attack must be the immigrants themselves. If this is done regularly, effectively and brutally, the aliens will respond by attacking whites at random, forcing them off the fence and into self-defence ...The race war is not about to happen so we must start it ourselves. Sophisticated weaponry is not necessary to start the ball rolling ... Anything which stirs the racial pot is justified. (80).

However these groups have yet to prove that they are capable of sustaining a campaign of violence sufficient to achieve these goals.

The far right and NBC weapons
Whilst groups belonging to the Christian right wing have never previously used NBC weapons, they appear to have the motivation to use them, because their religious leaders preach violence to be a divine duty that is executed in direct response to a theological imperative. Their belief in an impending apocalyptic war in which their enemies will be destroyed, leaving them to fulfil their objective of creating a new white state as God's kingdom on Earth, establishes a powerful religious imperative to conduct terrorist attacks involving mass casualties. To this end, many of them are learning practical survivalist skills, with some even

making shelters to protect themselves from NBC weapons. Their objective of initiating a race war, or war against the federal government and its allies in the New World Order, would certainly result in mass casualties. Therefore they constantly proclaim their willingness to initiate events which could potentially lead to thousands being killed. Whilst that is not the same as killing thousands in a single incident, the theological underpinning of their belief system will make it easier for them to engage in mass-casualty attacks.

Yet these groups have not shown much of an interest in causing mass casualties. Of the previous incidents of NBC terrorism involving right-wing groups, most appear to have involved discriminate targets, although the militia of Montana was alleged to have been trying to recruit the guards at the Rocky Flats nuclear facility, where large quantities of weapons- grade plutonium are stored. (81). Instead, their strategies are more diverse, and have primarily focused on acts of controlled violence. One of their primary tactics for initiating the war with the federal government is to attack federal buildings. Conventional weapons are more suited to these roles, although NBC weapons are also capable of being used in such a controlled fashion. Oklahoma-style attacks are possible using CBW, if access can be gained to the building. If these groups are interested in attacking specific, well-guarded facilities, CBW released into air conditioning or water supplies, could even be the most effective way for them to carry out an attack. Therefore, if these groups are seriously interested in procuring NBC weapons, it is not necessarily the case that they would use them in indiscriminate attacks. The use of NBC weapons in these roles could also be perceived to confer prestige on the groups, and provide the qualitative escalation which they might consider necessary to start the race war.

The Aryan Nations leadership has strongly refuted federal government allegations that its members are developing BW, and would use them. They consider that President Clinton's anti-WMD terrorism programme is actually part of a broader conspiracy by the federal government to destroy their movement. The Aryan Nations website states that: 'Aryan Nations here charges the US government, et al, for conspiracy in setting up Aryan Nations for a "fall guy" in a government orchestrated (or otherwise) attack against the USA – with anthrax.' It fears that the federal government would use an attack as a justification for clamping down on the movement 'Waco-style', as part of the federal government's war against the white race.

Individuals such as Thomas Lavy and Larry Wayne Harris have proved that some of these US groups could develop CBW if they wanted to. (See Appendix for details) But their compatriots in the UK do not present the same level of threat because the technical skills of their membership are poor. The nail bombs used in 1999 were crude, and it will be many years before they can develop even sophisticated conventional bombs. In addition, the extremely narrow popular base of these groups, comprising predominantly of under-educated individuals, suggests that they might find it difficult to attract individuals with the skills required to develop NBC weapons. The question of most concern with respect to the UK far right is the level of assistance they might receive from the USA.

General strategic motivations to use NBC weapons
Despite the apparently stronger political motivations of religious orientated groups to use NBC weapons, it would be unwise to rigidly differentiate between groups that are predominantly religious in character, and those that are predominantly and secular in nature. Some secular groups have goals which are as revolutionary as the goals of these predominantly religious groups, and could therefore be subject to similar motivations to use NBC weapons. In an interview, the sole surviving Japanese Red Army Terrorist who took part in the 1972 Lod airport massacre in Israel, in which 26 people were killed and 80 wounded, indicated that:

> Because he foresees total overthrow of the existing arrangements of society, he does not feel bound in any way by the moral values of the present world....(but) he is not really certain of what society will be like after the revolution has occurred. This uncertainty about what will come after the all-important revolution requires that he suspend judgement about revolutionary methods. Since his revolution is not being fought in the name of any specific values, there are no constraints on how it may be fought.
>
> (82).

Within secular terrorist groups there will also generally exist individuals or factions who are prepared to commit the most extreme acts within their capacity. In many cases these elements are kept under control by a less extreme leadership, but occasionally they can gain control of the group, or break away to pursue their own campaign of violence. One incident which particularly illustrates the danger of NBC terrorism posed by such splinter groups and rogue elements was the 1998 bombing of the town of Omagh in Northern Ireland. An IRA splinter group known as the Real IRA planted a bomb in the town centre, which exploded in the middle of the day, killing 28 people. What was significant about the attack was not only that the IRA itself had previously moved away from indiscriminate bombings, resulting in civilian casualties, but that Omagh has a mixed population of Protestants and Catholics, and therefore an indiscriminate attack would kill a number of Catholics who are the constituency of the Real IRA. They could have chosen to conduct the attack in another town which was predominantly Protestant, but chose not to.

This radical change of tactics on the part of the Real IRA was driven by the burgeoning peace process in which Sinn Fein, the political wing of the IRA, had secured a ceasefire from the IRA and were actively seeking compromise with their Unionist enemies, and the governments of Eire and the UK. The Real IRA comprised a core of IRA hardliners who wanted to continue the war to secure the unconditional acceptance of all Republican goals. Their marginalization within the Republican movement, coupled with growing public support for the peace process, meant that they could build support for their position only by derailing the peace process. This combination of factors led them to consider that only an extreme act of violence would suffice to turn the tide of opinion.

This case raises questions about individuals and splinter groups within other groups, who might be willing to accept extremely high levels of indiscriminate casualties in planning attacks against specific targets. As has been stated earlier, the perpetrators of the US embassy bombing in Kenya, were willing to accept the risk that some African Muslims might be accidentally killed in the blast. It is perhaps these individuals and groups, often driven by the specific political and strategic context at any given time, which pose the greatest threat in terms of NBC terrorism, because they will operate under fewer moral and intellectual constraints. This might help to account for some of the instances where secular groups have been linked to NBC plots, although these individuals and splinter groups might not have the resources and capability to develop NBC weapons. For instance, the Continuity IRA and Real IRA in Northern Ireland did not have access to the majority of the IRA' s weapon stockpiles. But individuals such as Larry Wayne Harris, Adam Busby and William Levitt Jr (see Annex) have demonstrated the capacity of individuals to develop or acquire chemical agents and biological pathogens which could have been used as contaminants. Therefore, whilst technical difficulties might be heightened for this category of groups, they will not necessarily be prohibitive.

Even if disagreements over strategy do not lead to the break-up of a group, divisions and rivalries are capable of leading to escalation as each faction competes for control, and this could conceivably lead to the use of NBC weapons. There have been examples of this phenomenon at the conventional level, such as in Lebanon, where the Muslim militia Amal, and Hezbollah, sought to outdo each other with suicide bombings. (83) The less cohesive a group, the more this is likely to occur.

What these cases suggest is that at certain times, even predominantly secular groups may perceive politico-strategic incentives to use NBC weapons. Konrad Kellen argues that the specific tactics which a terrorist group will employ also depend upon the strategic situation in which the group finds itself. (84). Groups that consider themselves to be on the defensive or under threat of extinction are willing to undertake more extreme or riskier attacks than groups on the offensive, which might be deterred from riskier types of attack. This phenomenon can be applied to all types of terrorist groups, and has already been apparent in the history of a number of groups. (85) This also links in with the observation that terrorists might resort to escalation when they perceive that other tactics have failed. There is some evidence of this at the conventional level, although it mainly leads to a shift between different strategies and tactics.

Palestinian violence reached its height in the years 1972–73, when the PLO found itself isolated amongst the international community and shunned by many Arab states following its expulsion from Jordan. Similarly, the Omagh bombing was a direct result of the marginalization of the IRA hardliners by the Northern Ireland peace process, which put them on the defensive. These arguments would seem to apply particularly to Islamic fundamentalist groups, which perceive themselves to be on the defensive in their conflict with the West and the USA. (86). Therefore this might be a factor in the higher lethality of Islamic fundamentalist attacks. When the secular PLO engaged in the Middle East peace process, the Islamist group Hamas was put on the defensive and responded with a series of indiscriminate suicide bombings against Israeli civilian targets, in an effort to derail the process.

Kellen argues that these groups will go further, and escalate the level of violence that they employ, more than those groups which consider their campaigns to be succeeding. (87). But most terrorists generally operate below their potential capacity for violence, and retain considerable capacity for escalation below the NBC-WMD threshold. Any group considering escalation will most likely look at the conventional options for escalation first, especially if technical factors make the acquisition of NBC weapons difficult. But in certain situations where a group's capacity for escalation through conventional forms of violence might be limited by technical, strategic or tactical factors, NBC weapons might offer better options for escalation, despite being less accessible.

Analysis of incidents from the past record of NBC terrorism does not unequivocally prove Kellen's conclusions. 1977 witnessed the height of the terrorist campaign by the left wing in West Germany, and partial explanations for the occasional RAF (Baader Meinhof gang) interest in CBW during the 1970s and 1980s could be sought in their steady decline from that time. Whilst several of the alleged threats preceded this high point, there is no publicly available corroborating evidence that they constituted anything more than threat or hearsay. However, the most serious of the incidents – the discovery of a bathtub full of botulinum in a safe house –occurred in the 1980s when their campaign of violence was in decline. In contrast, the sporadic interest of secular, racist far-right groups in developing CBW from the 1970s through to the 1990s is probably better explained by their racist motivations, rather than their general strategic situation, which is invariably poor in the majority of states which suffer from this form of violence. At first sight, the various Aum Shinrikyo attacks seem to support Kellen's hypothesis. Asahara ordered the major attacks because the authorities were closing in on the cult, and he feared that police and legal investigations would destroy it. Yet Aum Shinrikyo was always intending to unleash its CW because of its belief system, the police investigations merely brought forward the date of the Tokyo attack. What this indicates is that at least in a tactical sense, being on the defensive can influence the timing and targets of any attack.

Conclusion
This analysis indicates that all types of terrorist group can be subject to political and strategic motivations to use NBC weapons, although it appears that groups which are predominantly religious in nature, generally have stronger motivations than their secular counterparts, because they identify a more open-ended range of targets. In conjunction with this fact, they can also be less willing to compromise on their objectives than secular groups such as the PLO and IRA, whose campaigns of violence eventually led to a change of approach to seek their goals through dialogue and diplomacy, which by its nature has required compromises. It is also evident that some groups may experience strong motivations to use NBC weapons only when they are faced with specific politico-strategic situations. Therefore for all types of groups, the balance between politico-

strategic motivations and disincentives to using NBC weapons is constantly shifting, and can potentially lead to heightened risks at different times.

Yet despite the dogmatic nature of their objectives, religious motivations to use NBC weapons are not overwhelmingly strong or universal. Some predominantly religious groups pursue limited political goals, particularly in the short and medium term, and the strategies of most groups incorporate a wide range of tactics. Whilst some might consider undertaking indiscriminate mass-casualty attacks, for most, they are typical of only part of a wider strategy, rather than the sole tactic. In addition, the influence of political and strategic disincentives could also limit how and where NBC weapons would be used. Therefore, even when groups experience strong motivations to use NBC weapons, their use in discriminate attacks might be the preferred tactical option. Only some religious cults have an overriding imperative to use WMD for indiscriminate attacks, but these cults will always be very few in number at any given time. For the majority of other types of groups there are strong incentives to limit tactics and weapons in pursuit of limited goals. In general it is always the extremists from any type of group who espouse the apocalyptic or genocidal objectives which establish strong motivations to use WMD for indiscriminate attacks.

Notes and references

1. The term 'Islamist' is a generic term for a politically active Muslim who seeks to right the wrongs of a wayward society and government. The range of Islamism is broad, extending from protest within the system, to a violent rejection of it.
2. Reuven Paz, 'Is There an Islamic Terrorism?,' International Policy Institute for Counter Terrorism, internet site: <http://www.ict.org.il/articles/isl-terr.htm> (7 September 1998)
3. Amir Taheri, *Holy Terror: The Inside Story of Islamic Terrorism* (London: Hutchinson, 1987) p 192
4. Bruce Hoffman, *Inside Terrorism*, (London: Indigo, 1998) p 96
5. Hoffman: *Inside Terrorism*, p 97
6. Ely Karmon, 'Bin Laden Is Out To Get America!,' The International Policy Institute For Counter-Terrorism, internet site: <http://www.ict.org.il/articles/isl-terr.htm> (1998)
7. Hala Jaber, *Hezbollah: Born With A Vengeance* (London: Fourth Estate, 1997) pp 70–71
8. Taheri: *Holy Terror*, p 191
9. Jaber: *Hezbollah*, p 209
10. Ibrahim A Karawan, 'The Islamist Impasse,' *Adelphi Paper* 341, The International Institute for Strategic Studies (London: Oxford University Press, 1997) pp 7–20
11. Paz: 'Is There an Islamic Terrorism?'

12. Gavin Cameron, *Nuclear Terrorism* (Basingstoke: MacMillan, 1999) p 139

13. Taheri: *Holy Terror*, p 191

14. Interview, name withheld by request (23 March 1999)

15. *Qur'an*, 2:190

16. 'Refugee Calls For Biological Weapons Against the West,' Metro (London) (6 September 1999)

17. Hoffman: *Inside Terrorism*, p 96

18. Hoffman: *Inside Terrorism*, p 98

19. Hoffman: *Inside Terrorism*, p 98

20. James Adams, *The New Spies: Exploring the Frontiers of Espionage* (London: Hutchinson, 1994) p 175

21. Yael Shahar, 'Osama bin Laden: Marketing Terrorism,' The International Policy Institute For Counter-Terrorism, internet site: <http://www.ict.org.il/articles/isl-terr.htm> (7 September 1998)

22. 'Terror Leader Plots Attacks on British Targets,' *Sunday Times* (7 February 1999)

23. 'Bomb Plot Tip-Offs Fuel Airline Safety Fears,' *Observer* (15 August 1999)

24. Osama bin Laden, quoted in *Daily Telegraph* (26 December 1998)

25. In the USA, the Moonies gave money to US President Nixon's election campaign, in an attempt to influence US policy on the Republic of Korea; in Japan, the Soka Gakkai cult is a powerful political actor whose philosophy is to take over the world, and some of its members have been elected to the Japanese parliament. Aum Shinrikyo had members in the bureaucracy, judiciary, and the military. David Kaplan and Andrew Marshall, *The Cult at the End of the World* (New York: Crown Publishers, 1996) pp 47, 187. In China, the Falun Gong has members who are government officials.

26. Interview with Ian Haworth, Founder of the Cult Information Centre (1 October 1999)

27. Many of Charles Manson's devotees seem to have suffered from emotional or even psychological problems even before entering the cult. Many were drop outs, often from broken homes, see Vincent Bugliosi with Curt Gentry, *Helter Skelter: The Shocking Story of the Manson Murders* (London: Arrow, 1992) pp 403, 182. Bugliosi, the Chief Prosecutor, felt that most of Manson's devotees were weak and easily led.

28. Interview with Ian Haworth, Founder of the Cult Information Centre (1 October 1999)

29. Kaplan and Marshall: *The Cult at the End of the World*, p 74

30. Interview with Mr Ian Haworth, Founder of the Cult Information Centre (1 October 1999)

31. In May 1999, China experienced an unexpected demonstration by 15,000 members of the Falun Gong sect outside the compound of the communist party leadership in Peking. Headed by Li Hongzhi who is exiled in the USA, the sect has millions of members and preaches salvation from an immoral world on the brink of destruction. China has a long history of instability caused by religious cults such as the Taiping and Boxer rebellions, and responded by arresting key leaders and destroying its literature. 'Beijing Steps Up Security After Protest by Sect',

The Times (3 May 1999); 'Thousands Protest At Swoop On Chinese Sect',
The Daily Telegraph (22 July 1999); China Seeks Cult Leader's Arrest,'
The Times (30 July 1999)

32. Jessica Stern, *The Ultimate Terrorists* (Cambridge Ma: Harvard
University, 1999) p 72

33. Andrew Hubback, 'Apocalypse When? The Global Threat of Religious
Cults,' *Conflict Studies* 300, Research Institute For the Study of Conflict
and Terrorism (June 1997) p 21

34. Interviews with Ian Haworth (1 October 1999), and Alan Meale MP,
former Secretary of the House of Commons All-Party Committee on
Religious Cults (14 April 1999)

35. Brian Jenkins, 'Foreword,' in D.W.Brackett, *Holy Terror,
Armageddon in Tokyo* (New York: Weatherhill, 1996) p xi

36. *Guardian* (13 October 1998)

37. Cameron: *Nuclear Terrorism*, p 92

38. Stern: *The Ultimate Terrorists*, p 72

39. In the early Middle Ages when millenarian emotions simmered it
took little to stampede huge crowd movements. One such event was set
in motion by the preaching of the first crusade at the end of the eleventh
century. The idea of liberating the holy city of Jerusalem and the
Sepulchre of Christ from the infidel Turks had a millenarian tone about
it, especially as the Pope promised complete absolution of sins for all
who took part. So long before regular armies were formed to march to
the Holy Land, mobs of townsfolk and peasants moved in what they
believed to be the direction of Jerusalem. But unable to get their hands
on the Turks, they attacked the Jewish communities of the Rhineland
and elsewhere, murdering merchants and money lenders and stealing
their cash.

Throughout the Middle Ages and the Renaissance, and right into the
Reformation in the sixteenth century, rogue monks or unscrupulous
charismatic friars could easily persuade credulous mobs to form and go
on the rampage. Some of them prophesied that the millennium was a
time when all property, including wives and daughters, would be held in
common. Consequently, millennium mobs sometimes took over entire
towns indulged in looting and rape. In 1534, Anabaptist extremists
seized the German town of Munster and established a millenarian kingdom under a fanatic called John of Leyden. He claimed direct inspira-
tion from God and set up an egalitarian, polygamous city state. As usually happens with millenarian societies, the experiment degenerated into
terror and mass executions. After a year of horror the town was taken
back by the local bishop who had the 'king' publicly tortured to death
with red hot irons. Munster's experiences were a foretaste of what was
to happen when the millenarian idea was secularized and political ideo-
logues began to imagine perfect societies that would last forever.

In practice, the Munster horror was repeated on an enormous scale. A
recent authoritative calculation puts the number of victims of Marxist
communism at about 100 million, 60 million of them in China, where
the millenarian experiment continues. The term 'a thousand years' was
not used by Marx, Lenin or Stalin, although Ceaucescu of Romania,
claimed that he was building a new state for 'many centuries, ten or
more'. Mussolini founded the Fascist movement, inspired by the 'thou-

sand-year-old Roman Empire'. Fascism was in turn the germ of Nazism, designed by Hitler to create his Third Reich which would last a thousand years. The concept of the 'Thousand-year Reich'   in which his master race of people would be saved, was the central essence of Hitler's vision and also the true stuff of millenarianism.

40. Hubback: 'Apocalypse When?,' p 18
41. 'Official Warns of Cult Attack in Moscow,' *Moscow Times* (2 April 1995) ITAR_TASS, 1431hrs GMT (4 April 1995)
42. 'Israelis Fear Worst As End of Time Draws Near,' *Sunday Telegraph* (3 January 1999)
43. Interview with Ian Haworth, Founder of the Cult Information Centre (1 October 1999)
44. Robin McKie and Hadley Freeman, 'Millennium Madness Starts Here' *Observer* (27 December 1998)
45. Michael Jordan, *Cults From Bacchus to Heaven's Gate* (London: Carlton, 1999) p 133
46. McKie and Freeman, 'Millennium Madness Starts Here;
47. Interview with Ian Haworth, Founder of the Cult Information Centre (1 October 1999).
48. Hoffman: *Inside Terrorism*, p 123
49. Interview with Ian Haworth, Founder of the Cult Information Centre (1 October 1999)
50. Judy Kerr, 'Prophet Margins,' *Time Out* (15–22 March 2000) p 18
51. 'Sister of Death,' *The Sunday Telegraph* (2 April 2000)
52. Gail Bass et al, *Motivations and Possible Actions of Potential Criminal Adversaries of US Nuclear Programmes* (Santa Monica, CA: The Rand Corporation, 1980)
53. Hubback: 'Apocalypse When?,' p 22
54. Cameron: *Nuclear Terrorism*, p 102
55. Hubback: 'Apocalypse When?,' p 4
56. Hoffman: *Inside Terrorism*, p 117
57. Hoffman: *Inside Terrorism*, p 5
58. Aryan Nations webpage www.christian-aryannations.com
59. Hubback: 'Apocalypse When?,'p 5
60. The link between Christian Identity and the Oklahoma City bombing has been established by US intelligence sources, which claim that the Reverend Robert Millar, the leader of Christian Identity, had links to Timothy McVeigh, who himself has admitted to a belief in Christian patriotism. These sources indicate that in 1994 Millar wanted the state of Arkansas to grant clemency to his best friend, Richard Snell, who was on death row for the killing of a black police officer. According to FBI informant Carol Howe, Millar planned a massive terrorist attack in case Arkansas proceeded with Snell's execution. After all his appeals had failed, Snell was given a lethal injection on 19 April 1995. Later that day the Alfred P. Murrah federal building in Oklahoma City was engulfed by the biggest act of domestic terrorism ever seen on US soil.
According to Howe, the Murrah building had been on Millar's hit list for three months. Howe claims that the FBI knew this because Millar is also an FBI informant, which is why he has never been arrested. Millar was disillusioned with constitutional government and Washington's alleged

contempt for its citizens. The FBI's failure to act against Millar has produced dozens of malcontents amongst the Murrah victims. They have gathered evidence which proves the FBI knew from Howe and Millar that the Murrah bomb was coming and botched its interception. Daniel Jeffreys, quoted in *Daily Mail* (21 November 1998, pp 12–13)

61. Hubback: 'Apocalypse When?,' p 10
62. Cameron: *Nuclear Terrorism*, p 113
63. Aryan Nations webpage www.christian-aryannations.com
64. Aryan Nations webpage www.christian-aryannations.com
65. Hubback: 'Apocalypse When?,' p 5
66. Hoffman: *Inside Terrorism*, p 114
67. Quoted in Hoffman: *Inside Terrorism*, p 114
68. Hoffman: *Inside Terrorism*, p 114
69. Hoffman: *Inside Terrorism*, p 119
70. Hubback: 'Apocalypse When?,' p 6
71. Frank Barnaby, *Instruments of Terror: Mass Destruction Has Never Been So Easy* (London: Vision Paperbacks, 1996) pp 98, 102
72. Cameron: *Nuclear Terrorism*, p 95
73. Falkenrath, Newman and Thayer, *America's Achilles Heel* (Cambridge, MA: MIT Press, 1998) pp 196–97
74. 'Special branch Had No Idea,' *The Times* (1 July 2000)
75. Stuart Miller, 'We're at War and if That Means More bombs, so be it,' *Guardian*, G2 (27 April 1999). 'Hunt is Hampered by Secret Cells of Neo-Nazis', *Guardian* (1 May 1999); 'Police Check International Neo-Nazi Links', *Guardian* (27 April 1999)
76. Miller: 'We're at War and If That Means More bombs, So Be It'
77. Miller: 'We're at War and if That Means More Bombs, so be it'
78. 'Hunt Is Hampered by Secret Cells of Neo-Nazis'
79. 'Police Check International Neo-Nazi Links'
80. 'We're at War and if That Means More Bombs, so be it'
81. Stern: *The Ultimate Terrorists*, p 58
82. Patricia Steinhoff, 'Portrait of a Terrorist: An Interview With Kozo Okamato,' *Asian Survey* (September 1976) pp 844-855.
83. Cameron: *Nuclear Terrorism*, p 91
84. Konrad Kellen, 'The Potential For Nuclear Terrorism: A Discussion,' in Paul Leventhal and Yonah Alexander (eds), *Preventing Nuclear Terrorism* (Lexington, MA: Lexington Books, 1986) p 113
85. Al Jihad and Al Gamaa Islamiya in Egypt escalated their level of violence, particularly against the tourist industry when their position within mainstream society began to deteriorate in 1992. Richard Engel, 'Egypt Digs For the Truth,' *Jane's Defence Weekly* (24 February 1999) p 22
86. Interview, name withheld by request (23 March 1999)
87. Kellen, 'The Potential For Nuclear Terrorism: A Discussion,' p 115

7. Psychological Motivations and Inhibitory Controls

One of the least understood dimensions of the NBC terrorism threat, is the role of organizational and other psychological factors on terrorists' decision making. Chapters 4–6 suggest that any group considering the use of NBC weapons, would be subject to a conflicting set of tactical, strategic, political and theological motivations and disincentives. For any group, the balance between these factors will vary according to the decision making of the individuals involved, or between the different members of the group, which will be conditioned by a range of psychological factors. Studies of terrorists' memoirs, and interviews, have given psychologists a broad understanding of the variety of motivations that lead individuals to join terrorist groups and engage in acts of violence. Yet psychological analyses of terrorists and NBC weapons has been limited, and tend to extrapolate from analysis of conventional acts of terrorism. These analyses are the subject of contention, not least because they are highly speculative, although generalized psychological explanations about how terrorists might come to a decision to use these types of weapons, are possible, and the potential psychological motivations and disincentives can be identified.

The other psychological dimension of the NBC terrorism debate is how it has affected public opinion and decision makers in the West. One of the most interesting psychological issues which arises is that it is extremely difficult to have a rational debate about NBC terrorism. Psychologists would argue that the psychological condition of needing complete protection from an absolute threat to one's survival cannot be argued against rationally. It can only be dismantled piece by piece. Thus, perhaps one of the major drawbacks of this debate has been that many analysts have simply lacked the ability to stand back and then discard their fears. This has been a stumbling block particularly to the debate on NBC terrorism in the USA, which has not had a major history of domestic terrorism. European states on the other hand, which have had years of direct experience of terrorism, are not so psychologically conditioned by a state of fear and imminent threat. In the USA, however, the shock and psychological trauma of dealing with domestic terrorism led some of the US debate in the early 1990s into implausible rhetoric and gross overestimations of the threat.

Trying to find measures to counter the possibility of an NBC terrorist attack is also influenced by a psychological dimension. Arguably, a change in thinking is a necessary precondition for any departure from the dangerous politics of confrontation. And this change must be radical, otherwise any anti-terrorist treaty will be ineffective, and any counter-measures somehow contravened. Mutual trust is not a secondary but a primary concern, and efforts must be made to strengthen it.

The psychological difference between conventional and NBC weapons
At the heart of a psychological analysis of whether terrorists would use NBC weapons is whether there is a psychological distinction between using conventional weapons and using NBC weapons, particularly WMD. Some analysts argue that this would be a fairly easy transition to make, whilst others suggest that it is in fact a major psychological step. Previous terrorist incidents, most notably the bombing of the World Trade Centre, indicate that it is possible to cause mass casualties using conventional explosives. This would seem to suggest that for terrorists willing to conduct indiscriminate attacks involving large numbers of casualties it is indeed only a small step upwards to using WMD. Yet there are indications that the use of NBC weapons can be perceived differently from the use of conventional weapons, for a number of closely interrelated reasons.

The principal reason is the potentially higher destructive capacity of WMD, which is closely linked to the uniquely horrifying nature of the consequences of all NBC weapons, not only in terms of casualty levels, but also because of the horrendous nature of the deaths, injuries and contamination that they can cause. Whilst conventional weapons are capable of causing large number of deaths and appaling injuries, the type of injuries and levels of deaths caused by WMD can far exceed the consequences of conventional weapons.

These two factors underpin a third, a perceived societal taboo against the use of NBC weapons within many different cultures. This taboo is derived from a mixture of moral, religious, political and strategic considerations. These weapons are considered to be morally reprehensible, in part because of a visceral disgust of poisons and disease, and because societal values and moral norms dictate that even when violence is justified, it should to be proportionate. The use of WMD would under normal circumstances be a totally disproportionate response to most acts of violence or other grievances. In addition, the use of poison is often seen as unworthy of decent or heroic people, and is rather seen as the weapon of the weak and deceitful, something that is unnecessarily vicious and morally unacceptable. (1) Yet societal taboos have always been challenged and broken. The Aum Shinrikyo attack on the Tokyo subway was so important because it was perceived to weaken this psychological taboo. Yet it has not yet been broken, and the taboo should still influence many terrorist groups, particularly the predominantly secular groups. (2) However, it must be stressed that the more frequently that NBC weapons are used, the weaker the taboo becomes, and the easier it will be for terrorists to cross the moral threshold.

These considerations would seem to suggest that there are strong psychological inhibitions to using NBC weapons, and that one of the principal variables in determining whether terrorists will resort to using WMD is whether they can overcome the psychological objections to using them. However there are a number of other psychological factors which could come into play, which might establish conflicting motivations and inhibitions. Individuals have previously used NBC weapons, and considered it justified to do so. This not only includes during war situations such as the First and Second World Wars and the Iran-Iraq war, but they have also been used for political assassinations and murders. Therefore the strength of these inhibitions is likely to vary depending upon a number of factors: the personal belief system of the individual; the organizational factors influencing the individual; the lethality of the NBC weapon; and the target that is selected. They are likely to be strongest in respect of WMD attacks against population targets and weakest in respect of more controlled attacks – for example, against military and political figures.

Decision making dynamics within terrorist groups
One of the principal factors that will influence the terrorists' choice of weapons and tactics is the dynamics of the decision making process within the group. Many predominantly secular terrorist groups have 'democratic'-style decision making structures. (3) For example, the Provisional IRA is run by a seven-man Army Council, which is responsible for strategy and the planning of all operations, including when bombing campaigns will be conducted, and which targets are chosen. In the 1980s the IRA adopted an organizational structure based upon cells of eight people each, but central control over the cells was exercised by the operations officer, who would know of every operation being planned, and had the authority to approve or cancel any operation. (4)

Within such groups, decisions on whether to use NBC weapons would depend upon the balance of beliefs amongst the group leadership. Whilst groups with this type of decision making structure might contain individuals who would countenance the use of NBC weapons or WMD, the group itself would use them only if the balance of opinion amongst the leadership was in favour. This makes it less likely that such a group would resort to using NBC weapons. Yet this does not necessarily exclude 'democratic' style groups from adopting specific tactics, such as indiscriminate attacks against population targets, it merely makes it more difficult for these groups to adopt the most extreme tactics. Hence, it is only when the group's leadership contains a majority of hardliners that the most extreme tactics will prevail. But whilst the leadership of a specific group might reject the use of NBC weapons at any given time, individuals in positions of authority within the group can change, as some are killed or internal power struggles bring new cliques into power. Therefore the balance of opinion within groups can change.

In contrast, other groups have a more authoritarian structure. For instance, the Palestinian ANO is run by Abu Nidal himself, supported by four top aides. Under the aegis of a general council, his orders are passed to underground cells which operate in different countries, planning and executing attacks.5 Many of the new terrorist groups that are predominantly religious in character, that are so closely linked to the rise in lethality of modern terrorism have such authoritarian command structures. Although in some groups with authoritarian command structures, such as the Red Brigades, operational decisions are often taken near the bottom of the structure rather than descending from the top. (6)

Within these authoritarian types of decision making structures, decisions to use NBC weapons will primarily be derived from the attitude of the leader, since he/she cannot be effectively challenged by other individuals within the group hierarchy. As a consequence, groups with this type of decision making structure could be considered to represent more of a threat in respect of NBC terrorism, because once the leader decides to use these weapons, organizational dynamics will have little impact upon the decision. The potential threat is heightened because these groups are frequently amongst the most extreme. They often come into being as a result of breaking away from other groups, when they disagree over goals and strategies, and many are led by hardline personalities who do not want to be constrained by more moderate personalities in democratic decision making structures.

One of the characteristics of terrorism that emerged strongly in the 1990s was the rising number of lone terrorists. To date, the most famous has been the Unabomber, Theodore Kaczynski, who conducted a 20-year bombing campaign in the USA. The potential threat of NBC attacks from lone terrorists is perceived to be higher than that from established groups because they operate outside of the potential constraints of group dynamics, although the extent to which some of these individuals do operate alone is debatable. They are often part of 'communities of belief' which communicate their ideas to one another and interact without actually meeting, often through the internet. These 'virtual communities' have a shared sense of belonging and a distinct group dynamic despite the absence of a significant command structure or physical organization. For example, Timothy McVeigh did not belong to any particular group, but was a member of an unofficial community of like-minded individuals who shared information. These communities have less group loyalty, cohesion and social function than traditional terrorist groups, but they do serve as a motivating force. (7)

This phenomenon is actually a feature of another development that emerged strongly in the late 1980s and early 1990s, that of individuals operating in very small groups, loosely organized, and with less discipline than their traditional counterparts. This has particularly been the case with the far right in the USA. Following its failure to sustain a campaign of violence in the 1980s, it remained quiet until the early 1990s, spending its time maintaining and building support and preparing for a second wave of violence. Learning from the mistakes of the 1980s, Louis Beam, a former Grand Dragon of the KKK and ambassador at large for the Aryan Nations, pioneered a new strategy known as 'leaderless resistance'. This strategy posited a mass movement which would be led by a Christian Identity vanguard, but which would be unconscious of this fact. Sub-units would have a great deal of autonomy and anonymity, enabling the easy creation of terrorist cells comprising between four and six members. These cells would commit acts of terror on their own initiative without waiting for orders from a hierarchy. (8) The movement would be less vulnerable to penetration, because not even the individual cells would fully understand their interrelation with other parts of the movement, and their missions. Beam's theory was that individual acts of violence would initiate a chain reaction, leading to a white supremacist revolution. His ideas finally blossomed into the militia movement following the Ruby Ridge incident. (9)

There is clear evidence that small groups acting outside of a hierarchical decision making structure can lead to an escalation in violence. For example the attack by members of Al Gamaa Islamiya at Luxor in Egypt, which killed nearly 100 foreign tourists, was carried out by young members of the group who had apparently acted on their own initiative. (10) This tendency has also been manifest in other developments in terrorist organization. The World Trade Centre bombing was perpetrated by an ad hoc group of individuals who shared common beliefs and goals, and who came together only for that specific attack and had little connection to a controlling authority. As has been stated earlier, these ad hoc groups operate under fewer constraints than groups which are part of a rigid command structure. It has also been suggested that these new terrorists are more inclined to be driven by a desire for revenge, and are hence more interested in causing mass casualties.

The principle of 'leaderless resistance' is a particular concern in respect of NBC terrorism because small groups of extremists or individuals might not choose to operate under the same political, strategic or moral constraints as the majority of the movement. This is evident from the cases of Larry Wayne Harris and Thomas Lavy, who were apprehended in possession of plague and ricin, whilst acting independently. These cases indicate two things: that individuals within a broader group or movement might develop and use NBC weapons whatever the views of the leadership on the issue; and that the lack of a formal infrastructure will not necessarily inhibit technologically capable individuals from developing NBC weapons.

Therefore, in general terms, strong hierarchical command structures mean that the group leadership can maintain its authority and either keep extremist individuals under control, or lead the group to higher levels of violence. The looser and more diffuse the nature of the group, the more freedom that individuals or small groups have to conduct their own campaigns of extreme violence. Whilst an individual might be part of a 'community of belief,' the potential constraining influence of the community would probably be weaker than is the case within formal group structures.

Groups with a whole range of different types of organizational structures and dynamics have been linked to previous cases of NBC weapon threats and use. Democratic-style predominantly secular groups such as the West German, RAF (Baader-Meinhof gang), have been linked to a number of plots, although none of these cases involved their actual use (see Appendix for full details). It remains unknown whether an ostensibly democratic style of decision making would inhibit the actual use of NBC weapons. What is more evident from the past record of NBC terrorism is that the most serious cases involved groups with authoritarian decision making structures, particularly religious cults. Individuals acting in isolation have been proven to pose a threat, but there are technical limits to what an individual can achieve in developing NBC weapons, especially WMD. US white supremacists have synthesized ricin, but never managed to develop a dispersal mechanism to enable it to be used for indiscriminate attacks. Therefore attacks by individuals are likely to be crude, and unlikely to cause large numbers of casualties.

The psychology of the individual
The fact that using WMD runs so completely counter to conventional notions of morality and social values, would suggest that they are most likely to be used by individuals who are seriously mentally ill, or even psychotic. Certainly, a number of terrorists do exhibit such psychological characteristics. For these individuals, the extremity of their violence is a result of their illness. Buford Furrow, a member of the Aryan Nations who murdered a Filipino postman and injured five Jewish children at a day care centre in Los Angeles, during a shooting spree in 1999, had a history of mental illness. He was a known psychotic who fantasized about mass killings, and was undergoing treatment which included anti-psychotic drugs. (11) Thomas Leahy, who was convicted in the USA of possessing ricin, had a history of schizophrenia, and alcohol and drug abuse. As a result he was delusional, and believed himself to be surrounded by enemies. (12) There is some evidence that right-wing groups which emphasize violence tend to attract more psychopaths than other types of terrorist groups. Psychiatric studies of imprisoned neo-Fascist

Constraintsterrorists in Italy discovered that many of them exhibited 'free floating feelings of aggression and hostility', although this evidence remains fairly weak. (13)

However, these states of mind are incompatible with working effectively within a group. Chapter 3 indicated that acquiring an NBC weapon, and then successfully executing an attack, would require protracted planning and a high level of caution. The success of such an operation would require thought, reflection, and rigorous planning, yet psychotics tend to be impulsive and are not team players. This suggests that a successful NBC attack would typically need to be carried out by psychologically 'normal' people. Many terrorist groups would not in any case knowingly choose to work with psychotics, because of the potential security risk. As a result, the majority of terrorists are not psychotic, (14) however they may display other forms of personality disorders, such as mood disorders, anxiety disorders, and paranoia, which might influence their behaviour and belief systems. Sociopaths for instance, display continual antagonism with society, tending to be callous, impulsive and irresponsible. They exhibit little guilt or anxiety about their actions, because they have no genuine feelings of love or loyalty for any person or group. Consequently they tend to be loners, although they are adept at personal interaction and can possess above average intelligence. (15)

It is often considered that terrorists are influenced by unconscious and irrational thought processes, and that this irrationality could lead them to use NBC weapons, because of some perceived advantage that they would confer. Certainly, the past record of NBC terrorism contains numerous incidents of individuals and groups choosing to use NBC weapons in roles to which they are not suited. This suggests that terrorists do not necessarily act rationally in choosing to use NBC weapons. But the concept of rational choice does not necessarily equate to the 'right' decision, based upon which weapon will be most effective in achieving which goal. Instead, rationality assumes only a judgement of how to effectively tie ends to means, the conclusions of which are followed through consistently. Therefore, any decision needs only be the optimal one at that given moment, and then followed through. (16)

There appear to be two major sources of bias leading to apparently irrational decisions. The first is identified by psychologists as 'cognitive bias,' whereby individuals attend to certain stimuli but ignore others, thereby distorting reality. The second is known as 'motivated bias,' which occurs when the fulfilment of emotional needs and desires dominates the decision making process. There is evidence to suggest that some individuals and groups have been interested in NBC weapons as a result of an innate curiosity or fascination with the technology, or a perceived need to demonstrate their competence or worth to society. (17) Part of the reason why the Aum Shinrikyo conducted so many CBW attacks was because of Shoko Asahara's personal fixation with these type of weapons, whilst for other groups they could also serve as a source of self- esteem and group cohesion.

This raises questions about how psychologically 'normal' individuals could bring themselves to commit an act of mass destruction. It has been suggested that individuals and groups from heavily brutalized societies will have the kind of psychological mindset to use WMD, because they are driven by a greater sense of hatred and desire for justice or revenge. Of these types of groups, those that might have been subjected to NBC attack themselves, such as the Kurdish people of Northern Iraq, might be the most likely to use them. Theoretically, this would make it easier for them to morally justify the use of extreme levels of violence, and overcome the psychological disincentives to causing mass casualties. For them, an act of mass destruction would be proportionate to what they themselves had suffered, and could be morally justified in those terms. The plans of the Jewish reprisal organization, Nakam, to poison the water supply of German cities in 1946, fits neatly into this explanation. It might be a partial explanation for why individuals such as Osama bin Laden, who fought in the war against the Soviet Union in Afghanistan, have sought NBC weapons; and why some of the new, ad hoc, Islamic groups which contain Afghan war veterans, are more radical than other groups. Yet the Chechens were heavily brutalized in their two wars with Russia during the 1990s, but chose not to use NBC weapons against civilian targets. Neither does it help when trying to explain why US Christian white supremacists or the RAF, who have not been brutalized in the same way, have been linked to NBC weapon plots (although it might be a partial explanation for their apparent reticence to use them).

This suggests that there are other psychological factors at work, which stem from an elaborate set of cognitive devices that the individual uses to re-interpret a given situation, and his role within it. In particular, groups tend to justify their violence in terms of warfare against an evil oppressor, thereby freeing their violence from conventional moral constraints, by shifting responsibility for the consequences of their actions to their opponents. This is typically achieved by emphasizing the target groups' oppression of the terrorists' constituency. (18) There is a strong element of this phenomenon in the rhetoric of Christian Identity groups, Islamic fundamentalists and a range of other groups, which perceive themselves to be on the defensive against a more powerful and aggressive enemy.

However it is the belief system of the terrorist group which forms the basis of the primary justificatory mechanism for the individual committing violent acts. Terrorists openly reject conventional societal norms and values, undergoing a gradual but steady disengagement from moral realities. (19) One of the key features of terrorist belief systems is their idealizing of the goals of the group, and the devaluing or demonizing of their opponents. This polarizes the world into an us-versus-them scenario. The psychologist Dr Joel Simon Hochman testified at the Charles Manson trial in 1969–70 that, 'I think that historically the easiest way to program someone into murdering is to convince them that they are alien, that they are them and we are us, and that they are different from us.' (20) Whilst Jerrold Post argues that 'To the extent that the terrorist ideology devalues and dehumanizes the establishment and identifies it as the cause of society's [the terrorists'] problems, it is not only not immoral to attempt to destroy the establishment, it is indeed the highest order of morality.' (21)

Within this process, conventional notions of morality are replaced by the morality derived from the group and its ideology, and it is these moral norms and values which are used to justify terrorist violence. Analysis of some left-wing West German terrorists showed that they acted as though they were absolved of responsibility for their actions by the group's ideology. (22) This cognitive re-orientation does not take place suddenly, but comes about in gradual steps, often starting with quite minor acts with escalatory steps that are sometimes so small that they seem only slightly different from the one before. (23) Theoretically, such a 'slippery slope' could lead the individual all the way to the use of WMD. What is sometimes lost in this process is the element of proportionality which conventional notions of morality apply to acts of violence. (24) Terrorists are more likely to be absolutists, for whom the ends are more important than the means, which implies that no act of violence would necessarily be ruled out on moral grounds. (25) Therefore, the extent of this rejection of conventional morality is potentially the key factor in determining whether individual terrorists will choose to use NBC weapons, particularly indiscriminate WMD attacks.

Yet these new moral values can also act as a strong inhibitory control to using NBC weapons. Terrorists tend to perceive and present themselves as being held to a higher moral standard than their adversaries. It is this, after all, which enables them to justify their violence against the evil oppressors. They attempt to present themselves as champions of justice within an unjust society, rather than barbarians engaging in violence for the sake of violence. If their aim is to establish their legitimacy as a political actor, and reinforce their position as a moral force, then certain actions would be precluded. (26)

The extent to which these new values subsume the traditional societal norms and values with which the individual grew up, is also likely to vary widely. The normative social values which individuals acquire through their lifetime are so deeply ingrained within the personality that they can never be completely subsumed. As a result, they can still influence the individual. Hence, there have been instances in which terrorists have refused to carry out certain kinds of attacks. Hans-Joachim Klein, a member of the RAF, threatened to inform the authorities if the group carried out a threat to bomb Lufthansa passenger jets, and he left the group shortly afterwards. (27) If any act of violence is likely to lead to conflicts between terrorists' objectives and these deeply ingrained social values, it is the use of NBC weapons.

However the social values and moral norms of different societies can vary widely over time, for a whole range of cultural, religious, societal, political or socio-economic reasons. When the Red Brigades were operating in Italy, violence was seen as a societal norm, rather than an aberration. In fact, many terrorists come from societies and communities where personal and structural violence is the norm, from Palestinian refugee camps in Israel, to Chechnya in the 1990s and intercommunal violence in Northern Ireland. In societies where violence is the norm, it is significantly easier for the individual to resort to a more structured campaign of violence. Yet there does not appear to be any obvious link between individuals coming from these backgrounds and acts of NBC terrorism, otherwise it would be much more prevalent than it has been.

As a result of these conflicting moral imperatives, terrorists have to reconcile their desire to commit acts of violence with such normative values. Therefore, even if the tactical, strategic and political motivations favour the use of NBC weapons, the possibility that an individual will use them will also be determined by the strength of the justificatory mechanisms that (s)he employs. But the more extreme the level of violence, the more difficult it is to reconcile with these normative values. Therefore terrorists also calibrate their level of violence to what they can morally justify to themselves. These moral conflicts will be most extreme when considering using WMD for indiscriminate attacks, but where the target is more discriminate these conflicts might be easier to reconcile. Therefore, a basic inability to reconcile these competing imperatives could have contributed to the relatively low incidence of NBC use by terrorists.

Whether religious belief systems constitute stronger justificatory mechanisms for committing acts of NBC terrorism than political belief systems, because of their divinely inspired nature is a matter of conjecture, although most analysts assume that they do. It has been argued that the transcendental nature of the objectives of religious terrorism releases the perpetrators from political and moral constraints, and that they are unconstrained by conventional norms of proportionality, instrumentality and societal acceptability, because for them violence can have a cleansing and redemptive element. (28) Religion can be used to establish stronger motivations for carrying out indiscriminate attacks against population targets, since it can potentially be used to identify open-ended categories of targets, and can employ powerful de-humanizing terminology in its rhetoric and teachings. Islam has been misused by some groups to portray all non-believers as enemies of Allah, whilst Christian Identity make spurious claims that the non-white races are not really human, referring to Blacks and Hispanics as 'mud people' and 'Latrinos'. These factors can remove the sense of proportionality in how these groups conduct their campaigns of violence. Whilst not all religious groups might choose to use NBC weapons, or engage in indiscriminate attacks, the emergence of more of this type of group increases the probability that some of them might turn to using NBC weapons if they can acquire them.

In contrast, the belief systems of secular terrorists generally identify discriminate categories of targets. Their dehumanizing terminology tends to be directed at the political establishment and security forces of the state, although racist secular groups will emphasize the biological inferiority of their ethnic victims. This establishes a form of 'bounded morality' which, whilst not generally being understood or accepted by society, does constrain their acts. Because they commit their acts for their perceived constituency, they generally accept principles of proportionality and justice which typically preclude indiscriminate attacks, particularly mass-casualty attacks. (29) However they still perceive themselves to be outsiders, and are irretrievably hostile to the establishment. This implacable opposition might have an impact on their willingness to escalate the level of violence that they employ, but this does not appear to have been the case. (30) Therefore, the justificatory mechanisms of secular groups are significantly weaker, although not necessarily so absolutely weak as to completely rule out the use of NBC weapons.

In conjunction with the justificatory mechanisms derived from the group's ideology, individuals can also be decisively influenced by a figure who they deem to have a legitimate authority. These figures can make it very difficult for individuals to question what is required of them. Stanley Milgram's seminal experiments in the 1960s demonstrated the potential power of an authority figure over the individual. Milgram asked participants to deliver an 'electric shock' to a subject in another room when they made a mistake in a task. The 'shocks' were not real, but the actor in the other room performed as if they were. Despite being of above-average intelligence, two-thirds of the subjects were prepared to deliver 'shocks' that they knew were dangerous, whilst pleading with the experimenter to stop the study. (31) Individuals who obey an authority figure and commit an act which they personally object to, absolve themselves of responsibility by transferring it to the person who sanctioned the act. This resolves any moral conflicts for the individual, who also becomes less constrained by any potential political disincentives. The fact that many religiously motivated terrorists actively seek prior sanction for their attacks from a religious figure, indicates the critical psychological significance of this justificatory mechanism. It also suggests that if the group cannot obtain explicit sanction from a religious figure, the individual will have greater personal difficulty carrying out the attack, and might refuse.

In addition, all terrorists sometimes attempt to justify their acts by deliberately disregarding or misrepresenting the damage that they have caused. By minimizing the damage in this way, they avoid the full implications of their actions. When they do not know the harm that they are causing, it becomes de-personalized and consequently less difficult to overcome moral inhibitions. To an extent this is achieved through de-humanizing the victim. Some of the subjects of Milgram's experiments attempted to shut out the awareness that the victim was a fellow human being, and one of them commented, 'You really begin to forget that there's a guy out there, even though you can hear him. For a long time I just concentrated on pressing the switches and reading the words.' (32) Similarly, if the terrorist who gives the order to carry out an attack is not one of those who actually executes the act, it could be morally easier for that individual. (33) Yet there must be considerable doubt about whether this would apply to using WMD, because the consequences of using them would be so dramatic and extreme, that terrorists would know the likely consequences of their actions. There would be no escaping the moral dilemmas in ordering and executing such an attack.

Group decision making

Despite the emergence of more lone operators in the 1990s, terrorism primarily remains a group activity. This renders the individual susceptible to the powerful influences of group and organizational dynamics. Some of the strongest psychological motivations and disincentives to using NBC weapons, that will influence the individual, will be derived from the dynamics of decision making within the group.

Wanda Baeyer-Kaette identifies an 'upside down logic' that characterizes terrorist decision making. The group decides what is good and bad, and if the cause is served by a particular act, the act is considered good by definition. (34) One of the principal reasons why the group is so influential, is that the individual is driven by a strong motivation to belong, because it consolidates an incomplete psycho-social identity. This creates the foundation for especially powerful group dynamics, suggesting that the group is an unusually powerful setting for producing conforming behaviour. Memoirs and interviews with terrorists suggest that individuals have a tendency to submerge their personal identity into a group identity, and in the process subordinate their own judgement to that of the group. (35) This suggests that in debates about whether to use NBC weapons, individuals might ignore their own personal objections.

Within any terrorist group there are great pressures for compliance and conformity that mute dissent. Features of this ' group think' are illusions of invulnerability leading to excessive optimism and risk taking and collective rationalization of efforts to dismiss challenges to key assumptions; the presumption of the group's morality; the unidimensional perception of the enemy as evil or incompetent (thereby justifying risky alternatives); intolerance of challenges to shared beliefs by a group member; unwillingness to express views that deviate from the perceived group consensus; and a shared illusion that unanimity is genuine. Some members might also withhold adverse information concerning the instrumental and moral soundness of a decision from the group. (36) The key features are the reduction of critical judgement, the assumption of the group's morality and the illusion of invulnerability leading to excessive risk taking. All three of these factors will play a significant role in group decisions about whether to use NBC weapons.

Occasionally, unanimity within a group can be lost. This can lead to the emergence of factions under charismatic individuals, which break away, and in many cases prove to be more extreme than the parent group. Divisions however, do not invariably lead to the break-up of the group. When factions exist within an organization, competing viewpoints have to be reconciled, and it is through this process that the group leadership might escalate levels of violence, as a means to prevent divisions. (37) As rivals or different factions compete for influence, they might reach a situation in which they consider that displaying a stronger commitment to the cause through higher levels of violence is the best means of gaining influence. Yet this would also be partly dependent upon the politico-strategic context within which the group is operating. When the IRA considered calling a ceasefire as part of the Northern Ireland peace process, there was competition for control of the organization, between the advocates of the peace process and the hardliners who wanted to continue the war. This competition did not lead to an escalation of IRA violence because the political context had created an opportunity to explore political solutions, and that was what the majority of its constituency favoured.

The pressures for conformity with the collective belief are also closely linked with a phenomenon known to psychologists as 'risky shift', by which groups often make riskier decisions than individuals preferred privately. Terrorist memoirs and interviews provide plenty of evidence of this phenomenon. Adriana Faranda, a member of the Red Brigades, stated that you accept decisions, even if you are a dissenting minority: 'You support the others. It's a kind of pact of obedience.' (38) The individuals concerned are able to justify their more extreme actions by the knowledge that all members of the group will share responsibility, thereby lessening personal guilt for the consequences. A wish by the group to define its identity more clearly, peer pressure, the individual desire to conform or appear decisive are also other factors which can account for this phenomenon. (39) Conformity to the collective belief increases with the length of time that the individual remains in the group. Similarly, in groups that contain individuals with poor self-esteem, who depend upon the group for their sense of significance, these tendencies will be magnified. (40) C.J.M Drake suggests that the concept of risky shift will ultimately lead terrorists towards increasingly greater risks. (41)

Further work into this phenomenon by Solomon Asch in 1951 demonstrated that many subjects would yield to a majority, even when the group is patently wrong. The subject sees the world as it is, but has every reason to believe that the others see it differently, and will not dissent for fear of appearing foolish. (42) Asch's work indicated that the degree of conformity increases with the size of the group, up to a maximum of seven members, and thereafter does not rise. Most importantly, it was the desirability of belonging to the group, and the level of confidence of the individual in his/her own ability, that affected conformity. Asch found that when his subjects complied with a judgement with which they disagreed, many participants underestimated the extent to which they conformed. However more recent work has suggested that Asch's findings were misinterpreted, and that participants in fact managed to resist pressures to conform on about two-thirds of the judgements, and that conformity was the exception rather than the rule. Ability to resist group pressure is made easier if the individual has an ally. If two naive participants were present in an Asch -type experiment, conformity dropped to 5.5 per cent of the judgements given. (43) These findings indicate that conformity is not guaranteed, and that individuals will reject some decisions taken within groups. This implies that there is no guarantee that decisions to escalate levels of violence or risk taking within terrorist groups will find compliance with all members of the group.

The concept of risky shift ties in with the concept of the 'diffusion of responsibility', by which an individual might consent to commit an act which (s)he would otherwise reject, because an authority figure had stated that it was justified to commit the act. Again, the individual justifies perpetrating the act by shifting responsibility to the leader, or group, which ordered the act. Yet these factors do not invariably lead to escalation. The IRA was subject to these psychological dynamics but maintained constraints on its level of violence. Similarly, despite apparent escalatory pressures, terrorists remain, on the whole, conservative in their choice of tactics and weapons.

The critical significance of the group in the psychology of the individual members provides additional evidence for why groups that are in decline might resort to heightened levels of violence, including NBC weapons. As the group falls into decline, the individual is faced with the fear of losing all that (s)he gains from membership. It is the fear derived from their deep psychological need to belong to the group, which might drive them to consider any measures to ensure the group's survival.

The relationship between the group and society can also strengthen the power of the group over its members. Group dynamics are most powerful within groups that have been gone 'underground' and are cut off from society. This has included groups such as the RAF and the Symbionese Liberation Army (SLA); small cells which are operating outside of their own countries; and even right-wing groups in the USA that have established their own communities. Isolated from society, group cohesion develops in response to shared danger, and the members come to rely more upon themselves. The group and its ideology then becomes the individual's life, a source of safety and security. Because of this reliance, the fear of expulsion from the group can become all-encompassing. (44)

This group cohesiveness encourages the pursuit of violence because news is filtered through the group, leading to increased misperceptions of the outside world, reinforcing the beliefs of the group and creating the conditions in which ideology can become corrupted and abstract. (45) Martha Crenshaw notes how 'ideology may become increasingly corrupted and surrealistic, it is used to escape a disconcerting reality rather than to guide actions. The extreme abstractness of such beliefs ... disconnect their holders from objective reality.' (46) Consequently, isolation from society could be one of the key factors leading to NBC terrorism, because it also isolates the group from societal norms and values, strengthening the individual's acceptance of the group's morality and potentially corrupting that ideology.

Therefore, operating 'underground' establishes a pattern of behaviour in which the predominant determinant is the internal dynamics of the group. From only mixing with like minded individuals, group judgements are affected by self-reinforcing group values rather than conventional societal values. (47) But, even more significantly, it is possible for the members to conform to the agenda of just a few individuals, or even of just the leader. The leader is likely to be highly influential in determining how an individual views the organization and its goals, and can exploit the members' reliance on the group in order to ensure compliance. Voices of opposition are often muted because of the fear of jeopardizing their position within the organization, consequently the group might engage in levels of violence that none of the individual members believed were justified. (48) Groups such as the RAF and SLA operated under the leader's force of personality. (49) Andreas Baader used the threat of expulsion to ensure compliance from the Baader-Meinhof gang, 'whoever is in the group simply has to be tough, has to be able to hold out, and if one is not tough enough, there is not room for him here,' In some cases dissension might go beyond expulsion from the group to include the threat of death. One former member of the RAF commented on the pressures that 'can lead to things you can't imagine ... the fear of what is happening to one when you say, for example, "No I won't do that, and for these reasons." What the consequences of that can be.' (50) For groups that are predominantly religious in character, members might not dissent for fear of appearing unfaithful. Under these conditions, if the leader is interested in using NBC weapons, the group is more likely to follow that course. These factors might help to explain the previous RAF interest in NBC weapons, and why religious cults, and some Islamic groups, have also previously displayed an interest in them.

In contrast, terrorists who live within their own community, who probably have family lives and interact socially with people outside of the group, are continually exposed to societal norms and values. It can be noted that groups such as Hezbollah, ETA and the IRA, whose members generally live within their communities, have never previously been linked to NBC threats. Most right-wing terrorists are not complete outsiders, and also live as part of their communities. Therefore the close-knit insular organization of left-wing groups which go 'underground' is less of an aspect of right-wing terrorism. However some skinhead groups and extreme neo-Nazis are extremely alienated. Some of them live together, and the group becomes a surrogate family for them, when they break their ties with the outside world to become more centred on the group. (51) Some individuals and groups of this type have previously been linked to NBC plots.

However, the individual's reliance on the group could produce conflicting escalatory pressures. Whilst it might ensure compliance and greater risk taking, it might also be a factor in why terrorists have generally proven to be risk averse, because they will do all that they can to ensure the survival of the group. Engaging in a programme to develop and use NBC weapons entails a higher degree of risk, in terms of being discovered, killed by their own weapons, or provoking a governmental or societal backlash against the group which could lead to its destruction. Equally, debates about escalation might risk splits within the group, therefore the issue of using NBC weapons, might never really be debated within some groups. Hence, psychological factors associated with group dynamics can also act as powerful inhibitors. The new type of ad hoc groups, such as the perpetrators of the World Trade Centre bombing, pose a potentially greater threat because they operate underground and thus experience the most extreme consequences of group dynamics outlined above, but their members are not psychologically reliant upon the group in the same way, therefore considerations about preservation of the group are nowhere near as powerful.

Yet despite the fact that group dynamics can distort individual decision making, this is not necessarily irrational. As noted in Chapters 4–6, most terrorist groups will be subject to a conflicting mix of political, strategic and tactical motivations and disincentives to using NBC weapons. Group dynamics will help the individual to resolve these conflicting priorities. Consequently, there is a rational decision making process that could persuade terrorists that using WMD would further their aims, and it is psychological factors that will determine which political and strategic factors are most important in any decision, and whether it should outweigh other factors.

But whilst group dynamics can act as a powerful motivational factor, the social and moral beliefs of the individual will not necessarily be totally submerged, and can still act as strong disincentives upon the individual. There is some evidence to support this contention from past cases of NBC terrorism. When the Rajneeshpuram cult discussed the use of BW, part of the reasoning for using salmonella rather than typhoid, AIDS, hepatitis or giardia was the level of damage that would result. They were prepared for some incidental fatalities, but their intention was not to kill anyone. (52) This is a strong indication that moral factors derived from conventional societal norms do provide constraints within groups. For individuals acting alone, the psychological inhibitors to using NBC weapons are stronger, because the powerful justificatory mechanisms outlined cannot be employed to dominate personal moral objections.

Religious cults and mind control

Religious cults pose one of the potentially greatest threats in respect of NBC terrorism because of the confluence of many of these psychological motivations and escalatory pressures within their group dynamics. The leadership of a powerful, authoritarian, religious figure, coupled with the individual's strong sense of belonging to a cohesive group, means that diffusion of responsibility and risky shift would be powerful influences for conformity on cult members. Most cults also tend to isolate themselves from society, thereby magnifying these tendencies. As is the case with other religious terrorists, cults that perpetrate acts of violence employ explicit clerical sanction to justify their actions. Shoko Asahara instructed his top disciples that killing by the enlightened few was justified because it helped send victims to a higher plane: 'It is good to eliminate people who continue to do bad things and are certain to go to hell' and in doing so he also assured them that they themselves would rise another level towards Nirvana. (53) When Asahara ordered the murder of a lawyer called Sakamoto and his family, for working on behalf of the families of cult members, Asahara justified the murder of the baby, by claiming that it was holy work, because it prevented the child being brought up by Sakamoto, who was attempting to repeat bad deeds from a previous life, and that it would be born again in a higher world. (54) Similarly, cult leader Charles Manson's philosophy incorporated the notion that it was acceptable to kill, because one is killing only part of one's self, and death liberated the soul. He told his followers that they were above the law because they were divinely guided, and they followed his directives without question. (55)

However religious cults also differ significantly from conventional terrorist organizations, because of their use of mind control, which exacerbates the effects of these other group dynamics. Cult watchers contend that sophisticated mind-control techniques will work on anyone, given the right circumstances. (56) The two basic principles of psychological coercion are that if you can make a person behave the way that you want them to, you can make them believe the way you want them to; and that sudden drastic changes in environment lead to heightened suggestibility, and drastic changes in attitude and beliefs. Cults employ mind-control techniques in an atmosphere of intense group pressure to conform at all times to the desires of the leader. The victim is broken down physically and mentally, thereby becoming susceptible to the leader's suggestions and wishes. This process can take a little as three to four days. The end result is a sudden drastic personality change, referred to by Conway and Siegelman as 'snapping'. The new personality is unable to reason, to choose, or to critically evaluate, and is dependent upon the cult to interpret reality. Having lost the freedom of choice, cult members simply do what they are ordered to do by the leader. (57) Once in such a condition, the cult comes to dominate and control all aspects of the individual's life.

The Aum employed a wide variety of mind-control techniques which included separating members from their families, sleep deprivation, minimal diets, an unceasing barrage of cult teachings, extensive use of psychoactive drugs including Lysergic acid diethylamide (LSD) and thiopental and various physical punishments including confinement, scalding baths and immersion in near-freezing water. In conjunction with this treatment they were also subjected to a constant barrage of Aum Shinrikyo teachings and religious initiations. The Aum Shinrikyo even explored the possibility of using electricity to control brainwaves, and produced electrode caps which regularly administered an electrical discharge into the brain of the wearer. This was purported to tune the wearer's brainwaves into those of Asahara. (58) One member described her experience of an Aum Shinrikyo initiation ceremony, in which she was administered unknown drugs: 'Gradually a vision like hell came to me. I began to see scenes of hungry demons. I thought that the Guru's teachings must be right and true. Then I began to hear the Guru's mantra , then two sets of the mantra at once. I felt I must do better in Aum.' (59) Similarly, the techniques employed by the Us cult the Concerned Christians included building up people's confidence, building dependency on the leader and the group, threatening terrible things if individuals leave and isolation from the outside world. One member said, [The leader] 'Miller told me my father hated me, that he was a paedophile and would molest me if I ran to him. Any children who say something against him are forced into isolation.' (60)

As a result, the membership acts upon the imperatives of the belief system by which the cult lives. As was noted in Chapter 6, these belief systems are heavily influenced by the state of mind of the leader. One of the prime reasons why a cult will resort to violence is the leader being prone to violence. Whilst cult leaders tend to be very charismatic, they are also typically driven by egomania and even megalomania. After reading the Bible, Asahara wrote that 'I hereby declare myself to be the Christ', because he felt that the similarities between their lives were so close, and that 'I am the last Messiah in this Century'. On another occasion he also declared himself to be Buddha. (61) David Koresh, leader of the US cult the Branch Davidians claimed to have been the recipient of the final message of God – the Seventh Seal and had therefore been appointed to be the seventh messenger of the Book of Revelation, (62) whilst Charles Manson claimed to be Jesus Christ himself. Manson's control over his group was such that his followers testified in court that they truly believed that he was Jesus Christ. (63)

Jessica Stern identifies the nature of cult leadership as one of the key indicators in determining the latent potential for violence within a cult. She suggests that a single leader is more dangerous than a group in which a number of disciples are granted sacred authority. (64) Ian Haworth, founder of the Cult Information Centre in the UK, suggests that it is very common for cult leaders to suffer from some form of mental illness. Some of them become delusional and actually begin to believe that they are who they claim to be, or can even perform the miracles that they claim. He suggests that some of them suffer from profound problems in their lives, and that others develop problems during the lifetime of the cult. There are strong indications that the Reverend Jim Jones, the US leader of the People's Temple cult, was seriously mentally ill in the period leading up to the mass suicide of his followers at Jonestown in Guyana. (65) Yet despite indications of emotional traumas and maladjustment in the past of many of these leaders, most of them did not have backgrounds marked by extreme violence. Asahara was a bully during his time at school, whilst Manson had engaged in armed robbery, homosexual rape and wife beating, but had no sustained past record of violence. (66) Instead, their murderous tendencies seem to have emerged only during the lifetime of their cult activities.

Because of the role of the leader within the cult, the delusions which affect the leader can grow to dominate the life and behaviour of the cult. Paranoia can be a dominant feature of cult thinking, which is frequently manifest in extreme forms of behaviour. The Aum Shinrikyo was riven by paranoia, fuelled by Asahara's predictions of Armageddon. Enemies were perceived to be everywhere. Members suspected of breaking cult laws, disloyalty, spying, or dissent, were confined, tortured, and even killed. Immediately prior to the Tokyo subway attack, this even included persecuting members with the wrong blood type, after Asahara had declared that people with blood group O were bound to break Buddhist laws. (67) This sense of paranoia was fuelled by the cult's isolation from the outside world. Police raids, a critical press, along with angry neighbours and parents, fostered these feelings of persecution and alarm. Similarly, Jim Jones the leader of the People's Temple became increasingly paranoid and delusional, believing that the CIA was poisoning him, and imagining that he was the former Russian revolutionary, Lenin. (68) This sense of paranoia can also fuelled by external factors, and most cults that have resorted to violence: Aum Shinrikyo, The People's Temple, Rajneeshpuram, the Branch Davidians and the Solar Temple (many of whose members died in a mass suicide) have done so when they were under investigation by the law enforcement agencies of the states in which they were operating.

Yet evidence from the trial of Charles Manson and three female members of his cult, known as the Family, suggested that the exercise of mind control is not enough in itself to lead an individual to murder at the behest of a leader. Manson had control over the hardcore members of the Family, yet several of them refused to kill for him. Analysis of the three women convicted of the Sharon Tate murders indicated that none of them was psychotic, but all of them were predisposed to murder before meeting Manson. All of them had a history of alienation which was manifest in anti-social or deviant behaviour. Leslie Van Houten had extreme difficulties with impulse control, and there was a deep anger and rage within her. Analysing her relationship with Manson, the psychologist Dr Joel Simon Hochman argued that, 'His ideas, his presence, the role he played in his relationship to her, served to reinforce a lot of her feelings and attitudes. It served to reinforce and give her a way of continuing her general social alienation, her alienation from the establishment.' Hochman stated of Sadie Glutz that 'One is struck by the absence of a conventional sense of morality or conscience in this girl.' The conclusion drawn from the psychological evidence presented at the trial was that decisions to kill ultimately come from the individual. (69)

These psychological features serve to heighten the potential threat from cults. The use of mind control suggests that the psychological inhibitors to using violence and NBC weapons which would otherwise inhibit the individual are removed, because for the individual member societal norms are replaced by the cult belief system. Several Aum Shinrikyo members displayed indications of moral objections to their actions, yet still went through with them anyway. After producing a stockpile of sarin, the Aum Chief Chemist, Hideo Murai, phoned an old friend and warned him to 'Stay away from crowded places ... Aum Supreme Truth is out of control.' Dr Nakagawa, whose responsibility was to act as Asahara's personal doctor and provide medical care for his family, was riven with guilt after the murders of the Sakamoto family, yet failed to admit this to Asahara and went on to play a key role in other Aum attacks. Moreover, one of the Tokyo subway attackers, Dr Ikuo Hayashi, head of the Aum Shinrikyo's Healing Ministry, recounted that 'I didn't know why I was chosen for the attack. I wanted to refuse, but the atmosphere didn't allow it.' (70)

However mind control is not unbreakable and it does not always completely replace the conventional societal norms and moral values which were previously governed the behaviour of the individual. Some members, known as 'walk-aways,' leave cults, typically as a result of something unusual they have seen, heard, or experienced, which provided information directly opposed to what they were led to understand about the cult. (71) Many members left, or attempted to leave, Aum Shinrikyo. One member lost faith after witnessing the killing of another member, whilst another was appaled at the physical mistreatment of patients in the cult's hospital. (72) This typically involved rank and file members of the cult but, significantly, one of the individuals who was chosen to execute a BW attack on Kasumigaseki station on the Tokyo subway realized that what he was doing was wrong, and deliberately neglected to arm the botulism bombs. (73) However it appears that the number of 'walk aways' is typically only a fraction of cult membership.

Conclusion

This analysis suggests that terrorists also operate under strong psychological motivations and disincentives to using NBC weapons. The nature and consequences of NBC weapons suggest that psychological factors might be amongst the most powerful group of influences acting on terrorist decision making. Individual terrorists and groups will have to undergo a process of reconciling these conflicting influences, at the same time as tying them into the conflicting political, strategic and tactical motivations and disincentives to using NBC weapons which will also impact upon their decision making. Ultimately, it could be psychological factors which determine how terrorists balance the conflicting imperatives of the political, strategic and tactical motivations and disincentives to using NBC weapons.

The likelihood of NBC terrorism is obviously strongest when strong psychological motivations tie in to strong political, strategic and tactical motivations to use these weapons. But psychology is a wild card in assessments of the threat because individuals could choose to use these types of weapons when there is no ostensibly rational political or strategic reason to do so. Equally, when other factors might be pushing terrorists to use NBC weapons, psychological disincentives could prove to be the decisive factor in decisions not to use such weapons, or else might influence decision making in terms of the type of weapon used, and the target that is chosen. The presence of moral constraints would be another factor leading groups to use lower-order NBC weapons rather than WMD, and choosing discriminate targets.

Whilst it is impossible to quantify the precise psychological characteristics which will determine whether a group will engage in NBC terrorism, it is possible to identify combinations of factors which make it more likely. The profile that emerges suggests that authoritarian groups, cut off from society, with psychotic leaders, represent the biggest threat. It is also possible to argue that the psychological justificatory mechanisms of religious terrorists are stronger than the psychological disincentives which might influence them. Yet it is quite clear that all types of terrorist groups could operate under psychological motivations to use NBC weapons, depending upon the individuals who comprise the group and the conditions under which it operates. Equally, many individual terrorists will operate under strong psychological disincentives to using NBC weapons.

The psychological effects of NBC terror on the target state
Terrorists typically commit acts of violence in order to achieve certain effects within their 'psychological target,' (74) and as a means to achieve their political goals. Knowing that they cannot defeat the state militarily, most terrorists aim to win a battle of wills with government and society. NBC attacks, particularly involving mass casualties, could have a profound psychological effect on the target population, and an equally profound effect on the nation's politics and law. Public fear of attack will create political pressure for stronger counter measures, or even unleash powerful forces within society, including paranoia, xenophobia, isolationism and fury. The inability to prevent NBC

terrorist attacks, or to respond to them effectively, could even cause the population to lose confidence in its government, and initiate a chain of reactions leading to a shift in the relationship between citizen and state. Therefore NBC terrorism is of heightened interest to terrorists precisely because of its higher psychological impact value.

Drawing on a comparison with nuclear weapons and the Cold War, it is evident that nuclear weapons were born of the urgent fears which drove the Allies in the Second World War, and built up to the inflated numbers seen in the 1970s and 1980s as a direct effect of the deeply split and antagonistic Cold War political climate. According to Hugh Beach and Nadine Gurr, these Cold War fears have not been altogether laid to rest. We still live in fear, but it is much more generalized. It has been made clear to us that what has happened is not simply a rational response to matters outside our control. There is wrong in the world and some of it is our own doing, and states need to 'take back' in some sense the evil they have projected upon others. This is an uncomfortable, even perhaps a chaotic, psychological state to be in. In the post-Cold War world, fear is unfocused, and this results in anxiety. (75)

A useful starting point is the British experience during the Second World War. This cannot be explained simply in terms of international relations, but also needs to be understood on a psychological level. There have been wars throughout history and civilian populations have been treated appallingly. Territories have been overrun, and families, villages and communities broken up. But there has always been the knowledge that families who had fled could regroup in new areas, and the physical infrastructure could be rebuilt. Despite the damage that might be incurred, war was survivable.

In a psychological sense, the belief in 'survivability' was undermined by the end of the Second World War and the advent of the nuclear age, and this has been the framework from within which people have viewed all future threats. The sense of security and safety was undermined on a very personal level. The very structures on which people relied for their personal safety and security were assaulted, and at the end of 1945 there was a sense that an enemy could destroy one utterly. This applied not just in material or economic ways, not just destroying houses and cities, though certainly the mass indiscriminate bombings became lodged deeply in the collective mind. But beyond that, the sense of inner integrity and safety had been destroyed. If one were to compare the sense of threat in 1930 and 1950, the two would be very different. In 1950 any threat could be comprehensive and utterly destructive, and this deeply affected peoples sense of security.

A good example of this was the creation of the Iron Curtain by the Soviet Union. Psychologists argue that 'perception' is very important and the standpoint from which one comes when making a judgement. From one perspective it can be argued that the Soviet Union was forced to throw up a defensive glacis by British and American policies. Having defeated the enormous threat that Hitler's Germany had presented, these countries seemed to feel the need for a new and equally powerful threat. Stalin, the president of the Soviet Union and the totalitarian regime that he created, fitted the bill, and certainly the Soviet Union did enough to confirm this fear.

Today we are the product or children of the Cold War, and when we are in the middle of something it is difficult to stand apart and view it. The way that we have survived with this awfulness however has been to split into two, a righteous self and a projected evil. Hence we (the West) coped by making ourselves not only in the right but also the place of complete virtue. This psychological dimension seen in terms of military threat assessments, is influenced by our desire to think well of ourselves, and attribute the characteristics we dislike in ourselves, to others.

> This process of large group formation, of mindlessness and of leadership that has as its unconscious task the acting out of the psychotic elements of the group, is not confined to any one side or any one conflict. It happens on both sides of every divide. We find it not only within group processes but also between group processes. Put into a world perspective, therefore, we have a system in which nations act as defensive co-operatives for their own citizens and contract as an unconscious group to deny personal and national responsibility for themselves, instead projecting all negatives into the other side, in this instance the other nation. (76)

If we think in these terms the Cold War was a classic example of splitting between the righteous self (the West) and a projected evil (the East). We made ourselves absolutely self-righteous. We declared ourselves arbiters of complete virtue in terms of decency and democratic political values. We made ourselves the repository of all things good, of all civilized values, whilst the Soviet Union became the place of absolute evil. Whilst there might have been some justification for these simplistic categorizations, it hugely exaggerated the reality and somehow locked it in. In response to that universalistic totalizing view what was needed was absolute weapons. Nuclear weapons measured up to this.

In the 1980s the President of the USA, Ronald Reagan, famously described the Soviet Union as an 'evil empire'. According to one school of thought he induced its collapse through an unyielding determination to build up American offensive and defensive military strength, thus spending the Soviets into the ground. On a more sober reading the Soviet Union collapsed as a result of its own inherent contradictions and weaknesses, most notably the total unsuitability of a command economy to the information age. Nonetheless, following the end of the Cold War these same psychological mechanisms continued to dominate politicians' views of the world.

With notions such as Samuel Huntingdon's 'clash of civilizations,' being debated amongst the international relations and policy community, some would say that militant Islam is now being forced into the role that communist internationalism played during the previous 70 years. Some Islamic states are implacably hostile to the West, and some have ambitions to acquire NBC weapons. It is also true that Muslim fundamentalists are a growing menace in several regions. Christian Arabs in Egypt, Lebanon, Jordan, Iraq, Syria and Palestine have come under serious pressure, and hundreds of thousands have emigrated. Perhaps half a million Coptic Christians have left Egypt in the last ten years. This is a by-product of the militants' challenge to secular Arab governments – Syria, Jordan, Egypt, Tunisia, Algeria – as well as to pro-western fundamentalist nations like Saudi Arabia and the Gulf States. The radical leaders cannot operate in most of the Arab world nor in much of Europe. The newspaper *Egyptian Jihad* is published in New Jersey, USA, and mailed to the Middle East; Jordanian and Algerian members of the Islamic Front operate out of New York, USA; whilst sermons of a Lebanese radical are distributed from Dallas, USA. In Egypt militants have been striking at the tourist industry, costing the state billions of dollars in lost revenue. France is seriously concerned about the network of clandestine terrorists in Paris, linked to Algeria's GIA. The bombing of the World Trade Centre in New York seems to have been an Islamic atrocity, carried out by an anti-Israeli group from Pakistan. In that limited sense there is an international conspiracy. But Arab and Muslim nations are notoriously bad at co-operating together, and have spent much of their history in competition with each other for political influence in the Middle East. To paint their activities on anything like the canvas of former Soviet communism is the purest 'rent-a-threat,' demonizing for the sake of needing an enemy.

Much the same is true when it comes to personalities. Saddam Hussein, and to a lesser degree the Libyan leader, Colonel Ghaddafi, have been turned into demonic figures, men you can not negotiate with because there is no humanity in them. Admittedly these targets are well chosen; the psychological mechanism is intelligent and picks the people who best fit the bill. These men are unpredictable and can be prone to catastrophic errors of judgement. They are also implacably bent on acquiring WMD, regardless of what cost it will inflict on their own people. Saddam Hussain has twice ordered attacks on Iraq's neighbours, attacked Iraq's Kurdish population with CW, waged long and bloody wars to no advantage and proved infinitely duplicitous. The unstinting adulation of him in Baghdad is driven mostly by fear, whilst support for him in other parts of the Arab world, owes more to disillusionment with the policies of the USA (mainly in regard to Israel), than to any virtue on his part. That Britain is at ease with this situation, and backs the threat of military strikes against the Iraqi regime, must owe something to the success which the image of an evil empire has been propagated. It is not wholly tendentious to point out – as Arab commentators habitually do – that Israel also is an expansionist power, liable to engage in bloody frontier wars, which has long flouted resolutions of the UN Security Council mandating a political settlement and is in possession of WMD acquired clandestinely. Somehow however, the Israelis are 'one of us' and not part of the 'evil other'.

The same demonization process has also been applied to the shadowy terrorist leaders, such as Osama bin Laden and Ramseh Youssef. These figures have been demonized and made into apocalyptic figures with the ability to wreak havoc and chaos. They are the men who could, and would, without conscience create a nuclear, chemical or biological Armageddon. It is necessary only to read a newspaper report to see the type of highly emotive language that is used when discussing these figures, and the kinds of images that are presented alongside them: mad, bad, evil, pathological, cruel, without conscience and on the edge of reality and sanity.

Guided by a psychological perspective we can see, however, that the world is more complex than this, and humankind is good and bad and shades of grey. This is not as comfortable as if we were all good and others absolutely bad. Once we realize that there is good and bad in all and that things are not all black and white, then we all have to share responsibility for fighting terrorism. At a national level states are moving into a confused, uncertain way of looking at things, and it is through this confusion that we have to aim to somehow prevent the possibility of any other NBC terrorist attack.The psychological reaction to the threat from terrorism, and NBC terrorism in particular, has fostered a sense of societal vulnerability in many states, especially the USA. Most societies however, can become inured to terrorist violence. The IRA and ETA were no nearer achieving their goals despite decades of violence, because societies were willing to bear the cost of the violence, and even reacted against it, by demanding that no concessions be made. NBC terrorism offers a more profound threat to society, because no-one knows the precise ramifications of WMD terrorism and society's sense of survivability has been weakened. NBC terrorism creates the political conditions in which governments have to be seen to respond to the real or imagined threat. But in doing so, states are frequently in danger of losing their sense of perspective in assessing the precise nature of the threat that they have to address. As a result, psychological reactions within states can adversely impact upon governmental responses to the potential threat. This has already been manifest in military strikes which have achieved little, economic sanctions on state sponsors of terrorism that have had little effect, and tougher anti-terrorism legislation which creates constituencies of support for terrorists.

Notes and references
1. Jessica Stern, *The Ultimate Terrorist* (Cambridge, MA: Harvard University Press, 1999), pp 37–39
2. Brad Roberts, 'Has the Taboo Been Broken?', in Brad Roberts (ed), *Terrorism with Chemical and Biological Weapons* (Alexandria Va: Chemical and Biological Control Institute, 1997), p 130
3. Brigitte Monhaupt of the Red Army Fraction (RAF) stated that: 'Any concept of action ... is of course subject to discussion by everyone ... Leadership ... not domination. It is determined by what all members want.' Jerrold Post, 'Prospects For Nuclear Terrorism: Psychological Motivations and Constraints', in Paul Leventhal and Yonah Alexander (eds), *Preventing Nuclear Terrorism* (Lexington, MA: Lexington Books, 1986), p 96
4. Martin McGartland, *Fifty Dead Men Walking* (London: Blake, 1997) pp 217, 218, 221, 255
5. Yossi Melman, *The Master Terrorist: The True Story Behind Abu Nidal* (London: Sidgwick & Jackson, 1986) pp 72, 75, 78, 83
6. C.J.M. Drake, *Terrorists' Target Selection* (London: St Martin's Press, 1998) p.164
7. 'The New Terrorism: Does It Exist? How Real are the Risks of Mass Casualty Attacks?', Panel 4, 'Lone Operators and Mass Casualties', Proceedings of a Conference Co-Sponsored by Chemical and Biological Arms Control Institute and the Center For Global Security Research, Lawrence Livermore National Laboratories (29–30 April 1999) <http://www.cbaci.org/Newterrorism.htm>
8. Andrew Hubback, 'Apocalypse When? The Global Threat of Religious

Cults', *Conflict Studies* 300, Research Institute For the Study of Conflict and Terrorism (June 1997) p 6

9. The concept of 'leaderless resistance' has also spread to other states. In the UK, one issue of the Combat-18 magazine, *Strikeforce*, carried an editorial demanding an 'international terror/sabotage campaign by TOTALLY anonymous cells and groups'. Having emerged in 1995 the White Wolves kept a low profile, and attempted to prevent infiltration by adhering rigidly to this doctrine. Its activists are organized into small, self-contained cells with a maximum of five members, none of which is aware of the existence of the others, and with no central leadership issuing commands.

10. Richard Engel, 'Egypt Digs For the Truth', *Jane's Defence Weekly* (24 February 1999) p 22. There was an escalation in IRA violence in 1971–72 after many of the IRA's leadership were interned, and young, aggressive, and undisciplined terrorists were freed from the constraints that the leadership had imposed. Drake: *Terrorists' Target Selection*, p 165

11. 'Gun Ban On Furrow Was Ignored', *Sunday Telegraph* (15 August 1999)

12. 'Janesville Man Gets More Than 12 Years for Making Toxic Chemical', Special Issue to the journal *Sentinal* (8 January 1998)

13. Gavin Cameron, *Nuclear Terrorism* (Basingstoke: MacMillan, 1999) p 104

14. Drake: *Terrorists' Target Selection*, p 83; Cameron: Nuclear Terrorism, pp 20–22

15. Henry Gleitman, *Psychology*, Fourth Edition, (London: W W Norton, 1995) p 758

16. Cameron: *Nuclear Terrorism*, p 57

17. Richard A. Falkenrath, Robert D. Newman and Bradley Thayer, *America's Achilles Heel* (Cambridge, MA: MIT Press, 1998), p 210

18. Cameron: *Nuclear Terrorism*, p 55; Drake: Terrorists' Target Selection, p 28

19. Cameron: *Nuclear Terrorism*, p 53

20. Vincent Bugliosi with Curt Gentry, *Helter Skelter: The Shocking Story of the Manson Murders* (London: Arrow, 1992) p 56

21. Jerrold Post, 'Prospects For Nuclear Terrorism: Psychological Motivations and Constraints', in Paul Leventhal and Yonah Alexander (eds), *Preventing Nuclear Terrorism* (Lexington, MA: Lexington Books, 1986) p 96

22. K. Wasmund, 'The Political Socialization of West German Terrorists', in P. Merkl (ed), *Political Violence and Terror*, p 19

23. Gleitman: *Psychology*, p 476

24. Cameron: *Nuclear Terrorism*, p 18

25. Cameron: *Nuclear Terrorism*, pp 18–19

26. Brian M. Jenkins, 'Understanding the Link between Motives and Methods', in Roberts: *Terrorism with Chemical and Biological Weapons*, pp 46–47

27. Drake: *Terrorists' Target Selection*, p 171

28. Bruce Hoffman, 'Terrorism and WMD: Some Preliminary Hypotheses', *The Nonproliferation Review* (Spring–Summer 1997), p 48; Cameron: *Terrorists' Target Selection*, pp 85, 114

29. Cameron: *Terrorists' Target Selection*, pp 129–30

30. Cameron: *Terrorists' Target Selection*, p 127

31. Julia Berryman, David Hargreaves, Kevin Howells and Elizabeth Ockleford, *Psychology and You: An Informal Introduction* (Leicester: The British Psychological Society, 1997) p 116

32. Gleitman: *Psychology*, p 476

33. Cameron: *Terrorists' Target Selection*, p 53

34. Post: 'Prospects', p 95

35. Post: 'Prospects', pp 93–94

36. I. Janis, Groupthink: *Psychological Studies of Policy Decisions and Fiascos* (Boston: Houghton Mifflin, 1982) Post: 'Prospects', p 97

37. Cameron: *Nuclear Terrorism*, p 51; Drake: Terrorists' Target Selection, p 170

38. Drake: *Terrorists' Target Selection*, p 169

39. Berryman, Hargreaves, Howells and Ockleford: Psychology, p 113; Cameron: Nuclear Terrorism, p 45; Drake: *Terrorists' Target Selection*, p 170

40. Post: 'Prospects', p 98

41. Drake: *Terrorists' Target Selection*, p 170

42. Gleitman, *Psychology*, p 469

43. Berryman, Hargreaves, Howells and Ockleford: *Psychology*, p 115

44. Cameron: *Nuclear Terrorism*, p 27. Cameron also suggests that this is reflected in the type of individual who joins such groups. RAF and Red Brigades' terrorists came from incomplete family structures and had backgrounds of social isolation and personal failure. In contrast, those in nationalist separatist groups represent less of an extreme break with society and can come and go from the group with relatively more ease. pp 32, 44; Drake: *Terrorists' Target Selection*, p 167; Adrian Guelke, *The Age of Terrorism* (London: I.B Tauris 1998) p 93

45. Cameron: *Nuclear Terrorism*, p 46; Drake: *Terrorists' Target Selection*, p 168

46. Martha Crenshaw, *Terrorism and International Cooperation* (New York: Institute for East–West Security, Inc, 1989) p 16

47. Drake: *Terrorists' Target Selection*, p 168

48. Drake: *Terrorists' Target Selection*, p 43

49. Drake: *Terrorists' Target Selection*, p 164

50. Post: 'Prospects', p 94

51. Cameron: *Nuclear Terrorism*, pp 104–05, 110

52. W. Seth Carus, 'A Case Study in Biological Terrorism: The Rajneesh in Oregon, 1984', paper summary, Center for Counterproliferation Research, National Defense University (29 July 1997) p 5-6

53. David Kaplan and Andrew Marshall, *The Cult at the End of the World*

(New York: Crown Publishers, 1996), pp 50, 251

54. Kaplan and Marshall: *The Cult at the End of the World*, p 42

55. Michael Jordan, *Cults: From Bacchus to Heaven's Gate* (London: Carlton, 1999) pp 95, 104

56. The Cult Information Centre identifies 26 different forms of mind control: Hypnosis – inducing a state of high suggestibility, often thinly disguised as relaxation or meditation. Peer-group pressure – suppressing doubt and resistance to new ideas by exploiting the need to belong. Love bombing – creating a sense of family and belonging through hugging, kissing, touching and flattery. Rejection of old values – accelerating acceptance of new lifestyle by constantly denouncing former values and beliefs. Confusing doctrine – encouraging blind acceptance and rejection of logic through complex lectures on an incomprehensible doctrine. Metacommunication – implanting subliminal messages by stressing certain key words or phrases in long, confusing lectures. Removal of privacy – achieving loss of ability to evaluate logically by preventing private contemplation. Time-sense deprivation – destroying ability to evaluate information, personal reactions and body functions in relation to passage of time by removing all clocks and watches. Disinhibition – encouraging childlike obedience by orchestrating childlike behaviour. Uncompromising rules – inducing regression and disorientation by soliciting agreement to seemingly simple rules which regulate mealtimes, bathroom breaks and use of medication. Verbal abuse – desensitizing through bombardment with foul and abusive language. Sleep-deprivation and fatigue – creating disorientation and vulnerability by prolonging mental and physical activity and withholding adequate rest and sleep. Dress codes – removing individuality by demanding conformity to a dress code. Chanting and singing – eliminating non-cult ideas through repetition of mind-narrowing chants and phrases. Confession – encouraging the destruction of individual ego through confession of personal weakness and innermost feelings or doubts. Financial commitment – achieving increased dependence on the group by burning bridges to the past through donation of assets. Finger pointing – creating a false sense of righteousness by pointing to the shortcomings of the outside world and other cults. Flaunting hierarchy – promoting acceptance of cult authority by promising advancement, power and salvation. Isolation – inducing loss of reality by physical separation from family, friends, society and rational references. Controlled approval – maintaining vulnerability and confusion by alternately rewarding and punishing similar actions. Change of diet – creating disorientation and increased susceptibility to emotional arousal by depriving the nervous system of necessary nutrients through the use of special diets and/or fasting. Games – inducing dependence on the group by introducing games with obscure rules. No questions – Accomplishing automatic acceptance of beliefs by discouraging questions. Guilt – reinforcing the need for 'salvation' by exaggerating the sins of the former lifestyles. Fear – maintaining loyalty and obedience to the group by threatening soul, life or limb for the slightest 'negative' thought, word or deed. Replacement of relationships – destroying pre-cult families by arranging cult marriages and 'families'

57. Ian Haworth, 'Caring For Cult Victims', *Carer and Counsellor* 7/3

(Summer 1997) p 28

58. Kaplan and Marshall: *The Cult at the End of the World*, pp 22, 62, 183

59. Kaplan and Marshall: *The Cult at the End of the World*, p 82

60. 'The Domes-Day Cult,' *Daily Mail* (16 January 16 1999)

61. Kaplan and Marshall: *The Cult at the End of the World*, p 67

62. Jordan: *Cults*, p 112

63. Bugliosi with Gentry: *Helter Skelter*, pp 107, 449

64. Stern: 'Apocalypse Never', p 72

65. Interview with Ian Haworth, (1 October 1999)

66. Bugliosi with Gentry: *Helter Skelter*, p 199

67. Kaplan and Marshall: *The Cult at the End of the World*, p 172

68. Jordan: *Cults*, p 119

69. Bugliosi with Gentry: *Helter Skelter*, pp 597–603

70. Kaplan and Marshall: *The Cult at the End of the World*, pp 140, 240; W.D. Brackett, *Holy Terror: Armageddon in Tokyo* (New York: Weatherhill, 1996) p 22

71. Haworth: 'Caring For Cult Victims', p 29

72. Kaplan and Marshall: *The Cult at the End of the World*, pp 35, 114

73. Kaplan and Marshall: *The Cult at the End of the World*, p 236

74. Drake: *Terrorists' Target Selection*, p 39

75. Hugh Beach & Nadine Gurr, *Flattering the Passions: Or the Bomb and Britain's Bid for a World Role*, (London: I.B Tauris, 1999) pp195-220

76. Anton Obholzer, in Barnett, 'The Nuclear Mentality,' p 36 Kellen, 'The Potential For Nuclear Terrorism: A Discussion,' p 115

8. External Motivations:
State-Sponsored NBC Terrorism

One of the independent variables at work in calculating potetial motivations for NBC terrorism, is the possibility that a state, or even an agency of a state acting independently, will supply a non-state actor with an NBC weapon. In 1987, the International Task Force on the Prevention of Nuclear Terrorism, identified evidence of state support and even sponsorship of terrorism, as one of the factors which was contributing to the increasing probability of nuclear terrorism. (1) This is the easiest means by which a group can acquire an NBC weapon, making questions about how easily terrorists could develop such weapons redundant in assessments of the threat. Consequently, the possibility of state-sponsored NBC terrorism brings, a much wider range of groups into calculations about the nature of the threat, because it brings in those groups that might have the motivation to use them, but otherwise lack the technical sophistication to develop them independently. Therefore, as concerns about terrorist use of NBC weapons increase, inevitable concerns about state-sponsored NBC terrorism arise.

State sponsorship of terrorism
State sponsorship of terrorism has increased since the 1970s, much of it with broad political objectives such as the overthrow of specific regimes, and the extension of the political influence of the sponsoring state. Bruce Hoffman argues that for state sponsors,

> terrorism remains a useful and integral tool of their respective foreign policies: a clandestine weapon to be wielded whenever the situation is appropriate and the benefits palpable, but remaining sheathed when the risks of using it appear to outweigh the potential gains and the possible repercussions are likely to prove counterproductive. For the state sponsor, much as for the terrorist group itself, terrorism is not a mindless act of fanatical or indiscriminate violence but a purposefully targeted, deliberately calibrated method of pursuing specific objectives at acceptable cost. (2)

During the Cold War the USA funded and armed numerous anti-communist groups in the developing world such as the Contras in Nicaragua and the Afghan Mojahedin. The Soviet Union is also considered to have done likewise, and the collapse of communism in eastern Europe in 1989 and 1990 brought new evidence to light of eastern intelligence agencies supporting terrorist groups in the West, although it fell short of proving that they actually controlled the activities of groups such as the RAF. (3)

In the post Cold War world, there has been a shift in state sponsors of terrorism, to states in the developing world. The seminal event in the history of these states using non-state actors to pursue their foreign policy goals, was the seizure of the US embassy in Iran by radical 'students' in 1979, and their holding of the occupants as hostages for 444 days. The apparent success of this act did not go unnoticed by radical states in the developing world, who realized that it could be an effective way, if not the only effective way, that they could strike at the west, and the USA in particular. Therefore, whilst the embassy hostage crisis was the beginning of a long campaign of state-sponsored terrorism by the Islamic regime in Iran, it was also crucially significant as a precedent for a host of other radical regimes in the Middle East and elsewhere, who realized that the West was vulnerable to terrorism.

In 1999 the USA designated Cuba, Iran, Iraq, North Korea, Libya, Sudan and Syria as state sponsors of terrorism, and stated that Afghanistan was not co-operating in anti-terrorist activities. (4) With the exception of Sudan, all of these states have been on the list for a decade or more. Iran and Sudan also appear to be co-operating in sponsoring terrorism, with training camps in Sudan being financed and run by Iran. (5) Similarly, the Palestinian Islamic Jihad has received offices in Damascus from the Syrian government, and also receives arms and money from Iran. (6) However, on the basis of the type of support that the US State Department uses to justify the inclusion of a state on the list, such as the provision of safe havens, it would be possible to argue the case for many more states to be added. This has led to the conclusion that to a large degree, the inclusion of a state on the list was also a reflection on its relations with the USA. (7)

Many of these states have religious and ideological motivations for sponsoring terrorism. Pakistan, for instance, has supported Muslim groups fighting in Kashmir, as well as the Fundamentalist Taliban movement which seized control of most of Afghanistan. In other instances, states can have revenge motives for supporting terrorism against a particular state. In the wake of the US bombing of Tripoli in 1986, Libya funded the Japanese Red Army, which re-invented itself as the Anti-Imperialist International Brigades, to conduct a series of terrorist attacks, particularly against diplomatic and military sites, which included the US and Japanese embassies in Jakarta. Because of UK complicity in the bombing, Libya also sent several large shiploads of weapons and explosives, including semtex and surface-to- air missiles (SAMs), to the IRA in Northern Ireland. But behind these motivations most of these states also have strong political and foreign policy objectives, such as undermining hostile regimes and extending their national influence. The motives of Syria, for instance, are closely bound up with its interest in regaining control of the Golan Heights, cementing its control in Lebanon and generally enhancing its power in the Middle East.

It is Iran, however, that is generally considered to be the most active sponsor of terrorism, supporting numerous Islamic fundamentalist groups, such as Hezbollah in Lebanon. This also makes it one of the most dangerous, because it supports those types of group which are associated with the steady increase in the lethality of modern terrorism. The Iranian revolution is held up as an example to Muslims around the world to re-assert the fundamental teachings of the Koran, and since Iran is the only state to have begun the process of redemption by creating a 'true' Islamic state, it must be the advocate of the oppressed and aggrieved everywhere. (8) Consequently, exporting the Islamic revolution became an Iranian foreign policy goal, which is manifest in its support for Islamist causes. But in 1990 there were indications that Iran had shifted its policy to support not only Shi'a groups, but any individuals or groups who shared the common faith. This was interpreted as a move to increase Iranian influence in the region following the Gulf War. It also filled a vacuum following the 1991 Gulf War, when Iraq could no longer continue to sponsor some groups, and Syria cut its ties to the ANO, for example, because of its interest in developing closer relations with the USA. (9)

R. James Woolsey, a former Director of the CIA, stated in evidence before the Committee on the Judiciary of the US Senate that,

> Iran is by far and away the most active and dangerous state sponsor ...Tehran supports Lebanese Hezbollah both financially and militarily. In large part because of this support over the past decade, Hezbollah now poses a greater threat to US and Western interests than any other Middle Eastern terrorist group ... and senior Iranian officials and Tehran's media organizations are funnelling propaganda to the rest of the Islamic world that the US is the 'Great Satan' whose policy is to oppress Muslims. (10)

The support that Iran provides is diffuse in nature. In 1999 it was alleged to have provided US$4.4 million to Hamas, in order to fund additional attacks against Israeli targets, in an attempt to undermine the Middle East peace process. (11) Iran's terror network comprises individuals or small groups who operate largely independently, with support for large and established groups being an exception, although they do appear to have a headquarters in Peshawar in Pakistan. (12) This has also meant that Iran is casting its net so wide that it is drawing unprofessional groups into its network. (13) The Iranian purpose in sponsoring terrorism is the belief that by supporting attacks in different states it will encourage governments to clamp down on their Muslim populations, and subsequently enable Iran to act as a focus for the exploited and repressed Muslims in those states. (14) However western sources are reluctant to claim the existence of a grand conspiracy behind all terrorist attacks, because of a lack of co-ordination and professionalism amongst the different groups. (15)

The majority of the alleged sponsors of terrorism also possess, or are believed to possess, CW, and in some cases BW, and all have access to radioactive materials of some description which could be used in a contamination bomb (notably radioactive sources in hospital X-ray machines). Dame Stella Rimington, the former head of the UK security service, MI-5, has stated that 'some two dozen governments are currently trying to obtain such technology. A number of these countries sponsor or even practice terrorism and we cannot rule out the possibility that these weapons could be used for that purpose.' (16) In January 1999, however, British intelligence sources were still reporting that there was no indication that states were prepared to pass on the expertise of how to develop NBC weapons to terrorist groups. (17)

There are powerful advantages to be gained by terrorists in seeking the support of a state. This can come in two basic forms: active and passive support. The latter includes the provision of safe havens, whilst more active support can include the provision of logistical support, financing, training, arming, possible access to the intelligence agencies of those states, use of diplomatic bags, and false papers. Since 1986 Syria has apparently provided only passive support to terrorist groups, and many terrorist groups train in camps in states such as Sudan and Afghanistan. In contrast, Iran provides extensive active support to its clients, particularly through training, arms shipments and finance, (18) which it arranges through its network of safe houses, embassies, consulates, mosques, special schools, tourism companies and other activities such as newspaper publications, which are spread around many states in Europe and North America. (19)

Terrorists do not necessarily have to identify with their patron's cause, and neither do they have to be a rabid ideologue. All they have to be willing to do is perform a service for a price. As such, it adds a new dimension to international terrorism because it was not geared to seeking publicity, but to achieve the foreign policy goals of their patron, by covertly bringing pressure to bear by acts of violence. Consequently it operates under fewer constraints than ordinary terrorism. Bruce Hoffman argues that,

> because state-sponsored terrorists do not depend on the local population for support, they do not concern themselves with the risk of alienating popular support or provoking a public backlash. Thus the state-sponsored terrorist and his patron can engage in acts of violence that are typically more destructive and bloodier than those carried out by groups acting on their own behalf.

In fact, Hoffman points out that overall, state-sponsored attacks were eight times more lethal than those carried out by groups without state support or assistance. (20) Yet despite these figures, this does not necessarily mean that state-sponsored terrorists are unconstrained killers, or that their patrons are interested in causing indiscriminate mass-casualty attacks.

Yet the extent of state-sponsored terrorism must not be exaggerated. The US State Department admits that there is no evidence of Syrian officials involved in planning or executing terrorist attacks since 1986. North Korea has not been conclusively linked to, or known to have sponsored, any international terrorist attacks since 1987. There has been no direct evidence of Cuba's sponsorship of terrorism in 1995 or 1996. Iraq's ability to execute terrorist attacks abroad has been curbed by UN sanctions, whilst Sudan was not involved in any acts of international terrorism in 1996. An analysis of the chronologies of 330 significant terrorist incidents identified by the State Department from 1992 to 1996 revealed only six in which states were purported to have had direct control over potential perpetrators. Over two- thirds of incidents classified as international terrorism are directly attributable to non-state actors. (21)

Previous cases of states using NBC weapons
Outside of war situations, states have used NBC weapons for covert operations many times. These include the attempted assassinations of the Director of the Bulgarian National Intelligence Service and the presidential spokesmen using benzol, in 1993; Libya's murder of a PLO official with a 'poison gas letter'; a 1981 attempt by the East German Stasi to murder a dissident and his family with thallium; and the use of a ricin tipped umbrella to kill the Bulgarian dissident Georgi Markov by the Bulgarian secret service. (22) But with one notable exception, (outside of war situations) states appear to have never used NBC weapons for indiscriminate attacks against population targets. The only cases which fall outside of this category have been targeted against agriculture. However, such BW attacks could appear to be a naturally occurring phenomenon, and so cannot be identified as a state-sponsored attack. In the 1970s, Cuba accused the USA of being responsible for blue mould found on their tobacco crops, and cane smut on sugar cane. But since these blights are not unknown in Cuba, it is impossible to tell if this was a covert BW attack. (23)

One of the principal global developments which has underpinned the debate on terrorism and NBC weapons has been the heightened interest in CW following their acquisition and use by states in the developing world, notably by Iraq during the Iran-Iraq war. Some commentators, such as Leonard Cole, have argued that terrorist interest in NBC weapons, 'seems in large measure to be a consequence of state actions.' (24) The most worrying feature of this development has been that Iraq has also employed NBC weapons for the purposes of terror against its civilian population. In March 1988 the Kurdish town of Halabja in Northern Iraq was bombarded with CW over a period of two days, killing 6000 civilians. (25)

Any regime which is prepared to commit such an atrocity might also choose to engage in other acts of NBC terrorism, perhaps against another state. In 1998 this led to a scare after UK intelligence sources indicated that Iraq was planning to smuggle anthrax into the UK in duty- free goods. An 'all ports' warning was issued to UK customs and excise, but government Ministers subsequently downplayed the reports and stated that there was 'no evidence to indicate that any attempt to smuggle anthrax into this country' or that such an attack 'might be in prospect.' (26) Whilst the incident turned out to be a false alarm, the Iraqi regime is inherently unpredictable because its policy making depends upon the state of mind of Saddam Hussein. Consequently, concerns remain that some states will resort to NBC terrorism if they feel threatened enough.

There have been several unconfirmed reports of states assisting terrorists with NBC training, or the planning of attacks. There had been an allegation that the Former East German secret police, the Stasi, had set up a camp which trained terrorists in using CBW against civilian targets. (27) Yet there have been no indications of the complicity of any state in an actual attack, or even of an incident in which a non-state actor came into possession of an NBC weapon, despite the fact that several proliferators allegedly sponsor terrorism. This indicates that states have previously proved to be unwilling to release CBW to terrorist groups under their control.

Factors leading to state-sponsored NBC terrorism
One of the key factors which could impact upon the frequency and nature of state sponsorship of NBC terrorism, is the actions of powerful rogue, or otherwise independent, elements within governments and bureaucracies The intelligence services of many states are frequently accused of operating independently, often outside of the rule of law. The actions of Colonel Oliver North of the US National Security Council, during the Iran-Contra scandal in the mid 1980s in the USA are indicative of the potential of such rogue elements, even within democratic societies. In this operation Colonel North sought to secure the release of US hostages being held in Lebanon, by selling arms to Iran, contrary to US law, and then using the money to fund the Contras in Nicaragua. In other states it has also been shown

that ideologically driven agencies and individuals are an independent variable in assessing future terrorist threats. Occasionally, the security services of some states have been implicated in terrorist campaigns. In Italy during the 1970s and 1980s, elements of the Italian Intelligence Service (SIS) were directly involved in the campaign of violence being undertaken by various neo-fascist groups. (28)

One of the most worrying examples was the covert BW attacks launched by the former apartheid regime in South Africa. In 1989 the ANC-led government of President Nelson Mandela, established the Truth and Reconciliation Commission to investigate the abuses committed by all sides, during the apartheid era. This included uncovering the details of the old regime's covert BW programme. What emerged was a startling picture of how easily a state-sponsored programme can be set up, and what happens when it runs out of control.(29)

The principal figure in the government's official BW programme was Dr Wouter Basson, a former Special Forces Army Brigadier and heart specialist to President Botha, who was tried for murder. The Commission discovered that he also ran his own unofficial BW programme; which was set up in an attempt to develop BW that could be specifically targeted against South Africa's indigenous black population. The man in charge of the official South African BW programme was General Neils Knobel, Surgeon General of the South African Defence Forces from 1988 to 1997. He gave Basson the necessary autonomy to organize the deceptions, which gathered together BW knowledge from all around the world. Knobel admitted that South Africa covertly penetrated the programmes of many countries. He also organized a fertility control programme which he intended to target against the black population. The scientists working on this unofficial programme admitted that they would have administered an infertility drug that would make black Africans sterile, without them knowing it. They also admitted to making poisons to kill and paralyse.

The Truth and Reconciliation Commission discovered that Dr Basson's unofficial programme had committed several murders and had compiled a list of enemies of the state who were to be murdered. The programme also conducted research into toxins which are untraceable and which mimic death by natural causes. The Reverend Frank Chickane, a senior ANC activist, now Director General of the Office of Deputy President in South Africa, was twice targeted with thallium, a deadly organophosphate poison, which was administered in his underpants. Fortunately for Reverend Chickane, the toxin had not been distributed properly, and was discovered by the staff working in an

American hospital. If he had been treated in a hospital with less sophisticated facilities for identifying poisons, the outcome might have been different. Basson's ultimate target was Nelson Mandela, and there were plans to contaminate his medication which were never carried out. It is also possible that thallium could have been administered to another senior ANC activist, Steve Biko, whose strange behaviour in a police station before he was beaten to death has been identified by some as being symptomatic of thallium poisoning.

In other operations anthrax spores were put into the food of three Russian advisors to the ANC in Zambia, whilst the cigarettes of some other individuals were tipped with anthrax. They also put toxins into sweets, chocolates and screwdrivers. Cholera is endemic in South Africa, and there is now little doubt that it was used deliberately to contaminate local water supplies in some areas. The members of Basson's unofficial programme also released hepatitis and anthrax spores near hostile villages and enemy encampments. In 1979 anthrax which had been produced at Porton Down in the UK, was used by African intelligence services to kill cattle in Zimbabwe.

By 1994 South Africa's dirty war was over, but a new problem emerged. Concerns were raised that the South African programme could proliferate to the rogue states. British intelligence discovered that Basson had visited Libya, which led the USA and the UK to confront President de Klerk some time between 1993 and 1994, about the extent of South Africa's CBW programme. Western intelligence agencies claimed that Colonel Ghadaffi had been trying to set up a BW programme for years. Basson was subsequently apprehended by police in February 1997 during a sting operation in a Pretoria park, while conducting a drugs deal involving 1000 Ecstasy tablets. When the police raided his house, they found documentation of the entire South African BW warfare programme, along with files and photos of people killed during experiments and operations. Currently, South Africa's CBW programme is held on 12 CD ROM disks, under triple lock and key, and if it is ever opened the President must be present.

But whilst Basson acted independently of the official BW programme, he still did not release BW agents to any of the extremist Afrikaaner groups which were opposed to the transition to majority rule. This might have been due to the fact that they were under heavy police surveillance and any links they had to Basson might have been discovered. In addition, Basson might have been concerned about how effectively these groups would use any weapons that he passed on to them. There was every chance that they would not have been as professional as the agents working in Basson's programme, and would have been quickly discovered by the security forces. Therefore, even in this case a degree of restraint was being exercised in deciding not to release pathogens to groups or individuals who they might not have been able to control – although Basson's objectives and targeting choices were probably as extreme as any of the Afrikaaner groups. Consequently, the Apartheid regime falls within the definition of a terrorist state rather than a state sponsor of terrorism.

Another alleged actor in state-sponsored terrorism is Pakistan's powerful Inter Services Intelligence (ISI) agency, which observers claim has been taken over by Islamic fundamentalists, and is run as almost a private fiefdom by its leaders. It now conducts what are apparently autonomous covert operations. In particular it has been accused of funding, arming and training Islamic fundamentalists in the disputed province of Kashmir. This takes place through an umbrella organization called Harakat ul-Ansar (HUA) which is closely linked to Osama bin Laden and who himself has close links with ISI. (30) The HUA has now expanded beyond its remit in Kashmir, and is considered to pose a threat to Pakistan itself and the wider South Asia region. It has training camps in Afghanistan, and the US Tomahawk cruise missile raids against bin Laden's camps in 1998, killed seven HUA members. As a consequence it swore revenge on the USA. (31)

But whilst the ISI is argued by some analysts to be out of control, it is a wholly different proposition to suggest that it would extend its assistance to non-state actors to include NBC weapons. Even if allegations of Pakistan's CW programme are true, it is a big assumption to make that ISI could, or would, supply a terrorist organization with a CW or other materials such as nuclear isotopes. These weapons and materials are very well administered, even in developing states, because they are too sensitive to leave under an ordinary security regime. Therefore doubts must be raised about whether ISI actually has access to such weapons. Equally, Pakistan is now in a state of overt mutual deterrence with India, and the use of an NBC weapon by any of the militant groups in India such as the Kashmiris or Sikh militants, would without doubt provoke a response from India. The ISI should be aware of the logic of deterrence, and limit its activities accordingly.

In non-crisis situations it is hard to conceive of an incentive for a rogue state to engage in an act of NBC terrorism, since the likely disincentives will outweigh all other factors. Instead, for many of the states of concern, the principal factors which might lead them to resort to NBC terrorism, are probably linked to specific political scenarios. The principal situation in which a state might resort to NBC terrorism is one in which the regime is threatened, and it lashes out in a final act of revenge. However none of the states of concern have so far been pushed into such a situation, and therefore it remains a hypothetical concern only.

Factors against state-sponsored NBC terrorism
Whilst a number of proliferators are alleged to be state sponsors of terrorism, there is no record of any of them supplying NBC weapons to terrorist groups, and all of them seem inhibited from doing so. Even during the Gulf War and in the numerous subsequent stand-offs with the UN, Iraq has retained tight control of its residual NBC weapons. It is difficult to determine the precise conditions under which Saddam would release these weapons to terrorists.

One of the principal factors inhibiting state sponsors from NBC terrorism, is the fear of retribution if they were ever discovered to be responsible for such an attack. Whilst rogue states might hope that they could use terrorists to either threaten or use an NBC weapon, they could not be assured of being able to maintain deniability. Neither would retaliation by the target state necessarily be dependent upon proving the guilt of the sponsor state beyond all doubt.

In the Middle East there is a long history of Israeli military action against neighbouring Arab states from which Palestinian terrorists launched attacks against Israel. Following the 1948-49 Arab-Israeli war, Egypt was unable to achieve its goals militarily, and instead armed Palestinian fedayeen commando units. One of the factors leading to the 1956 Arab-Israeli war was an increasing cycle of fedayeen raids and Israeli retaliation, which had begun in 1953. This same pattern of events was repeated in the 1960s, culminating in the 1967 Arab-Israeli war. Whilst state sponsorship of terrorism was not the primary cause of these wars, it was a factor in decision making. The lesson from both cases was that the state sponsor of terrorism ultimately reaped the backlash of being defeated in war.

Because Israel has contiguous borders with some of the alleged sponsors of terrorism, it has the ability to conduct a sustained military campaign; however, western states are geographically removed from these states, which makes going to war for limited objectives much harder to countenance. Therefore western responses to state sponsors have focused on economic sanctions, political isolation and even punitive military action, but these have had limited success. In 1986 the USA launched bombing raids on Libya, following allegations of its complicity in terrorist bombings against US targets. However they resulted only in an increase in Libyan support for international terrorism. The same is also true following the Tomahawk cruise missile attacks on bin Laden's training camps in 1999.

A state-sponsored terrorist incident involving an NBC weapon would be such a major escalation in violence that it would provoke the most severe backlash from the victim, and the international community at large. It would also be unlikely that the state would be able to maintain the support of its erstwhile allies. US power in the Middle East is very strong, and the need of the Arab states to maintain good relations with the USA and the West would force them to oppose any Middle East regime that sponsored such an attack. (Although it must be noted that states such as North Korea and Iraq have few allies anyway.)

The outcome of Allied airstrikes on Iraq in 1999 following its non-compliance with the UNSCOM inspection regime, has also demonstrated that a committed regime is capable of surviving punitive military action. Therefore fear of the consequences of an NBC attack will have a varying impact in different states. However, even Saddam Hussein has on occasion shown himself to be sensitive to the costs of defying the international community. He has been prepared to risk airstrikes, but in the periodic bouts of brinkmanship that have occurred over UNSCOM access to suspected WMD sites inside Iraq, he has frequently accepted compromise rather than risk the total retribution of the international community.

It must also be remembered that not all state-sponsored terrorist attacks are targeted against the West. Iran and Iraq both support opposition groups in each other's territory. Iran, in particular, is alleged to sponsor attacks throughout the Gulf region and the Middle East, particularly in those states that supported Iraq, in the Iran-Iraq war. (32) Yet even in regional scenarios, reactions to a state-sponsored NBC attack are likely to be so strong that they would have to be a factor in the policy decisions about whether to sponsor such an attack. In 1999, Iran launched SCUD missile attacks against camps in Iraq housing the Mojahedin Khalq, an Iranian opposition group which is backed by Iraq. (33) But whilst Iraq is willing to use CW against internal dissidents, it has been deterred from sponsoring such attacks in Iran.

Another factor which might inhibit state sponsors is that the weapons they pass on could be turned against themselves one day, because of a lack of control over their proxies. The USA has already learned this lesson, to its cost. Similarly during the Afghan war, the CIA operated an arms supply pipeline to the Afghan Mojahedin, which included sophisticated Stinger anti-aircraft missiles. Following the cessation of the war, the CIA realized that Islamic militants now possessed the surplus stocks that had not been used in the war, and that they could be used for terrorist purposes. The CIA attempted to buy the missiles back from the Mojahedin, but was unsuccessful. During the time when he lived in Sudan, Osama bin Laden was under observation by the Sudanese Intelligence Service, apparently because he was so extreme, that even the radical Sudanese government considered that he might become a threat to them one day. (34)

The extent of this risk will be dependent upon the level of control which the state sponsor maintains over the terrorist group. Iran does not appear to maintain tight control over its proxies. In fact, the Iranian regime deliberately avoided the creation of a unified central command, because it considered that groups should be left to plan their own campaigns, and it satisfied itself with maintaining a small degree of influence through its ability to manipulate its ideological and financial powers. (35) One intelligence source has commented that, 'The Iranians do not appear to select the targets ... Rather they hand out the equipment and the knowledge and each group get on with it. Sometimes the cash disappears, sometimes nothing happens but sometimes the terrorists attack.' (36)

Yet if a state did pass an NBC weapon to a terrorist group for a specific attack, the state sponsor would in all probability attempt to mitigate this possibility, by exercising some additional form of control over its proxy. Part of the reason why Iraqi-sponsored terrorist attacks did not occur during the Gulf War, was because the Iraqis maintained strict control over the supply of arms to their client groups through their embassies, and insisted on giving the go-ahead for all attacks. When communications between the Iraqi foreign ministry and its embassies and intelligence agencies were destroyed, that permission was never received. (37) Therefore problems derived from a loss of control over their proxies, should not be a major problem. In turn, this means that state sponsors should be able to ensure that the acts they sponsor meet their foreign policy objectives.

Most state sponsors of terrorism also have some form of relationship with the West which they would not want to jeopardize. Both Syria and Iran became involved in the hostage crisis in the Lebanon during the early 1990s, because President Assad of Syria needed US backing for his political role in Lebanon, and President Rafsanjani of Iran wanted to open up his country to the western world in order to rescue its economy. (38) Sudan has also expressed an interest in negotiating with the USA. (39) Even isolated states are in this position. Iraq is dependent upon the west to secure an end to sanctions, and North Korea needs food aid. Therefore all of these states have something to lose from alienating the international community, and the West in particular. The use of an NBC weapon would be such a major act, that it would probably irrevocably damage relations with the West, and undoubtedly provoke the strongest reaction. Therefore, despite the increasing levels of lethality associated with state-sponsored terrorist attacks, these sponsors still seem willing to calibrate levels of violence to acceptable levels, and will rein it back completely when political conditions require it.

Yet despite seeking some form of accommodation with the West, Iran remains ideologically opposed to any form of accommodation with Israel. Indications that the Israeli Prime Minister, Ehud Barak, was anxious to resolve all outstanding issues in the Middle East peace process and reach an all-encompassing agreement with the Palestinians, allegedly prompted Iran to invest US$ 4.4 million in funding a new wave of terrorism. (40) Therefore, whilst state sponsors might be willing to restrict their acts in respect of the West, this will not necessarily apply to all states, although in this instance Iran might also have to consider how attacks which it might sponsor inside Israel, could still alienate the USA and the West.

Conclusion
State sponsorship is a wild card in any assessment of the potential threat of NBC terrorism. Despite the fact that state-sponsored terrorist attacks are amongst the most lethal, this is no indication that a state would release an NBC weapon to a non-state actor, and it can even be considered that state sponsorship might act as an inhibiting factor on such attacks. Yet whilst it is unlikely that a state would sponsor such an attack, the possibility cannot be ruled out, particularly as a result of the actions of ideologically driven government agencies acting independently. There are a number of conceivable scenarios in which desperate leaders in these states might release NBC weapons to terrorist groups to further their goals, particularly if their regime was threatened, and they wanted to exact final revenge against their enemies. But in general it could be concluded that an act of state-sponsored terrorism would be such an extreme act that it would be an option of last resort for any of these states.

Notes and references
1. Paul Leventhal and Yonah Alexander (eds), *Preventing Nuclear Terrorism* (Lexington, MA: Books, 1986), p 8 Lexington
2. Bruce Hoffman, *Inside Terrorism* (London: Indigo, 1998) p 197
3. Adrian Guelke, *The Age of Terrorism* (London: I B Tauris, 1998) p 40

4. 'US Terror League,' *Sunday Telegraph* (2 May 1999)

5. James Adams, *The New Spies* (London: Hutchinson, 1994), p 180

6. Adams: *The New Spies*, p 184

7. Guelke: *The Age of Terrorism*, p 148

8. Hoffman: *Inside Terrorism*, p 96

9. Adams: *The New Spies*, p 183

10. Quoted in Peter Taylor, States of Terror (London: BBC Books) p 197

11. 'Iran Funds Hamas Terror Group To Sabotage Peace Process,' *Sunday Telegraph* (15 August 1999)

12. Adams: *The New Spies*, p 185

13. Adams: *The New Spies*, p 188

14. Adams: *The New Spies*, p 188

15. Adams: *The New Spies*, pp 186, 188

16. Gavin Cameron, 'Nuclear Terrorism: A Real Threat,' *Jane's Intelligence Review* (September 1996), p 424

17. 'Russians Help Syria To Make Chemical Arms,' *The Times* (25 January 1999)

18. For a description of Iran's network of terrorist training camps, see Amir Taheri, *Holy Terror: The Inside Story of Islamic Terrorism* (London: Hutchinson, 1987) pp 90–102; 'Iran Funds Hamas Terror Group To Sabotage Peace Process,' *Sunday Telegraph* (15 August 1999)

19. Taheri: *Holy Terror*, pp 103–09

20. Hoffman: *Inside Terrorism*, p 189

21. Thomas J.Badey, 'US Anti-Terrorism Policy: The Clinton Administration,' *Contemporary Security Policy* 19/2 (August 1998) pp 53–55

22. Ron Purver, 'Chemical and Biological Terrorism: New Threat to Public Safety?,' *Conflict Studies* 295 (December 1996–January 1997),Research Institute for the Study of Conflict and Terrorism, p 15

23. Wendy Barnaby, *The Plague Makers: The Secret World of Biological Warfare* (London: Vision Books, 1997), p 15

24. Leonard Cole, 'Überterrorists,' Review of Jessica Stern, *The Ultimate Terrorists*, *The Bulletin of the Atomic Scientists* (September–October 1999) p 67

25. According to Israeli sources, Iran has been attempting to expand its nuclear weapons programme since 1988, but despite its efforts to procure technology from Russia, China, North Korea and Europe, its programme remains at a preliminary stage.The CIA has also reported that Iran has an extensive CW programme, despite signing the CWC in 1993. It is also considered to have conducted research on anthrax and biotoxins, and is suspected of producing BW at a pesticides facility near Tehran.Under the terms of the 1991 cease-fire which ended the Gulf War, Iraq must destroy all of its CW and BW, and any potential nuclear weapons, if it wants international sanctions to be lifted. Iraq is now closely monitored by the UN, but despite intrusive verification measures, has shown many indications that it intends to rebuild its WMD capabil-

ities. Unconfirmed reports indicate that Iraq recruited 50 scientists from the FSU in 1991, whilst another claimed that an Iraqi delegation travelled to the FSU to purchase nuclear waste in 1992. It also appears that Iraq did not destroy some of the pre-1991 calutrons manufactured for enriching uranium. Whether or not these reports are true, the fact remains that Iraq possesses the most advanced workforce in the Arab world, with hundreds of scientists and engineers experienced in the production of fissile material and nuclear technology. It is possible that Iraq would be able to weaponize very quickly, should Baghdad manage to obtain fissile material smuggled from the FSU. Iraq's CW and BW capability also remains a cause for concern. By May 1994, all known Iraqi chemical munitions, agents and precursors, were believed to have been destroyed by UNSCOM. Iraq also claimed that it had destroyed all of its bacteriological agents after the Gulf War, but has yet to produce evidence to support this claim. Whatever the facts are, it is generally accepted that Baghdad has retained dual-use production facilities and the experts capable of renewing production of both CW and BW. Therefore although Iraq has been forced to accept ongoing UN monitoring of its weapons programmes this does not mean that Saddam Hussein intends to forgo rebuilding Iraq's WMD capabilities. Syria's nuclear programme remains at an embryonic stage and is limited in scope..There are no indications that Syria is attempting to construct facilities that would enable it to produce fissile material, and given the financial and strategic constraints, it is unlikely to do so in the near future. However it is considered to have a chemical warfare programme which has been active for at least a decade, which according to Israeli sources has now successfully produced VX nerve agent. Libya dedicates several hundred million dollars annually to developing WMD. Uranium deposits were discovered in Libya in 1985, but its nuclear weapons programme did not begin in earnest until 1992. Libya is believed to have recruited nuclear scientists from the Commonwealth of Independent States (CIS), and unconfirmed reports claim that it has attempted to acquire HEU and a nuclear reactor from China. The IAEA has conducted inspections in Libya, but the results cannot be ascertained from open sources. However Libya does tend to be characterized as having embarked on a slow-moving nuclear weapons programme. Although this programme is not an immediate threat because Libya lacks well-developed plans, technological expertise and consistent financial support. Moreover, Tripoli's reliance on foreign assistance is a major constraint, particularly as acts of terrorism have led to US pressure and UN sanctions which deter foreign support. Libya's BW programme also appears to be at an early stage of development, hampered by an inadequate biotechnical foundation, and technical short-comings. This precludes the production of a militarily-effective BW system for the foreseeable future. But its CW programme is of more immediate concern, and Ghadaffi has proved that he is prepared to use such weapons. Iran is believed to have supplied Libya with chemical agents in the 1980s, and since then Libya is thought to have developed an extensive indigenous CW programme. According to US government figures, by 1991 Tripoli had manufactured at least 100 tons of blister and nerve agents at its facilities in Rabat. The USA also believes that work is currently underway on the construction of a large underground chemical warfare plant at Tarhuna.

26. 'Ministers Sound Retreat on Anthrax Warning,' *Guardian* (25 March 1998)

27. Jessica Stern 'Will Terrorists Turn To Poison,' *Orbis* (Summer 1993) p 2

28. Guelke: *The Age of Terrorism*, p 65

29. *'Special Investigation Into Project Coast,'* Truth and Reconciliation Committee Final Report, Volume 2, Chapter 6 (29 October 1998)

30. 'Bin Laden Shielded By Cult Status in Pakistan,' *Sunday Telegraph* (20 February 2000)

31. 'Pakistan Funds Islamic Terror,' *Sunday Telegraph* (16 May 1999)

32. Hala Jaber, *Hezbollah: Born With A Vengeance* (London: Fourth Estate, 1997) p 111

33. 'Iran-Iraq Strains Grow as Report Says Scuds Fired,' *Guardian* (11 June 1999)

34. Frank Smyth, 'Culture Clash, bin Laden, Khartoum and the War Against the West,' *Jane's Intelligence Review* (October 1998) p 22

35. Taheri: *Holy Terror*, pp 100-101

36. Adams: *The New Spies*, p 180

37. Adams: *The New Spies*, p 167

38. Jaber: *Hezbollah*, p 143

39. Smyth: 'Culture Clash,' p 25

40. 'Iran funds Hamas Terror Group To Sabotage Peace Process,' *Sunday Telegraph* (15 August 1999)

9. External Constraints:
The Security Environment Created by Governmental Counter-Measures

Should terrorists manage to develop or otherwise acquire NBC weapons, they are confronted by a final series of constraints if they decide to actually use them – the security environment of the state in which they operate. Societal vulnerability might make defence more problematic, but acts of NBC terrorism are much more difficult to plan and execute than conventional attacks, thereby providing greater opportunities for detection. Therefore, despite the vulnerability of society to terrorist attacks, they can be prevented, and the future scale of the threat from NBC terrorism will also be determined by the effectiveness of the regime of counter-measures that governments implement. It is impossible to permanently protect all potential targets, but the threat can be contained using the same basic approaches used to combat conventional terrorism, with the addition of some special measures. To this end, governments are pursuing a multi-layered, integrated strategy of policy responses at national, bilateral, multilateral and global level. Each level of response has its individual strengths and weaknesses in contributing to strengthening this regime. Writing about building a regime to combat the threat from transnational crime, Phil Williams and Ernesto Savona argue that 'For the most part bilateral, regional and global approaches can be regarded as overlapping strategies that generally complement each other.' (1) They argue that a multi-level approach of this kind has a synergistic effect, especially when co-operative ventures feed back into the national level, encouraging states to develop domestic law with the obligations that they have accepted internationally.

Prevention and consequence-management measures at the national level
The primary, and most critical, level of defence is at the national level. No two states will respond to the threat in exactly the same way because deficiencies in existing policies, organizational structures and operational capabilities will vary considerably between states, as will threat perceptions, and the levels of resources which can be devoted to the problem. For each state, implementing an effective defence is predicated upon the establishment of a coherent national strategy and programme of long-term planning. The range of scenarios which states might have to confront could vary considerably depending upon the type of agent used and the nature of the target,therefore, states are going to have to analyse the whole range of potential scenarios and response measures. (2)

The multi-faceted nature of the threat means that governmental responses require the co-ordination of the activities of a wide range of departments and agencies. John Deutch, a former director of the CIA, argues that it is not necessarily a bad thing that a number of different agencies are involved, because they each have different areas of expertise and responsibility. (3) But in practice, this tends to create problems of intra and inter-agency co-operation. Therefore, one of the first challenges confronting governments is to establish strong bureaucratic structures, with clear lines of authority and responsibility. This is best achieved with a 'top-down' approach, to co-ordinate the mixture of prevention and consequence- management measures that are implemented.

The principle means for preventing terrorist attacks taking place are intelligence and good police work, backed up by legislation, which provides the necessary authority for these agencies to do their work effectively.

Whilst terrorism and the proliferation of NBC weapons has always been a major target for intelligence agencies, the end of the Cold War led to additional resources and assets being focused on these issues. Yet this has not been sufficient to prevent all acts of terrorism, or bring a halt to proliferation. The intelligence community faces immense problems in penetrating terrorist organizations, particularly those with cell structures and those that are transnational in nature. Yet these problems are not insurmountable. The UK security services have heavily infiltrated the IRA and right-wing extremist groups, to the extent that the IRA once admitted that 90 per cent of its operations were cancelled because of security force activity. (4) Similarly, the FBI has been successful in infiltrating right-wing Christian militia groups and some religious cults.

Monitoring communications traffic has traditionally been a prime source of intelligence, but as terrorist groups become more sophisticated it is becoming increasingly difficult to intercept anything of value. Groups are now using the internet, and can download virtually unbreakable encryption codes with which to mask their communications. However such monitoring is still a profitable source of information. Operations by Osama bin Laden's network in 1998 and 1999 were severely curtailed by the interception of communications traffic. (5)

Beyond these traditional activities, intelligence and law enforcement agencies now need to watch for technical indicators from small-scale, NBC weapon development activities. This will be difficult because CBW programmes can be easily disguised as legitimate commercial activities. However in retrospect, there were plenty of technical indicators which could have alerted the Japanese authorities to the existence of the AUM programme, but because the Japanese law enforcement agencies were not looking for covert CW development activities they were overlooked. In general, the limited and ambiguous indicators of covert NBC weapon development that are likely to be apparent, will tend to make sense only if they can be linked to specific individuals or groups. Therefore it is primarily by monitoring the activities of known terrorists that clandestine NBC development programmes will be identified.

Additional sources of intelligence can also emerge from terrorist defectors, or from the interrogation of captured terrorists. The plot by members of the Patriots' Council to murder federal officials using ricin was uncovered when the wife of one of the members informed on them and took a jar of ricin to the FBI. (6) whilst the planned CW attacks by the Covenant, the Sword, and the Arm of the Lord were thwarted because two members of the group revealed the plan to the FBI after their arrest on unrelated charges. (7) Standard industrial regulatory activities and the awareness of the general public, could also be a major source of information on suspicious activities. It was members of the public in Japan who warned the police of noxious odours emanating from AUM buildings. The current debate on NBC terrorism, despite its apparent exaggerations, therefore serves a useful purpose in raising public awareness of the dangers. This concept of 'societal verification' might prove to be one of the key sources of intelligence on covert NBC acquisition activities, so long as the information that is received is passed to the relevant agencies and investigated properly.

The work of law enforcement agencies is underpinned by anti-terrorism legislation. The consequences of inadequate legislation were made painfully apparent by the Japanese experience with Aum. One of the reasons why Aum avoided close police scrutiny was because of Japanese laws relating to religious activities. The 1947 draft constitution provided strong unambiguous guarantees of religious freedom, and the 1951 Religious Corporation Act further strengthened the rights of religious organizations by giving them tax exemptions and strong protection from state intrusion into their affairs. This gave Japan's religious organizations unprecedented legal protection, and a high degree of autonomy. In conjunction with these legal measures, Japanese culture is extremely bureaucratic, and Japanese officialdom obeyed these legal dictums literally. (8) This confluence of factors is unlikely to be repeated in other states, but it is indicative of how anomalies in national legislation can seriously hinder efforts to contain the threat.

There has always been a lack of uniformity in anti-terrorism legislation between different states. This often begins with the very definition of the term 'terrorism' itself, but also encompasses broader issues such as willingness to extradite terrorist suspects or suppress fundraising activities by groups linked to terrorism. The USA has frequently had difficulty in co-ordinating international economic sanctions against alleged state sponsors of terrorism, whilst the UK has previously had difficulty extraditing IRA suspects from the USA, on the grounds that their crimes were political in nature. This creates inconsistencies and loopholes which terrorists can exploit.

There is an inherent tension between strengthening anti-terrorism legislation and maintaining civil liberties. Legislation in virtually all democratic states is capable of being strengthened in areas such as the provision of greater rights of surveillance, 'stop and search' powers, the banning of specific groups, and the banning of activities such as fundraising, that are being undertaken on behalf of these groups. Therefore public opinion on terrorism is a key determinant on the limits of anti-terrorism legislation. Consequently, each state differs in how far it is willing to encroach on civil liberties. As a result, many democratic states do not suppress the activities of all militant groups that operate on their territory. In the 1990s, the UK in particular became a centre for the activities of some Islamic groups that are alleged to support fundamentalist causes. This includes groups such as Hizb-ut-Tahrir, al-Muhajiroun, and Al Ansar al-Shariah, whose leader Abu Hamzah al-Masri has been accused of recruiting young British Muslims to commit terrorist attacks in the Yemen. (9)

Ironically, legislative provisions in respect of NBC terrorism should be uniform because most states have signed the CWC, the Biological and Toxin Weapons Convention (BTWC), and the 1980 Convention on the Physical Protection of Nuclear Material. The CWC and BTWC ban the production and possession of these weapons in all signatory states. Consequently, the legislative instruments which states have introduced in order to meet their obligations under these treaties and conventions enhances the authority of law enforcement officials to investigate and prosecute individuals and groups for the possession or production of CBW, or the possession of fissile material. The CWC also enables the improved tracking of precursor chemicals because it requires companies to report their transfers and use of such chemicals to the CWC organization, thereby obliging governments and companies to be more vigilant about transactions and could be used to introduce tougher measures to monitor domestic activities with dual-use chemicals. (10)

However the implementation of these treaties and conventions at the national level has been variable. In 1995, a US federal court found two members of the Patriots Council guilty of possessing ricin in violation of the CBW Anti-Terrorism Act (the legislation which implemented the BTCW into US domestic law), yet at the time of the Aum attacks, Japan had no law making it illegal to produce or possess sarin. (11) The effectiveness of the national authorities that are required to implement the provisions of the CWC and BTWC can be seriously undermined by factors such as the distribution of power between them and other government departments or agencies, which have overlapping responsibilities, and by the bureaucratic culture of the state. Therefore, in most states, greater steps could be taken to enhance legislation. There is also still considerable scope for tightening national controls on the supply of BW agents. However, there will be opposition from industry in the negotiation of verification and disclosure obligations under the BTWC because they can be onerous and intrusive. The economic power of the global biotechnology industry is such that it could prevent the introduction of strong enough legislation. In some states there are legal obligations upon individuals to uphold the prohibition on offensive application of agents, but outside of the USA the direct regulation of biological pathogens is largely restricted to imposing standards for biosafety containment. (12)

Physical security measures designed to protect individuals, important sites, or even geographical areas, can add yet another level of practical difficulty for terrorists planning to carry out an NBC attack. As well as posting guards at strategic sites and the installation of truck bomb defences, governments can also institute mass searches of buildings, control traffic flows in and out of specified areas, establish checkpoints, flood areas with police and army units, and install CCTV cameras. These measures can all seriously complicate the task of executing a terrorist attack, and increase the chance of detection. It is difficult to maintain these measures over a long period of time, therefore it could be the case that governments use such measures only when they have received specific intelligence of an attack, although thoughtful terrorists should be able to breach most defences of this type, given time.

Additional physical security at nuclear power stations has been identified as a necessary requirement in several states. The US Nuclear Regulatory Commission has been analysing precautions to protect reactors against the threat posed by truck bombs. This includes creating buffer zones around the vital areas of a facility, although this could prove difficult at some small ones. Its rules require facilities to be prepared for a small group of trained terrorists, possibly working with a confederate inside the plant. (13) Additional protection from the insider threat can also be provided by measures such as further compartmentalization to restrict personnel from key areas, and the adoption of a 'two-person' rule. However, there will be resistance to these measures because of the costs, although it is also possible to design out vulnerable areas in new plants, (14) which is a better long-term solution.

Security forces can also be used to conduct pre-emptive and punitive attacks on terrorist bases and suspects. This can take a number of forms, from the use of special forces units, to airstrikes using aircraft or missiles. The use of airstrikes is particularly useful where the opportunities for using special forces are limited. However the utility of military options is limited. Successful pre-emption relies on intelligence to identify the precise location of an NBC production facility or weapon storage site, and in many circumstances the use of military force is placed within tight legal constraints.

Ultimately it will be impossible to prevent all future acts of NBC terrorism, therefore states also require a system of consequence-management capabilities. If a BW attack does occur, it will probably be first detected by epidemiological surveillance systems. When casualties begin arriving at hospitals it is only through quick diagnosis of the disease and recognition that an attack has occurred, that its consequences can be managed and contained. Since the incubation period of some diseases can be days, many lives can potentially be saved. This makes specialists in infectious diseases a critical part of the front line of defence. Most developed states already have some systems in place to detect, contain and treat natural outbreaks of disease, but in general the epidemiological surveillance systems in most states are inadequate to deal with the massive consequences of a WMD attack.

Therefore, strengthening public health systems is one of the foremost consequence- management measures available to states. No-one is sure how effectively existing medical infrastructures could deal with massive numbers of NBC casualties. No state has enough isolation beds to cope with a massive outbreak of infectious disease, and most doctors have a lack of knowledge about uncommon CBW, such as anthrax. (15) Specialized equipment held at a few sites such as the US Centers for Disease Control and the US Army Medical Research Institute of Infectious Diseases can identify an agent within three hours, although standard enzyme based immuno tests can take 18–24 hours. (16) The ability to cope with large numbers of casualties, and quickly vaccinate significant numbers of people (if that is deemed necessary), will also depend heavily upon the availability of antibiotics and vaccines.

Consequently, states need to invest in improving the speed and accuracy with which their epidemiological surveillance systems can detect BW attacks, and link them into central control centres, from which nationwide resources can be mobilized. Similarly, most states will have to enhance their emergency medical systems, so that they are capable of mounting an effective no-notice response. This requires stockpiles of vaccines and antibiotics, trained personnel and programmes of high-readiness mobilization. (17)

Following any NBC attack, the most important operational community will be the first responders, since there would be little or no time to bring in outside experts to deal with the immediate consequences. This includes the local police, hazardous material specialists, fire and medical services. In all states, the vast majority of these people have no specialist training or equipment to deal with such a contingency. However it is possible to create a layered system of preparedness which would start with broad-based awareness training, the provision of specialized equipment and training for local specialists (eg HAZMAT hazardous materials teams, bomb squads and emergency management officials) and specialized medical units at the regional level. (18) Some states are also beginning to establish specialized anti-WMD terror response units at the national level, to supplement these local forces.

The military have a lot to offer these civil defence plans because of their specialized knowledge, training, and equipment, related to operating in a NBC environments. Therefore as states improve the capabilities of their armed forces to cope with NBC threats, they will also enhance their domestic capability to cope with the problem. (19) If governments intend to integrate their armed forces into civil defence programmes, however, they are going to have to grapple with civil liberties' issues, as they examine ways to clarify the legal provisions which govern the role of the military in domestic security operations.

Technical fixes can greatly enhance prevention and of consequence-management programmes. Such technologies are invariably expensive, and policy makers have to strike a balance between the resources that they can afford to invest in the technology and its inherent limitations. The key technologies are detection devices, protective suits, decontamination systems and bomb disposal equipment. (20) Other US development programmes include an escape hood that can be used by evacuees from an incident, a hazardous materials database that is accessible on a hand-held computer, and a simulant kit to ensure that detectors are working. (21) Some detection devices for CW and nuclear weapons have already been developed, but they only have a short range, some only have a limited lifespan, whilst others will detect only specific agents, although improved models are under development.

Planners have to address the question of where to deploy detection devices, given that states will be able to afford only a limited number. The obvious choices are at facilities which store WMD and the materials necessary for their production; at all entry points to a state; as well as with the first-responder and specialist security force units which will have to deal with any attacks. The utility of detection devices will be enhanced if intelligence can narrow down the search parameters. What remains an unknown factor is whether it will be technically feasible to develop detection devices that can monitor the entire territorial space of a state, and detect the presence of NBC weapons and development facilities. This seems unlikely, although clouds of airborne biological agents can be mapped with lasers.

The other main technical response is the physical control of the materials required for producing NBC weapons. Most states already exercise strong physical protection measures over fissile materials, and effective accountancy and control procedures, through the acceptance of IAEA safeguards. The same level of control is impossible to achieve in respect of CW, which can be developed from commercially available chemicals, although it is possible to achieve a certain measure of monitoring and control through systems of supplier awareness and self-regulation. Chemical suppliers generally know who they are dealing with, and can monitor what they are supplying, and to whom. This can make it more difficult for terrorists, and could potentially lead to the detection of some clandestine programmes. Equally, whilst biological pathogens can be acquired from the environment, those that have already been isolated are generally contained in secure areas of government and commercial facilities, because of standard biosafety regulations.

Bilateral measures
Since terrorism often has a transnational dimension, national efforts to combat the threat can be enhanced by international co-operation. Considerable progress has already been made in efforts to internationalize and harmonize law enforcement efforts to combat terrorism, but there is considerable scope to expand it to deal with new threats. Bilateral agreements have been the most prevalent method of supporting national counter-terrorism programmes. The bilateral approach to regime-building is based on an evolutionary model in which there is a gradually thickening web of agreements, an incremental process marked by the gradual extension of norms, mechanisms and instruments of co-operation. It works from the bottom up, focusing on what is immediately achievable, without losing sight of the overall objective. (22)

Bilateral agreements can cover issues such as law enforcement co-operation, extradition treaties and the training of law enforcement officials and judges, and have proved highly successful in combating international terrorism. In the investigations following the Kenya and Tanzania embassy bombings in 1999, the USA exploited bilateral links to extradite several suspects from Pakistan, and subsequently co-operated with the UK in extraditing a key player in bin Laden's organization working from London. It then passed information to Uruguay, leading to the arrest of another suspect with alleged links to bin Laden.. (23) However there is scope for broadening the nature of bilateral co-operation in the specific area of NBC threats. This could encompass the provision of advice, funding for procuring relevant technologies, and the sharing of the results of national anti-terror exercises.

Evidence from efforts to combat transnational crime indicates that not all bilateral agreements work as effectively, or have the same positive and beneficial results. In some cases asymmetry in law enforcement capabilities or asymmetrical commitments to co-operation can lead to frustration and disappointment. (24) Whilst the UK had difficulty extraditing IRA suspects from the USA, there was effective co-operation between the law enforcement agencies of the two states. The FBI broke up a number of IRA arms deals being brokered in the USA, often in co-operation with British law enforcement officials.

Nevertheless, this incremental approach to building an integrated regime can have some real strengths. It is highly flexible and can be tailored to the specific needs and objectives of each state. The commitment of both states is also likely to be stronger, owing to the recognition of a mutual interest, and because of this, such agreements typically establish clear obligations for each partner. Therefore, provided the implementation of these agreements is effective, they can have an enormous impact. (25)

One of the principal areas where bilateral measures should have a great impact by linking directly into national counter-measures, is in technical co-operation and financial assistance agreements. The main example of this has been the Nunn-Lugar programme, through which the USA is investing financial and technical assistance into Russian nuclear facilities. The goals of the programme are to assist the destruction and dismantlement of Russian nuclear weapons, to strengthen the chain of custody to ensure proper control and safeguards over nuclear materials, and to facilitate the demilitarization and defence conversion process. (26) These objectives are interlinked, but the most important element in respect of NBC terrorism are the programmes to re-establish effective systems of accountancy, control, and physical protection of nuclear materials. The programme has approached the problem with a 'layered defence' concept which, US Assistant Secretary of State Thomas McNamara argues, has 'sought to control the sources of supply material as well as technology and items used in the production or use of special nuclear materials; to reduce demand; to ease economic dislocation that followed the break-up of the Soviet Union; and to strengthen law enforcement and intelligence capabilities needed if the security of the material is breached.' (27)

In 1996, Graham Allison stated that these programmes were hampered by a lack of co-ordination and funding, as well as the absence of a concerted high-level effort to overcome obstacles. (28) Since then, co-operation on nuclear safety and security issues has expanded, and many of its shortcomings have been rectified. However much still needs to be done in respect of materials accountancy, protection and control, which has led to calls for it to be given greater levels of funding. However it remains a source of contention within the US Congress, where some Congressmen consider that it has not been effective, or because it releases Russian funds for re-constructing its armed forces. (29) Therefore, whilst the programme is a priority of the Clinton administration it could run into obstruction in Congress.

Intelligence-sharing is another area where bilateral agreements can directly enhance national prevention measures. This was evident in 1999 when the USA, UK and Israel shared information on a number of religious cults, which led to Israel deporting several members of the Concerned Christians group. It has also led to both Israel and the UK increasing security at sites which were considered to be potential targets for these cults. (30) There are problems associated with revealing sensitive sources of information, therefore co-operation is really effective only where the parties have confidence that their reports will remain secret, and that they can maintain the integrity of their sources. It is therefore likely to take place only between trusted and like-minded states. Consequently, it is most likely to be fully implemented within bilateral arrangements.

There are also some shortcomings to using bilateral agreements. The main problem is that this approach can create gaps or loopholes which terrorists can exploit. Most notably, not all states have extradition treaties with each other, and the same standards are not universally applied. Consequently, the whole could be less than the sum of the parts, since the ad hoc quality of this form of co-operation can produce inefficiencies, notably from a lack co-ordination and the potential overlapping of different measures. The result is that it can be consuming in both time and resources, making it difficult for smaller states which have neither the resources nor the expertise to engage in multiple bilateral negotiations. The implication is that although the web of bilateral agreements is thickening, it needs to be structured by multilateral forms of co-operation. (31)

Multilateral co-operation and regional integration
Multilateral co-operation is a means to resolve the shortcomings of bilateral measures, by establishing a more systematic approach which will provide a clear structure within which the web of bilateral agreements can be developed. (32) Yet such approaches face a number of problems: some states might apply double standards because they sympathize with some groups but not others; and some could also suffer from a lack of political will to address the problem owing to differing perceptions of the threat. This makes the negotiation of multilateral and glob-

al agreements difficult, because they frequently reach consensus through compromises based upon the lowest common denominator.

International approaches need not necessarily be based upon a global model, but can be regional in scope. Efforts have already been made to create a 'common judicial space' in Latin America and western Europe. This extends webs of bilateral agreements to a wider group of like-minded states facing similar threats. Problems associated with co-operation increase with the number of states involved, but if they already have some kind of regional identity the problems can be managed more easily. (33) Yet even so, co-operation on many matters within the European Union (EU) still shows a propensity to reach solutions based upon the lowest common denominator. Although the history of political co-operation in Latin America and western Europe means that their regional efforts at co-operation are more likely to have positive outcomes than in regions such as eastern Europe or central Asia where there is no history of voluntary national co-operation.

Regional co-operation on judicial and criminal matters would appear to be a natural progression from efforts to achieve political and economic integration, and a response to the recognition that something needs to be done to address the increased regional vulnerabilities accompanying the opening of internal borders. But complete uniformity of national legislation is neither feasible nor desirable. Each national criminal law system is finely tuned to the specific characteristics of each state, and this delicate equilibrium should not be disturbed unless a substantial advantage is to be gained. (34)

Most western European states have a long history of dealing with terrorism, and share a common interest in controlling it. Consequently, the EU has enhanced levels of co-operation on law enforcement and anti-terrorism issues amongst its member states. In 1975 the European Community (EC) set up the TREVI group, to provide a basc for co-operation between EC states in their handling of subversion in all its forms. Under its aegis, meetings are held between EC interior and justice ministers and senior police officers. It provides for the pooling and exchange of information, and has proved remarkably effective. (35)

In 1998, the EU's police agency, Europol, came into being after operating in embryo form since 1995. Its mission is to co-ordinate intelligence on organized crime, but it has been given powers that fall far short of a federal police force. Europol acts as an information clearing house, monitoring the activities of traffickers in narcotics, illegal immigrants, stolen vehicles, transnational sexual crime and nuclear materials. From 1999 it also began to co-ordinate intelligence on terrorist organizations. Several technical issues remain unresolved, and the member states are jealously guarding their sovereignty over criminal matters. Europol has no authority to initiate investigations, and whilst some hope that its powers will ultimately be expanded, it is nowhere near being a European FBI, although it is hoped that it will establish links with eastern European states. (36)

Some regional initiatives have the advantage of being relatively easy to formulate and implement, because the states have a broad convergence of interests and relatively homogeneous needs and problems. However the experience of the EU indicates that regional bodies will only be able to develop within constraints, and there are limits beyond which states will cede authority to transnational organizations. Yet even in its limited form, Europol will be of major significance if it operates effectively, and the member states provide it with all available information.

States do not necessarily need contiguous borders to engage in such agreements. The Clinton administration has used the G7 forum as its principle vehicle for pursuing multilateral co-operation on terrorism. At the Ottawa Conference in December 1995 a 'Declaration on Countering Terrorism' was drafted, which among other things called upon states to join existing international treaties; promote mutual legal assistance and extradition; strengthen the sharing of intelligence and other information, pursue measures to prevent terrorist use of NBC materials; refuse to make substantive concessions to hostage takers; inhibit the movement of terrorists and prevent falsification of documents; counter terrorist attacks against public facilities and infrastructures; deprive terrorists of funds; and increase counter-terrorism training and assistance. (37) At the Paris meeting in July 1996, the Ministers agreed a 25-point programme to fight terrorism and transnational crime, including a convention to declare terrorist bombings an international crime, joint databases on forensic evidence and to consider criminalizing the possession of BW.

One meeting that was specifically related to the issue of NBC terrorism was the G8 Moscow Nuclear Safety and Security Summit which was held in 1995. The main purpose of the summit was to promote an effective nuclear safety culture in every country with nuclear installations, and to ensure the long-term viability of nuclear power. A Programme For Preventing and Combating Illicit Trafficking in Nuclear Material was agreed, which stated that, 'The criminal diversion of nuclear material could assist states or terrorist groups to bypass the carefully crafted controls of the international nuclear non-proliferation regime and permit them to construct or otherwise acquire a nuclear or radiological weapon.' (38) The summit aimed to promote co-operation, to combat illicit trafficking and to identify areas where it could be enhanced. This included: safe and secure storage of nuclear material; effective material protection and accounting; co-operative intelligence-sharing; enhanced customs and law enforcement efforts to prevent the transportation and sale of diverted materials; and joint efforts to identify and suppress the illicit supply of, and demand for, nuclear materials. The G8 states have similar needs and problems, particularly because they consider themselves to be among the principal targets of nuclear terrorism. This has enabled them to develop a common approach, and they are also in a position to provide funding and technical expertise to states that need it, which is why it was a useful forum for pursuing these goals.

Global responses
The rationale for the negotiation of global conventions in response to transnational threats is that it will enable states to proceed with other forms of co-operation in a more systematic and effective manner, by creating a framework which bridges the gaps between existing agreements. Global conventions provide a way of mobilizing mutual support and assistance for what individual states are unable to do alone. They focus attention on the problem, legitimize national actions and the greater interaction between governments and particular government departments in ways that could lead to enhanced co-operation. (41) International conventions also establish a set of standards and expectations, providing an important regularizing effect and standardized forms of co-operation.
A useful model is provided by the UN Convention Against Illicit Traffic in Narcotic Drugs and Psychotropic Substances of 1988 (Vienna Convention), which has given rise to a wave of legislative activity at the national level, supported by the legal assistance programme of the UN International Drug Control Programme. (39) Thanks to the commitment and political will of a large number of signatory states, it has had a major impact in bringing about concerted action against drug trafficking, (40) but there has been only partial progress in global efforts to combat terrorism through the UN.
International conventions dealing with terrorism have always been stymied by the lack of an internationally agreed definition of terrorism. Because of this, global responses to terrorism have had to focus on specific terrorist crimes, which led to the enactment of five conventions: the Convention on Offenses and Certain Other Acts Committed on Board Aircraft (Tokyo

Convention); the Convention for the Suppression of Unlawful Seizure of Aircraft (Hague Convention); the Convention for the Suppression of Unlawful Acts Against the Safety of Civil Aviation (Montreal Convention); the Convention on Prevention and Punishment of Crimes Against Internationally Protected Persons, Including Diplomatic Agents (New York Convention); and the International Convention Against the Taking of Hostages (Hostages Convention). (42)

Global responses to the threat posed by NBC terrorism have followed this same pattern. The principal mechanism has been to exploit global non-proliferation norms, rather than anti-terrorism norms, through provisions in the CWC, the BTWC and the 1980 Convention on the Physical Protection of Nuclear Material, even though none of these instruments was specifically designed to combat the threat from terrorism. The loopholes in these instruments are being addressed, which in conjunction with the 1998 convention on Terrorist Bombings, means that international instruments to combat the threat from WMD terrorism are well in hand.

The CWC bans the production and possession of CW by all of its signatories, and provides for the destruction of existing stockpiles and control of the international trade in precursor chemicals. Article VII of the Treaty provides, that states party shall prohibit persons anywhere on their territory, nor permit in any place on their territory, activities that are prohibited to states party. This obliges signatories to enforce the provisions of the convention on all non-state actors. Similarly, the BTWC also bans the production and possession of BW. Its Article IV provides, that states party shall take all necessary measures to prohibit and prevent the development, production, stockpiling, acquisition or retention of the agents, toxins, weapons, equipment and means of delivery specified in Article I, within its territory, under its jurisdiction or under its control. Again, this obliges the states party to enforce the provisions of the convention on non-state actors.

The first instrument to deal with nuclear terrorism was the 1980 convention on the Physical Protection of Nuclear Material. This contains an annex which establishes general levels of physical security to be provided during the shipment of nuclear material used for peaceful purposes. States party also have to co-operate in the recovery and return of stolen material. They are also required to enact legislation that criminalizes certain acts such as the theft or any other unauthorized transfer of nuclear material, attempts to obtain nuclear material by force, and threats to use nuclear material to cause serious harm to people or property. These crimes are extraditable in any extradition treaty between the parties, and must be included in any future extradition treaties. (43)

It has been recognized for a long time, that the scope of the 1980 convention is inadequate for dealing with the threat of nuclear terrorism. In 1998, Russia put forward a proposal in the UN to negotiate a Convention on the Suppression of Nuclear Terrorism. Its intention was to cover the gaps left by the 1980 convention, which is limited to nuclear material in peaceful uses, and does not cover nuclear material of a military nature. The 1980 convention also does not distinguish acts of nuclear terrorism from other criminal acts involving nuclear material; and it was considered necessary to deal with a wider range of measures for combating nuclear terrorism than are covered in the 1980 convention. (44) Discussion of the proposal ended abruptly after considerable doubt was expressed over the need for a definition of the term 'terrorists,' whilst other states questioned the very requirement for the treaty, whilst others considered that its provisions could best be met through protocols to the 1980 convention and the 1998 International Convention for the suppression of Terrorist Bombings. (45)

The objectives of these conventions are supplemented by the International Convention for the Suppression of Terrorist Bombings which was opened for signature in 1998. Article II states that 'Any person commits an offence within the meaning of this Convention if that person unlawfully and intentionally delivers, places, discharges or detonates an explosive or other lethal device in, into or against a place of public use, a state, or government facility, a public transportation system or an infrastructure facility.' Article I identifies an 'explosive or other lethal device' as 'A weapon or device that is designed, or has the capability to cause death, serious bodily injury or substantial material damage through the release, dissemination or impact of toxic chemicals, biological agents or toxins or similar substances or radiation or radioactive material.' (46)

These instruments ensure uniformity of obligations amongst the states party, but the question of whether they go far enough remains unanswered. The provisions of these conventions are largely in line with the other five conventions dealing with terrorist acts. One area of difference lies in the New York Convention, which requires members to co-operate in order to prevent within their territories, preparations for attacks on diplomats within or outside their territories. But none of the conventions obliges states to extradite suspects. (47) Most of the conventions also include relatively strong provisions for settling disputes that allow for binding arbitration or adjudication, but they make no provision for sanctions.

At the global level, the regime is now moving from the phase of enacting the necessary instruments, into the phase of implementing them. In order to be effective, states need to exhibit the will and capacity to meet their obligations. (48) The general acceptance of the non-proliferation norm, has meant that the majority of states have signed the CWC, BTWC and the 1980 convention, although ratification has been slow in coming. The main effort has shifted towards ensuring uniformity of implementation. The conventions provide guidance for a programme of implementation that would assist in harmonizing law enforcement measures., many governments do not view the threat and national financial and strategic interests can also have a tendency to take priority in some instances. Some states lack the resources for effective implementation, whilst some states' responses are undermined by official corruption and organized crime.. Russia being a good example in both cases. In order for international conventions to work effectively, each party has to make sacrifices commensurate with those of others. The acid test will come when member states find themselves on opposite sides of a particular case.

Besides these conventions, other global arrangements are in place to deal with specific aspects of the threat. The IAEA has been co-ordinating the global response to the problems posed by the trafficking of nuclear materials. It has been providing assistance in drafting laws and regulations, helping states to apply effective physical protection measures, accounting and control procedures on nuclear materials, and effective import and export controls. It also helps states to respond quickly and effectively to any incident that occurs, as well as providing training in prevention and response measures, and promoting an information exchange. In 1992 it also began the systematic collection of incident reports.

In December 1994 the IAEA Board approved a number of proposals to enhance the services that the IAEA could offer in helping member states to improve the protection of nuclear material, and to detect and suppress trafficking. In 1995 the functions of the database were expanded to enable the IAEA to provide its member states with authoritative information about reported smuggling attempts. Governments agreed to provide information on the date and place of any incident, and a description of the material involved. The IAEA also held a number of meetings with members states, the UN, the European Atomic Energy Agency (EURATOM), and international law enforcement organizations such as of the International Criminal Police Organization INTERPOL. These meetings were used to assess the extent of the problem, and to recommend further action, such as the systematic sharing of information, improved detection of smuggled material at frontier crossings, fuller use of the database and prompt notification of incidents.

One area where additional international co-operation is required, is in the establishment of an effective and reliable system for collecting, sharing and analysing information on terrorism. One proposal has been the possibility of establishing an international clearing house to collect and share more reliable information. However, John Deutch argues that established channels of international co-operation mean that states can be reasonably sure that any terrorist group can be identified and tracked. (49). Information-sharing already occurs with illicit transfers of fissile material, but global information sharing on a broad range of terrorist activity is required. At the international level the practical and political problems associated with sharing intelligence are compounded however. Article 3 of the INTERPOL constitution states that 'it is strictly forbidden for the organization to undertake any intervention or activities of a political, military, religious or racial character'. Because of this restriction, INTERPOL has been constrained to proceed cautiously in its involvement with combating terrorism. INTERPOL would not involve itself in any intelligence activity aimed at preventing terrorist acts, although once an act occurred it would assist law enforcement efforts. Terrorist suspects are excluded from its files, and only those directly implicated in a crime are held. This greatly inhibits the effectiveness of preventive action by the international police community. But whilst it is difficult to envisage formal institutional arrangements to share intelligence, it does take place for non-proliferation purposes.

Global prevention measures are strongly enhanced by measures to control access to the necessary materials, with the aim of establishing transparency and verification mechanisms to verify that no NBC weapons are being produced within a state. In respect of nuclear weapons, the IAEA operates a safeguards system on nuclear facilities to ensure that fissile material is not diverted for clandestine purposes, although it does not have access to military nuclear facilities. In addition, the Nuclear Suppliers' Group (NSG), an export control cartel, controls the global transfer of special fissionable material. Yet there is currently no international legal agreement establishing standards of physical protection for nuclear materials. Such an instrument would harmonize existing practices and remove potential weaknesses in the national systems of some states.

However the focus of these activities is on clandestine programmes being run by governments. Questions must be raised about whether they would be effective against small- scale programmes being run by non-state actors. Consequently, it is down to the capabilities of nation states themselves, to locate and prevent clandestine NBC weapon production by non-state actors. The vigour with which any state will pursue this, will depend upon a number of factors, including its national threat perception, and the resources which it is willing to invest.

In July 1998 the Rome Statue of the International Criminal Court was adopted. It was established 'with jurisdiction over the most serious crimes of concern to the international community as a whole'. These include genocide, crimes against humanity, war crimes and the crime of aggression. Whilst not specifically identifying terrorism, the definition of 'war crimes' includes the employment of poison or poisoned weapons, and employing asphyxiating, poisonous or other gases and all analogous liquids, materials or devices.. The advantage of such a move would be that states will take collective responsibility for the fight against terrorism, and therefore will all share the risk of terrorist retaliation. (50)

Striking the balance between costs and effectiveness
When considering a prudent level of investment in countermeasures, the balance between the costs and effectiveness of different programmes becomes important. Different policy responses will have varying levels of effectiveness. The lowest-cost measures are legislative and organizational, but ironically, these are probably amongst the most effective measures that have been proposed. The best means of defeating the terrorist are good intelligence, effective law enforcement, effective anti-terror laws, and international co-operation to share intelligence and extradite suspects. One of, the most effective use of resources has been the Nunn-Lugar programme which has led to a marked improvement in Russian control of nuclear materials, although there are limits to its scope. One analysis of the problem concluded that 'as long as Russia continues to be touched by turbulence, uncertainty, and disorder, the risk of serious nuclear leakage will persist' (51). Stockpiling vaccines and antibiotics also has variable utility, because it will require enormous quantities to deal with a mass casualty attack. In a scenario involving a city of 50,000 people, an effective BW attack might cause 30,000 casualties, which would require 84 grammes of antibiotic per person, making a total of 2 tonnes of antibiotic which would have to be delivered overnight. There is not that much antibiotic stored anywhere in the USA. If a major city was hit, the casualties and amounts of antibiotic required would rise considerably. In just one example, if one person were infected with smallpox they could infect 20 others, and each of

those could infect 20 others. In 1970 the German authorities had to vaccinate 100,000 people after a single case appeared in hospital, and in 1972 virtually the entire population of Yugoslavia was inoculated over a period of three weeks to prevent a similar outbreak. There are currently 7 million useable doses of smallpox vaccine stored in the US at one location in Pennsylvania. If an outbreak occurred it would be impossible to vaccinate all 270 million US citizens within a matter of weeks. (52)

Stockpiling also assumes that terrorists will use a BW for which there is a stockpiled vaccine. There is no vaccine to most likely BW, and even the vaccine for anthrax is of doubtful effectiveness. For all states, but particularly the geographically large ones, logistics is also a problem. Response teams need to have fast access to the vaccines and antibiotics in case of an attack. VX is the easiest CW to treat if atropine is administered immediately, but if the stocks were held too far away from the site of an attack, they would be useless by the time that the medical services received them. Therefore stockpiles of antibiotics and vaccines can only help to limit casualties rather than prevent them.

The history of terrorism demonstrates that it is impossible to stop a determined terrorist. The security forces in Northern Ireland have excellent intelligence of terrorist activity which enables them to pre-empt many attacks, yet atrocities such as the 1998 Omagh bombing still occur. The problems of acquiring good intelligence at a transnational level are multiplied considerably. Consequently, there will always be intelligence failures, such as the one which occurred in respect of the bombings of the US embassies in Kenya and Tanzania, followed by the mistake in identifying the Shaifa pharmaceutical plant as a covert CW production facility. (53).

Counter-measures also have to be flexible enough to deal with an incident at any location. One of the significant points about the Oklahoma City bombing, was that it was not considered to be a major target for an attack on the federal government.

Equally, it is impossible to hermetically seal off a state through border controls. This is already apparent from terrorists' ability to acquire conventional weaponry. The problem is compounded by the fact that it only requires one NBC weapon to slip through the cordon. Current detection devices have only short ranges, and their targets can be shielded from them relatively easily. (54). In addition, the huge amount of legitimate commerce that passes through airports and ports, makes it impossible to screen all incoming items effectively. They are most usefully deployed at sensitive facilities and storage sites, as a means to prevent theft. Neutron activation is the best means of detecting nuclear weapons and samples of fissile material but it is prohibitively expensive. Therefore, it is impossible to have adequate detection at all conceivable entry points into a state, because of the huge numbers of devices that would be required. The question must be asked, whether it is worthwhile deploying any at all, at those points, since a terrorist could theoretically choose an entry point where there are no detection devices. (Although how a group would know where, detection devices, were, or were not, deployed is uncertain.)

Border controls will also be of limited utility, since a terrorist group is most likely to produce NBC weapons within the borders of the state that it intends to attack, if access to the necessary raw materials and facilities can be achieved within its borders. The weapons used in Tokyo, Oklahoma and the World Trade Centre were all produced inside the state. In developing NBC weapons it would be easier for a terrorist to acquire the necessary raw materials, expertise and facilities to produce a weapon inside the USA, or a European state, which are also amongst the most likely targets.

It has been argued that tougher physical security measures will enhance the ability to prevent NBC terrorism. But terrorism feeds off repression and injustice, and there is a risk that excessive anti-terrorism legislation, especially if it is perceived to be abused by the security forces, might prove to be counter-productive. Evidence from Northern Ireland shows that the checking of identity documents, vehicle road blocks and other checkpoints caused resentment, and perhaps created sympathizers for the IRA.55 A balance needs to be struck between implementing strong counter-terrorism measures, and maintaining basic civil liberties. Consequently, states first have to identify the limits of democracy, before enacting anti-terrorism legislation.56 Equally, there is no guarantee that repressive measures will be successful in pre-empting an attack; states therefore have to weigh the likely advantages of enacting stronger legislation with the likely costs.

In certain circumstances events might create the conditions under which public opinion will accept stronger anti-terrorism legislation. The UK and Eire introduced their strongest-ever legislation in 1998 after the Omagh bombing, because public opinion was prepared to accept the consequences in the final drive to achieve peace, and a political consensus could be built, but even then it was the subject of considerable debate. Individual states and societies have to decide for themselves whether the potential threat from NBC terrorism and its likely consequences, justifies state encroachment on civil liberties. The differing nature of societies, combined with different perceptions of the threat, will lead to different outcomes in this debate.

Pre-emptive or reactive military action will also have varying degrees of success. The US cruise missile attacks in response to the bombings of the US embassies in Kenya and Tanzania in 1998, successfully destroyed the Shaifa chemical plant but the attacks on bin Laden's camps in Afghanistan were ineffective; bin Laden survived and only 21 terrorists were killed. Use of special forces units to attack terrorist bases would be the most effective option, but as the Israeli experience in southern Lebanon proves, this involves a high risk of casualties. The backlash in generating support for bin Laden amongst radical regimes, and public opinion in many Muslim states, ultimately made the attacks an even bigger failure.

US efforts to impose unilateral economic sanctions on alleged state sponsors of terrorism, have also failed. Significant changes in behaviour or policy have not been noted in any of the states that have been the target of these policies, nor has there been a drastic change in the number of incidents of international terrorism which could be attributed to these efforts. In the case of Iran, the result was actually a backlash against US interests. (57). It has also caused problems with allies who do not agree with it. It could be argued that the lack of multilateral sanctions undermines the US policy, but this cannot be proven.

Comparing responses

Most of the states that have acknowledged a potential threat from NBC terrorism have broadened their general anti-terrorism programmes to incorporate some specific anti-NBC measures. These programmes share a core of common elements, such as the use of intelligence warning and strong law enforcement, backed by effective anti-terrorism legislation. But there are also significant differences in the effectiveness of these programmes in each state, and also in the degree of emphasis which different policies have been given.

The USA

The USA has instituted the most ambitious and well-funded response programme of any state. But despite the abundance of disparate policies that have been implemented, it is disorganized. This has stemmed from the lack of an integrated long-term plan. Most new initiatives have been driven by activist legislators, individual federal agencies, or even public opinion, with the result that the programme lacks coherence. (58) Of all the states being considered here, the US response is most driven by these internal political pressures, with has sometimes led to the administration making poor policy decisions.

In an effort to enhance co-ordination, President Clinton appointed the first terrorism 'Czar,' but the programme remains hampered by the lack of clear lines of bureaucratic authority and responsibility. The US National Security Council is supposed to co-ordinate all counter-terrorism programmes; the FBI has been designated as the lead agency for crisis management in case of an attack; the Federal Emergency Management Agency (FEMA) has responsibility for consequence management; and a host of other departments such as the Department of Energy (DoE), Department of Health and Human Services and the Environmental Protection Agency are also involved in enhancing overall terrorism-response capabilities. The USA probably faces the greatest difficulties in co-ordinating its bureaucracy, which contains over 40 different federal agencies, bureaus and offices, all with a role to play. This contributes to the existence and confusion of overlapping programmes. (59)

The USA has enacted a wide range of anti-terrorism legislation. The FBI definition of the term 'terrorism' is one of the most all-encompassing, covering the use of serious violence against persons or property, or the threat of such violence, to intimidate or coerce a government, the public, or any section of the public for political, religious or ideological goals. This definition is flexible enough to deal with emerging threats and issues, but whilst it has been adopted by the UK, (60) it is not universally accepted. It has also enacted a number of executive orders to impose economic sanctions on states which it considers to sponsor terrorism. Executive Order 12947 'Prohibiting Transactions With Terrorists Who Threaten the Middle East Peace Process', was enacted through the provisions of the 1996 Anti-Terrorism Act, and prohibits fundraising in the USA by terrorist groups that might threaten the peace process, and provides powers to freeze bank accounts and seize assets. (61)

However, civil liberties' issues have led to the watering down of anti-terror legislation. In the wake of the Oklahoma City bombing in 1995, an anti-terrorism law passed by Congress did not include several key provisions, such as enhanced federal wiretap authority, permission for the military to help local law enforcement agencies deal with CBW attacks, and the use of chemical tracers in gunpowder, which the Clinton Administration had sought. (62) However in 1999, the first report of the US Commission on National Security suggested that when faced with an imminent act of terrorism, the government may need to suspend many freedoms and rights. (63) Yet it is precisely this alleged erosion of civil liberties which is fuelling the growth of the right wing in the USA. However the USA is a state which rigorously maintains its civil liberties, therefore the limits to legislation are greater than in some other states.

It has also made great efforts to tighten legislation on the supply of NBC weapon materials. In the past it was not illegal for US citizens to acquire pathogens from biological supply houses, only the possession of weaponized versions of pathogens and toxins was a crime. The 1996 Anti-Terrorism and Effective Death Penalty Act made it a crime to threaten the use of BW, and established greater controls on the transfer of pathogens. (64) In April 1997, operating under the authority of this legislation, the Centers for Disease Control and Prevention of the US Public Health Service issued regulations specifying 24 infectious agents and 12 toxins that pose an unusually great risk to health, requiring individuals and organizations dealing with these agents, to register with the federal government for licensing. (65) Each transfer of these agents now requires certificates from both the recipient and the shipper, including details of proposed use, which will be made available to federal and state officials. (66) Yet the resources to enforce the legislation and regulations were not forthcoming, leaving the situation much the same as before. (67)

The USA places a much higher emphasis on civil defence than European states. A programme of training, planning and exercises is being pursued at all levels of response, and is co-ordinated between national and state level, in order to ensure the optimal sharing of knowledge. (68) FEMA has developed a Federal Response Plan which is to act as a template to co-ordinate the delivery of Federal assistance in the event of an attack, (69) and also works at the local level to enhance response capabilities. The 1996 Defense Authorization Act called for the Department of Defense (DoD) to manage the training of the civilian authorities in 120 US cities to respond to an NBC incident, (70) whilst the Nunn-Lugar-Domenici amendment to the 1997 Defense Authorization Act also provided for training, equipment and co-ordination of emergency-response personnel and more funds for the customs service. (71)

Local defences are supported by specialized national response teams such as the DoD's Nuclear Emergency Search Teams (NEST), the Chemical Biological Rapid Response Teams (CBRRT); the National Guard's Rapid Assessment and Initial Detection Teams (RAIDS), the FBI's Domestic Emergency Support Team (DEST), the State Department's Federal Emergency Support Team (FEST); the Marine Corps' Chemical Biological Incident Response Force (CBIRF) and the Army's

Technical Escort Unit (TEU). (72) The Public Health Service has also created Metro medical-response teams, capable of organizing an effective operational response to a large-scale attack. It is intended to establish 100 teams in the largest cities. (73) All of these response teams are being equipped with NBC-related equipment.

Linked in with this approach, the USA also places a greater emphasis on searching for technical fixes to help manage the threat. Research and development (R&D) on technical measures has been identified as a key requirement for funding. In early 1998 the DoE, demonstrated a range of technologies for detecting NBC weapons and preventing the illicit movement of nuclear materials. This included radiation-detection portal monitors, and a wide-area tracking system that is designed to intercept vehicles transporting nuclear weapons, (74) and track nuclear material movements through ports, airports and metropolitan areas. (75) The DoE has also established a requirement for the national laboratories to develop sensors and computer software for detecting BW. (76)

However, Surgeon General David Schacter, the former Direct of the Centers for Disease Control and Prevention has stated that the US public health infrastructure has deteriorated, to the extent that it is inadequate to even detect natural outbreaks of disease. (77) This has left it ill-prepared to cope with the consequences of a major BW attack, although it has instituted a programme to stockpile vaccines and antibiotics.

The USA is considering appointing a commander-in-chief to oversee domestic defence in the event of a terrorist attack. (78) This would give the military unparalleled powers on American soil; despite the Posse Comitatus Act of 1878 which barred federal troops from domestic policing, although the DoD has argued that military units would not have a policing function, which would remain in civilian hands. (79) The USA has demonstrated a willingness to occasionally use military action outside of its own borders, particularly when pressured by public opinion and Congress; this has previously included airstrikes against Libya, Afghanistan, and Sudan. It has modified its nuclear doctrine to provide the option of using nuclear weapons to combat terrorism, but it is almost inconceivable that it would actually do so. (80) More significant has been the creation of special mission units for counter-WMD terrorism and counter-pro-liferation roles around the world. (81) These responses are typically driven by public opinion and political pressure from Congress,

The USA's other major policy difference with European states is its greater emphasis on deterring and punishing state sponsors of terrorism. In 1979, legislation was enacted which requires the secretary of state to impose sanctions on any state which he considers to have provided consistent support for international terrorism. This was directed not at 'state terrorism,' which is defined as the use of terror by the apparatus of the state within a domestic context, but at state support for terrorist acts in an international context. (82) This has primarily focused on economic sanctions and diplomatic efforts to isolate those states politically and economically. In contrast, Europe has preferred a strategy of political engagement with states such as Iran, rather than the confrontational approach of the USA, which has not reaped significant gains. Despite the high level of expenditure, it is apparent that the USA is singularly unprepared for a major incident. In March 1998 it conducted an exercise to respond to terrorist use of BW along the Mexico-American border. As the scenario unfolded state and local officials were quickly overwhelmed, and huge gaps were discovered in logistics, legal authority and medical care. Towards the end of the 1990s however, criticism of this focus on worst case scenarios began to emerge. The General Accounting Office of the US Congress issued a report which criticized plans by the DHHS for being 'geared toward the worst-possible consequences from a public health perspective and do not match intelligence agencies' judgements on the more likely biological and chemical agents a terrorist group or individual might use.' (83) Consequently, officials began moving the focus of their attention away from mass casualty attacks, to focus on the smaller scale threats that terrorists are technologically more capable of developing. Although spending on counter measures continued to rise.

The UK

The response in the UK has been markedly more low-key than in the USA, and is being implemented after a period of careful study. Owing to the different nature of the legislative process in the UK, it is also a top-down approach, rather than the bottom-up approach which sometimes characterizes the US response. A comprehensive plan to combat the threat is being developed, and clear lines of authority and bureaucratic responsibility have been established. A new organization within the Ministry of Defence (MoD) has been established to co-ordinate anti-CBW efforts with the biological and chemical warfare research centre at Porton, and other government departments such as the Home Office and Department of Health. (84)

The primary focus of the UK response is on intelligence warning, although this is supplemented by a modest civil defence programme. The MoD operates the Nuclear Emergency Unit which is equivalent to the US NEST, and a joint-service NBC defence unit of regular troops has also been established. (85) This is supported by modest investments in technology, such as 150 vehicle-mounted detectors, (86) and a programme to stockpile vaccines and antibiotics for the civilian population.

In 1998 the governments of the UK and Eire implemented even more restrictive anti-terrorism legislation which included five new offences: directing an unlawful organization; possessing items for purposes connected with gun and explosive offences; withholding information about illegal terrorist activities, collecting information for unlawful purposes; and training people to use weapons and explosives. There are also changes to make it easier to prove membership of a terrorist organization. Courts will be able to draw inferences if a suspect relies on facts not mentioned when charged or questioned, and to treat a defendant's failure to answer relevant questions as corroboration of police claims that he or she belongs to an illegal organization. Detention without charge for a terrorist suspect is increased from 48 to 72 hours, and bail denied to those considered dangerous. (87) The new legislation also included unprecedented powers to convict people guilty of conspiracy within the UK, to commit terrorist offences anywhere in the world (the 1978 Suppression of Terrorism Act allows only the offence of conspiracy to commit murder abroad in specific countries – mostly in Europe – to be subject to criminal charges). (88) This was partly a response to criticism that the UK has been too lax in allowing Islamic extremists to operate virtually unhindered in the UK. Further proposals aim to make it an offence to raise funds for a banned organization. (89)

The UK experience with the IRA has also led to a radically different use of physical control measures than is the case in the USA. The security forces have made extensive use of security cordons, checkpoints and the control of traffic flows in and out of specified areas throughout the UK, in order to control terrorist activity. In 1993, entry into the City of London was controlled through only seven vehicle-entry points which were guarded by police checkpoints, and West Belfast is permanently ringed by security force checkpoints. (90) These measures did not prevent all attacks, but certainly made it more difficult for the terrorists. In Northern Ireland itself, attacks are deterred by flooding specified areas with troops after specific intelligence has been received.

The situation in respect of controlling the materials for producing NBC weapons is similar to that in the USA. Most chemical companies know who they are supplying their products to, and there is a similar kind of self -regulation. The UK has also ratified the CWC, which will enhance reporting in this area. However any company that wants to store lethal biological pathogens simply has to prove to the government's Health and Safety Executive (HSE), that it has adequate containment facilities. The HSE itself has no jurisdiction over private citizens who keep lethal pathogens at home, although threats to do harm with those pathogens, transporting or storing them improperly, or obtaining them by fraud or theft are illegal.91 UK nuclear facilities are under strong physical security, and operate strict accountancy and control mechanisms, therefore leakages of fissile material are unlikely, although civil nuclear reactors are less secure than military ones.

In contrast to the USA, the UK has used its military extensively to combat domestic terrorism in Northern Ireland, and has no compunction about using it for a whole range of domestic emergency situations, including fire-fighting, and driving ambulances during industrial disputes. In Northern Ireland they have been an essential component of controlling the conflict, even though it has had to operate within the rule of law. The military has not really been used on the mainland UK for anti-terrorism purposes other than bomb disposal, and even in Northern Ireland law enforcement has always remained in civil control.

Russia

Of all the principal states under threat, Russia is probably the least prepared. It needs to create a counter-terrorism programme from the bottom up, improving its general anti-terrorism measures, as well as instituting some specific NBC programmes. However a chronic lack of resources means that the government cannot invest heavily in a comprehensive programme of counter-measures.

When first confronted with a significant terrorist threat, Russia's basic anti-terrorism legislation was poor. In 1997, it still did not have a law on terrorism, and a draft law being debated by the Duma did not include any specific provisions relating to NBC terrorism. Instead, the situation is regulated by the Law on the Creation, Functioning, Destruction and Security of Nuclear Weapons, adopted in 1997. (92) However, Russia has enacted legal obligations upon individuals to uphold the prohibition on offensive application of CBW agents, complete with penalties for violations (although systems for licensing firms and individuals who deal with the relevant agents are not yet in place). (93)

Russia's compliance with international treaties is also poor. It has not fully met its obligations under the CWC, and for years it operated a covert BW programme in breach of the BTWC. It also cannot meet international standards on accountancy and control of nuclear materials. Similarly, the physical protection measures at the majority of nuclear power plants are inadequate. (94) One of the principal tasks for Russia has been to re-establish its accountancy, control and physical protection systems.

Russia also faces problems in co-ordinating its federal bureaucracy, although perhaps not to the same extent as in the USA. There are three departments in the Russian federal security service (including the counter-terrorist centre) involved in combating NBC terrorism, but there is no department specializing in only this area, and there is no co-ordination between the federal security service, the Security Council, the Ministry on Emergency Situations, and other agencies on this issue. (95) However an Inter-agency Anti-Terrorism Commission has been established which could take the lead. (96) The military is being integrated into the counter-terrorism programme with the creation of specialist anti-terrorism forces within the V Directorate of the Federal Security Bureau. (97)

Russia also needs to develop greater levels of co-operation with other states particularly in the west, through bilateral and multilateral agreements; as when the Cold War ended there were virtually none in the field of terrorism. Russia has been a willing participant in the G7 agreements, and has attempted to work with the UN on the Nuclear Terrorism Convention and it has also engaged in the Nunn-Lugar programme. But it still needs to build and integrate itself into a much wider and firmer web of agreements, such as bilateral agreements on sharing intelligence, extraditing suspects and clamping down on terrorist fundraising.

Owing to the lack of funds, the Russian programme seems to rely more on prevention than consequence management. It has no programme of specialized training for emergency response teams, has no specially trained personnel (98) and no special stockpiles of drugs.

Israel

Israel has adopted the same approach as the US, giving equal attention to rigorous prevention, and strong consequence management, measures. It has implemented the most widespread and effective programme of consequence- management measures of any state, because of its extensive civil defence programme to deal with the perceived CBW threat from its Arab neighbours. All Israeli citizens are issued with protective kits which include gas masks, atropine injections and powder to treat chemical burns, (99) and the home front command has systems for distributing antibiotics within a very short space of time. Israel has the advantages of both small population size, and limited geographical area, in implementing its civil defence programme; and because of this, the Israeli programme cannot be replicated in most other states, least of all the USA.

Israel is also the state which relies most on the use of military force to combat terrorism, both within its own borders and against neighbouring states. This has involved using both airpower and special forces to attack terrorist bases and specific individuals. Some of these attacks are merely punitive, but some are designed to destroy known sites or kill specific individuals. The close interrelationship between the military and society in Israel means that there have been few problems using troops in domestic security situations.

Israel also maintains very high levels of physical security at likely targets within its borders. In 1999, the Israeli government instituted additional physical security programmes around the Al Aqsa mosque and other key religious sites, owing to the influx of religious fanatics prior to the millennium; US$10.2 million was spent on an additional 400 security force personnel, close circuit television and sensor pads, (100) although these measures were primarily concerned with conventional terrorist threats. These physical security measures also include searches of homes, vehicle checkpoints and the checking of identification documents at border entry points. Israeli public opinion accepts this, because of the general acceptance that such measures are needed. They might alienate Palestinians, but they are already alienated from the Israeli state anyway, so it probably makes little difference to their attitudes.

Conclusion
Government counter-measures will never be able to prevent all potential NBC terrorist attacks, but some future attacks will be prevented by this regime of counter-measures. Every minor improvement in capabilities could increase the chance of detecting an attack. Similarly, consequence management will never be wholly effective, yet continued improvements in response capabilities will help reduce the potential casualties from any attack. Governments need to achieve coherence in their programmes, and even if they do not have significant resources can at least focus on the lower cost responses, which will enable them to maximize the value of the resources that they can invest. Whilst

the current regime of counter-measures is far from complete, the costs of implementing a fully comprehensive programme of counter-measures are enormous, and will be disproportionate to the reality of the threat. Even to guarantee a reasonable level of protection, states are going to have to invest considerably more resources than they have hitherto. Fortunately, many of the costs are shared with other programmes, such as non-proliferation and general anti-terrorism, which greatly reduces the direct cost. Equally, a number of counter-measures do not appear to be cost-effective, and so can be minimized in the planning process. Many policies responses, however, are based upon worst-case scenario planning of a highly effective WMD attack against a population target, resulting in high casualty levels. This is the least likely of the threats to occur, and can never be dealt with effectively. Effective management of the more likely mid-level threats, such as poorly disseminated CBW or radiological weapons, perhaps targeting discriminate targets, is much more achievable. Programmes of responses therefore need to be tailored to objective estimates of the threat.

Notes and references
1. Phil Williams and Ernesto Savona (eds), *The UN and Transnational Organized Crime* (London: Frank Cass, 1996) p 142
2. Robert Taylor, 'All Fall Down,' Special Report, *New Scientist* (11 May 1996) p 36
3. John Deutch, 'Terrorism', *Foreign Policy* (Fall 1997) p 15
4. C.J.M. Drake: *Terrorists' Target Selection* (London: St Martin's Press) 1998 p 123. The Royal Ulster Constabulary claims a ratio of four out of five attacks; whilst some of these cases might have been incidental many were based on intelligence of the IRA's intentions.
5. 'US Foils Spate of Bin Laden Bomb Attacks,' *The Times* (25 February 1999)
6. 'Next Dominant Domestic Terrorism Fear: Biochemical Weapons,' Gannett News Service (28 March 1997)
7. Jessica Stern. 'Apocalypse Never, But the Threat is Real,' *Survival* 40/4 (Winter 1998–9) p 178
8. D.W. Brackett, *Holy Terror, Armageddon in Tokyo* (New York: Weatherhill, 1996) p 52
9. 'Muslims Who Find A Haven in London,' *Guardian* (26 August 26 1998)
10. Ron Purver, 'Chemical and Biological Terrorism: New Threat to Public Safety?,' *Conflict Studies* 295, Research Institute For The Study of Conflict and Terrorism (December 1996–January 1997), p 23
11. Brackett: *Holy Terror*, p 147
12. Brackett: *Holy Terror*, p 94
13. 'US Studying Truck-Bomb Defenses at Reactors,' *New York Times*,

Special Edition – Terrorism (23 April 1993)

14. Daniel Hirsch, 'The Truck Bomb and Insider Threats to Nuclear Facilities', in Paul. Leventhal and Yonah. Alexander (eds), *Preventing Nuclear Terrorism* (Lexington, MA: Lexington Books, 1986) p 214

15. A. Henderson, 'Bioterrorism as a Public Health Threat,' Journal of Emerging Diseases 4/3 (June–September 1998)

16. 'Wargame Finds Large Holes in US Counter-Bioterrorism,' *Defense News* (1999)

17. Richard A. Falkenrath, 'Confronting Nuclear, Biological and Chemical Terrorism,' *Survival* 40/3 (Autumn 1998) p 60

18. Falkenrath: 'Confronting Nuclear, Biological and Chemical Terrorism,' p 60

19. Falkenrath: 'Confronting Nuclear, Biological and Chemical Terrorism,' p 61

20. See *Jane's Defence Weekly* (14 May 1997) p 8; & (8 October 1997) p 5

21. 'Agencies to Centralise for CBW Rapid Response', *Jane's Defence Weekly* (12 November 1997) p 11

22. 'Agencies to Centralise,' p 142

23. 'The Global Terrorist,' *Sunday Times* (7 February 1999)

24. Williams and Savona: *The UN*, p 145

25. Williams and Savona: *The UN*, p 146

26. Jason Ellis, 'Nunn-Lugar's Mid-Life Crisis,' *Survival* 39/1 (Spring 1997) pp 88–92

27. Ellis: 'Nunn-Lugar's Mid-Life Crisis,' p 91

28. Frank Barnaby, *Instruments of Terror: Mass Destruction Has Never Been So Easy* (London: Vision Paperbacks, 1996) p 164

29. Barnaby: *Instruments of Terror*, p 100

30. 'Millennium Death Wish Cults Put the Dome Under Siege,' *Sunday Telegraph* (17 January 1999)

31. Williams and Savona: *The UN*, p 146

32. Williams and Savona: *The UN*, pp 146–47

33. Williams and Savona: *The UN*, p 143

34. Williams and Savona: *The UN*, p 147

35. Conor Gearty, Terror (London: Faber & Faber, 1991), p 136

36. The Times (2 October 1998)

37. Thomas J. Badey, 'US Anti-Terrorism Policy: The Clinton Administration', *Contemporary Security Policy* 19/2 (August 1998), pp 60–61

38. Communiqué of the Moscow Nuclear Safety and Security Summit (April 1996)

39. Williams and Savona: The UN, p 150

40. Williams and Savona: The UN, p 149

41. Williams and Savona: The UN, pp 151–52

42. John F.Murphy, 'Co-operative International Arrangements: Prevention of Nuclear Terrorism and the Extradition and Prosecution of Terrorists,' in Leventhal and Alexander (eds): Preventing Nuclear Terrorism, p 363

43. Murphy: Co-operative International Arrangements,' p 365

44. Programme for Promoting Nuclear Nonproliferation, *Newsbrief* (First Quarter 1998) p 18

45. 'UN Split on New Plan To Fight Nuclear Terrorism,' *Jane's Defence Weekly* (18 March 1998) p 6

46. Graham Pearson and Malcolm R. Dando, 'National Implementation Measures: An Update,' Strengthening the Biological Weapons Convention, Briefing Paper 14 (October 1998) Department of Peace Studies, University of Bradford

47. Pearson and Dando: 'National Implementation Measures,' pp 363–64

48. Williams and Savona: *The UN*, pp 150, 152; John F. Sopko, 'The Changing Proliferation Threat,' *Foreign Policy* 103 (Winter 1996–97) p 17

49. Deutch: 'Terrorism,' p 21

50. United Nations, Rome Statute of the International Criminal Court, A/CONF.183/9 (17 July 1998)

51. Graham T.Allison, Owen R.Cote, Richard A.Falkenrath, Steven E.Miller, *Avoiding Nuclear Anarchy* (Cambridge Ma: MIT Press, 1996) p 31

52. Richard Preston, *The Secret War*, Arena, (1998) p 212

53. 'US Cruise Attacks "Ignored Warnings"' *Guardian* (6 October 1998)

54. Allison, Cote, Falkenrath, Miller: *Avoiding Nuclear Anarchy*, p 67. Allison et al outline how plutonium and HEU are difficult to detect because of their low radiation signatures which will be reduced further by effective shielding.They conclude that it requires physical searches in conjunction with the detectors to provide sufficient guarantees, but this is logistically impossible.

55. Drake: *Terrorists' Target Selection*, p 129

56. Interview with Professor Frank Barnaby (25 January 1999)

57. Badey: 'US Anti-Terrorism Policy,' p 59

58. Richard A.Falkenrath, 'Confronting Nuclear, Biological and Chemical Terrorism,' *Survival* 40/ 3 (Autumn 1998) p 59

59. James H. Anderson, 'Microbes and Mass Casualties: Defending America Against Bioterrorism,' *The Heritage Foundation Backgrounder* 11 (26 May 1998) p 10

60. 'Animal Activists Face Ban as Terrorists,' *The Times* (18 December 1998)

61. Badey, 'US Anti-Terrorism Policy,' pp 56–60

62. Chuck McCutcheon, 'Homeland Defense: Mobilizing Against Terrorism,' *Congressional Quarterly Weekly* (6 March 1999) p 527

63. First Report of the Federal Commission on National Security (20 September 1999) <www.nssg.gov>

64. Anderson: 'Microbes,' p 14

65. John Steinbruner, 'Biological Weapons: A Plague Upon All Houses,' *Foreign Policy* 109 (Winter 1997–98) p 93

66. Purver: 'Chemical and Biological Terrorism,' p 21

67. Anderson: 'Microbes,' p 14

68. Report to Congress on Response To Threats of Terrorist Use of Weapons of Mass Destruction (31 January 1997), reprinted in *The Monitor* 3/2 (Spring 1997) Center For International Trade and Security at the University of Georgia, p 19

69. Anderson: 'Microbes,' p 10

70. McCutcheon, 'Homeland Defense,' p 527

71. Sopko, 'The Changing Proliferation Threat,' p 18

72. 'Agencies to Centralise for CBW Rapid Response'; Anderson: 'Microbes', p 11. The USA will spend $250 million over six years to train ten, 22-member National Guard RAIDS Units, which will be able to react to any CBW incident within four hours, 'US Plans Force To Beat Germ Terrorists,' *The Times* (2 February 1999)

73. Richard A. Falkenrath, Robert D. Newman and Bradley Thayer, *America's Achilles Heel* (Cambridge, MA: MIT Press, 1998) p 305

74. *Nuclear Fuel* 23/3 (1998)

75. 'USA to Develop System to Track Loose Nukes,' *Jane's Defence Weekly* (8 October 1997) p 5

76. McCutcheon: 'Homeland Defense,' p 528

77. Sydney J. Freedberg, Jr and Marilyn Werber Serafini, 'Be Afraid, Be Moderately Afraid,' *The National Journal* (27 March 1999)

78. McCutcheon: 'Homeland Defense,' p 526

79. 'US Plans Force To Beat Germ Terrorists,' *The Times* (2 February 1999)

80. Perhaps the only instance is where the target is buried deep underground and an earth-penetrating device such as the US B-61 is the only means of success. However, the USA is currently developing new generations of conventional earth-penetrating weapons which should make even this redundant. In addition, there are legal and moral issues which would constrain US actions in employing nuclear weapons in this role. Perhaps the great inhibitor will be the taboo against the use of nuclear weapons. This is considered to be a pillar of the regime to prevent the use of nuclear weapons' proliferation. Any use of nuclear weapons will weaken, if not destroy, the taboo.

81. 'Revealed: USA's Overt Squads To Counter WMD,' *Jane's Defence Weekly* (11 March 1998), p 12

82. Adrian Guelke, *The Age of Terrorism* (London: I.B Tauris, 1998) p 148

83. Jonathan B.Tucker & Amy Sands, 'An Unlikely Threat,' Bulletin of the Atomic Scientists (July/August 1999) p 47

84. *Sunday Telegraph* (11 October 1998)

85. *Sunday Telegraph* (11 October 1998); 'UK Bio-Agent Detector System Is Delivered,' *Jane's Defence Weekly* (13 January 1999) p 17

86. *Sunday Telegraph* (11 October 1998)

87. *The Times* (20 August 1998)

88. *Guardian* (26 August 1998)

89. 'Animal Activists Face Ban as Terrorists,' *The Times* (18 December 1998)

90. Drake: *Terrorists' Target Selection*, pp 108–09

91. Taylor: 'All Fall Down,' Special Report, *New Scientist* (11 May 1996) p 36

92. Vladimir Orlov, 'Preventing The Threat of Nuclear Terrorism: The Case of Russia,' *Disarmament Diplomacy* (November 1997) p 15

93. Masha Katsva, 'Threat of Chemical and Biological Terrorism in Russia,' *The Monitor* (Spring 1997) p 16.

94. Orlov: 'Preventing The Threat,' p 15

95. Katsva, 'Threat of Chemical and Biological Terrorism,' p 14

96. Orlov: 'Preventing The Threat,' p 16

97. Orlov: 'Preventing The Threat,' p 16

98. Katsva: Threat of Chemical and Biological Terrorism,' p 16

99. 'US Evacuates Diplomats in Anthrax Alert,' *The Times* (19 December 1998)

100. 'Jerusalem Tightens Security Against Doomsday Cult, *Guardian*, (24 November 1998)

10. The Future

It is clear from Chapter 9 that in all states the current efforts to control the potential threat from NBC terrorism are partial and often incomplete. An embryonic regime is forming, but its effectiveness is at times limited by its shortcomings. Policy makers need to invest additional resources and further attention into counter-measures. But in order to be effective, such programmes need to be based upon a realistic assessment of the potential threat, and they will have to strike a balance between what they consider to be the likelihood and nature of any future attack, and what is a reasonable level of investment to make in counter-measures. In turn, calculations concerning the cost and relative effectiveness of any specific measure will also need to be weighed up. In many cases this can be achieved by strengthening general anti-terror measures, a process which is underway in most states anyway. But in addition, there are some WMD-specific measures which need implementing. Traditional methods of controlling terrorism however, prove that states cannot provide 100 per cent effective safeguards against attacks. Therefore states are going to have to accept a certain level of vulnerability.

The future threat from NBC terrorism

Terrorism is likely to remain a threat to many states for the fore-seeable future, because the issues which generate terrorism are unlikely to be resolved. Uncertainty and confusion will persist in many states as the world continues to change, because there no 'quick fixes' for the profound economic, political and social problems which afflict many peoples' lives. Paul Schulte of the UK MOD argues that,

> Globalization, or accelerating world wide contacts, transactions, and interpretations; the expanding flows of information, people, goods, ideas, images, behaviour, and money will call forth many different local responses and various demands for protection. Failure to provide protection from perceptions of the corrosiveness of globalism and the resulting feelings of powerlessness may result in violent reactions. (1)

As a result, ethnic, political, religious and nationalist move-ments will continue to emerge in all parts of the world.

Some of these movements and groups might resort to violence because of the inability of national governments and the inter-national community to meet their aspirations. In particular, US and western influence in the Middle East will continue to be a source of contention. The strategic significance of the region, and the investments of the large multinational companies, means that the West just cannot totally disengage from the region, even if it wanted to. This in turn means that Arab and Muslim opposition to western 'interference' in the region will continue, particularly because the West is unlikely to totally withdraw its support from Israel. Similarly, the demands of the US far right cannot be met by the federal government, because they will require a root and branch transformation of American society, culture and politics. Moreover, in being self-contained, and driven by internal factors, the much smaller threat from religious cults will also continue.

Whilst it is impossible to extrapolate future trends in terror-ism from past history with any reasonable degree of assurance, there is no indication that the trend in terrorist incidents towards fewer attacks involving higher numbers of casualties will be reversed, although the world could witness at least tem-porary reversals in this trend. Equally it is impossible to deter-mine that the trend will lead to larger numbers of mass-casual-ty attacks, involving higher and higher levels of casualties. If anything, current evidence indicates that the trend is not having an impact on the number of the most lethal attacks, which declined in number in the 1990s. Instead, what might happen is that mass-casualty attacks with the potential for causing significantly higher casualties than the average will continue to occur very infrequently.

Similarly, it would be wrong to categorically state that a trend of increasing numbers of NBC attacks, particularly from BW, will emerge, but there is no reason to suggest that it will not. The precedent of acquiring and using NBC weapons has already been set. But groups are not being inexorably driven towards using NBC weapons, by a perceived requirement to ratchet up their levels of violence, in order to ensure continued press coverage. Whilst some groups might make that calculation, many will not. Target type rather than levels of lethality will be the primary consideration for many groups. Therefore, in all probability, small numbers of individuals and groups will continue to attempt to develop or otherwise acquire these weapons.

Any assessment of the future threat is inherently problematic because specific threats will emerge only as an outcome of the internal decision making of individual groups, and the technical opportunities that are available to them. Therefore future threats will be a function of the kinds of NBC weapons that terrorists can acquire, and the tactical, strategic and political decisions by the terrorists on how and where to use them.

An analysis of NBC weapon technology indicates that, on the basis of a number of broad assumptions, the development of NBC weapons is achievable by increasing numbers of terrorist groups, as they reach a certain level of technical sophistication. However any analysis needs to be critical of these underlying assumptions. It is undeniable that the theoretical knowledge required to develop NBC weapons is readily available, and that given time, skilled individuals can engineer that knowledge into a weapon. What is more problematic is whether groups can recruit the necessary individuals. It would seem to require at least two individuals to successfully develop a CBW, although an individual could develop an agent or pathogen, without a sophisticated delivery mechanism, on their own, and nuclear weapons would seem to require a team of at least three people. Whilst there might be increasing numbers of people with the necessary skills within society, it cannot simply be assumed that all terrorist groups would have access to them. There are indications of some groups that are interested in acquiring NBC weapons lacking the necessary technical skills.

In addition, the development of NBC weapons requires a significant investment of finance and time. It is not an easy task, and therefore the quality of the weapons that groups might prove to be capable of producing could vary considerably. Technical constraints mean that most NBC threats are likely to be low level: crude CW and poor BW, and perhaps radiological weapons, if terrorists can acquire nuclear materials. Consequently, they are most likely to be used as contaminants, or employed in discriminate attacks against individuals or buildings. Occasionally, it is possible that groups might be able to produce weapons equivalent to those developed by Aum, that are capable of being used for indiscriminate attacks outdoors, although the number of fatalities that these weapons could produce is likely to be relatively small because of either poor-quality agents or ineffective dispersal mechanisms. The likelihood of a terrorist group being capable of manufacturing a WMD is likely to remain very small.

Technical opportunities and constraints will therefore have a decisive impact on the nature of the potential future threat. But whether any particular group will choose to use an NBC weapon, and the way in which it chooses to use it, will be the result of a decision making process of reconciling the motivations to using NBC weapons, and the disincentives to using them. These are determined by a number of variables which include: the political goals of the groups; the tactics and strategies which they employ; the perceived advantages that would accrue from using NBC weapons; the organizational dynamics of the group; the psychology of the group and its leadership; and the politico-strategic situation in which the group operates. Different types of group, and even individual groups of the same type, can reach radically different decisions on whether to use NBC weapons. In addition, terrorists' decision making could also change over time, since the balance between motivations and disincentives to using NBC weapons is a dynamic one, which could easily shift owing to changes in these variables.

Analysis of terrorist goals and strategies paints a confusing picture. It suggests that all types of terrorist groups might have motivations to use NBC weapons, although they appear to be strongest in groups that are predominantly religious in character. For some groups, the motivations will come to outweigh the disincentives to using them only when the group falls under the threat of defeat, or is forced onto the defensive. Yet these motivations are not overwhelmingly strong, because a number of disincentives to using NBC weapons will also influence most types of terrorist group. Therefore decisions on whether to use NBC weapons will only emerge from how individual groups balance the imperatives of these conflicting motivations and disincentives.

NBC weapons confer decisive military advantages for only one type of attack – indiscriminate mass-casualty attacks. For all other military objectives, conventional weapons should be the preferred option. The strategies and tactics of most groups incorporate a wide range of targets, and many groups choose not to conduct indiscriminate mass casualty attacks, because of what they know they can achieve by attacking more discriminate targets. Similarly, even when groups do strike at indiscriminate population targets, it cannot simply be assumed that they would be interested in causing casualty levels that could be defined as 'mass destruction.' For many groups, indiscriminate attacks causing limited casualties could equally serve their purposes. Yet the past record of NBC terrorism also indicates that terrorists have been willing to use them in roles to which they are not particularly suited, ostensibly because of the propaganda and heightened intimidatory effects.

In general it can be argued that groups with more limited goals appear to have fewer motivations to seek and use NBC weapons, because their goals are best achieved through controlled and limited acts of violence. This strongly suggests that secular groups will be disinclined to use NBC weapons, although racist secular groups, who have broader objectives and a broader target set, are less inclined to keep their violence within strict limits. But whilst they might be more interested in perpetrating indiscriminate acts of violence against their ethnic enemies, they would still want to be discriminate in restricting violence to these enemies. In general terms, considerations of losing political and material support from the international community, and alienating their domestic constituency, will undoubtedly inhibit groups that are predominantly secular in character, from using NBC weapons for indiscriminate mass-casualty attacks. However these considerations will not necessarily inhibit them from using them in more discriminate roles. In fact, the strong propaganda value to be gained from using such weapons could make them distinctly attractive for such use. Therefore, the balance of motivations and disincentives should generally deter predominantly secular groups from using them in indiscriminate roles, but the disincentives seem to be distinctly weaker in respect of using them in discriminate roles.

Groups that are predominantly religious in character appear to have stronger motivations to use NBC weapons than groups that are predominantly secular in character because of their more all-encompassing objectives. At its most extreme, the rhetoric of some of these individuals and groups displays genocidal goals. But even these groups operate under constraints. Most religious groups have a constituency which they are attempting

to appeal to, some seek support from the international community, and religious dictums do not necessarily establish imperatives to conduct indiscriminate acts of violence. As is the case
with secular groups they also operate under practical disincentives to using NBC weapons, particularly the fact that it would
result in the contamination of the land, or state of which are
attempting to gain control. In addition, there are also operational factors which would limit how and where they might want
to use NBC weapons. Therefore, whilst the motivations certainly appear to be stronger than in respect of secular groups, they
still operate under strong disincentives which cannot be
ignored. The exception are religious cults, which if they do
decide to lash out violently against society operate under no
political or ideological constraints, and will use NBC weapons
indiscriminately. But these cults will always be very few in number at any given time.

Ultimately it may well be psychological factors and the internal dynamics of group decision making, which determine how
terrorists balance the conflicting imperatives of the political and
strategic motivations and disincentives, which impact upon
their decision making. Terrorists will not come to decisions to
use NBC weapons, especially WMD, easily. They are going to
have to reconcile conflicting psychological motivations with a
number of inhibitors, which are amongst the most powerful and
deeply held beliefs for the individual. Moral and other psychological factors will be a significant constraint on terrorists' willingness to use NBC weapons. But psychological factors are a
wild card in assessments of the future threat from NBC terrorism, because of the inherent difficulty of pre-judging how an
individual will think and act.

In many cases, NBC threats are most likely to be a consequence of the emergence of specific political, strategic and technological circumstances, in conjunction with a mindset amongst
the terrorist group that is willing to use such weapons. In particular, groups have previously proved to be more inclined to
perpetrate indiscriminate acts of violence when they are in
decline, or feel that they have no other recourse to achieve their
goals; equally, if hardliners seize control of the groups, or break
away to form splinter groups. Under these conditions groups are
less concerned with losing international political support and
alienating their domestic constituency. But equally as important
will be sudden changes in technological opportunity – particularly if groups gain sudden access to NBC materials, or individuals with the necessary technical skills, or even if state sponsors
suddenly prove to be willing to release NBC weapons to their
proxies under extreme conditions, when their regime is threat-

ened or perhaps when they perceive that they have no other recourse.

Since the motivations to use NBC weapons appear to be stronger amongst groups that are predominantly religious in character, and there has been a steady growth in the numbers of these groups, it could be concluded that the potential risk of NBC terrorism is increasing. But in general it is impossible to unequivocally identify specific future threats by studying the motivations and disincentives which will influence terrorist groups, because the goals and tactics of all types of groups establish potential motivations for all of them to use NBC weapons, and the disincentives to using them will remain strong. The crucial determining factors are the technical opportunities that are open to them, and the decision making of the individuals involved. This is in turn influenced by two other variables: the nature of decision making within the group, and the strategic situation in which the group operates. In addition, government counter measures are likely to prevent some attacks taking place. What emerges from these general considerations, is that the threat from NBC terrorism is very limited, technical constraints and tactical choices by groups will mean that indiscriminate WMD incidents are not imminent and are likely to be very rare. The consequences of the type of lower-order threat are more likely to occur can be managed by states with reasonable response capabilities.

Improving counter-measures
Chapter 9 demonstrated that it is impossible to implement a programme of counter-measures sufficient to prevent all future NBC attacks and cope with the consequences of a WMD attack, but this analysis suggests that states could instead implement programmes of counter-measures geared towards coping with irregular occurrences of intermediate levels of threats, involving casualty levels similar to those caused by the Aum attack on the Tokyo subway.

To a large extent, governments have already identified the necessary policy responses, but they need to strengthen their responses in key areas, and make clear decisions about what they can, and cannot do, because of financial restrictions and other limitations. Since each level of the regime is mutually supporting, owing to the synergistic effect between them, governments must implement and strengthen measures at national, bilateral and multilateral levels. But in doing so they must not allow these measures to consume huge amounts of resources. Instead, governments must focus on prudent and cautious investment in counter-measures at all levels. This also means that states will not necessarily respond in exactly the same way, or commit equivalent resources to managing the threat. A state's ability to meet any of these policies is dependent upon their resources. Russia has already proved that its lack of resources prevents it re-establishing accountancy and control over its fissile materials. Although whatever level of resources which a state has at its disposal, however, there are a number of low-cost measures which they should be able to implement.

At the national level, states need to start with a coherent national plan, but there is no model programme which can be readily applied to all states. Responses will be slightly different in each state, depending upon the specific threats that they face, the weaknesses that already exist in their own national and bilateral measures, as well as the resources which they have available to devote to the problem. There are good models for some specific programmes, for example the US nuclear emergency search teams, and US anti-terror legislation, which is being adopted in other states. But not all of the programmes can be re-created in other states. The Israeli model of civil defence represents the optimum programme, but it is probably impossible to re-create it in other states for societal and financial reasons. Therefore, because of peculiarities in each state, generalized responses are impossible.

The best place for governments to start are low-cost measures such as creating effective bureaucratic structures, with clear lines of responsibility and authority. This can optimize the impact of the limited resources which they can devote to the problem, by preventing overlapping jurisdictions, bureaucratic infighting, and a general lack of coherence in the overall strategy to meet the threat. The enactment of strong and all-encompassing national legislation will give governments the legal authority to combat terrorism without infringing on civil liberties. By establishing a clear and effective framework in this way, the value of investments in other counter-measures will be maximized.

The primary call on resources for prevention should be on early-warning measures. This should focus on enhancing the collection and analysis of intelligence, and the creation of structures and mechanisms to facilitate sharing it with other states. The value of current electronic methods of gathering intelligence is declining, because terrorists are learning to use encryption and alternative means of communication. Therefore further investments in new technologies are required, and a greater emphasis needs to be placed on human intelligence, particularly through the infiltration of agents into these groups. (2)

Most states still have inadequate anti-WMD terrorism consequence-management measures, such as technologies for detection, bomb dismantlement and decontamination; training and
exercises for responder units; changes to the public health system; and to a limited extent the stockpiling of vaccines and
antibiotics. Governments need some capacity in these areas, but
these are among the more expensive counter-measures, and
states must be careful not to over-invest in this area, and allow
them to consume a disproportionate amount of resources.

In general terms, governments need to guard against over-
committing resources to searching for technical solutions to the
threat. Whilst they can go some way to containing various
aspects of the problem, they cannot provide anything like a comprehensive solution. There is a place for technical measures, but
they are disproportionately expensive for the advantages they
offer in containing the threat. Whilst states require some equipment, training and other preparedness measures to cope with
the consequences of an attack, no amount of preparation will
ever enable a state to cope as quickly and efficiently as is
required to deal with a WMD attack against a population target.
In particular, NBC detection devices can probably be deployed at
only a limited number of key targets, entry points into the state,
and with specialized response units, because of their cost.

The most effective technical measures comprise the accountancy, control and safeguards technologies relating to nuclear
materials. The prospect of nuclear terrorism could be virtually
eradicated if states with stockpiles of fissile material prevent it
leaking on to the black market. Most states with nuclear industries already maintain tight controls over nuclear materials,
which need to be maintained and enhanced, therefore this is
primarily an issue for Russia and other states of the FSU, where
they have broken down. Once these measures are in place and
working effectively in all states, the flow of fissile material on to
the black market should be cut off at source. This includes
increased physical protection of nuclear materials, facilities and
weapons. Work also needs to be undertaken to implement
essential safeguards. The IAEA could play a more active role in
developing and implementing future schemes of nuclear materials safeguarding, and coping with the problems of nuclear terrorism.

There can be no really effective controls however, on the materials required to develop CBW. National control procedures and
supplier self-regulation and reporting on chemicals could inhibit terrorists' access to large quantities of precursors, but it is
impossible to monitor and verify all transactions of precursor
chemicals. Control of commercially available pathogens will be

of variable effect, because whilst it is possible to tightly monitor and control existing samples, it is also possible to acquire them from natural sources. Although forcing terrorists to do this, will introduce another technological barrier which they will have to cross. This could force them down the route of choosing more easily acquired pathogens such as botulinum, ricin and anthrax, which in turn will assist in response planning.

It is possible to expand and institutionalize the system of self-policing by suppliers of dual-use equipment and materials. These companies are in a position to gather and report information on their transactions, and to seek details of their customers. Governments can supply guidance on the most likely technical options which terrorists are likely to take, so that suppliers can report on suspicious orders. (3) This could never guarantee that all terrorists would be caught, but it might lead to the uncovering of at least some planned attacks, especially if the terrorists do not take enough care in their technological choices. This system could utilize existing export control systems, but would need to include items below the normal quantity thresholds. It would also need a central point of contact for companies to report to.

Consequence-management measures also need strengthening in all states. Epidemiological surveillance systems need to be improved to work better and faster so that diseases are identified quicker and responses mobilized faster. Many treatments need to be administered before the onset of symptoms, therefore medical practitioners need to be trained to speed up their responses, which would generally require that they receive better briefing on recognizing early indicators of a BW attack, and that they report all cases to a central authority. Hospitals can also be issued with portable test kits for identifying major BW. To this end, central authorities need to improve their ability to test and identify diseases, and establish enhanced links to the response capabilities of other agencies. (4) It will be impossible to train all first responders, but states must make some provision for adequately trained personnel to be available at local and regional levels to deal with any incident. Equally, the first responders need immediate access to a central point of contact, so that national resources can be mobilized as quickly as possible, and specialized advice be passed to those dealing with the incident. (5)

Strong and effective measures at the national level create the basis for enhancing the effectiveness of measures at other levels of the regime. Considerable developments can be made at bilateral level. Decades of co-operation on anti-terrorism between some states has led to the creation of strong and effective bilateral channels of communication and co-operation between them. Additional bilateral extradition and information-sharing agreements could be negotiated, perhaps under the provisions of international conventions.

Perhaps the most important bilateral agreement concerning the issue of WMD terrorism in the short term is the Nunn–Lugar programme which, if successful, will have a dramatic impact on lessening the threat. It needs to be expanded and made more efficient, and could perhaps be expanded to cover CW and BW stocks and facilities. There is also considerably greater scope for WMD-specific technical, financial and other assistance such as the sharing of information from exercises, and the supply of specialized equipment. This already occurs between some states and can help reduce the general levels of costs.

At the international level, considerably more work is needed in completing and implementing international treaties. The Convention for the Suppression of Terrorist Bombing needs to be signed, ratified and implemented effectively, although the more important treaties are the CWC and the verification protocol of the BTWC. The Organisation for the Prohibition of Chemical Weapons (OPCW) needs to ensure that states implement the legislative and administrative measures to implement the CWC, and that they are comprehensive enough for the state to enforce the convention effectively in its jurisdiction. Through harmonizing national measures, it should prevent the creation of safe havens and facilitate co-operation and legal assistance between states. The verification protocol for the BTWC needs to be completed, and the demands of industry managed. The protocol needs to ensure that each state party implements measures necessary to enforce Article IV, and possibly harmonize the current national variations. For these treaties to be effective it requires the enactment of appropriate national measures, and the creation of a national authority which can function effectively. Each national authority must possess statutory powers of investigation, and a degree of statutory protection sufficient to ensure that other organs of government do not interfere in the effective performance of its functions. It must be sufficiently independent of other agencies within the machinery of government to command confidence, and steps need to be taken to ensure that implementation is uniform, which the OPCW is already doing. There is also potential scope for negotiating other international Treaties such as a Nuclear Terrorism Convention that closes the loopholes in the 1980 Convention on the Physical Protection of Nuclear Materials, and a treaty establishing standards of physical protection for nuclear materials.

The events on September 11 2001 heralded a fundamental change in the global response to terrorism. The extremity of the destruction forced the USA to respond swiftly to seek justice and prevent future attacks. President Bush declared that 'We're at war ... There's no question about it, this action will not stand. We're going to find those who did it, we're going to smoke them out of their holes, we will get them running and we will bring them to justice.' (6) The avowed goals of the war were to bring bin Laden to justice, destroy al-Qaeda, replace the Taliban regime in Afghanistan, and more broadly to destroy terrorism wherever it might be found in the world. In a reflection of the changed nature of international relations, the USA was supported by a global coalition that included Russia and many Muslim states.

The political and military leadership in the USA recognised that in order to achieve these goals it would have to send troops into Afghanistan to directly engage al-Qaeda and the Taliban. They also acknowledged that it would be a long war in which American and British troops would be killed. However the severity of the attacks on September 11 coupled with the anticipation of future attacks which might involve NBC weapons, created a groundswell of public and political opinion in the USA that was willing to accept casualties in order to achieve these goals.

It is unlikely that military action alone will defeat terrorism or totally destroy al Qaeda, although it can disrupt the al Qaeda network by forcing it onto the defensive and denying it a safe haven. Hence, the more fundamental long-term dimension of the war against terrorism involves a hardening of the whole spectrum of political, legal and economic counter-terrorism measures. The attacks forced many states to accept that they can no longer accept some of the constraints that they had previously placed on their counter-terrorism activities, and that they will have to act together if they are to succeed. A greater number of states are now willing to accept the economic, political and social cost of implementing stronger counter-terrorism programmes. Over the long term it is the combination of military, political, legal and economic measures, rather than any of them in isolation, that offers the potential to contain terrorism and make it much more difficult for al Qaeda to plan and successfully execute attacks of the complexity required to cause mass casualties.

Political approaches to defeating terrorism
This regime of counter-measures and use of military force are treating the symptoms, rather than the causes of the problem.

A number of analysts have argued for more radical measures to address the threat. Professor Paul Rogers argues that governments should pay attention to the root causes of insecurity – those conditions of society, especially the deepening wealth-poverty divide, which are dispossessing hundreds of millions of people and inciting them to extreme violence. (7) Louis Rene Beres, in particular, has been a long-standing advocate for changes in US foreign policy, which he identifies as being one of the primary causes of the conditions which generate terrorism. He suggests instead a move from the use of force to the use of diplomacy in foreign policy, and entering into negotiations on terrorist grievances. (8)

Yet this is already evident in the policies of many governments. The UK government engaged in several attempts at dialogue with the IRA during the course of the conflict in Northern Ireland, which led to a number of political compromises by both sides and resulted in the Anglo-Irish agreement and the Good Friday agreement. Alongside the successful engagement of secular and ethno-nationalist groups in some other states, this indicates that political solutions can be effective in resolving conflicts involving this type of group, although the emergence of the Real IRA and the Continuity IRA in Northern Ireland indicates that political engagement will not necessarily draw in all of the most extreme elements within these groups. Therefore the success of political approaches may well remain partial.

Engaging groups that are predominantly religious in character, however, appears to be an entirely different proposition. At the UN General Assembly in New York in 1998, President Clinton attempted to reach out to the Arab world by insisting that there was no clash of civilizations, only a choice between good and evil, and that there must be greater efforts to tackle 'the sources of despair'. (9) But beyond the rhetoric it is difficult to envisage how the US can successfully engage the Muslim world to defeat terrorism without fundamental changes in US foreign policy, particularly in respect of Israel. The strong focus in US foreign policy on sanctioning the alleged state sponsors of terrorism also perpetuates the sense of grievance amongst many people in the Muslim world. The efficacy of this policy is doubtful, and could conceivably be dropped. Therefore, at first sight, changes in the foreign policy of western states could have an effect on some terrorist groups. But it is uncertain how the new generation of hardline terrorist leaders, such as Osama bin Laden, would be satisfied with anything short of their optimum demands. This approach assumes that these individuals and groups can be meaningfully engaged. (10)

Islamic terrorists would want an anti-Israel policy from western governments. But they will never get this. Western interests in the Middle East are governed by a diverse mix of considerations, which will not accept the destruction of the state of Israel, which is the primary goal of the Islamist groups. Public declarations indicate that Hezbollah will not accept peace with Israel, 'Even if it [Israel] withdrew from Lebanon it will never end as an enemy which is occupying Palestine. If it withdrew from South Lebanon we would have achieved a certain victory. But the problem in the region would not have finished.' (11) However, some Islamist groups have demonstrated an ability to evolve, and to accept compromise, therefore there is some potential for engagement in the future.

The US government will have similar problems meeting the demands of the Christian far right within its own borders. Their racist agenda is not acceptable within a democratic society, and neither is the federal government going to legislate itself out of existence by devolving its powers to state and local levels. There does not seem to be room for compromise, since the paranoia which fuels the beliefs of many of these individuals is derived from the very existence of the federal government. Worse still, political solutions offer absolutely no solution to the threat posed by millennial cults, because they are internally driven by religious-based doctrines of Armageddon. They cannot be engaged because they seek no political goals, and the social goals that they seek will be fulfilled only in the aftermath of Armageddon. Therefore they have no interest in bargaining with governments for concessions.

The shortcomings of such a radical approach are summed up by Joshua Lederberg, a Professor at the Rockerfeller University in Manhattan, who argues that, 'There is no technical solution to the problem of biological weapons. It needs an ethical, human and moral solution if it's going to happen at all. But would an ethical solution appeal to a sociopath?' (12) Paul Wilkinson similarly argues that it is a dangerous illusion to believe that it will be possible to find the perfect political solution that would meet the underlying grievances of terrorist groups. He goes on to argue, however, that political approaches are an underestimated element of counter-terrorism programmes, and can greatly reduce the level of violence. (13) Conor Gearty also suggests that 'the evidence points to the fact that no political solution will ever obliterate the militant factions altogether. There are too many complex additional factors, such as psychological maladjustment, daring macho personalities, criminal tendencies or the pursuit of material gain, which can interpose themselves between at least certain subversives and the acceptance of even a totally generous political solution.' This is amply borne out by the Northern Ireland peace process, which has capped the campaigns of violence by the mainstream Nationalist and Unionist groups, but is having difficulty containing the violence of hardcore splinter groups.

However all counter-terrorism programmes should have a political element, and responses to terrorist incidents must not alienate moderate opinion. Whilst it may not be possible to engage all groups, governments must be careful not to over-react with repressive measures, or punitive military action which might lead to a growth of support for these groups, although governments do also need to be robust in pursuing suspects and preventing attacks from taking place. In this respect, governments need to be strong in confronting their public opinion, which might demand such punitive action. It is perhaps through engaging with the moderate opinion within terrorists' own communities that the problem can be managed.

Conclusion

It is a reasonable assumption that at some stage there will be further terrorist incidents involving WMD. Richard Falkenrath describes it as a 'low-probability, high-consequence threat'. The likelihood of an attack is quite small, because most terrorist groups lack the expertise and resources to acquire WMD, and use of WMD is not necessarily a means by which they can pursue their goals. But there is a small cadre of groups and individuals who could develop them, and would use them, and therefore the threat is real. Consequently, the costs of providing counter-measures will be disproportionate to the likely number of terrorist incidents involving WMD. But the potentially high consequences of even a single attack justifies the investment of resources into combating the threat. The enormous difficulties faced in attempting to defeat terrorism means that there can be no complete safeguards. Even to guarantee a reasonable level of protection, states are going to have to invest considerably more resources than they have hitherto. Fortunately, the costs are not as high as is apparent at first sight, because many of them can be shared with other programmes, and resources can be focused on the most effective measures. But at the end of the day, there must be limits to what is spent, and the resources which are invested in the problem must not be allowed to draw resources away from other valuable policy issues. Ultimately it will be impossible for governments to spend their way out of the problem, and it must accept a degree of vulnerability whilst keeping spending at a reasonable level.

Notes and references

1. Paul Schulte, 'Motives and Methods of Future Political Violence: Landscapes of the Early 21st Century,' Address at Conference, 'The New Terrorism: Does It Exist? How Real Are the Risks of Mass Casualty Attacks?' (29–30 April, 1999) <http://www.cbaci.org/Newterrorism.htm>

2. James Adams, *The New Spies: Exploring the Frontiers of Espionage* (London, Hutchinson, 1994) p 312

3. Richard Falkenrath, Robert D. Newman and Bradley Thayer, *America's Achilles Heel* (Cambridge, MA: MIT Press, 1998) pp 288–89

4. Falkenrath, Newman and Thayer: *America's Achilles Heel*, pp 295–96

5. Falkenrath, Newman and Thayer: *America's Achilles Heel*, pp 301, 304–05

6. 'Bush Finalizes Battle Plan', *Daily Telegraph*, September 16, 2001

7. Paul Rogers, 'The Next Terror Weapon Will Be Biological. And it Could be Used Soon,' *Guardian* (18 August 1998) p 14

8. Louis René Beres, 'Preventing Nuclear Terrorism: Responses to Terrorist Grievances,' in Paul Leventhal and Yonah Alexander (eds), *Preventing Nuclear Terrorism* (Lexington, MA: Lexington Books, 1986) p 154

9. 'Terror is World's Problem,' *Guardian* (22 September 1998). For instance, the principal grievance underpinning the activities of Hezbollah and Islamic Jihad in the Lebanon is the Israeli military occupation of South Lebanon which has killed many civilians, displaced considerably more and destroyed numerous villages. But significantly, they are also aggrieved by western complicity in those actions, which stretches back to the mid-1980s when the multilateral force in the Lebanon was seen to take sides in the civil war, which led directly to the bombing of the US and French marines barracks. The dichotomy between the west forcing Iraq to comply with UN resolutions to leave Kuwait and failing to force Israel to comply with various UN resolutions is also not lost on the Muslim community. This is exacerbated by current Israeli and US policies to put pressure on key states such as Syria and Iran to curb the activities of terror groups. According to the deputy Secretary General of Hezbollah, Naim Qassem, 'The issue of the hostage crisis was basically a result of the West's general performance. Their handling of issues concerning our region sparked a reaction against the West. For example, they brought the multinational forces and then used them to pressure us to accept certain conditions.'5 In various punitive military operations since 1982 Israel has penalized the residents of southern Lebanon by bombing their villages and forcing them to flee their homes, in an attempt to turn them against Hezbollah.6 Following Operation Accountability in 1993, in which 50 villages were bombarded, the lack of a western response to the Israeli operation was perceived as tacit collusion by the Lebanese Muslims, and re-awakened bitterness against the west. The UN Security Council did not even meet to discuss the offensive. Israel hoped that the estimated 200,000 refugees would ultimately pressure the Lebanese and Syrian government to curb Hezbollah attacks

10. Falkenrath, Newman and Thayer: *America's Achilles Heel*, p 208

11. Richard Preston, 'The Secret War', Arena. (1998) p 212

12. Paul Wilkinson, 'Terrorist Targets: New Risks to World Order.' *Conflict Studies* 236 (December 1990) p 15

13. Conor Gearty, *Terror* (London: Faber & Faber 1991) p 129

Epilogue

The 1990s marked a transition period in terrorist activity in which the potential to acquire NBC WMD realistically came within the grasp of a number of terrorist groups, and there were a number of attempted acts of mass destruction. Al-Qaeda came close to achieving it at the World Trade Centre in 1993, as did Aum Shinrikyo in 1995. But it was not until 11 September 2001 that the world finally crossed the threshold into the era of mass destruction in which terrorists proved to be both willing and able to execute their plans.

The attacks on the World Trade Centre and the Pentagon confirmed many of the assumptions that underpinned the debate on WMD terrorism in the 1990s. As many people feared, it did prove to be only a matter of time before a terrorists act of mass destruction was successful, and NBC weapons were used again. Equally, the apparent culprits were motivated by an explosive mix of religious and radical politics and it now seems very likely that they will use an NBC weapon of mass destruction in the future. The World Trade Centre was an economic target and was also symbolic of US power, but it was primarily a population target. Taken together, these facts indicate that terrorists would use an NBC weapon of mass destruction against the population at large. At the same time these events also cast doubt on a number of other widely accepted assumptions. This first act of mass destruction terrorism was caused by a conventional weapon rather than an NBC weapon, and despite possessing a high quality anthrax, those responsible for the subsequent BW letter campaign appear to have been unable to weaponise it into a WMD. This suggests that there is still a technological barrier in developing NBC weapons of mass destruction that terrorists have not yet managed to cross, and it will continue to be a powerful constraint.

It has also been argued that terrorists might be deterred from perpetrating acts of mass destruction by the prospect that it would alienate members of their constituency, leading to a loss of international political support, and because the inevitable counter-terrorism backlash might destroy them. True enough, the level of destruction on 11 September, coupled with the realisation of what al Qaeda could achieve if it acquired an NBC weapon of mass destruction, convinced many states that they would have to be considerably more aggressive in order to prevent future attacks. Consequently, al-Qaeda was widely denounced and the US received political, logistical, or military support for the war on terrorism from a wide range of states.

Yet al-Qaeda was not intimidated by these risks. Instead it appears to have hoped that the attacks would act as a catalyst to rally popular Muslim support to expel western influence from the Middle East and Gulf region, with the ultimate goal of replacing current Arab governments with Islamist regimes. These objectives were reflected in statements released by bin Laden and the Taliban shortly after the initial bombing of Afghanistan. Bin Laden declared that 'God has blessed a group of vanguard Muslims, the forefront of Islam, to destroy America' ... 'Every Muslim must rise to defend his religion. The wind of change is blowing to remove evil from the peninsula of Mohammed.' Similarly, the Taliban leader Mullah Mohammed Omar accused the US of wanting to 'eliminate Islam, and spreading lawlessness to install a pro-US government in Afghanistan'. In response, President Bush and Prime Minister Blair had to engage in a political struggle with bin Laden to win the support of moderate Islam.

The war against terrorism is beset by a number of unknown problems. Foremost amongst them was whether it would gradually evolve into the clash of civilisations that was predicted by Samuel Huntingdon. It is widely acknowledged that military measures alone cannot defeat terrorism, but can only manage the symptoms. Therefore it threatens to become a war without end. Even if bin Laden is killed there will be others to replace him. For the present at least, the radical Islamists remain a minority in the states in which they operate although they have the potential to cause significant civil unrest. Faced with the prospect of being locked in an enduring struggle against Islamic radicalism, the alternative courses of action that are available remain unclear. It would be impossible to meet al Qaeda's political objectives in full, and there is no evidence that al-Qaeda are prepared to compromise in any meaningful sense. Consequently, a diplomatic approach also offers only limited opportunities to contain terrorism.

Despite what has happened, future terrorist activity still needs to be viewed in perspective. It is certain that there will be further attacks involving NBC weapons, possibly including WMD if terrorists can acquire them. Yet acts of mass destruction will probably continue to be very rare. It is apparent that attacks of this magnitude consume significant resources, require highly professional operatives, and take several years of planning. Even al-Qaeda has only rarely managed to execute an act of mass destruction. The 1993 bombing of the World Trade Center is the only other attempted act of mass destruction that came close to succeeding. In the intervening years the security forces in several states have proved to be successful in pre-empting numerous al-Qaeda attacks, some of which involved, CW. Significantly, individual terrorist groups should continue to find it technologically difficult to develop NBC weapons of mass destruction. Therefore the majority of future NBC weapon threats are likely to continue to fall below the WMD threshold. States are also going to have to invest more resources in safeguarding against acts of mass destruction involving conventional weapons. Neither should governments lose sight of the fact that whilst Islamic groups or networks such as al-Qaeda undoubtedly pose the most potent threat, the future might yet herald threats from a range of other types of groups or individuals.

Appendix 1: DATABASE OF CHEMICAL, BIOLOGICAL, AND NUCLEAR, TERRORIST INCIDENTS

The following database is a list of not only the most notable and successful terrorist incidents, but also includes unsuccessful attempts to acquire NBC weapons; attempted use of such agents; threats to use NBC weapons without any evidence of actual capabilities; threats of use involving actual possession of NBC agents; hoaxes; and near incidents. There are also a few very early CBW incidents mentioned, in order to give the database a historical context, but it mainly focuses on the twentieth and twenty first centuries. However it does not include criminal use of NBC weapons, even though there have been many cases of murderers using poisons, going back hundreds of years; and extortion attempts, involving threats to contaminate foodstuffs or water supplies with CBW.

It is also important to note that there is a distinction between the use of NBC agents for purposes of mass destruction and their use in smaller, more limited attacks. For example, there have been many cases of terrorist 'threats' to use NBC weapons in mass destruction attacks; and their actual use in more limited roles, such as for individual assassinations, murder, extortion, incapacitation, to terrorize, as a political statement, and product contamination. (Moreover, in addition to the incidents mentioned there are some which cannot be discussed at this time, and many other incidents which go unreported).

There has also been considerable confusion surrounding the past use of NBC weapons by terrorists. Some of this confusion, is due to vague ness and ambiguity in semantic terms, such as what is meant by WMD and NBC, and what is meant by the term terrorist. For the purposes of this database, however, an incident of terrorism presupposes a political motive in the broadest philosophical or religious sense. Moreover, any CW, BW, nuclear weapon or nuclear material, is considered to be a WMD by virtue of its inherent potential, whether it is ultimately used, or intended to be used, to inflict or threaten mass destruction, or confined to some lesser role.

By drawing on past patterns of NBC acquisition and use, the incidents in this database might highlight warning signs, and provide a more comprehensive understanding of motivations underlying the threat. Drawing on past NBC terrorist threats then, we the authors, have then tried to identify and quantify the trends that may feed into one another, and heighten the profile of this threat.

CASES INVOLVING THE USE OR THE THREAT OF THE USE BIOLOGICAL WEAPONS, PATHOGENS AND TOXINS

1999: According to an article published in *Jane's Intelligence Review*, elements in Egypt loyal to Osama bin Laden, have acquired BW through the mail. There is however, no mention, as to what has been intercepted by the Egyptian security forces. According to the report, factories in former Warsaw Pact countries, and some Eastern states, supply diseases such as ebola, anthrax and salmonella to whoever wants them without verifying the identity of the importer. An organisation with close ties to the bin Laden terror group, that has been active in Egypt until fairly recently, was able to acquire anthrax from a source in an east Asian country, for the equivalent of US $3,695, plus freight. A Czech laboratory apparently agreed to supply what appeared to be botulinum toxin for $7,500 per sample. (1)

1998: August 17, 200 people were evacuated from the Joan Finney State Office Building in Wichita, Kansas USA, after a state employee discovered a package containing white powder, and a note warning that the substance was anthrax. The substance was also found on the control panels of three lifts in the same building. Between two and four blocks were cordoned off while local and military officials investigated. On August 18, a letter claiming responsibility was sent to a local television station from the so-called "Brothers for the Freedom of Americans," a neo-Nazi militia group. Their target was symbolic of the government in general, and their motive was to overthrow the government. The package was found to be non toxic, and there were no injuries or fatalities. (2)

1998: A leader of the Islamic Jihad Movement, stated that the Islamic movements have found WMD to be the secret for defeating their enemies. During April, they allegedly threatened to use BW against Israel. April 8, the Jordanian newspaper *Al-Bihad* reported that Asad Bayud At-Tamimi, (a leading figure in Islamic Jihad-Jerusalem) talked about the possibility of using BW agents at a memorial service for Muhyuddin Ash-Sharif, the bomb maker who was supposedly murdered by a competing group within Hamas. (3)

1998: July 1, in Olmito, Texas, USA, law enforcement officials arrested John Wise, Jack Abbott Grebe Jr. and Oliver Dean Emigh, who were members of a separatist militia group seeking Texan independence, called the Republic of Texas. The men planned to kill federal agents and their families, including specific government officials, such as US Attorney General Janet Reno: FBI Director Louis Freeh; directors of the CIA; Texas Attorney General Dan Morales; Cameron County Court at Law Judge Migdalia Lopez, their families; other local, state, and federal officials; even US President Clinton and his family. The plot was uncovered by the FBI, who received letters in which the group threatened to hurt government officials, and mentioned the use of WMD. According to the arrest affidavit, the investigators were looking for biological agents when they searched the homes of the perpetrators. Among the items sought were containers of HIV infected blood, rabies virus, and anthrax spores. In addition federal agents were looking for instruction manuals, written threats, and production equipment. Authorities reportedly seized a syringe and a container marked DMSO. According to press reports the group were developing a needle and a cactus spine launched by an altered propane cigarette lighter, to shoot barbs coated with anthrax spores, the HIV virus and the rabies virus, to kill President Clinton. (4)

1998: It was alleged that an Iraqi terrorist network is being maintained in the US, which is equipped to conduct acts of bio-terrorism, with BW agents that have been smuggled into the US by Iraqi women. (5)

1998: May 26, a Belgian Radio station issued a report claiming that in March 1998, the Belgian authorities searched a building associated with the Algerian terrorist organisation, the GIA. The group had allegedly tried to grow Clostridium botulinum, but police only confirm possession of a document on how to grow the botulinum. (6)

1998: March, in the USA, agents of the Bureau of Alcohol, Tobacco and Firearms bureau, the FBI, the Internal Revenue Service, the Michigan State Police and local law enforcement agencies arrested three men who were part of an organisation called the "North American Militia of Southwestern Michigan". The terrorist group possessed a video tape describing techniques for manufacturing ricin. There is however no evidence that the group had any interest in manufacturing ricin. (7)

1998: March, Lawrence Pagnano, of Phoenix, Arizona, USA, attempted to acquire anthrax. Despite hoax letters in which the recipients were supposed to have been exposed to anthrax. Pagnano never acquired any anthrax, and there is no evidence of any malicious intent. (8)

1998: February 5, John Bernard Koch, walked into the Civil Courts Building at Charlotte, North Carolina USA, with a bomb that may have contained an unknown amount of biological and chemical agents. Koch's target was the judicial system, and his motive was revenge for losing custody of his children. There were no injuries and no fatalities. At his home in Rock Hill, South Carolina, at least one book on CBW, and bomb making instructions from the internet were discovered. Koch may have had connections with a militia group. (9)

1998: January, there were claims that manufacturers of illicit drugs were contaminating material in their laboratories with ricin, to poison law enforcement officials. There is no evidence that anyone actually has acquired ricin for that purpose. (10)

1997: According to a report published in an Arabic newspaper in

France. Dr Hasan al-Turabi, a leading figure in the Sudanese Islamic government, hosted a meeting with several terrorist heads including Osama bin Laden. The paper claimed that terrorists groups may be constructing a 'bacterial' laboratory. The terrorist groups have also provided funding for construction of the CBW facility in the Sudan. (11)

1997: September, the UK newspaper the *Guardian*, published a story which featured an interview with a man who claimed to have been a bomb maker for the anti Turkish terrorist organisation, the PKK. The 31 year old Kurd, Seydo Hazar, claimed that his people were receiving assistance from the Greek Government and that they were considering the use of CBW in the struggle against Ankara. German resident, Hazar, told the newspaper that the PKK now had a splinter faction which was targeting civilians with chemical bombs. He claimed the PKK, which was fighting a war against the Turkish state (at the time), has links with the Marxist, Greek, November 17 group; the Palestinian Hamas organisation; and the Tamil Tigers in Sri Lanka. He said his claims provide the most complete picture of collaboration between international terrorist organisations. He also claims that one NATO power may have been harbouring militants from a group waging a war against the government of another NATO member. He made his revelations to the newspaper because he was disgusted by the use of chemical bombs, including the nerve gas sarin, against civilians. He said the group was targeting British interests in Turkey, and in the UK because London extradited a Turkish Kurd leader to Germany. He also claims his group was funded by elements close to the Greek security services. The Greek government does not believe his claims, but western intelligence agencies took the allegations seriously, according to the *Guardian*. (12)

1997: August 26, the New Zealand Ministry of Agriculture and Forestry (MAF) confirmed that it had identified the presence of Rabbit Haemorrhagic Disease virus (RHD), also known as Rabbit Calicivirus Disease (RCD), on the country's South Island. The New Zealand authorities believed that someone smuggled the RCD into New Zealand, probably from Australia, and introduced it into the rabbit population. Farmers allegedly told journalists, however, that the RCD had been brought into the country two months before its release. It was the New Zealand farmers however who admitted to propagating the disease, and illegally spreading the RHD. There is overwhelming evidence to support the fact that the farmers intentionally introduced this prohibited pathogen. (13)

1997: April 23, in Washington D.C. USA, a group of religious extremists called the Counter Holocaust Lobbyists of Hillel, planned an Anthrax hoax. The groups target was the Jewish community and the motive was to scare members of the Jewish community. The group posted a petri dish labelled 'anthrachs' to the Washington offices of B'nai B'rith, a Jewish organisation. A mail clerk noticed the package was leaking a red strawberry gelatin substance from the broken petri dish. The package also contained a two page letter from the group, identifying the contents of the dish as an agent of 'chemical warfare.' Authorities sealed off the building for eight hours, quarantined 100 people, and hosed down another 14. There were no injuries, and no fatalities. The substance in the dish was later confirmed to be Bacillus Cereus which is harmless.

(B.cereus is closely related to B.anthracis, and this suggests the possibility that the perpetrator may have believed that it was anthrax). There was considerable publicity surrounding the incident, but no prosecution. (14)

1997: February, Steve Quayle, a survivalist in the USA, who produces a shortwave radio broadcast known as 'Blueprint for Survival' claimed that unspecified 'Middle Eastern Terrorists' allegedly used Bacillus anthracis, in a BW attack on Ames, Iowa. As yet there is no evidence of such an attack, and it would appear as though the episodes were fabricated. (15)

1997: February, libertarian extremist, terrorist James Dalton Bell wrote an internet essay about killing government officials called 'Assassination Politics.' Bell who was also active in anti government forums on the internet, (where he posted the essay), told participants how they could send encrypted messages to each other, and Bell also offered donations to whoever 'predicted' how long a targeted official would live. Bell also allegedly investigated toxins. (Bell who was a Massachusetts Institute of Technology (MIT) graduate, had previously been arrested for possessing ingredients with which to manufacture methamphetamine.) On April 1, 1997, Internal Revenue Service investigators searched Bell's home in Vancouver, Canada, and found a cache of chemicals which included 500 grams of sodium cyanide, diisopropyl fluorophpsphate, and a range of corrosive acids, sarin, two precursors, possibly ricin and botulinum toxin. Subsequent analysis of computer files confiscated from his residence, revealed that Bell expressed interest in acquiring castor beans, and cultivating botulinum toxin. According to Gordon, Bell's target was the government, and Gordon believes that Bell had already set in motion his plans to facilitate its collapse. Bell denied the allegations and asserted that he merely wanted to explore his interest in chemistry and libertarian ideals. (16)

1997: February 18, Larry Wayne Harris, (a lieutenant in the white supremacist group the Aryan Nations, and a member of the Christian Identity Church), and William Leavitt Jr, were arrested by the FBI in Henderson, Nevada, USA. The FBI believed that the men had 8-10 flight bags of Bacillus anthracis in the trunk of their car. Subsequent analysis proved the material to be harmless veterinary anthrax vaccine. Harris claims that he wanted to test the anthrax in order to develop a vaccine for humans. When this incident came to the attention of the press, there were repeated news reports claiming that the two men were planning a terrorist attack on the New York Subway, which proved to be false, and the US Justice Department dropped the case. (17)

1997: In Ramalla, an anaesthetic substance was discovered in the possession of Palestinian terrorists affiliated with Hamas. (18)

1997: January 17 in Janesville, Winsonsin USA, the FBI, the local police and a hazardous materials team from the Madison Fire Department, searched the home of Thomas.C.Leahy. (Leahy had first come to the attention of the FBI in 1997 when he was arrested for shooting his teenage stepson in the face). In the basement of Leahy's home the law enforcement officials found a make-shift laboratory where tests indicated that he had produced approximately 0.7 grams of pure ricin. After further laboratory analysis, it was determined that he had also attempted to grow botulism, and had produced a lethal mixture of nicotine sulphate which he mixed with dimethyl sulphoxide (DMSO) and placed in a spray bottle. Animal viruses and vaccines, staph bacteria cultures, fungicides, insecticides, hypodermic needles and gas masks were also found. Leahy was initially indicted for possession of ricin for use as a weapon in violation of Title 18, Section 175, The Biological Weapons Anti-Terrorism Statute, the legislation which enacts the BTWC into US domestic law. On April 28 1997, he was charged with possession of ricin to use as a weapon. He was indicted on May 15, by a Federal Grand Jury. On October 28, he entered a guilty plea admitting that he possessed ricin, and intended to use it as a weapon. At his sentencing January 7, 1998, Leahy claimed that he wanted the poisons to 'kill his enemies' through the United States Postal Service and also to 'protect' himself. It has been alleged that Leahy had had a lifelong fascination with poisons, he had also taken medication for schizophrenia, and had a history of alcohol and drug abuse. Leahy was sentenced to 55 months in prison for possessing toxin as a weapon. (19)

1996: August 28, in Dallas, Texas, USA, 12 laboratory workers at St Paul's Medical Centre became ill as a result of eating muffins and doughnuts in their cafeteria. Apparently the food was intentionally contaminated with Shigella dysenteriae type 2 (a type of bacteria which causes diarrhoea), by Diane Thompson, a disaffected worker. Thompson is believed to have gained access to the Shigella dysenteriae type 2 from the culture collection of the hospital where she worked. An epidemiological study of the case supports the theory of intentional contamination. Thompson was indicted by the state of Texas, on charges of tampering with a food product. (20)

1996: In August, there was report that Israel's defence minister had warned the CIA of a plan by Iran to poison water resources in Western Europe and America with a biological pollutant, and that that both the CIA and Israel believed that Iranian defence scientists had developed a deadly BW aerosol that can be carried by a terrorist. (21)

1996: In March, an unknown perpetrator, stole a package of botulinum toxin from Florida Institute of Technology, USA. The toxin was returned to the university after publicity surrounding the theft. There is no evidence to suggest that the perpetrator even knew that botulinum was present in the stolen package. (22)

1995: In Lancaster Ohio USA, Larry Wayne Harris. (See Harris's details in 1997 case above), acquired freeze dried bubonic plague bacteria (Yersinia pestis) from the American Type Culture Collection (ATCC), Rockville, Maryland. (The ATCC is a non profit making organisation. It has the USA's leading collection of cultured diseases and acts as a library of about 1,000 microbes for institutions worldwide. The ATCC sells approximately 130,000 cultures annually, and ships orders to 60 nations. It was the ATCC, that drew US congressional criticism for sending Iraq dozens of dangerous biological cultures shortly before the Persian Gulf War).

The bacteria was delivered by Federal Express, but the plot was foiled because Harris became impatient and telephoned the ATCC to ask where the parcel was. This alerted the company, and after consulting with the Centres for Disease Control and Prevention (CDC), law enforcement was contacted. On investigation three vials of the plague were recovered from the glove compartment of Harris's motor vehicle. Although Harris claimed to be a microbiologist who was writing a training manual for the Aryan Nations, he did not have a facility, or the necessary training to properly handle the material. However he had broken no law in possessing the agent. After a plea bargain he was charged under the Fraud by Wire statute, for fraudulently using a laboratory registration number when ordering the agent. (Since Harris' case a misdemeanour would exist today for such conduct under CDC transfer regulations.) He received a six month suspended sentence. This was dropped however by a US District Judge who rejected the agreement. Harris was tried April 1997, and convicted of fraud for acquiring y.pestis from the ATCC. He was sentenced to eighteen months probation and 200 hours of community service. Harris, police said, had ordered the plague germs from the ATCC, for US$240 dollars. There are a number of different accounts of why wanted the bacteria. Harris does not appear however to have had any plans to use the bacteria, and claimed to have purchased the bacteria to support his research on the development of medical treatments for the plague, (although treatments already exist). It is alleged that he said he needed the bacteria to develop an antidote to Saddam Hussein's invasion of germ carrying mice, or because he was undertaking research for a book. Harris has since written and published a book on the subject called "Bacteriological Warfare: A Major Threat to North America," which he says is a manual for surviving BW. The Southern Poverty Law Centre's Klan Watch however, say the book is a DIY manual for mass destruction through biological terrorism. (23)

1995: March, members of the Aum Shinrikyo religious cult, in Japan, left three briefcases designed to release Botulinum Toxin in Kasumigaseki subway station. Apparently, the perpetrator had qualms about the planned attack and failed to arm them with the agent. (24)

1994: The Animal Liberation Front (ALF) allegedly mailed fragments of hypodermic needles contaminated with HIV. This incident is recounted in an article by Ron Purver, but his account does not say in what country the needles were mailed, although it was probably the UK since the ALF are a UK animal rights group. This incident does not however, appear on the list of ALF activities maintained by the ALF Information Service. (25)

1993: In June, an attempt was made by the Aum Shinrikyo to disrupt the planned wedding of Prince Naruhito, Japan's Crown Prince, by spraying botulinum toxin from a specially equipped vehicle cruising central Tokyo. This attack also failed. (26)

1993: In June, the Aum Shinrikyo attempted to release anthrax spores from an industrial sprayer fitted with a powerful fan, over a period of four days, from the roof of a building that it owned in eastern Tokyo. The attack killed only birds and plants. When the police raided the Aum Shinrikyo compound they discovered 160 barrels of media for growing Clostridium Botulinum bacteria, which produces Botulinum toxin. A US Senate Committee has also alleged that cult members had also tried to obtain the Ebola virus from Zaire (now called Congo). The virus causes an infection whereby the body disintegrates into pools of blood. Unconfirmed reports state that Aum Shinrikyo scientists went to

Africa to obtain samples of the virus, and certainly there were Aum Shinrikyo agents in Kikwit in Congo when the virus was at its worst. (27)

1993: 8th April, Thomas Lewis Lavy, an electrician working in Valdez Alaska, for an oil pipeline company, was apprehended by Canadian Custom's officials at the Alaskan-Canadian border. (Other reports indicate that he might have been a farmer). On investigation, customs officials found, neo-Nazi white supremacist literature, 'how to' manuals which purport to describe techniques for producing botulinum toxin or extracting ricin from castor beans. ('The Silent Death' by Uncle Fester and 'The Poisoners Handbook'), US $98,000 in cash, court documents, four guns, 20,000 rounds of ammunition, and a bag of white powder which was identified as 130 grams of ricin. The Canadians took the powder and released him. Lavy claimed that he had intended to use the ricin on coyotes threatening his chickens. The FBI, were later advised of the incident, and the investigation was re-opened on 20th December 1995. Near Onia, Arkansas USA, FBI agents arrested Lavy at his farm, and a search was conducted. A large quantity of castor beans, from which ricin is derived, were discovered, but Lavy stated that he had not produced any more ricin. According to Richard Falkenrath et al, after a two year investigation by the FBI, Lavy was arrested and charged under the 1989 Biological Weapons Anti Terrorism Act with possession of a biological toxin with intent to kill. He later hanged himself whilst in a detention facility awaiting adjudication, two days before Christmas 1995. It is alleged that Lavy is alleged to have had links to survivalist groups, and it is suspected that he had connections with right wing Christian Fundamentalists. (28)

1992: May, in Alexandria, Minnesota, USA, a US court found two people guilty of possessing ricin in breach of the Biological Weapons Anti Terrorism Act 1989. The production of the ricin was linked to a survivalist militia group of radical tax protestors known as the Patriots Council. Founded by Frank Nelson, the members of the group were Douglas Allen Baker, Leroy Charles Wheeler, Dennis Brett Henderson, (first co-founder of the local chapter), and Richard John Oelrich (the second co-founder of the local chapter). Two of the group (Baker and Wheeler) were convicted of conspiracy to assassinate federal law enforcement officers (who had served papers on the group) with Ricin. According to an FBI informant, a dozen castor beans ordered by mail had been planted on land owned by one of the defendants, and 0.7 grams of ricin was extracted from it, made from a recipe found in a book by Maynard Campbell, called 'Catalogue of Silent Tools of Justice.' The group had been planning to poison US government agents by smearing the ricin mixed with the solvent DMSO, on doorknobs, expecting that it would be absorbed through the victims skin. The plot was foiled when an angry wife turned in her Patriot husband after a marital fight, and delivered the suspicious powder he was keeping in a baby food jar to the police. (29)

1992: March 2, Henry D Pierce of Vienna, Virginia, USA, was arrested and charged with malicious wounding, after he sprayed ten people, with a liquid that he claimed was anthrax. When police were called to the scene, Pierce was confrontational with the police, and he had to be subdued with a stun gun. The Fairfax County Fire and Rescue

Department decontaminated the people in the house, and sent them to hospital. Nine other people in the neighbourhood were also kept at the hospital for treatment. Subsequent analysis by USAMRIID, Fort Detrick, Maryland, showed that the substance was not anthrax. (30)

1992: 15 January, the British Colombia News received a report that the Animal Aid Association (AAA) had injected `Cold Buster' chocolate bars with HIV, in order to protest against the use of animal research, and the diversion of funds from AIDS research. According to a publication of the Canadian Intelligence Service, this incident involved oven cleaner, not a biological agent. The ALF Information Service does not list this incident (31)

1991: April, a scientist called John Gunnar Limnner, Ph.D, was found in possession of Tetrodotoxin and botulinum toxin, he also had a recipe to make botulinum. The perpetrator had an interest in poisons but was never convicted of a criminal offence. (32)

1991: According to the Congressional testimony of Steven Emerson, (an investigative journalist who focuses on Islamic terrorist groups), the Palestinian group Hamas have allegedly shown an interest in CBW. As evidence, he cites Israeli documents that record the interrogation of a senior Hamas official Muhammad Salah. Although the statement clearly suggests an interest in CW, there was insufficient evidence to suggest an interest in biological agents. (33)

1990-1991: Between August 1990 and February 1991, during the Gulf War there were reported plans to use bacteriological bombs against airports, airlines, airline offices, schools, trains, railroads, oil refineries and hospitals in Europe. There was also an anonymous threat to biologically contaminate the water supply of a city in British Colombia. The discovery was reported by UNSCOM inspectors who found plans to use such agents in terrorist activities. (34)

1990: In June, in Edinburgh Scotland, nine people were infected with Giardia lamblia, (which causes severe diarrhoea), when the water supply of their apartment building was deliberately contaminated with giardia infected faeces. There is no evidence that the perpetrator knew that this would cause an outbreak of disease. (35)

1990: In the UK, Kevin Denton, masterminded a plan to blackmail the UK government with the threat of germ warfare. Denton planned robberies and burglaries with the aim of stealing large amounts of cash to finance Operation Grand Slam, a scheme to unleash the Legionnaires Disease virus on buildings, unless he received US$1.5 million in payment in diamonds from the government. Denton took his idea from the James Bond film Goldfinger. Denton broke into two schools to steal chemicals and laboratory equipment, and he obtained a copy of an international terrorist manual to learn how to make bombs. Bomb experts found handwritten instructions on how to make chemical bombs from ingredients such as flour, linseed oil and bleach. He also concocted recipes for germs that he would unleash into the air cooling system of several large buildings. Denton had also made detailed drawings which included matchstick men lying on the ground and arrows pointing to graves with crosses on the top. Denton was jailed for four years. (36)

1990: April, the Aum Shinrikyo sprayed a solution of Botulinum toxin from a vehicle through the engine's exhaust, the car was then driven around the Diet building, where the Japanese Parliament sits. (37)

April 1990-March 1995: the Aum Shinrikyo produced biological agents and tried to use them. According to press reports the cult's membership included skilled scientists, and technicians, including some with training in microbiology. Aum Shinrikyo attempted various terrorist attacks (possibly nine attacks) with botulinum toxin and anthrax. Some reports state that these early efforts were set up to try to set off an apocalyptic war between the US and Japan. The group also sought to genetically enhance bacteria they had acquired, but failed. there have been numerous press reports of these cases but no official indictment. (38)

1989: November, in Los Angeles County, California USA, in late 1989, an unknown group called the Breeders, who were agricultural activists, sent letters to Los Angeles Mayor Tom Bradley, agricultural officials, and members of the media, claiming responsibility for spreading Medfly through Southern California. The incident was a protest against California's agricultural policies. This was not strictly a BW terrorist attack, because Medflies are not a biological agent, pathogen or toxin. (39)

1988: November 6, Colonel Jean-Claude Paul, the retired commander of Haiti's elite Dessalines Battalion was murdered by an unspecified poison, administered to his pumpkin soup. Paul was the leader of the notorious Tontons Macoutes, a terror squad created by President Baby Doc Duvalier's regime to maintain power. Paul was also until his retirement one of the most powerful figures in Haiti. At the time of his death, the US had been trying to extradite Paul for his involvement in South American drug smuggling. In this case there was sufficient evidence to identify the type of poison involved. It is believed that it may have been a chemical, or it may have been one of the toxins known to Haitian practitioners of Voodoo. (40)

Mid 1980s: There were threats from the USA Minutemen (a politically right wing group) to disperse an unknown virus that had been developed by their leader Robert De Pugh (the owner of a veterinary drug firm), by sprinkling it on the floors of major airline terminals. The motive for this attack is unknown, and the target would have been indiscriminate casualties. De Pugh claims that the group were working on seven agents, including equine encephalitis, and Sarin, and they were also genetically engineering viruses to increase their virulence and resistance to antibiotics. However none of these claims were ever proved, and there was no evidence that any of these agents had been produced and no attack ever took place. (41)

1984: November 21, two Canadians were arrested by the FBI at the Buffalo, New York, USA, Federal Express Office, for attempting to procure tetanus and Clostridium botulinum cultures from the ATCC, by falsely claiming to be working for a research firm. Although the botulinum culture was not sent, reportedly the first phone order of deadly cultures was fulfiled, and one ampoule of frozen tetanus culture was sent, and never recovered. (Officials claimed that it could be reproduced in quantities sufficient to be dangerous). It was not until the second order however, that ATCC employees became sufficiently suspicious to notify the authorities. The two were indicted by a federal Grand Jury on April 18, 1985, on charges of telephone fraud. They negotiated a plea bargain agreement, and pleaded guilty to the charges. They were both fined. (42)

1984: September, followers of the Rajneeshpuram Cult in Oregon, USA, carried out a terrorist attack on the salad bars of restaurants in The Dalles; the seat of the local government. Around September 12, members of the cult contaminated the salad bars in two restaurants. About twenty five people became sick as a result of eating food in these restaurants. Around September 20, just as health officials thought the outbreak was coming to an end, the Rajneeshees contaminated the salad bars at ten local restaurants, (including the two previously contaminated) with Salmonella Typhimurium, which causes a diarrhoeal disease (this was their trial run before poisoning the water supply of the entire town). They purchased their seed stock of salmonella, (which is not on a control list), from a medical supply company. The Rajneeshees also had a state certified clinical laboratory, which gave them a legitimate reason to acquire agents like salmonella. Their goal was to make local townspeople ill, preventing them from voting in a local referendum in November, and throwing the election their way. The attack resulted in serious food poisoning (salmonellosis) to 751 people, in Wasco County (although the actual number could have been higher, since the community is on an interstate and some of the infected travellers may not have reported their illness). 45 people were hospitalised. This was the largest outbreak of salmonellosis in Oregon history, and it overwhelmed the local medical establishment. Fortunately there were no fatalities, but the main attack of poisoning the water supply, was never undertaken. For some time afterwards, public health officials believed that the salmonella outbreak in The Dalles was of natural origin, until a former member of the cult confessed. A year after the outbreak an investigation was carried out and the two main culprits Ma Anand Sheela, the ringleader, and Ma Anand Puja, the cult's nurse, who was instrumental in the plot, were convicted of attempted murders in both state and federal courts for participation in the plot. They were sentenced to long prison sentences. Other members admitted to participation but were never tried. This is the only bioterrorism incident in which human illness has been verified. There are also reports of efforts by the Rajneeshees to develop a means to disperse AIDS through aerosolized HIV contaminated blood. (They also considered using hepatitis and giardia). The Rajneeshees had a powerful and charismatic leader, who maintained strict internal controls on the cult members but there is no evidence to suggest that the cult's religious leader Bagwhan Shree Rajneesh was aware of, or involved in any way, in this plot. (43)

1984: August 29, members of the Rajneeshees used their biological agents against some individuals. The group gave water laced with Salmonella typhimurium to two hostile Wasco County commissioners. Both became sick; one required hospitalisation and might have died without adequate medical care. Although the Rajneeshees were suspected of deliberately poisoning the commissioners, there was no evidence to support such a claim and there was no criminal investigation. (44)

1984: Members of the Rajneeshees tried to spread Salmonella typhimurium around The Dalles. On one occasion, two members poured vials onto produce at a local grocery store. On another occasion, a Rajneeshees official put the mixture onto door handles and urinal handles in the Wasco County Courthouse. On a third occasion a Rajneeshees was instructed to visit schools and nursing homes to put Salmonella typhimurium into the food. These attacks were ineffective. (45)

1984: On two occasions, members of the Rajneeshees attempted to contaminate the water supply of The Dalles. They boke into one of the water tanks that supplied the city and poured an unknown substance onto it. It appears that the Rajneeshees did not have enough Salmonella typhimurium and so probably used sewage mixed with dead rats. This contamination does not appear to have caused any illness. (46)

1984: On January 16 in Australia, the Queensland State Premier, Bjelke-Peterson received a letter threatening to unleash foot and mouth disease in Queensland unless certain conditions, such as prison reforms, and the release of some prisoners were met. The perpetrator was Peter Vivian Wardrop, a murderer serving life in Townsville's Stuart Jail. (47)

1983: According to Douglas and Livingstone, sometime in 1983 or 1984 the FBI seized an ounce of ricin from two brothers in Springfield, Massachusetts, USA, who had manufactured it themselves. There is very little information about this incident, and no information is available on the disposition of the case. Nor is it indicated why the two had acquired the ricin. (48)

1981: October 10, a group of UK environmentalist terrorists left a sample of contaminated soil in a paper package inside a bucket. A statement given to the press indicated that a group calling itself Dark Harvest orchestrated the incident. According to the group they were returning the 'seeds of death' to their source; the Chemical and Biological Defence Establishment based at Porton, Wiltshire, in the UK. The soil the protestors claimed, was taken by two university microbiologists, from the Hebridean island of Gruinard. (The island had been closed to the public since germ warfare experiments involving anthrax, were conducted there in the early 1940s. It was not until 1990, that Gruinard was returned to civilian use). Press reports suggest that anthrax was found in at least on soil sample, and it was consistent with soil found on Gruinard. October 14, a second package was deposited at the site of a Conservative Party meeting. In this instance, police received an anonymous tip off about the presence of a metal box, containing the soil which was located on the roof of the meeting site. Subsequent analysis proved negative for anthrax. Very little is known about this incident, but it would appear that Dark Harvest were uninterested in causing harm to people or property, but they thought the appropriate use of a biological agent would send the right political message. (49)

1980-1985: A former member of the East German secret police (the Stasi) claimed that an East German terrorist camp had been teaching terrorists to use CBW against civilian targets. In a recorded interview (this was reported in a documentary directed by a British journalist Gwynne Roberts shown on January 30 1991, on the British Channel 4, as part of the *Dispatches* documentary). An unnamed former Stasi officer describes the Stasi's training of Iraqis and Palestinians. Terrorists were allegedly taught how to disseminate CBW agents in public places, such as airports, train stations, and how to poison water supplies. The officer also claimed that agents of the Iraqi secret police, the Mukhabarat, had been trained to use CBWs. This training allegedly took place in 1980-1985, after which it continued in Iraq, Syria and Yemen. Some experts believe that Stasi officials reluctant to return to a unified Germany are still training agents in Iraq. (50)

1980-1984: Ostensibly equally expert sources with access to classi-fied US government records dispute the date, but sometime between 1981-1984, police raided the Paris apartment of a cell of the West German RAF (Baader Meinhof gang). There, police found a miniature laboratory containing cultured Clostridium botulinum which produces Botulinum toxin. Notes about bacteria induced diseases were found in the apartment as well. Although the public record does not indicate that the material was produced at the location, the work is attributed to one of the group's members, Silke Maier-Witt, who was a medical assistant by profession. (51)

1980: In 1980 there was an allegation that Hezbollah had tried to acquire CBW. This has not been confirmed. (52)

1980: Abu Tayyib, the commander of Fatah's Force 17, stated in an interview that the PLO possessed CBW, and would not hesitate to use them in future wars. Other reports suggest PLO interest in WMD, but none have been proved. (53)

1980: In Sri Lanka, possibly between 1983 and 1987, a militant group of Tamil guerrillas threatened to use the biological agents, Schistisima worms, Yellow fever, leaf curl (to attack rubber plants) and unspecified agents against the Sinhalese dominated government of Sri Lanka. (There are five main Tamil groups, but which of them made the threat is not specified). According to Milton Leitenberg, the guerilla's released a communique threatening to wage biological warfare against the government. They described four operations that they would carry out. The series of BW attacks included the use BWs on the human pop-ulation: the transport and introduction of the natural vectors for River Blindness (a snail) and Yellow Fever (mosquitos) into the south of the country. The remaining two were threats of transporting and introduc-ing two anti plant agents, against the rubber plants and tea bushes and two pathogens that which make up two of Sri Lanka's major export products. There was no evidence that any such attacks were ever car-ried out. (54)

1979: November, the white government of Rhodesia claimed that Zimbabwean terrorists spread Bacillus anthracis, in 12 districts. Twenty people reportedly died form the disease, which also affected cattle. There is insufficient information to support these allegations, and the incident may have in fact been Rhodesian propaganda. (55)

1979: According to the RAND-St Andrews Terrorism Chronology, in July, the terrorist group the Aliens of America threatened to contami-nate the US consulate in Munich, Germany, with Legionnaires Disease bacteria. There is insufficient evidence to support the allegation. (56)

1978: September, in Tuscon, Arizona USA, an individual sent an undisclosed number of letters to Tuscon Mayor Lewis Murphy threaten-ing to contaminate the city with an unknown amount of bubonic plague carrying fleas unless a $500,000 ransom was paid, the poor were given food, and Kino Community Hospital resumed performing abortions. There were no injuries and no fatalities. (57)

1977: March, in the USA a letter was sent by a possible terrorist, to a US advertising firm claiming the discovery of a 'lethal bacterium capable of contaminating the fresh water of nuclear armed nations.' The target for this incident was the government in general and indiscriminate casualties. The motive was possibly to protest international nuclear policy. There were no injuries and no fatalities. (58)

1975: According to the RAND St-Andrews Terrorism Chronology sometime in February 1975 the western Sahara's Polisario Front made contact with ETA to plan poisoning water supplies of Paris, Madrid, Rabat in Morocco, and Nouakchott the Mauritian capital. These attacks were to be in retaliation for the policies of these countries regarding Polisario's guerrilla efforts. (59)

1974: The Rand-St Andrews Terrorism Chronology states that sometime in 1974, 'a Middle East firm was reported to be engaged in the development of means of poisoning the Jordan river by bacteria.' There is very little information about this incident. (60)

1974: The Rand-St Andrews Terrorism Chronology states that during a raid on a left wing revolutionary Symbionese Liberation Army's (SLA) safehouse, police allegedly found biological warfare manuals, and US technical military manuals on the production of BW agents. Press accounts based on information released by law enforcement officials. (61)

1974: The Rand-St Andrews Terrorism Chronology states that a terrorist group called the Legion of Nabbil Kadduri Usur threatened to release bacteria if its demands were not met. There is very little information to support this case. The original source of the report is unknown. (62)

1972: Two men affiliated with the US neo-Nazi group the Order of the Rising Sun, which was dedicated to creating a new master race, were arrested in Chicago with between 30 and 40 kg of Typhoid bacillus, that they had apparently produced themselves. The two who eventually fled to Cuba had conspired to contaminate the water supplies of some large Midwestern cities such as Chicago and St Louis, with stocks of Typhoid fever germs cultivated by one of them. Up to 40 kilograms of bacteria cultures were found in a college laboratory. (63)

1972: The Rand-St Andrews Terrorism Chronology states that an unnamed Middle East terrorist organisation, allegedly established a programme to develop CBW agents. (64)

1972: In the USA, in January, a white racist terrorist group called RISE, led by two students Steven Pera and Allan Schwander, who studied at a community college in Chicago, plotted to wipe out the entire human race with eight different microbial pathogens, and then repopulate the world with their own genes. Members of RISE were to be inoculated and immunised against the pathogens, they would then form the basis for a new master race. Their initial scheme was to use aircraft to disperse the agents on a global basis, but they scaled down their vision to killing the residents of the five states around Chicago by contaminating local water supplies with Salmonella. Some of the group members informed the FBI about the plot, and the groups apocalyptic ideology, before it was carried out, however, and the two ringleaders fled to Cuba. Schwander was arrested in Cuba and sentenced to six years in prison. Pera returned to the US and surrendered. (65)

1970: During November 1970, an informant warned the US Customs Bureau, that a revolutionary left wing group, called the Weather Underground, (led at the time by Bernardine Dohrn, one of many leaders for the Weather Underground) were attempting to blackmail a homosexual lieutenant at the United States Army Medical Research Institute of Infectious Diseases (USAMRIID) in Fort Detrick, near Frederick Maryland, into supplying organisms. According to reports, the organisms were to be used to contaminate the water supply of a city or cities, to incapacitate a population by infection for 7-10 days. The terrorist group hoped that the repressive reaction of the government to such an incident would radicalise the general population and create additional supporters for the cause. According to the Monterrey database, the entire event, which was widely reported in the media and referred to by academics, apparently never occurred. (66)

1970: There are numerous allegations that the RAF claimed an interest in BW, and, or, were receiving training in how to use BW. According to a story that appeared in Defence and Foreign Affairs. Several agencies report that West German terrorists, the remnants of the RAF (Baader-Meinhof gang) were preparing to use bacteriological weapons. At least 13 terrorists were being trained in a camp south of Beirut. which is run by the PFLP, the most radical Palestinian terror organisation. The account claims that Western security agencies treated this information with scepticism. Jeffrey Simon reports that a few years earlier the RAF had threatened to poison water in twenty West German towns if three radical lawyers were not allowed to defend a comrade on trial. But there are no sources for this allegation. Another source claims that 'an unconfirmed report denied by the authorities' alleges that domestic terrorist elements possibly hard core RAF members were planning to attack the Federal Research Institute for Animal Viruses in Tuebingen (Germany) to steal infectious viruses. The source claims that the targeted facility was photographed by an unidentified person planning the attack. The source of the allegation is not identified in the account. In 1980 there was reportedly a threat by the RAF to spread Anthrax through the German Mail system. The account does not specify the intended targets, nor does it clarify whether the terrorists intended to mail some kind of dissemination device or if they only intended to send contaminated letters. (67)

1970: Neil C Livingstone alleged in a book that the FBI and the Los Angeles police arrested someone who was preparing to poison the water supply with biological poison. No date or other particulars are given. (68)

1968: According to the newspaper Dagens Nyheter, an Arab Pharmaceutical Congress indicated its support for the PLO and advocated its training in biological warfare. There is very little information about the incident, and it is unclear whether the Congress was suggesting the PLO should undertake biological warfare, or if the suggestion was directed at Arab states. (69)

December 1964- March 1966: a Japanese doctor and bacteriologist

Mitsuru Suzuki confessed that he deliberately caused a series of dysentery and typhoid outbreaks by contaminating food, and administering injections. Dr Suzuki stole the S.typi cultures from the Japanese National Institute of Health. This reportedly affected 200 people, resulting in four deaths. Dr Suzuki appears to have been motivated by the desire for revenge. He was angry about the treatment he was receiving as a resident in his medical training, and allegedly retaliated by infecting other health care providers and patients. Suzuki's motivations are complicated by suggestions that he may have been creating clinical cases to further his academic research. The defendant was indicted and brought to trial for alleged use of pathogens. (70)

1961: In October, 'J.L,' was accused of contaminating food served at an officer's mess with the Hepatitis A virus. 22 US Navy personnel were stricken with the illness. There is no evidence to suggest that the perpetrator carried out the attack, and did deliberately transfer the virus to the food via urine. J.L did suffer psychological problems, but there is no evidence to support the allegation. (71)

1964-1969: Robert De Pugh, the owner of a veterinary medical products supply company named the Biolab Corporation, in the state of Missouri, USA, headed the largest paramilitary right wing organisation in the USA, the Minuteman of America. He claimed to have a 'number of our own physicians and bacteriologists working on the production of biological agents. Most of this research goes on after hours in public and private institutions where they hold a regular job during the day and have an opportunity to moonlight a few hours in the evening on their own.' De Pugh claimed that his associates were researching classical BW and research and development subject matters, 'such as...the selective breeding of various pathogens in order to increase or decrease their virulence and to render them resistant to antibiotics.' He referred to equine encephalitis virus as one of his seven agents his group had selected to work on. He also claimed that he had personally produced sarin at his company's facilities and elsewhere across the country. None of these claims were ever validated by any other source and there is no knowledge that any of the agents were ever produced, or used. (72)

1950s: In the 1950s British authorities in Kenya, Africa, discovered that the Mau Mau, a nationalist liberation movement originating with the Kikuyu Tribe; had used the plant toxin, African milk bush (Synadenium grantii) to kill livestock. This was a concerted campaign that often involved other poisons, including arsenic. This incident has been confirmed by scientific studies of the incident. (73)

1947-1948: Between November 1947-May 1948, it is alleged that Zionist terrorists planned to use biological agents against Egypt and Syria. The Palestinian Arab Higher Committee submitted a 13 page report to the UN at the time, claiming that the 'Zionists intended to use the inhuman weapon against the Arabs in the Middle east in their war of extermination.' The report contended that there was 'some' evidence to link Palestinian Jews to cholera outbreaks in Egypt in November 1947 and in Syria in February 1948. Not long afterwards, it was said that 'Zionists' had contaminated wells in Gaza with a liquid that the Egyptians maintained was 'discovered to contain the germs of dysentery and typhoid.' (74)

1945: There are two accounts of a Jewish resistance group who intended to use BW and poisons against Germans after the end of the Second World War. Michael Elkins, a correspondent for the BBC gives the first account. According to him, in early 1945, a group of Jewish resistance fighters operating in central Europe, organised a group to exact revenge on German officials involved in the Holocaust. They called the organisation Dahm Y'Isreal Nokam DIN, (Judgement) a biblical phrase from the Hebrew, meaning the blood of Israel will take vengeance. During 1945 the group were involved in plots to kill former Nazi officials, and they allegedly killed 100 people during this period. Elkins also recounts a plot by former Jewish resistance fighters to put biological agents into water. The terrorists planned to poison the water supply of five German cities to avenge the Holocaust. Technical problems foiled their plan. There is insufficient evidence to confirm the allegations. (The second account is available in the CW section of the database). (75)

December 1942 - September 1943: Polish resistance terrorists used pathogens such as Salmonella typhi to infect German soldiers during World War Two. One of the tactics used was to coat the glue on envelopes with a toxic carcinogen. The Polish resistance also succeeded in killing horses used for transport in the German war effort using Bacillus anthracis. (76)

1910: In Latin America, the terrorist Pancho Villa allegedly used botulinum toxin to attack Federal troops during the Mexican revolution. There is very little information about this incident. (77)

Early BW attacks: BW attacks have a very long history, and early Persians, Greeks, and Romans poisoned their enemies' wells by throwing corpses into them. The three year siege of Caffa (now Feodosija) was broken in 1346 when attacking Tartars slung the bodies of plague victims over the walls and infected the inhabitants. (78)

CASES INVOLVING THE USE, OR THE THREAT OF THE USE OF CHEMICAL WEAPONS.

2000: The Russian government and insurgents in the breakaway republic of Chechnya, both claimed that the other side waged chemical warfare. The latter charge stemmed from the bombing, accidental or otherwise, of some Chlorine tanks near the Chechen capital, Grozny. General Gennadi Troshev, Russian commander of the western front in Chechnya, said that his soldiers were forced to suspend operations in Grozny to protect civilians. He claimed that rebels were blowing up containers of toxic chemicals and using civilians as human shields. He informed NTV television that, 'Grozny has today been officially declared a risk area, an ecological danger zone. That chiefly affects civilians and children.' At the end of December 1999, as Russian and Chechen forces fought for control of Grozny, gas masks were distributed amongst Russians in case the Chechens, set off bombs at what were suspected to be chlorine filled chemical plants on the city's edges. (79)

1999: Adam Busby, leader of the Scottish National Liberation Army issued blackmail letters in the name of the Republican Revenge Group, which threatened to contaminate water supplies in the UK with the highly toxic weedkiller, Paraquat, unless British troops were withdrawn from Northern Ireland by mid June 1999. The letters contained a high level of technical detail which raised concerns that the threat was a real one, and whilst it is not known whether Busby actually had possession of the Paraquat, it is a commercially available weedkiller which he could easily have acquired. (80)

1998-1999: In Japan people were poisoned by beverages containing cyanide. The drinks had tiny holes drilled into them and the contents laced with poison. (81)

1998: November, the CIA confirmed that Osama bin Laden had attempted to develop or buy chemical weapons for use against US troops in the Persian Gulf area. US National Security Advisor Sandy Berger told a press conference in February 1999 that, 'we know bin Laden was seeking chemical weapons' and 'we know that he had worked with the Sudanese government to acquire chemical weapons.' Bin Laden was in Sudan between 1991 and 1996, and during that time he worked closely with Sudan's National Islamic Front (NIF) to obtain weapons and explosives, and most significantly CWs. The controversy over the El Shaifa Pharmaceutical plant near Khartoum notwithstanding, the evidence available suggests that Sudan had acquired and used CWs as early as 1992. Khartoum may also be developing CW production facilities. There is also evidence of Sudanese Iraqi CW co-operation and bin Laden-Iraqi connections. In December 1998, bin Laden is reported to have met with the Iraqi ambassador to Turkey who is believed by some to be an agent of the Iraqi intelligence service. There are also reports of contacts between bin Laden's operatives and Iraq's special security organisations, which is responsible for protecting Iraq's CWs, BWs and nuclear programmes. Bin Laden is also believed to have had numerous contacts with Iraqi agents during his years in Sudan. The available evidence, including bin Laden's links to Sudan, Iraq and Iran suggests that his organisation may well have acquired a CW. (82)

1998: August, in retaliation for the bombing of the US embassies in Nairobi, Kenya and Dar-es-Salaam, Tanzania, the US bombed the El Shaifa Pharmaceutical plant near Khartoum which is owned by Osama bin Laden, the prime suspect in several anti-US attacks including the Kenya and Tanzania embassy bombings. The US justified this action by claiming that the plant was producing VX nerve gas, following the alleged discovery of the chemical Empta, in soil samples taken from the plant. Since then, considerable doubt has been cast on the validity of this analysis. (83)

1998: 8 July 1998, a group suspected of being the Army of God, a group of anti-abortion activists, sprayed three to four gallons of butyric acid, through holes drilled in the doors of abortion clinics. The four abortion clinics in Houston Texas, USA, which included Concerned Women's Centre, America's Women Clinic, A to Z Women's Services, and one unidentified clinic, were vandalised only days after five clinics in New Orleans, Louisiana, were similarly attacked. Officials reported that the attacks could be related; the terrorists apparently were travelling along the Interstate-10 corridor. Their aim was to disable the clinics and to protest against abortions. The attacks injured between 11-14 people, according to different sources, but there were no fatalities. (84)

1998: 6 July, in New Orleans, Louisiana, USA, a group suspected of being the Army of God, delivered an unknown amount of butyric acid through the mail slot by hand. When the workers at the five women's clinics in the New Orleans, Louisiana area arrived at work on the 6th July, they found that the clinics had been vandalised using butyric acid. The aim of the terrorists was to disable the clinics and to protest against abortions. There were no injuries and no fatalities. (85)

1998: On the 16-23 May, in Orlando, Daytona Beach, St Petersburg, Clearwater and Miami Florida, USA, a group suspected of being the Army of God, poured an unknown amount of butyric acid through holes in the wall of abortion clinics. The terrorists aim was to sabotage the abortion clinics, and between the 16th and the 22nd May, ten women's clinics in Florida were attacked with the acid. The attacks resulted in three injuries and no fatalities. (86)

1998: On the 26th March, in Washington DC, USA, a 34 year old homeless man is alleged to have left a plastic container labelled 'Chemical Warfare Agent,' (the substance was found later confirmed to be tap water), near a telephone kiosk only one block form the White House, in front of the Treasury Department. The suspect's target was government officials and indiscriminate casualties, but his motive is unknown. There were no injuries and no fatalities. (87)

1998: A local law enforcement officer in Wisconsin City USA responded to a complaint of spousal abuse. The wife was the complainant and when the law enforcement officers arrived on the scene, the wife opened the door to the law enforcement officer, wearing a gas mask. When the police asked why she was wearing the mask, she responded, 'because my husband is in the basement making poison gas.' An investigation followed, and the FBI were brought in. Multiple chemical and biological agents were recovered from the scene as were assorted precursors and chemicals likely to be used as solvents, in particular DMSO. The suspect, the husband, had graduate training in science, and had been a professor of science at a local university. The evidence was most convincing for ricin; therefore, officials decided to prosecute under charges related to ricin alone. The subject pleaded guilty in early 1998 and was sentenced. (88)

1997: Israelis affiliated with an extreme non political organisation sprayed harmful chemicals on Palestinian owned vineyards. (89)

1997: Terrorist Adil Mahjub Husayn, a hijacker of the Sudan Airways flight from Luxor in Egypt April 1994 made a confession after being arrested. He claimed that he had managed to hijack the aircraft, saying the motive for the hijack had been political. He claimed that the trial he had been subjected to was a mere formality after which he was released. He was directed by Egyptian security agents to join the proscribed (Democratic) Unionist Party, after having refused to join the proscribed Ummah Party. He was forced to join the forces of the so-called (National Democratic) Alliance in Eritrea and received military training in sabotage and the use of explosives. He then travelled to Ethiopia and slipped over the border to Sudan. He confessed that he had planned to storm the National Assembly and blew up all its occupants. He claimed to have smuggled in automatic, and chemical, weapons, and phonetic explosives. (90)

1997: In 1997 new evidence given in court by cult member, Dr Ikuo

Hayashi, revealed that the Aum Shinrikyo had also planned to release nerve gas in the US, June 1994. The idea was planned out sufficiently, that the cult ordered one of its members to go to the US to pick up a shipment of sarin nerve gas that would be concealed in a Japanese ornament, and sent by sea mail. Dr Hayashi said, "The guru had ordered us to release sarin in several places in America." The plan was dropped for unknown reasons. (91)

1997: In Sydney, chlorine gas injured 19 people and forced the evacuation of more than 500 shoppers in a second attack in one week on a shopping centre. (The first attack carried out at the Randwick Village shopping centre left four people injured with minor respiratory problems as a result of the chlorine gas). The second attack was on the Eastgate Shopping Centre which filled with chlorine fumes. The authorities discovered the gas coming from a jar on the floor in the middle of the complex. The authorities did not disclose a motive for the attack. (92)

1997: Indian security forces seized four plastic jerrycans filled with chemicals used by militant ultras from a hide out in Baramulla district in North Kashmir. Earlier the Border Security Force claimed to have seized a probable 'chemicalized' grenade from a militant hide out in Srinagar in January. (93)

1996: According to the US Department of Defence, in February 1996 German police confiscated a coded diskette from a neo-Nazi group, that contained information on how to produce the chemical agent mustard gas. (94)

1996: Khmer Rouge guerrillas, in Thailand, poisoned streams being used by government troops with highly toxic insecticides. There were reports of eight soldiers being killed in one incident. (95)

1996: A sting operation by Turkish authorities in August, resulted in the seizure of 19 containers of mustard gas each strong enough to destroy life in an area of 5km, an one container of sarin from a smuggler in Istanbul, who claimed to have acquired them from an officer in Istanbul. (96)

1995-1996: July, and March 1996, Chechen separatists in Russia threatened to use CBW on Russian territory. In October 1995, the Head of the Russian Chemical Warfare Troops, Stanislav Petrov, denied that the Chechens could possess modern CW, but admitted they could have stocks of Chlorine and Prussic acid similar to that used in the first world war. (97)

1995: August, German police discovered instructions for 'poison gas production' during a search of neo-Nazi premises in Gorlitz. (98)

1995: July, There were unsubstantiated claims by Micmac Indians involved in a fishing dispute in New Brunswick, Canada, that they possessed stockpiles of chemicals including sarin.(99)

Date Unknown: There was an attempt by white-supremacist skinheads to disperse toxic chemicals through the internal ventilation systems of buildings in Arizona. (100)

1995: There was a threat by Chilean right wing groups, to release sarin in the Chilean underground system, if General Manuel Contreras, head of the secret police from 1973 to 1990, was imprisoned. The threat was empty as the general was sent to jail, and no action was taken. (101)

1995: On the 27th April, Paraguayan President Juan Carlos Wasmosy released a document that provided information, regarding a plan by unspecified terrorist groups to launch CBW attacks in several Latin American cities. Wasmosy told an international press conference that the Colombian military attache in Washington and several embassies, had received anonymous letters which provided details of the threatened attacks. The letters included a list of cities to be targeted with lethal chemical and biological agents to be used, such as cholera, typhoid, malaria and yellow fever, as well as the dates on which the attacks were to be carried out. The document which discussed the anonymous letters was sent to Wasmosy by the Paraguayan ambassador in Washington, and it states that the letters had been sent from California, but that they lacked addresses or other information that could help investigators. (102)

1995: On the 21st April 1995, according to newspaper reports, unnamed federal authorities, officially stated that they foiled an Aum Shinrikyo plot to use sarin, on Easter weekend at Disneyland, in Anaheim, California. The target of the two alleged members of the sect was indiscriminate casualties. Justice Department officials confirmed that Disney executives did receive a threat, but denied any real plot by cult members. (103)

1995: The Aum Shinrikyo led by Shoko Asahara, were the first group who fully developed both the capabilities and the intention to take tens of thousands of lives. In March, the cult planted sarin on the subway in Tokyo. Twelve people died and over five thousand were injured. This is a confirmed case. What motivated the cult to carry out this atrocity has been the subject of deep speculation. What is known is that the cult was led by a powerful charismatic leader. In this case the group had a sense of moral and religious superiority, and embraced an apocalyptic ideology of a better society. It involved individuals and an organisation who were not motivated by a traditional political goal, but rather by a broader religious, conspiratorial and supremacist ideology. The group possessed a sense of immense persecution and messianic frenzy, and held faith in salvation via Armageddon. The Aum wanted to kill large numbers of people, as part of their effort to seize control of Japan. (104)

1995: March, Aum Shinrikyo members released gas on board a train as a rehearsal for the Tokyo subway attack, and in May it conducted an attempted Hydrogen Cyanide attack on Shinjuku station in Tokyo which could have killed up to 20,000. There were also four more failed gas attacks on the Tokyo subway in July 1995. (105)

1995: In February, in a hotel room in Islamabad, Pakistan, which was formerly occupied by Ramseh Youssef, the man convicted of the World Trade Centre bombing, a draft letter was discovered which threatened the use of 'chemical and poison gas' against 'vital institutions and residential populations and drinking water sources' in the Philippines, unless the authorities released a co-conspirator of his, who had been arrested in January 1995. He also stated in interviews with the FBI that he planned to assassinate President Clinton, possibly by attacking the Presidential Limousine with Phosgene gas. (106)

1995: There was a reported use of tear gas against government troops, by the Tamil Tigers in Sri Lanka. (107)

1994: In September 1994, the Tamil Tigers threatened to poison exported tea bags with arsenic. The group's aim was to disrupt the Sri Lankan economy. After 200 random samples that were bound for the USA, Germany and Italy were checked, however, no evidence of arsenic poisoning was found. (108)

1994: Spring, the Aum Shinrikyo attempted to kill the leader of the Buddhist Soka Gakkai sect, by using an industrial spraying device to spray 2lbs of Sarin outside of a building in which he was giving a lecture. This was followed by an attempt to kill the writer Shoko Egawa, by using a small aerosol dispenser to pump Phosgene gas through the letterbox of her apartment; and by two attacks on individuals in Tokyo and Osaka, in Japan, using syringes filled with VX resulting in one death and one serious injury. This was followed by another unsuccessful attempt to murder a critic, by spraying him with VX. Also in this year, Aum Shinrikyo's first major attack used sarin on the town of Matsumoto. It resulted in the death of seven people, and injured more than 200 others. (109)

1994: On New Years Eve, cyanide laced champagne, killed at least nine Russian soldiers, and six civilians in Dushanbe, capital of Tajikistan. Another 53 were hospitalised. (110)

1993: On the 26th February a bomb was detonated at the World Trade Centre, New York. The bomber was a terrorist who has many different pseudonyms but is most commonly known by the name of Ramzi Youssef. Youssef represented a group called Shaykh Umar Abd-al Rahman. It is possible that this attack was state sponsored by Iraq. It has been alleged that the bomb contained an unknown amount of sodium cyanide packed with conventional explosives. The terrorists allegedly packed their bomb with cyanide, which was intended, but failed to spread poison throughout the building. The judge presiding over the case said, 'You had sodium cyanide around, and I am sure that it was in the bomb. Thank God the sodium cyanide burned instead of vaporizing. If the sodium cyanide had vaporized, it is clear what would have happened is the cyanide gas would have been sucked into the north tower and everybody in the north tower would have been killed. That to my mind is exactly what was intended.' According to Richard Falkenrath et al, however, the judge's claim does not appear to have been based on reliable technical analysis: even if the sodium cyanide could have been disseminated effectively by the bomb's explosion which it could not, the amount present was too small to be lethal except in a tightly confined space. (111)

1993: There was a report that proposals were made during early February, at a meeting of fundamentalist groups in Tehran, under the auspices of the Iranian Foreign Ministry, to poison the water supplies of major western cities. (112)

1992: September, there were reports that 19kg of Cyanide had disappeared from a chemical factory in Kyrgyzstan, where a month earlier 5kg of the substance 'intended to be used for terrorist purposes' had been seized by police. (113)

1992: In a mini market in Jerusalem, a Palestinian worker contaminated various food articles with parathion. (114)

1992: A Chilean judge investigated the use of sarin, which was produced by the secret service DINA, the sarin was bottled into a spray device, and blown into the faces of people from a political party. The victims died. (115)

1992: March, the PKK poisoned water tanks at a Turkish Air Force Compound in Istanbul, with lethal concentrations of Potassium Cyanide, which was discovered before any casualties were incurred. (116)

1992: The German authorities foiled a neo-Nazi plot to pump hydrogen cyanide into a synagogue. There was also a Neo-Nazi plot to 'use cyanide to murder children in a Jewish day-care centre' in Dallas, Texas, USA. (117)

1991: On 28 January, in Baton Rouge, Los Angeles, USA, Federal Agents uncovered a plot by a Louisiana biochemist, Stephen P Ashburn, to spray US President Bush with Sarin. His motive was unknown. The plot was prevented when Ashburn and an accomplice, possibly Jamal Mohammed Warrayat, a Palestinian living in New Jersey, contacted the Iraqi Embassy seeking support for their terrorist actions. (118)

1990: June, there were reports of the use of Chlorine Gas by the Tamil Tigers against Sri Lankan troops. (119)

1990: On the 22nd June in Milwaukee, Wisconsin USA, Milwaukee city council member Michael McGee, stated that he had received a phone call from a group of racial extremists calling themselves the "Militant African Underground Squared (Mau Mau)" with alleged connections to the Black Panther militia. The group threatened to contaminate sausage products made by "Usinger's Famous Sausages" by injecting them with rat poison, to protest against the cities attitude towards the black community. The groups target was perceived racism, and their motive was alleged retaliation for opposing the renaming of a city street after Martin Luther King Jr. The main suspect in this incident was McGee himself. (120)

1989: Atlanta August 21, radical extremists posted one parcel by the "Priority Mail" US postal service, to the southeastern regional Atlanta, GA USA, office of National Association for the Advancement of Coloured People (NAACP). The package held caustic gas tear in a canister that detonated when the package was opened, injuring fifteen people. Eight people were treated at hospitals, and seven were treated at the scene, after the canister sent a cloud of stinging fumes through a three storey building. Only two people were in the office of the (NAACP) when the package was opened, and they managed to escape with relatively minor injuries. It is speculated that the bomb was sent by a group of racial extremists calling themselves the Americans for a Competent Federal Judicial System, the target was the African American community and the motive was racially motivated revenge. (121)

1980s: There have been numerous threats by insurgent groups (or their sympathizers abroad) to contaminate the export products of a country in conflict, in order to damage its economy and /or simply draw attention to their cause. Numerous examples can be cited such as Uganda (coffee and tea), Sri Lanka (tea), South Africa (wine and fruit), the Philippines (pineapples), Israel (citrus fruits), France (various products, in protest against its nuclear testing programme of 1995, and Chile grapes. (122)

1989: In November, members of Aum Shinrikyo killed a lawyer along with his wife and child, in Yokohama, Japan, by injecting them with potassium chloride. (123)

1989: (This incident is reported to have occurred in 1988 and 1989 in different reports.) One of the most celebrated cases of food contamination occurred, when an unidentified person who claimed to be Chilean, called the US embassy in Santiago, (from Philadelphia on 2 March), claiming that he had poisoned fruit destined for the US and Japan. The caller claimed that killing policeman and placing bombs had not resolved the problems of Chile's lower classes, and that he wanted to involve other countries. It seems that the target of the incident was the Chilean government in general, and the motive was to disrupt the Chilean economy by attacking its main export, and to bring attention to the plight of the grape workers. An exhaustive search by the US Food and Drug Administration led to discovery of two grapes that contained minute quantities (0.003 mg of cyanide - not enough to kill an adult). The US, Canada, Japan, Denmark, Germany and Hong Kong suspended fruit imports from Chile, which the Chilean fruit industry claimed cost Chile an estimated US$333 million. In 1991 the Chilean government joined forces with fruit growers and exporters to sue the US for damages totalling $466 million. The caller's motivation is not known, and neither is it clear than any tampering actually took place. (124)

1989: There have been many threats by animal rights activists to contaminate food products, usually in protest against the use of animals in research. These have sometimes caused significant economic losses, as products were pulled from the shelves, but rarely has there been evidence of such contamination actually occurring. Numerous examples of this type of threat can be cited involving groups such as the Animal Aid Association (AAA) and the Animal Rights Militia (ARM) in Canada, and the ALF in the UK. One notable case involving the ALF was that the group were suspected by the UK police of poisoning eggs found in British supermarkets. The eggs were punctured and marked with skull and crossbones. An attached message signed ALF warned that the eggs had been poisoned. (125)

1989: A report stated that in recent years, Israeli security agents and police found canisters of a potent poison presumed to have been brought in by terrorists at a safe house in Tel Aviv: also allegations that Palestinian terrorists groups were known to have access to a nerve agents; or had been stockpiling nerve agents for years. (126)

1980's-1990s: There have been various unsubstantiated claims that Sikh and Kashmiri militants in India were using CWs. (127)

1988: On the 8 October 1988, in Dallas, Texas USA, racial extremist vandals, Sean Christian Tarrant, Jon Lance Jordan, Michael Lewis Lawrence Christopher Barry Greer, and Daniel Alvis Wood, calling themselves Confederate Hammerskins, carried out a racially motivated attack against the Jewish Temple Shalom, and the Mosque of Richardson in Dallas, Texas. On the 28 September, a federal grand jury indicted five skinheads for vandalism, and conspiracy to violate the civil rights of Jews, Hispanics, and African-Americans. During the trial which began in February 1990, former members of the Confederate Hammerskins, testified that the group planned to pump cyanide into Temple Shalom, through the air conditioning system. (128)

1988: April 1988, health authorities admitted that six grapefruits on sale in Italy, had been injected with a blue substance, but that it was not poisonous. It is believed that the act was carried out by Israeli citrus producers, who ship half the 53,000 tons of grapefruits to Italy every year, and was carried out to shake public confidence in the purity of their product. (129)

1987: An unknown perpetrator tried to poison the general population of the US with cyanide disseminated through teabags.

1987: 19 police recruits were killed and 140 hospitalized in the Philippines in what military officials believed could have been a mass poisoning by communist rebels, Muslim separatists, or one of several insurgent terrorist groups on the island of Mindanao. The poisoning took place in Zamboanga City, more than 700 miles south of Manilla. Officials said 225 recruits for the Philippine constabulary participated in a traditional fun-run for about four miles, and along the way were offered ice water in plastic bags, which contained poison, by an unidentified person. (130)

1987: A threat was made to fly over Cyprus with a microlight plane, that would saturate the area with aerosol borne poisons. The plot came to light mid May, when British police arrested five people and charged them with trying to extort (reports of the amount vary) of approximately US$21.9 million from the Cyprus government. If the money was not paid the plotters threatened poisonous gas, would be released under the heavily populated areas of the island. The group who were British subjects, with Greek names, also threatened to poison water supplies, with the aim of damaging tourism. (131)

1986: On the 11th June, East San Jose, California, USA, stores cleared their shelves of cigarettes after threatening letters were received by local shopowners claiming that they had been poisoned with sodium cyanide. The author made statements opposing the tobacco industry, and the US Government. The motive of the incident was to intimidate the American smokers and the US government. There were no injuries and no fatalities. (132)

1986: In February, in the UK, a Sainsbury's Supermarket in London, was warned that Bernard Matthew's brand chickens had been poisoned. Sainsbury's had established procedures for such a threat and internal investigation revealed that no poisoning had occurred. In another case, however, the threat had been carried out. In March a large quantity, perhaps as much as 24,000 pints, of Northern Dairies brand milk was contaminated by petrol. The contamination was discovered only after the tainted milk had been distributed to three communities. No one was injured and the milk was withdrawn. Although no group claimed responsibility, the British police believe that the contamination was deliberate. (133)

1986: In India the disclosure by a terrorist suspect that other terrorists might poison drinking watertanks led to a state-wide alert. (134)

1986: In January, the Australian, Canadian, US and UK embassies in Colombia, Sri Lanka, received letters purporting to be from the Tamil Tigers in Sri Lanka, claiming that they had put potassium cyanide in shipments of Sri Lankan black tea that were destined for export. There were no injuries and no fatalities. (135)

1985: An incident occurred in which the nerve agent Carbamate was added to the coffee at an Israeli military mess, but there were no indications of casualties. (136)

1985: In the Lebanon, Palestinian terrorists reportedly drugged the tea of Amal movement members and soldiers, and then slaughtered them. (137)

1985: British police charged four members of the ALF with injecting toxic mercury into turkeys sold at supermarkets. The ALF conducted the attack, as a protest against the slaughter of Turkeys for Christmas. (138)

1985: (This incident has been cited as occurring in 1984, 1985 and 1986 by different sources) On the 22nd April 1985, after a three day stand off at the white supremacist organisation known as the Covenant, the Sword and the Arm of Lord (CSA) compound, based in the Ozark Mountains, Arkansas USA. The CSA (who were led by Jim Ellison, were a Christian Identity, millenarian, neo-Nazi group) had their CW stockpile seized by the FBI. Reportedly the FBI found that the CSA, had acquired weapons, ammunition and gold. They also had 30 gallons of potassium cyanide to poison the water supplies of several US cities, believing that God would direct the poison to kill only the targeted individuals, who comprised non-believers, Jews and blacks living in major cities. Before the covenant could act, however, the FBI penetrated the group and arrested the leaders. The group embraced a survivalist ideology but the motive was to wage war and overthrow the federal government and to hasten the coming of the Messiah. The groups target was the government in general and indiscriminate casualties. There were no injuries and no fatalities. (139)

1984: The confectionery manufacturer Mars, reportedly lost US$4.5 million, after a hoax in the UK, in which the ALF purported to have spiked chocolate bars with rat poison, to protest against tooth decay experiments being carried out on monkeys. Eight bars were found to contain notes, allegedly from the ALF, claiming that "cruelty based products" had been adulterated. No poison was found however. (140)

1984: In the US, Tylenol contaminated with arsenic, was found in drug and grocery stores. (141)

1984: A Cuban CW instructor defected, and then testified that one third of the US could have been contaminated if a stockpile of toxins held by Cuba were to be strategically placed in the Mississippi River. (142)

1983: More than 300 schoolgirls in the Israel-occupied West bank were hospitalised suffering from nausea and dizziness, supposedly caused by a poison gas attack. A second wave of illness involving 394 others followed. Two doctors from the US Centres for Disease Control concluded that the incident may have been triggered initially either by psychological factors, or by subtoxic exposure to hydrogen sulphide from a latrine. (143)

1983: May, the Israeli government reported a plot by Israeli Arabs to poison the water supply in Galilee, with an 'unidentified powder'. Other reports indicating Palestinian links to CW include a report that Yasser Arafat's 'Force 17' had been trained in the use of CW and that East Germany had been providing such training to various terrorist groups including the ANO. In 1989 one report stated that 'in recent years Israeli security agents and police found canisters of a potent poison, presumed to have been brought in by terrorists, at a safe house in Tel Aviv.' There were even vaguer allegations that Palestinian terrorists were known to have access to nerve agents, and had been stockpiling nerve agents for several years. (144)

1983: A plot was hatched at a meeting of white supremacists from the US and Canada at the Headquarters of the White Supremacist group the Aryan Nations, in Idaho, USA< that included the 'polluting of municipal water supplies.' Four years later, this resulted in 14 individuals being indicted on Federal charges, of plotting to engage in indiscriminate mass killing through poisoning of municipal water supplies in two major American cities. (145)

1982: In the US, Members of Congress claimed that the Israelis had captured a PLO representative in Lebanon, in possession of CW.

1981: Thirty one neo-Nazi arms caches uncovered by West German police were said to have contained 'various poisons including arsenic, strychnine and cyanide.' A German neo-Nazi, Heinz Lembke, was arrested in connection with the find, but hanged himself in his cell in Luneburg gaol. (146)

1981: In Northern Ireland, acid bombs were thrown at security forces in Londonderry after days of street violence. The use of the acid, stolen from local schools was the work of youths in the Catholic Bogside district. Acid is customarily mixed with fuel to make Molotov cocktails. This is the first known use of acid itself. There are no firm indications that the IRA was behind the actions of the youths. (147)

1980: Contamination of the water supply of Pittsburgh USA, in December, may have resulted from a deliberate introduction of the insecticide chlordane, into the water system. Officials at the National Centres for Disease Control reported. Pittsburgh officials banned water use in two Pittsburgh neighbourhoods, and the adjacent town, for about two weeks as a result of the contamination. Over 10,000 residents were affected. Few health problems were associated with the contamination, and the insecticide was removed from the water system with prolonged and vigorous flushing. (148)

1980: Several embassies in Europe received threats of terrorist use of a mustard agent against them. (149)

1980: Gordon Liddy, the former White House staff member who masterminded the 1972 Watergate break-in, reported in a book, that there were plots to kill Howard Hunt, a fellow conspirator and Jack Anderson, newspaper columnists. Excerpts form the book which appeared in the US magazine *Time* tell of how Liddy had been prepared to be killed on orders from the White House, for the failure to break in to the Democratic National Committee headquarters, in Washington. Liddy also tells of detailed plans to discredit Daniel Ellsberg who discovered the Pentagon papers study of the Vietnam War, by using LSD. Charles Colson, President Nixon's counsel, was said to have developed a plan to drop the drug in Ellsberg's soup, at a fund raising dinner at which he was to speak. Liddy also tells how he planned to poison Howard Hunt by poisoning his food. He also tells how a CIA operative and himself, planned to kill Jack Anderson with LSD. When this was dismissed as impractical, they decided to spike the newspaper columnist with LSD, so he would become incoherent in a radio interview. (150)

1980: Throughout the 1980s and 1990s there have also been numerous threats by Animal Rights activists such as the Animal Aid Association and Animal Rights Militia in Canada and the Animal Liberation Front on the UK, to contaminate foodstuffs in shops with chemicals. Very few of these threats turned out to be real. Threats to contaminate export products of a state have also been common. There are numerous examples: Ugandan tea and coffee; Sri Lankan tea; South African wine and Fruit; Philippine pineapples; Israeli citrus fruits; various French products following French nuclear testing in the Pacific; and Chilean grapes. (151)

1979: The Arab Revolutionary Army Palestinian Commandos threatened to poison Israeli agricultural exports to the European Economic Community. There are differences in the literature about when this event took place, the number of people who were affected, and in which particular country. The general background to the incident was that exported Israeli oranges were poisoned after being injected with liquid mercury. Palestinian terrorists in cooperation with Iraq, calling themselves the Arab Revolutionary Army Palestinian Commandos stated that their goal was to damage Israeli fruit exports, and to sabotage the Israeli economy rather than killing European consumers. Poisoned oranges were found in Great Britain and West Germany, as well as in the Netherlands, where some children were killed. More than a dozen people were poisoned. The following year, the same terrorist group threatened to poison Israeli agricultural exports to Europe. (152)

1978: On the 18 November, in Guyana, nine hundred and eleven members of the People's Temple cult, led by the Californian cult leader, the Reverend Jim Jones, died in the 'Jonestown Massacre,' by drinking cyanide. The cult leader had decided that all his followers should die at their settlement in Guyana, so he provided quantities of soft drinks laced with the poison. How many of the cult members were murdered, and how many committed mass suicide is not known. In December 1978 in Washington DC, USA, a former member of the People's Temple alleged that the cult had planned to poison the water supply of Washington DC. (153)

1976: Late 1976, in San Francisco, California, USA, an unknown group released tear gas on one of San Francisco's major bridges. Authorities believed that the tear gas was stolen from the National Guard Armoury and that the incident was either a prank or a test performed by a terrorist organisation. Motorists experienced some eye irritation, but no injuries were reported. (154)

1976: In San Francisco, California, USA, the Police Department Counter-terrorist Unit apprehended a terrorist with nerve gas; another report states that the individual was on the verge of, but had not completed, his nerve gas production. The target and motive for this incident is unknown. (155)

1976: Sarin was brought into the US by Michael Townley, for use in an assassination plot against former Chilean Foreign Minister Orlando Letelier. The agent had originally been produced by Chile for possible use against Argentina or Peru, and was smuggled into the US in a Chilean Chanel Number 5 atomizer. Subsequent reports surfaced that anti-Castro Cubans in the US had learned of the Chilean produced sarin, and had asked DINA, the Chilean intelligence organisation, for some. (156)

DATE UNKNOWN: According to George Kupperman, the Red Brigades have tried seven times to poison reservoirs in Italy. The attacks were unsuccessful, since the toxins are quickly diluted. (157)

1976: The US postal authorities seized a suspicious package. When the package was X-rayed by The Treasury Department's Alcohol, Tobacco and Firearms Division, it was found to contain a small explosive. It was turned over to Army experts at the Aberdeen Proving Grounds in Maryland, USA, and on examination discovered to contain a small charge designed to explode one vial of nerve gas when the package was opened. An Arab terrorist group was suspected. There were no injuries and no fatalities. (158)

1975-1976: There are hazy reports from Vienna, usually dated 1975-1976, which claim that an Austrian chemist, Richard Konigstorfer, and a criminal gang led by his brother Johann Konigstorfer, attempting to sell the nerve agent tabun, sarin, or large quantities of diisopropyl fluorophosphate (DFP). According to Der Spiegel, it was DFP that was being secretly produced in Berlin-Neukolln, and a litre of DFP was found in the cellar of a Viennese house; spray cans and phials had already been filled with part of it 'ready for commercial use.' According to some reports the group were planning to sell the gases to terrorists, by one account to Palestinian terrorists in particular. *Der Spiegel* said the group had manufactured the gas for, 'interested parties in the criminal world' and the gang described the gas, 'as being particularly suitable for bank raids.' (159)

1975: A large quantity of mustard gas (according to the British newspaper the *Guardian* fifty three steel bottles each containing a litre of mustard gas) was stolen from a US army base in West Germany. The paper said they were of British origin and had been handed to the West German army to be destroyed. Other reports state that it was a West German material depot in France. This was followed by fears that the gas may be in the possession of terrorists. This was followed by threats from the RAF (Baader Meinhof gang) to use it against Stuttgart, and possibly other cities, unless an amnesty was granted to all political prisoners. (160)

1974: During August in Los Angeles, California, USA, a man known as the Alphabet Bomber (Muharem Kurbegovic), was arrested after bombing Los Angeles international Airport and killing three people. He also admitted that he had threatened to use nerve gas, and that he was going to go to Washington DC to kill the US President Gerald Ford, with the nerve gas. According to one account he was in the process of purchasing the last ingredient he needed, when he was arrested. (161)

1974: On the 24 June, in Washington DC, USA, United Press International received an audio cassette, claiming that nine postcards with nerve gas under their stamps were sent to all nine Supreme Court Justices. There were no injuries and no fatalities. The culprit was the Chief Military Officer of the Aliens of America, also known as the Alphabet Bomber, a politically left wing group. His target was specific government officials, and his motive was to take over the world.

According to a report in the *International Herald Tribune* written in 1989, Yugoslavian born Kurbegovic had also threatened to explode a nerve gas device on Washington, he said he would, 'bomb the Capitol building with projected nerve gas munition.' (162)

1973: On the 6th November 1973, two members of the left wing revolutionary terrorist group, the Symbionese Liberation Army (SLA), Joseph Michael Remio and Russell J Little (later acquitted), killed Oakland, California USA, school superintendent Dr Marcus A Foster with eight cyanide tipped bullets. The reason for the murder was that the SLA did not approve of Foster's performance as school superintendent. Deputy Superintendent Robert A Blackburn who was with Foster at the time of the attack, survived. (163)

1972: In Detroit, Michigan, USA, a radio station received a letter from Australia threatening to contaminate the Kenisco Reservoir in Winchester, New York, with a nerve agent. The FBI informed city officials of the threat, and a range of experts from a number of organisations, including the United Nations and the US Edgewood Army Arsenal, were brought in to offer assistance. The actors in this case are unknown, as is the motive. (164)

1972: There were indications of a terrorist plot to use chemical agents against a US army nuclear weapon storage site in Europe. (165)

1970: July, in the UK, philosophical/religious extremists tried to disseminate tear gas in the House of Commons.

1960s: According to former Klansman Tom Martinez, members of the racially extremist Klu Klux Klan (KKK) planned to poison water supplies of US cities, with an unknown agent in the 1960s. (166)

1969-1970: In Ashville, Alabama USA, beginning in November 1969, 30-55 cows from a farm owned by Black Muslims were poisoned with cyanide. It is believed that the culprits were the KKK, or another white supremacist group. The target of the plot was the African-American community and the motive was to drive the Black Muslims out of the town. In this case the perpetrators got their wish, when in March 1970, the manager of the farm announced that the farm was to be sold to the KKK, or any other group, as the group suffered too much harassment. (167)

1969: On the 28 January 1969, at San Francisco State College, California, USA, in response to an anonymous tip, police searched buildings at the college for a cyanide gas cylinder, three months into a militant strike by students at the college. On the same day, a stench bomb, and two tear gas bombs, exploded on the University of California campus in Berkeley, California, where a similar strike was in progress. The Third World Liberation Front, a group of minority organisations, had called the strike to call attention to ethnic studies programmes. The authorities did not find anything. (168)

1968: In Chicago, Illinois USA, two left wing revolutionary groups, the Weatherman Underground and The Yippy Movement (led by Abbie Hoffman) threatened to 'space out' delegates to the Democratic National Convention by dumping Lysergic Acid Diethylamide (LSD) into Lake Michigan. (169)

1967: In the USA, cyanide was found in the possession of the Revolutionary Action Movement. (170)

1960s: In the 1960s, a sub-group of the Minutemen, a right wing group, led by Robert De Pugh, planned to introduce hydrogen cyanide into the air conditioning of the United Nations in New York City, USA. De Pugh allegedly tested his homemade nerve gas on a dog in an attempt to determine the minimum lethal dosage of the gas. (171)

1946: These are two accounts of a Jewish resistance group who intended to use BW and poisons against Germans after the end of war in Europe. Michael Elkins, a correspondent for the BBC gives the first account, (see 1945 BW database). The second account is from Bar Zohar, who states that in July, the European Jewish reprisal organization Nakam, (the Hebrew word for vengeance) who fought as partisans during World War Two were set up. Nakam succeeded in poisoning the food of more than two thousand former SS storm troopers held in prison near Nuremberg by spreading arsenic on bread in the camp bakery. Several hundred are estimated to have died. Nakam were a group that burned with revenge following the genocide against their nation. The combination of unrestrained anger, and total powerlessness, may lead such groups to believe that their only option is to exact a horrendous price for their loss. Zohar also talks of a plot which is different to Nakam's, where a group of non Jews planned to poison the water supply of five German cities to avenge the Holocaust. In some articles the group are called The Avengers. (172)

CASES INVOLVING THE THREAT OF THE USE OF NUCLEAR WEAPONS AND NUCLEAR MATERIAL

1990s: Allegations surfaced that Osama bin Laden had paid US$2 million in an attempt to procure a tactical nuclear weapon from Kazakhstan, and had also made efforts to purchase enriched uranium. Recent reports which have come to light in the late 1990s, claim that bin Laden may have already acquired tactical nuclear weapons from this black market. The veracity of this reports cannot yet be ascertained. (173)

1998: A Radiological Dispersal Device was found in Chechnya in December. (174)

1997: The RAF (Baader-Meinhof gang) is reported to have attacked a US Army base in Germany in January 1988 in an effort to steal nuclear weapons. This incident cannot be confirmed with publicly available evidence. (175)

1996: September, a terrorist organisation called the Aryan Republican Army a neo-Nazi militia group, claimed to be in possession of radiological isotopes, and biological agents. There is very little information to support this incident. In 1995, Peter Langan, appeared in a recruitment video for the Aryan Republican Army, referencing a so-called Aryan super-bomb that contained yellow cake plutonium residue. The target is unknown but the motive was to establish an Aryan nation, and to exterminate all Jews. There is no evidence to suggest that the group acquired this material. (176)

1996: (In certain reports this incident is dated at occurring in 1994) On the 12 June, at Long Island, New York USA, a group of men were reported to have 5 canisters of radium, a radioactive material. The men, John Ford, Joseph Mazzuchelli, and Edward Zabbo, were part of a group called the "Long Island UFO Network" led by a president called John Ford. The men were arrested with the radium which was enough to fill several coffee cups, which they had planned to disperse, by putting it in the food, cars and toothpaste of prominent Long Island Republican Party politicians, John Powell, Anthony Gazzola, and Fred Towle. The ufologists motive was to reveal an alleged conspiracy by county officials who were covering up the crash landing of space aliens. Their ultimate objective was to seize control of the county government, but members were apprehended before they were able to poison anyone. There were no injuries and no fatalities. (177)

1996: May 9, a report produced by the FBI and the CIA, claims that agents for the Iraqi government, and the Islamic Jihad, offered rogue Russian nuclear scientists US$2 million US dollars for a nuclear warhead. (178)

1995: In November, on the first anniversary of the outbreak of fighting Russia and the break away Republic of Chechnya, Chechen separatists threatened to detonate radiological devices in and around Moscow. The Russians had been concerned about the possibility of a terrorist attack on their nuclear facilities from Chechen guerrillas. On 23 November, the Chechen guerrilla leader Shamyl Basayev, informed the Russian television network NTV that he had hidden four cases of radioactive caesium in Moscow. NTV, discovered a 32 kg case, wrapped in a plastic bag in Izmailovsky Park, emitting 310 times the amount of normal radioactivity. Basayev had frequently threatened to attack Moscow with nuclear weapons, but Russian officials dismissed the threat claiming that the material was caesium-137 used in x-ray equipment and that it was only capable of emitting 100 times the background amount of radioactivity. Western experts also dismissed the threat, doubting that the Chechens would have access to such material. The park is a popular recreational spot for Russians and tourists, and had Basayev disseminated the caesium he would have imposed heavy costs on the Russian government. (179)

1995: The Aum Shinrikyo sought to obtain a nuclear warhead, and they turned to the black market in Russia. The cult was reportedly co-operating with North Korea, with former Soviet Mafia Groups, and indirectly with Iran, in smuggling nuclear materials and conventional munitions out of Russia, through Ukraine. Moreover according to another source, members of the Aum had purchased nuclear materials during one of their numerous trips to Russia, although this allegation cannot be verified. It has also been reported that during raids on Aum Shinrikyo facilities, following the Tokyo subway attack, Japanese police confiscated technical information on uranium enrichment processes and a notebook that listed enquiries about the cost of obtaining a nuclear warhead. During the subsequent trial, former cult member, Dr Hayashi said, at the court hearing on 21 March 1997, that Shoko Asahara had asked him, 'What do you think would happen if an atomic bomb was dropped on Washington?' (180)

1994: Both units at the Ignalina nuclear power station in Lithuania, were closed down on government orders, because of the threat of a terrorist attack, that was made after the death sentence was given to an organised crime ringleader. No signs of sabotage were found but the plant remained shut for one week, while an anti terrorist group worked at the plant. Anti terrorist experts however, found no evidence of sabotage at the nuclear power station in Lithuania. (181)

1994: In the Slovak Republic: Greenpeace protestors have been accused of committing a terrorist act by staging a large scale demonstration at the Mochovce nuclear power plant, which was under construction. Three people were injured during the protest, and 30 demonstrators were arrested. The Slovak power utility SEP, stressed its commitment to complete the construction of the two units, despite the Greenpeace protest. (182)

1994: Power lines serving the German rail system were disrupted, poles cut down and barricades set up, against the first rail shipment of spent fuel from the Phillippsburg nuclear power station to the Gorleben interim storage facility. It was rumoured that a terrorist organisation may have been involved in the action. The Luneburg administrative court approved two applications opposing the storage of the Phillippsburg fuel, effectively halting transportation, but the federal office for radiation protection appealed against the ruling. (183)

1993-1994: Following the arrest of 989 members of the Byeloye Bratstva (White Brotherhood) cult in Ukraine, after they had converged on Kiev in anticipation of armageddon, bomb threats were made against the Chernobyl nuclear power station, but no attack was ever carried out. (184)

1993: February 7, one of the best documented examples of an attack on a nuclear power facility, occurred in Pennsylvania, in the United States. An intruder invaded the Three Mile Island nuclear power plant, remaining at liberty within the building for four hours. This attack was not successful, and was carried out by a single mentally ill man. Had the attack been carried out by professionally trained terrorists, the effects could have been devastating. (185)

1993: Recent reports state that members of the militant organisation al-Qaeda, which is closely linked to Osama bin Laden had attempted to purchase uranium. (186)

1991: In the USA, Dave Foreman, eco-terrorist, and founder of Earth First a radical environmental group, went on trial on federal charges of conspiracy to blow up power lines to nuclear plants in three Western state's. (187)

1990: Armenian rebels are reported to have attacked a Soviet base in Azerbaijan in January, with the aim of stealing nuclear weapons. This incident cannot be confirmed with publicly available evidence, and many experts question the accuracy of the reports. (188)

1985: In the USA, a letter was sent to New York City Water Authority on 1 April, threatening to contaminate New York's water system with plutonium trichloride, (traces of plutonium were later discovered in the drinking water). The letter was addressed to New York Mayor Edward Koch and stated that its author would carry out the plan unless charges were dropped against New York's 'subway vigilante,' gunman, Bernard H. Goetz. There were no injuries and no fatalities. (189)

1985: In their seminal work, Preventing Nuclear Terrorism; The Reports and Papers of the International Task Force on Preventing Nuclear Terrorism, Paul Levenethal and Yonah Alexander cite over 20 nuclear related terrorist activities. Most of these have been terrorist or radical activist attacks against commercial nuclear facilities, or the offices of nuclear power companies. Most of these incidents are not mentioned in this database, but they can be found in the papers of the International Task Force on Preventing Nuclear Terrorism. (190)

1984: The FBI investigated whether a group of Iranians were planning a nuclear attack on New York. They were allegedly going to smuggle radioactive material into the city and distribute it around Manhattan. The FBI was also concerned that the smuggling of fissile material out of the FSU would result not in a nuclear bomb, but in a nuclear enriched conventional explosive. (191)

1974: May 1974, the most famous extortion attempt was carried out by a person calling himself 'Captain Midnight,' who threatened to detonate an improvised nuclear device in Boston. This incident was a hoax, but was taken seriously enough to mobilise a major deployment of nuclear experts from the national weapons laboratories. It was this incident which led to the setting up of the US Nuclear Emergency Search Team (NEST) in 1975, to deal with a nuclear terrorism threats. In the years since, the FBI has continued to receive and evaluate nuclear terrorist threats, although most of these threats have been readily identified as hoaxes. NEST has been deployed approximately 30 times, between 1975 and 1993. (192)

Notes and references

1. Khalid Sharaf-al-Din, Al-Sharq-al-Awsat and Washington's Foreign Broadcast Information Service (FBIS), *Jane's Intelligence Review* (August 1999)

2. *Terrorism in the USA Involving Weapons of Mass Destruction*, A Publication of the Chemical and Biological Weapons Non Proliferation Project of the Centre for Non proliferation Studies at the Monterrey Institute of International Studies (October 1998)

3. Israel's Business Arena (13 April 1998) as found in <http://www.globes.com.il>, citing a report that appeared in the Jordanian newspaper, Al-Bilad

4. See Karisa King, 'Alleged Plot Involved Anthrax, HIV and Rabies,' *Brownsville Herald* (14 July, 1998). Diane Schiller, 'Anthrax and HIV are Suspected in Valley Plot,' *San Antonio Express* (13 July, 1998)

5. *Terrorism in the USA Involving Weapons of Mass Destruction Terrorism in the USA Involving Weapons of Mass Destruction*

6. Brussels La Une Radio Network in French 1200 GMT, 26 May, 1998. P.D.G and F.H, 'Fourteen Searched in Belgium Without Arrests,' *La Libre* (27 May 1998)

7. Lisa Singhania, 'Militia Member Admits his Role in Bomb Plot,' *Associated Press* (1998)

8. Susie Steckner, 'Arrest in Anthrax Threat: Collection Agency Got Tainted Letter,' *Arizona Republic* (12 March, 1998)

9. *Terrorism in the USA Involving Weapons of Mass Destruction*

10. W. Seth Carus, *Bioterrorism and Biocrimes: The Illicit Use of Biological Agents in the Twentieth Century*, Centre for Counterproliferation Research, National Defence University (August 1998) p 181

11. Al J. Venter, 'North Africa Faces New Islamic Threat,' *Jane's Pointer*

(March, 1998)

12. Shyam Bhatia, 'Bomber on the Run Has No Place to Hide,' *Observer*, (28 September, 1997) 'PKK member Says Splinter Group Planning Chemical Attacks,' <news://fas-news.harvard.edu/Qbritain terroristURn5G_7SS@clari.net, also C-afp'clari.net> (AFP). Shyam Bhatia and Leonard Doyle, 'Poison Bomber Offers Secrets for Sanctuary,' *Observer* (28 September 1997). Denis Staunton, 'Jailed Leader Denies Poison Bomb Plan,' *Observer* (28 September 1997)

13. Carus: *Bioterrorism and Biocrimes*, p 182

14. Michael Powell and Allan Lengel, 'Chemical Alert Traps Workers in Buildings, Discovery of Leaking Package at B'nai B'rith Turns into Nine Hour Ordeal in D.C,' *Washington Post* (25 April 1997)

15. *Terrorism in the USA Involving Weapons of Mass Destruction*; John Branton, 'Feds were Looking for Nerve Gas and Anthrax,' *Columbian* (8 May 1997)

16. *Terrorism in the USA Involving Weapons of Mass Destruction*; Richard A Falkenrath, Robert D Newman and Bradley A Thayer, *America's Achilles Heel, Nuclear, Biological and Chemical Terrorism and Covert Attack* (Cambridge MA: MIT Press, 1998) p 41

17. Danny Shoham, *Chemical and Biological Terrorism, An Intensifying Profile of a Non Conventional Threat*, The Arial Centre For Policy Research, (1998)

18. Carus: *Bioterrorism and Biocrimes*, p 57

19. *Terrorism in the USA Involving Weapons of Mass Destruction*; USIS Washington File, Excerpts: FBI Report on Domestic Terrorism, (17 April 1997)

20. Angela Lee, 'Shigella, Deliberate Contamination, USA Texas,' (12 November 1996) <finchley@aol.com>

21. Shoham: *Chemical and Biological Terrorism*

22. 'Botulism-Causing Powder Stolen from Lab,' *Miami Herald* (25 March 1996)

23. Ron Purver, 'Chemical and Biological Terrorism, New Threat to Public Safety,' *Conflict Studies* 295, Research Institute for the Study of Conflict and Terrorism, (December 1996) pp.12; Ron Purver, 'The Threat of Chemical and Biological Terrorism,' *The Monitor*, 3:2 (Spring 1997) pp 5-8. Wendy Barnaby, *The Plague Makers. the Secret World of Biological Warfare* (London: Vision Paperbacks, 1997) pp 54-55. Falkenrath, Newman and Thayer: *America's Achilles Heel, Nuclear, Biological and Chemical Terrorism and Covert Attack*, p 40

24. Carus: *Bioterrorism and Biocrimes*, pp 63-66

25. Purver: 'The Threat of Chemical and Biological Terrorism,' p 34

26. Carus: *Bioterrorism and Biocrimes*, pp 63-66

27. Carus: *Bioterrorism and Biocrimes*, pp 63-66

28. Statement for the Record of Robert M Burnham Chief, Domestic Terrorism Section before the United States House of Representatives, Committee on Commerce Hearing Witness, Subcommittee on Oversight and Investigations, Hearing Regarding: Threat of Bioterrorism America: Assessing the Adequacy of Federal Law Relating to Dangerous Biological Agents, 1 June 1999. Falkenrath, Newman and Thayer: *America's Achilles Heel*, p 39

29. Conrad deFiebre, 'Two Convicted of Possessing Deadly Poison,'

via Nexis, *Star Tribune*, (1 March 1995) p 1B

30. Steve Bates, 'Fairfax Man Accused of Anthrax Threat,' *Washington Post* (5 March 1992)

31. Purver: 'The Threat of Chemical and Biological Terrorism,' p 34

32. Carus: *Bioterrorism and Biocrimes*, p 159

33. Jilad Salim, 'Secrets of al-Manshiyah,' *Al-Watan al-'Arabi* (31 October 1997). Steven Emerson, 'Foreign Terrorists in America Five Years After the World Trade Centre Bombing,' (24 February 1998) a report submitted to the US Senate Judiciary Subcommittee on Terrorism, Technology and Government Information.

34. Venter: 'Biological Warfare: the Poor Man's Atomic Bomb,' p 42; William E Burrows and Robert Windrem, *Critical Mass: The Dangerous Race for Superweapons in a Fragmenting World* (New York: Simon and Schuster, 1994) p 49

35. Robert S Root-Bernstein, 'Infectious Terrorism,' *The Atlantic* (May 1991) p 48

36. Ray Clancy, 'Jail for Germ War Blackmailer who Planned £1m Gems Theft,' *The Times* (28 September 1990)

37. Carus: *Bioterrorism and Biocrimes*, pp 63-66

38. Carus: *Bioterrorism and Biocrimes*, pp 63-66

39. *Terrorism in the USA Involving Weapons of Mass Destruction*

40. Alan Tomlinson, 'Poison Suspicion after Haiti Colonel on Drug Charges Dies,' *The Times* (8 November 1988)

41. Milton Leitenberg, 'Biological Weapons Arms Control,' *Contemporary Security Policy*, 17:1 (April 1996) p 40

42. 'Two Canadians Held in US Over Bacteria,' *The Sun*, Vancouver, (24th November 1984)

43. W.Seth Carus, 'A Case Study in Biological Terrorism, The Rajneesh in Oregon, 1984,' Centre for Counterproliferation Research National Defence University (29 July 1997) pp5-6

44. Carus: 'A Case Study in Biological Terrorism, The Rajneesh in Oregon, 1984,' pp 5-6

45. Carus: 'A Case Study in Biological Terrorism, The Rajneesh in Oregon, 1984,' pp 5-6

46. Carus, 'A Case Study in Biological Terrorism, The Rajneesh in Oregon, 1984,' pp 5-6

47. *Defence and Foreign Affairs Daily*, Special Edition Terrorism (27 March 1984)

48. Carus: *Bioterrorism and Biocrimes*, p 127

49. Barnaby: *The Plague Makers. the Secret World of Biological Warfare*, pp 78-79; 'Ecologist Condemn Soil Dumpers,' *The Times* (16 October 1981)

50. Harvey Morris, 'Crisis in the Gulf: Saddam terrorists trained by Stasi,' *Independent* (30 January 1991)

51. Leitenberg: 'Biological Weapons Arms Control,' pp 1-79; Siegfried Buschschluter, 'Bacteria Lab Found in Terrorist Hideout,' *Guardian* (8th November 1980)

52. FBIS, June 23, 1987, p.L2, cited in Jeffrey D. Simon, 'Terrorists and the Potential Use of Biological Weapons: A Discussion of Possibilities,' R-3771-AFMIC, Santa Monica, California, RAND, 1989, p 19

53. See William H Thornton, *Modern Terrorism: The Potential for*

Increased Lethality (Langley Air Force Base, Va.: Centre for Low Intensity Conflict, 1987) p 7. Robert H Kupperman and R James Woolsey, Testimony before the Subcommittee on Technology and Law, Committee on the Judiciary, US Senate, (19 May 1988) in US Department of Justice, Federal Bureau of Investigations, Terrorism and Technology, (19 May, 1988) Foreign Broadcast Information Service (13 January 1988) p 47, cited in Jeffrey D. Simon, *Terrorists and the Potential Use of Biological Weapons: A Discussion of Possibilities*, R-3771-AFMIC (Santa Monica, California: RAND, 1989)

54. Leitenberg: 'Biological Weapons Arms Control,' pp.1-79. Rohan Gunaratna, *War and Peace in Sri Lanka* (Sri Lanka: Institute of Fundamental Studies, 1987) pp 51-52

55. *RAND-St Andrews Terrorism Chronology*

56. *RAND-St Andrews Terrorism Chronology*

57. *Terrorism in the USA Involving Weapons of Mass Destruction*

58. *Terrorism in the USA Involving Weapons of Mass Destruction*

59. *RAND St-Andrews Terrorism Chronology*

60. *RAND St-Andrews Terrorism Chronology*

61. W.Seth Carus, 'The Threat of Bioterrrorism', *Strategic Forum*, Number 127 (September 1997); Philip Hagar, 'Guns and Bullets Among Patty's Effects, FBI Says,' *Los Angeles Times* (30 September, 1975). *RAND St-Andrews Terrorism Chronology*

62. *RAND St-Andrews Terrorism Chronology*

63. Andrew Hubback, 'Apocalypse When? The Global Threat of Religious Cults,' *Conflict Studies* No. 300, Research Institute For the Study of Conflict and Terrorism, (June 1997) p 5, & Purver: 'The Threat of Chemical and Biological Terrorism,' p 12

64. *The Rand-St Andrews Terrorism Chronology.*

65. Ronald Koziol, 'Tighten Water Plant Guard After Poison Scare Arrests,' *Chicago Tribune* (19 January, 1972)

66. Joseph Douglass Jnr. and Neil Livingstone, *America the Vulnerable: The Threat of Chemical and Biological Warfare*, (Lexington, Ma: Lexington Books, 1987), 'Army Tells of Plot to Steal Bacteria from Fort Detrick,' *New York Times* (21 November, 1970) pp 31-32; *Terrorism in the USA Involving Weapons of Mass Destruction;* Jack Anderson, 'Weatherman Seeking BW Germs,' *Washington Post* (20 November, 1970)

67. Jeffrey D Simon, *Terrorist and the Potential Use of Biological Weapons, A Discussion of Possibilities* (RAND Corporation, December 1989);.*Risk Assessment Weekly* (19 May, 1989); Richard C Clark, *Technological Terrorism* (Old Greenwich, Connecticut: Devin Alder, 1980) p 137

68. Neil C Livingstone, *The War Against Terrorism*, (Massachusetts: Lexington Books, 1982) p112

69. *RAND-St Andrews Terrorism Chronology*

70. 'Suzuki Says He Fed Kin with Germs', *Japan Times* (21 April, 1966)

71. P.R.Joseph, J.D.Millar and D.A.Henderson, 'An Outbreak of Hepatitis Traced to Food Contamination,' *New England Journal of Medicine* (22 July, 1965)

72. Leitenberg: 'Biological Weapons Arms Control,' pp 1-79

73. Venter: 'Biological Warfare: the Poor Man's Atomic Bomb,' p 43

74. Venter: 'Biological Warfare: the Poor Man's Atomic Bomb,' p 43;

Barnaby: *The Plague Makers*, pp 114-116

75. Michael Elkins, *Forged in Fury, A true Story of Courage, Horror... and Revenge* (London: Piatkus, 1996) pp 168-169 and 194-210

76. Robert Harris and Jeremy Paxman, *A Higher Form of Killing, The Secret Story of Chemical and Biological Warfare* (New York: Hill and Wang, 1982) p 89

77. Benjamin Weissman, 'Dream Control,' *Los Angeles Times, Book Review*, p 15. The alleged use of botulism toxin by Pancho Villa's followers is mentioned in Uncle Fester's, *Silent Death*, revised and expanded 2nd Edition (Port Townsend, Washington: Loompanics Unlimited, 1997) p 93

78. Barnaby: *The Plague Makers*, p 7

79. Michael Wines, 'Kremlin Offers Video as Proof,' *Moscow Times*, reproduced in the New York Times Service, (14 January, 2000). Excerpt found on the internet at site HYPERLINK http://www.moscowtimes.ru/14-Jan-20000/stories/story8.html Alice Lagnado, 'Generals replaced after Grozny Setback,' *The Times* (8 January, 2000); Marcus Warren, 'Russians Attack Grozny From All Sides,' *Daily Telegraph* (27 December, 1999); Alice Lagnado, 'Moscow Steps up Bombing of Grozny,' *The Times* (3 January, 2000)

80. 'Water Terror Plot Foiled,' *Observer* (11 July, 1999); & 'Ex Soldier Held Over Poison Threat,' *Daily Telegraph* (12 July, 1999)

81. Venter: 'Biological Warfare: the Poor Man's Atomic Bomb,' p 43

82. Stefan Leader, 'Osama bin Laden and the Terrorist Search For WMD,' *Jane's Intelligence Review* (June 1999) pp 34-37

83. 'US Cruise Attacks Ignored Warnings,' *Guardian* (6 October, 1998)

84. *Terrorism in the USA Involving Weapons of Mass Destruction*

85. *Terrorism in the USA Involving Weapons of Mass Destruction*

86. *Terrorism in the USA Involving Weapons of Mass Destruction*

87. *Terrorism in the USA Involving Weapons of Mass Destruction*

88. Letter from Ben Garrett <garrettb@battelle-cc.org> to Julian Perry Robinson, Subject: Possible Misunderstanding in CBWCB (1 August 1998)

89. Shoham: *Chemical and Biological Terrorism*

90. Republic of Sudan radio, Omdurman in Arabic 1300 gmt 13 June 1997. 'Sudan: hijacker Confesses to Plan to Blow up Parliament-Radio' (207), Text of report by Sudanese radio (13th June)

91. 'Japanese Cult said to have Planned Nerve Gas Attacks in US,' *New York Times International* (23 March, 1997)

92. 'Chlorine Gas Fells 19 at 2d Mall in Sydney,' *International Herald Tribune* (1-2 March, 1997)

93. 'Chemicals Seized from Militants Hide Out,' *Hindu* (5 February, 1997)

94. Purver: 'Chemical and Biological Terrorism, New Threat to Public Safety,' p 16

95. Counterproliferation Programme Review Committee, *Report on Activities and Programmes for Countering Proliferation* (Washington D.C: US Department of Defence, May 1996) p 13

96. Purver: 'Chemical and Biological Terrorism, New Threat to Public Safety,' p 14

97. Purver: 'Chemical and Biological Terrorism, New Threat to Public

Safety,' p 13

98. Purver: 'Chemical and Biological Terrorism, New Threat to Public Safety,' p 11

99. Purver: 'Chemical and Biological Terrorism, New Threat to Public Safety,' p 12

100. Shoham: *Chemical and Biological Terrorism*, p 21

101. Purver: 'Chemical and Biological Terrorism, New Threat to Public Safety,' p 11

102. 'Paraguay: Chemical Warfare planned Terrorists, President Warns,' (28 April, 1995), Copyright 1995, Inter Press Service, via Nexis:/sr50503.

103. *Terrorism in the USA Involving Weapons of Mass Destruction*

104. Carus: *Bioterrorism and Biocrimes*, pp 63-66

105. Stern: *The Ultimate Terrorists*, p 64. Evelyn le Chene, 'Chemical and Biological Weapons Proliferation, and the Problem of Special Interest Groups,' Intersec, 7:6 (June 1997). Carus: *Bioterrorism and Biocrimes*, pp 63-66

106. Purver: 'Chemical and Biological Terrorism, New Threat to Public Safety,' p 16

107. Purver: 'Chemical and Biological Terrorism, New Threat to Public Safety,' p 14

108. *Terrorism in the USA Involving Weapons of Mass Destruction*

109. Kyle Olsen, Testifying at Hearings conducted by the US Senate Permanent Subcommittee on Investigations October 1995. 'Hearings on Global Proliferation of Weapons of Mass Destruction: A Case Study of Aum Shinrikyo,' *Senate Hearings* 104-422, 'Global Proliferation of Weapons of Mass Destruction, Part 1,' *Hearings before the Permanent Subcommittee on Investigations of the Committee of Governmental Affairs*, US Senate, 104th Congress, 2nd Session (Washington DC, US GPO, 31 October, 1995) pp 87-88. D.W.Brackett, *Holy Terror: Armageddon In Tokyo* (New York: Weatherhill, 1996) pp 27-43

110. Purver: 'Chemical and Biological Terrorism, New Threat to Public Safety,' p 14

111. *Terrorism in the USA Involving Weapons of Mass Destruction*; Quote found in the prepared statement of John F Sopko and Alan Edelman, Permanent Subcommittee on Investigations, in *Senate Hearings* 104-422, 'Global Proliferation of Weapons of Mass Destruction, Part III,' *Hearings before the Permanent Subcommittee on Investigations of the Committee on Governmental Affairs*, US Senate, 104th Cong; 2nd Sess, (Washington, DC: US Government Printing Office, US GPO, 1996) p 23; Falkenrath, Newman and Thayer: *America's Achilles Heel*, pp 32-33

112. Purver: 'Chemical and Biological Terrorism, New Threat to Public Safety,' p12

113. Purver: 'Chemical and Biological Terrorism, New Threat to Public Safety,' p 11

114. Shoham: *Chemical and Biological Terrorism*

115. Letter from Dieter Maier to Julian Perry Robinson, which outlines a press cutting from Chile about a sarin attack, (8 January, 1992)

116. Purver: 'Chemical and Biological Terrorism, New Threat to Public Safety,' p 14

117. Purver: 'Chemical and Biological Terrorism, New Threat to Public

Safety,' p 14

118. *Terrorism in the USA Involving Weapons of Mass Destruction*; Bill Gertz, 'FBI Foiled Plot to Kill Bush with Nerve Gas,' *Washington Times* (16 July, 1991)

119. Purver: 'Chemical and Biological Terrorism, New Threat to Public Safety,' pp 14

120. *Terrorism in the USA Involving Weapons of Mass Destruction*

121. 'Gas Canister Mailed to the N.A.A.C.P. in Atlanta Goes Off,' *New York Times* (22 August, 1989)

122. Jessica Stern, 'Will Terrorists Turn to Poison,' *Orbis*, 37:3 (Summer 1993) p 396

123. Brackett: *Holy Terror*, pp 20-24

124. Stern: 'Will Terrorists Turn to Poison,' p 396

125. Stern: 'Will Terrorists Turn To Poison,' p 4

126. Robert H.Kupperman & Jeff Kamen, *Final Warning: Averting Disaster in the New Age of Terrorism* (New York: Doubleday, 1989) p 101, & William H.Thornton, 'Modern Terrorism: The Potential for Increased Lethality,' Langley Air Force Base, VA: Army-Air Force Center for Low Intensity Conflict, *CLIC Paper* (November 1987) p 7

127. Purver: 'Chemical and Biological Terrorism, New Threat to Public Safety,' p 14

128. *Terrorism in the USA Involving Weapons of Mass Destruction*

129. 'Grapefruit Scare Over,' *The Times* (29 April 1988)

130. Keith B Richburg, 'Poison Used in 19 Deaths in Philippines,' *Washington Post* (7 September, 1987)

131. 'Four in Court Over Gas Plot,' *Guardian* (18 May, 1987)

132. *Terrorism in the USA Involving Weapons of Mass Destruction*

133. Joseph Pilat, 'World Watch: Striking Back at Urban Terrorism,' *NBC Defence and Technology International*, 1:3, (June 1986) pp 18-19

134. Jeffrey D. Simon, 'Terrorists And The Potential Use of Biological Weapons: A Discussion of Possibilities,' *TVI report*, 10:3 (1992) p 12

135. Stern: 'Will Terrorists Turn to Poison,' p 4

136. Purver: 'Chemical and Biological Terrorism, New Threat to Public Safety,' p 14

137. Stern: 'Will Terrorists Turn to Poison,' p 15

138. Stern: 'Will Terrorists Turn to Poison,' p 4

139. *Terrorism in the USA Involving Weapons of Mass Destruction*

140. Stern: 'Will Terrorists Turn to Poison,' p 4

141. Shoham: *Chemical and Biological Terrorism*, p 23

142. Shoham: *Chemical and Biological Terrorism*, p 23

143. *Terrorism in the USA Involving Weapons of Mass Destruction*

144. Purver: 'Chemical and Biological Terrorism, New Threat to Public Safety,' p 13

145. *Terrorism in the USA Involving Weapons of Mass Destruction*

146. Siegfried Buschschluter, 'Neo-Nazi Weapons Found,' *Guardian* (2 November 1981) and Robert Tilley, '230 bombs in Neo-Nazi Arms Caches,' *Daily Telegraph* (3 November 1981)

147. David Beresford, 'Acid bombs Used on Security Forces in Derry,' *Guardian* (24 April, 1981)

148. New York Times (28 November, 1981) and the Washington Post, (28 November, 1981)

149. Shoham: *Chemical and Biological Terrorism*, p 22
150. 'Liddy, in Book, Tells of Two Murder Plots,' *International Herald Tribune* (15 April, 1980)
151. Jessica Eve Stern, 'Will Terrorists Turn to Poison,' Pugwash Chemical and Biological Weapons Workshop (8-9 May 1993)
152. Shoham: *Chemical and Biological Terrorism*
153. *Terrorism in the USA Involving Weapons of Mass Destruction*
154. *Terrorism in the USA Involving Weapons of Mass Destruction*
155. *Terrorism in the USA Involving Weapons of Mass Destruction*
155. Purver: 'Chemical and Biological Terrorism, New Threat to Public Safety,' p 14
156. *Terrorism in the USA Involving Weapons of Mass Destruction*
157. Fred Kaplan 'Arsenals of Todays Terrorists,' *Boston Globe* (27 December 1983) pp 1-3
158. William Beecher, 'Terrorist Gangs, Reaching for Nerve Gas, Gruesome New Weapons,' *Boston Sunday Globe* (7 November, 1976). Ian Ball, 'Terror Gang Gets Nerve Gas,' *Daily Telegraph* (8 November, 1976)
159. 'Planned Bank Raids with Quick Killing Nerve Gas: Sellers Arrested in Vienna, Manufacture Taken into Custody in Berlin; Terrorist Groups also Interested,' *Der Spiegel* (8 March 1976). Kaplan: 'Arsenals of Today's Terrorists,' pp 1-3
160. Norman Crossland, 'Mustard Gas Theft Follows Terrorist Threat to Stuttgart,' *Guardian* (13 May 1975). Richard Falkenrath et al however argue that it is not clear that the terrorists even possessed the gas canisters, many of which were recovered later, Falkenrath, Newman and Thayer: *America's Achilles Heel*, p 37
William Beecher, 'Terrorist Gangs, Reaching for Nerve Gas, Gruesome New Weapons,' *Boston Sunday Globe* (7 November, 1976). Ian Ball, 'Terror Gang Gets Nerve Gas,' *Daily Telegraph* (8 November, 1976)
161. *Terrorism in the USA Involving Weapons of Mass Destruction*
162. *Terrorism in the USA Involving Weapons of Mass Destruction*
163. *Terrorism in the USA Involving Weapons of Mass Destruction*
164. *Terrorism in the USA Involving Weapons of Mass Destruction*
165. Purver: 'Chemical and Biological Terrorism,' p 11
166. *Terrorism in the USA, Involving Weapons of Mass Destruction*, p 98
167. *Terrorism in the USA Involving Weapons of Mass Destruction*
168. *Terrorism in the USA Involving Weapons of Mass Destruction*
169. *Terrorism in the USA Involving Weapons of Mass Destruction*
170. Shoham: *Chemical and Biological Terrorism*, p 20
171. *Terrorism in the USA Involving Weapons of Mass Destruction*
172. Michael Bar-Zohar, *The Avengers*, Translation. Len Ortzen (London: Arthur Baker, 1968) pp 43-58
173. Stefan Leader, 'Osama bin Laden and the Terrorist Search for WMD,' *Jane's Intelligence Review* (June 1999); & Bruce Hoffman with David Claridge, 'Illicit Trafficking in Nuclear Weapons,' Research Institute for the Study of Conflict and Terrorism, *Conflict Studies* 314/315 (January/February 1999) pp 30
174. Leader: 'Osama bin Laden and the Terrorist Search for WMD,' p 36
175. Andrew Cockburn and Leslie Cockburn, *One Point Safe* (New York: Doubleday, 1997) pp 1-12
176. Carus: *Bioterrorism and Biocrimes*, p 161; & *Terrorism in the USA*

Involving Weapons of Mass Destruction

177. Terrorism in the USA Involving Weapons of Mass Destruction

178. William Webster, *The Nuclear Black Market, International Task Force Study* (The Centre for Strategic and International Studies, USA, 1996)

179. Programme for Promoting Nuclear Nonproliferation, *Newsbrief* (Fourth Quarter 1995) p 15; Gavin Cameron, 'Nuclear Terrorism a Real Threat,' *Jane's Intelligence Review* (September 1996) pp 422-455

180. Stern: *The Ultimate Terrorists*, p 65; Hoffman with Claridge: 'Illicit Trafficking in Nuclear Weapons,' pp 30; Kaplan and Marshall: *The Cult at the End of the World: The Incredible Story of the Aum*, pp 190-198; 'Japanese Cult said to have Planned Nerve Gas Attacks in US,' *New York Times International* (March 23 1997)

181. *NucNet News*, 555/94 and 556/94 (17 November 1994); see also Uranium Institute, *News Briefing* (1994)

182. *NucNet News* 349/94 (8 July, 1994); & *NucNet News*, 350/94 (8 July, 1994). Uranium Institute, *News Briefing* (1994)

183. *NucNet News* 563/94 (24 November); *Nucleonics Week* (24 November) p 1; Uranium Institute, *News Briefing* (1994)

184. Hubback: 'Apocalypse When? The Global Threat of Religious Cults,' p 19

185. Paul Leventhal and Yonah Alexander, *Preventing Nuclear Terrorism; The Reports and Papers of the International Task Force on Preventing Nuclear Terrorism* (Lexington Mass: Lexington Books, 1987) pp 82-84, pp 123-133

186. Bruce Hoffman with David Claridge, 'Illicit Trafficking in Nuclear Weapons', Research Institute for the Study of Conflict and Terrorism, *Conflict Studies* 314/315 (January/February, 1999) pp 30

187. Jonathon Tilove, 'Tale of a Plot to Rid the Earth of Humankind,' *San Francisco Examiner* (14 April, 1991)

188. Andrew Cockburn and Leslie Cockburn, *One Point Safe* (New York: Doubleday, 1997) pp 1-12

189. Terrorism in the USA Involving Weapons of Mass Destruction

190. Leventhal and Alexander: *Preventing Nuclear Terrorism*, pp 82-84, pp 123-133

191. Jonathan Schelfer, 'Nuclear Terrorism,' *Technology Review*, Special edition Arms Control (April 1991); Neil C.Livingstone, 'USSR: The Next Terrorist Battleground,' *Seapower* (November 1991); 'Nightmare in a Suitcase,' *Daily Telegraph* (19 August 1994); 'Russian Nuclear Secrets for Sale' Sunday Express (9 June 1996); Tim McGirk, 'Iranian's Buying Ex-Soviet Uranium,' *Independent* (28 March 1996)

192. Falkenrath, Newman & Thayer: *America's Achilles Heel*, p 42

Appendix 2:BIBLIOGRAPHY

BOOKS

There are a number of books which provide an excellent overview of the nature and characteristics of modern terrorism. These include: Bruce Hoffman, *Inside Terrorism* (London: Indigo, 1998); Adrian Guelke, *The Age of Terrorism* (London: IB Tauris, 1998); and C.J.M.Drake, *Terrorists Target Selection* An increasing number of books which focus specifically on WMD terrorism have been published. Frank Barnaby, *Instruments of Terror: Mass Destruction Has Never Been So Easy* (London: Vision, 1996); and Wendy Barnaby, *The Plague Makers: The Secret World of Biological Warfare* (London: Vision, 1997), provide general and easy to read overviews of the subject. More detailed analysis of the subject, from a US perspective, can be found in Richard Falkenrath, Robert. D.Newman, & Bradley Thayer, *America's Achilles Heel: Nuclear Biological and Chemical Terrorism* (Cambridge MA: MIT Press, 1998); Brad Roberts ed, *Terrorism With Chemical and Biological Weapons: Calibrating Risks and Responses* (Alexandria Va: Chemical and Biological Control Institute, 1997); and Jessica Stern, *The Ultimate Terrorists* (Cambridge MA: Harvard University Press, 1999). The seminal work on nuclear terrorism is Paul Leventhal & Yonah Alexander, *Preventing Nuclear Terrorism: The Report and Papers of the International Task Force on Prevention of Nuclear Terrorism*, (Lexington: Lexington Books, 1987); whilst Gavin Cameron, *Nuclear Terrorism: A Threat Assessment for the Twentieth Century* (Basingstoke: MacMillan, 1999), includes a useful chapter on psychology.

Detailed analysis of specific dimensions of the threat from WMD terrorism can be found from a number of sources. Graham T.Allison, Owen R.Cote Jr, Richard A.Falkenrath, Stephen E.Miller, *Avoiding Nuclear Anarchy*, (Cambridge Ma: MIT Press, 1996), is the best work on the smuggling of nuclear material from the former Soviet Union. James Adams, *The New Spies: Exploring the Frontiers of Espionage*, (London: Hutchinson, 1994), contains useful information on intelligence and the prevention of terrorism. Phil Williams and Ernesto Savona eds, *The UN and Transnational Organized Crime*, (London: Frank Cass, 1996), provides insights on how a regime of counter-measures to combat WMD terrorism might be constructed. Amir Taheri, *Holy Terror: The Inside Story of Islamic Terrorism*, (London: Hutchinson, 1987), provides an insight into the various dimensions of Islamic Fundamentalism, whilst Hala Jaber, *Hezbollah: Born With a Vengeance*, (London: Fourth Estate, 1997), provides a counter perspective from the point of view of just one Fundamentalist group - Hezbollah. Tim Pat Coogan, *The IRA*, (Harper Collins: London, 1995); tells the history of the IRA; and Mark Tully & Satish Jacob, *Amritsar: Mrs Ghandi's Last Battle*, (London: Jonathan Cape, 1985), is an account of the Sikh insurgency in the Punjab.

Good accounts of the most serious terrorist incidents involving CW can be found in D.W.Brackett, *Holy Terror: Armageddon In Tokyo*, (New York: Weatherhill, 1996); and David E.Kaplan & Andrew Marshall, *The Cult at the End of the World*, (New York: Crown Publishers, 1996), these provide invaluable information on NBC terrorism based upon a case study of the Aum Shinrikyo attacks in Japan.

ARTICLES AND REPORTS

There are an enormous number of articles and report on all aspects of NBC terrorism. Worst case analysis of the threat from US sources includes Richard K.Betts, 'The New Threat of Mass Destruction,' *Foreign Affairs* (January/February 1998); David M.Rosenbaum, 'Nuclear Terror,' *International Security*, 1:3 (Winter 1977). John Sopko, 'The Changing Proliferation Threat,' *Foreign Policy*, No.103 (Winter 1996-97). John Steinbruner, 'Biological Weapons: A Plague Upon All Houses,' *Foreign Policy*, No.109 (Winter 1997-98). IPPNW Global Health Watch Report No.1, *Crude Nuclear Weapons: Proliferation and the Terrorist Threat*, International Physicians for the Prevention of Nuclear War (1996). *The Monitor*, Center For International Trade and Security at the University of Georgia, Special Issue, 3:2 (Spring 1997); & Richard Preston, "The Secret War", ARENA, (1998). UK sources include Frank Barnaby, 'Nuclear Terrorism,' *Safe Energy 95* (June/July 1993); James Langton, 'A Plague On All Our Houses,' The Sunday Review, in *Sunday Telegraph* (8 March, 1998); and Robert Taylor, 'All Fall Down,' Special Report, *New Scientist* (11 May 1996).

More down-beat assessments of the threat can be found in Richard A. Falkenrath, 'Confronting Nuclear, Biological and Chemical Terrorism,' *Survival*, 40:3 (Autumn 1998); Bruce Hoffman, 'Terrorism and WMD: Some Preliminary Hypotheses,' *Nonproliferation Review* (Spring/Summer 1997); Gavin Cameron, 'Nuclear Terrorism: A Real Threat?,' *Jane's Intelligence Review* (September 1996); Ron Purver, '

Chemical and Biological Terrorism: New Threat to Public Safety?,' *Conflict Studies No.295*, Research Institute For The Study of Conflict and Terrorism (Dec 1996/Jan 1997)

Details of existing counter-measures to combat the threat, and proposals for how to enhance them, can be found in Thomas J. Bady, 'US Anti Terrorism Policy: The Clinton Administration,' *Contemporary Security Policy*, 19:2 (August 1998).

Ashton Carter, John Deutch, & Phillip Zelikow, 'Catastrophic Terrorism: Tackling The New Danger,' *Foreign Affairs* (November/December 1998). Jason Ellis, 'Nunn-Lugar's Mid-Life Crisis,' *Survival*, 39:1 (Spring 1997); Chuck McCutcheon, 'Homeland Defence: Mobilizing Against Terrorism,' *Congressional Quarterly Weekly* (6 March, 1999). John Deutch, 'Terrorism,' *Foreign Policy* (Fall 1997). Graham S.Pearson & Nicholas A.Sims, 'National Implementation Measures: An Update,' *Strengthening the Biological Weapons Convention Briefing Paper No.14* (October 1998), Department of Peace Studies, University of Bradford.

More detailed information on specific dimensions of the threats was taken from a number of other sources. Ian Haworth, 'Caring For Cult Victims,'" *Carer and Counsellor*, 7:3 (Summer 1997); provided information on religious cults' use of mind control; and Andrew Hubback, 'Apocalypse When? The Global Threat of Religious Cults,' *Conflict Studies No. 300*, Research Institute For the Study of Conflict and Terrorism (June 1997) provided an general overview of the nature and threat from cults. Additional details of nuclear smuggling can be found in Bruce Hoffman & David Claridge, 'Illicit Trafficking in Nuclear Materials,' *Conflict Studies No.314/315*, Research Institute For the Study of Conflict and Terrorism (Jan/Feb 1999); & *ISIS Report*, 3:1 (May 1996). Additional information on Islamic Fundamentalism was obtained from: Ely Karmon, 'Bin Ladin is Out To Get America,' The International Policy Institute For Counter Terrorism, Internet Site: <http://www.ict.org.il/articles/isl-terr.htm> (29 October, 1998); Reuven Paz, 'Is There an Islamic Terrorism?,' International Policy Institute for Counter Terrorism, Internet Site: <http://www.ict.org.il/articles/isl-terr.htm> (7 September, 1998); & Ibrahim A Karawan, 'The Islamist Impasse.' *Adelphi Paper 341*, The International Institute for Strategic Studies, (London: Oxford University Press, 1997). Whilst Paul Wilkinson, 'Terrorist Targets: New Risks to World Order,' *Conflict Studies No.236* (December 1990), provided additional information on the nature of terrorism.

PRESS REPORTS
NBC Terrorism is a constantly evolving issue, and during the course of writing this book a number of incidents and developments occurred which were of potential relevance to this analysis of NBC terrorism. These were reported in the following news reports: 'US Studying Truck-Bomb Defenses at Reactors,' *New York Times*, Special Edition - Terrorism (23 April 1993) 'Militias and Messiahs,' *The Economist* (April 5-11, 1997) 'NBC Weapons Cannot be Reliably Destroyed,' *Jane's Defence Weekly* (14 May 1997). 'USA to Develop System to Track Loose Nukes,' *Jane's Defence Weekly*, (8 October 1997). 'Agencies to Centralise for CBW Rapid Response,' *Jane's Defence Weekly*, (12

November 1997) 'Ministers Sound Retreat on Anthrax Warning,' *Guardian* (25 March 1998). 'War Games Show up Germ Defenses,' *Guardian* (28 April, 1998) 'US to Guard Public From Germ Attack,' *The Times* (22 May 1998) Paul Rogers, 'The Next Terror Weapon Will Be Biological, And It Could be Used Soon,' *Guardian* (18 August 1998) 'Vaccines For All in Anti-Germ War Plan,' *Sunday Telegraph* (11 October 1998) 'Jerusalem Tightens Security Against US Doomsday Cult,' *Guardian* (November 24, 1998) 'Animal Activists Face Ban as Terrorists,' *The Times* (December 18, 1998) 'US Evacuates Diplomats in Anthrax Alert,' *The Times* (December 19, 1998) 'Muslims Told to Avenge Iraq Strikes,' *Daily Telegraph* (December 26, 1998) 'Hoax Callers Spread Anthrax Scare,' *Guardian* (December 29, 1998) Paul Johnson, 'A Time of Miracles, Madness and Danger,' Comment, *Sunday Telegraph* (January 3, 1999) 'Israelis Fear Worst as the `End of Time' Draws Near,' *Sunday Telegraph* (January 3, 1999) 'Cultists To Be Deported,' *Guardian* (January 5, 1999) 'The Domes-Day Cult,' *Daily Mail* (January 16 1999) 'Millennium Death Wish Cults Put the Dome Under Siege," *Sunday Telegraph* (January 17, 1999) 'US Plans Force To Beat Germ Terrorists,' *The Times* (February 2, 1999) 'The Global Terrorist,' *The Sunday Times* (February 7, 1999) 'US Foils Spate of Bin Laden Bomb Attacks,' *The Times* (February 25, 1999) 'We're At War And If That Means More Bombs, So Be It...," *Guardian G2* (April 27, 1999) 'Police Check International Neo-Nazi Links,' *Guardian* (April 27, 1999) 'Anti-Terror Police Seek White Wolf Racist Over Bombs,' *Guardian* (April 28, 1999) 'Hunt Is Hampered By Secret Cells of Neo-Nazis,' *The Times*, (May 1, 1999) 'Manifesto of Hate: The War Is On,' *Sunday Telegraph* (May 2, 1999) 'Water Terror Plot Foiled,' *Observer* (July 11, 1999) 'Ex-Soldier Held Over Poison threat,' *Daily Telegraph* (July 12, 1999) Programme for Promoting Nuclear Non Proliferation, *Newsbrief:* (1994-1999)

ACKNOWLEDGMENTS

The authors would like to thank a number of people who assisted in the production of this book: Mr Ian Haworth, the Founder of the The Cult Information Centre; Dr John Walker, Principle Research Officer in the Arms Control and Disarmament Research Unit, of the Foreign and Commonwealth Office; Professor Nicholas Sims, London School of Economics; Dr Trevor Findlay, Director, VERTIC; Professor Frank Barnaby; the Rt Hon Alan Meale MP; the Rt Hon Frank Cook; Mr Julian Perry Robinson, Senior Fellow, the Science Policy Research Unit, University of Sussex; Dr Alistair Hay, Department of Pathological Sciences, University of Leeds; Dr Darryl Howlett, Department of Politics, University of Southampton; Dr Jonathan Cole, Department of Psychology, University of Liverpool. Professor Adrian Guelke, University of Belfast; Carolyn Sansbury & Caitriona McLeish, the Science Policy Research Unit at Sussex University; Charu Jasani, assistant librarian, the Uranium Institute; Mr Ernest Bow, a freelance scriptwriter, for preparing the typescript for reproduction. As well as the anonymous reviewers of the manuscript, who provided invaluable comment.